THE MANAGERIAL EXPERIENCE

CASES, EXERCISES, AND READINGS

FIFTH EDITION

THE MANAGERIAL EXPERIENCE

CASES, EXERCISES, AND READINGS

FIFTH EDITION

LAWRENCE R. JAUCH
Northeast Louisiana University

SALLY A. COLTRIN
University of North Florida

ARTHUR G. BEDEIAN
Louisiana State University

THE DRYDEN PRESS
Chicago New York San Francisco Philadelphia
Montreal Toronto London Sydney Tokyo

Sr. Acquisitions Editor: Mary Fischer
Developmental Editor: Penny Gaffney
Project Editor: Karen Steib
Design Director: Jeanne Calabrese
Production Manager: Kathy Harsch
Computer Services: Sandra Lopez
Permissions Editor: Doris Milligan
Director of Editing, Design, and Production: Jane Perkins

Text and Cover Designer: Vargas/Williams Design
Cover Illustration: Pauline Phung
Text Type: 10/12 New Century Schoolbook

Library of Congress Cataloging-in-Publication Data

Jauch, Lawrence R.
    The managerial experience: cases, exercises, and readings. — 5th ed./
Lawrence R. Jauch, Sally A. Coltrin, Arthur G. Bedeian.
        p. cm.
    Rev. ed. of: The managerial experience/Lawrence R. Jauch . . . [et al.]
4th ed. 1985, c1985.
    ISBN 0-03-026617-3
    1. Management—Problems, exercises, etc. I. Coltrin, Sally A.
II. Bedeian, Arthur G. III. Managerial experience. IV. Title.
HD30.413.M36 1989
658.4—dc19   88-10846
                                                           CIP

Printed in the United States of America
890-066-987654321

Address orders:
111 Fifth Avenue
New York, NY 10003

Address editorial correspondence:
One Salt Creek Lane
Hinsdale, IL 60521

The Dryden Press
Holt, Rinehart and Winston
Saunders College Publishing

THE DRYDEN PRESS SERIES IN MANAGEMENT

PREFACE

Welcome to the managerial experience. The following pages present a variety of learning materials that we hope you will find interesting and valuable. The materials are designed as an aid to supplement your basic knowledge of the management field.

Our two major objectives in the preparation of this book were to promote skill development in the areas of leadership, communication, decision making, planning, and organization design; and to increase your understanding of the manager's job and environment, individual and group behavior, and staffing, conflict, control, and change processes. This understanding will help you to effectively apply the managerial skills you will learn.

You will be asked to think about managerial problems, make decisions, interview managers, and discuss various issues with your peers. Your understanding of management will be enhanced by active participation in the process you are about to undertake.

The following material is included in this book:

1. **Cases.** This volume includes short and medium length cases. They are designed to expose you to different problems that managers face. Some deal with single issues or concepts. Others require that you integrate the application of several concepts. Try to put yourself in the position of a manager of the group or individual in the case. You may be able to recommend solutions to the problems posed and thus apply the concepts you have learned.

2. **Exercises.** There are three kinds of exercises—field, individual, and small group. The field exercises ask you to interview a manager or visit an organization to gain insight into how managers function and how the organization operates. Individual exercises are those you can complete on your own, but may be discussed in class. Some of the exercises will be valuable to your own career and personal development in addition to helping you develop an understanding of basic managerial concepts. The group exercises (some of which relate to the individual exercises) are designed to give you experience in working with others toward a common goal and an understanding of how others' perceptions and approaches to problems may differ from yours.

3. **Readings.** Experts and practitioners in the field have written extensively about management issues. You will be asked to study a sampling of these articles. Some may be difficult to understand at first; others will present a viewpoint that challenges accepted thought and practice. We hope you will think about the readings and challenge the positions taken

in the discussions that will take place. One of our new readings ("Breaking Away") should be interesting to those contemplating a management career in the future.

Although you may not be assigned all of the experiences included in the book, we hope you will be stimulated to complete some of them on your own. Your interest in management and your ability to comprehend the world of the manager will be increased to the extent that you are involved with these situations. We trust that you will have a rewarding managerial experience.

An *Instructor's Manual,* which includes summaries of cases and readings, descriptions of exercise procedures, and sample test questions, is available upon adoption of the text.

We sincerely appreciate the cooperation of the authors and publishers who granted us permission to incorporate their material into this volume.

We would be remiss if we did not mention the role of Bill Glueck, for he was the driving force behind the book's original concept and its outline. We have continued to use some of the material he contributed and have made this revision adhere to the spirit of the first two editions, for which Bill provided guidance.

Of course, we are responsible for any omissions or errors in content. We hope the material included will help you develop your skills and understanding of the managerial job and stimulate your interest in a career in management.

Lawrence R. Jauch
Monroe, Louisiana

Sally A. Coltrin
Jacksonville, Florida

Arthur G. Bedeian
Baton Rouge, Louisiana

June 1988

CONTENTS

Chapter 4: Decision Making

Chapter 5: Organization Design and Change

Chapter 6: Staffing

Chapter 7: Leading and Interpersonal Influence with Groups and Individuals

Chapter 8: Communication 247

Chapter 9: Controlling 273

Chapter 10: Comparative Management and the Future 299

CHAPTER 1

WHAT MANAGERS DO

M
any of you using this book want to be managers. You may have seen managers at work or read about how managers act and live. This chapter examines what managers really do on the job and what life might be like for an entrepreneur.

Perhaps you think managers just deal with people, solve problems, and make decisions all day long. Certainly interpersonal skills, communication, motivation, decision making, and problem solving are important, but managers have other roles that may consume time and effort. Some of these are very productive, while others are less productive but a necessary part of the job. The first reading in this book presents one observer's conclusions about the role of a manager by discussing some of the folklore and facts about the job.

The subsequent exercise asks you to interview a manager, which gives you the opportunity to gather some firsthand data about the roles that managers perform. Hopefully, you and your classmates will begin to compile a profile of how managerial jobs vary by level of management, type of industry, size of company, tasks to be done, and so on. Through the use of such a profile, you will see the underlying patterns as well as the wide diversity in the job called manager. You might even begin to explore what makes some of these managers successful.

One of the significant differences in managerial jobs is determined by whether the manager can be classified as an entrepreneur. Many important businesses are still run by families or are closely controlled and influenced by them. In some ways entrepreneurs may differ from what might be termed professional managers. The case study on Si Schwartz in this chapter exposes you to what an entrepreneur might be like and points out special problems that may occur in conjunction with this kind of management. We suggest that you pay particular attention to the idea that entrepreneurs may be motivated by different factors than other managers.

As you may discover if you use the exercise, "Understanding Managerial Jobs," the middle manager's job can differ from that of the upper or supervisory manager. The case, "A Day in the Life of a Middle Manager," gives you a chance to see the various roles and activities of a typical middle manager. You can contrast this with your own findings, what Mintzberg discovered, and what you found out about

● **LEARNING OBJECTIVES**

When you have completed this chapter, you will have a better understanding of:

1. How managerial jobs are similar and how they differ.

2. How entrepreneurs may differ from managers.

3. The various roles managers perform at different levels.

4. The environment within which managers operate.

5. Various perspectives on social responsibility and ethical behavior of managers.

6. How managers might be more successful.

entrepreneurs. And in "The Perfect Pizzeria" case, you will get another glimpse of problems that managers can have in performing their functions.

The effective conduct of the roles managers play requires development of contacts and relationships between the manager and groups in the environment—governments, local communities, suppliers, customers, pressure groups, and even competitors. This is the environment within which managers function. The environment makes a significant impact on a business firm, and while managers cannot ignore it, they must decide how to react to these influences on the enterprise. Do they passively accept pressure or actively react through attempts to influence the environment in ways favorable to the firm?

For example, environmental protection, consumerism, civil rights, and women's rights are recent movements that affect business firms. Does the firm resist them, influence legislation, build its image, or just give up and follow the law? These decisions may depend on managerial values, ranging from "it's our responsibility to get involved" to "the business of business is business." If an active position is taken, then managers must decide which of the groups in the environment demand the most attention and what mechanisms of influence can be used to relate to those groups. These mechanisms include interpersonal influence, image building, direct political involvement, and, in some cases, illegal or unethical activities (*not* recommended).

A great deal of debate develops over the issue of "social responsibility." Those in favor of a profit ethic argue that executives exist to make profits for shareholders, that costs increase (thus raising prices) when firms engage in "socially responsible" activities, that power can become concentrated if social responsibility prevails, and that social responsibility is a form of "socialism."

Those with a social responsibility ethic contend that people expect business institutions to behave responsibly, that social responsibility prevents further governmental regulation, that long-run profits will be enhanced, and that firms have resources to be used for socially beneficial projects. You will get an insight into these arguments and other positions when you read "The Future of Private Enterprise Initiatives for the 1980s."

"Trouble in Toyland" presents a meeting of stockholders in which the executives are questioned about deceptive marketing, equal opportunity, and other issues affecting corporate image and credibility.

Another issue that has created problems is whether business people should behave ethically or legally. There is a difference. Behavior can be unethical but legal, or illegal but ethical. Identifying what is unethical often becomes a matter of personal beliefs. What are yours? The case "Flexithane Paint Company" addresses this issue. Flexithane's sales manager has just been informed by his staff that their president allegedly made donations to a political party in exchange for a promise of unlimited access to polyvinyl chloride, a crucial material for Flexithane. If these allegations are true, was the action unethical? Illegal? What should be done?

The next exercise in the chapter, "A University's Environment," is designed to provide you with the opportunity to evaluate the external environmental elements that influence an organization with which you are familiar.

The final exercise in this chapter is included to stimulate your thinking about what kinds of behaviors lead to success as a manager. Although success is an elusive concept, there are conceivably a certain set of abilities and attitudes which, when matched with the nature of the job to be performed, are more likely to lead to successful outcomes. Do you think you know what these abilities and attitudes are? Are they all in the exercise? ●

READING 1

THE MANAGER'S JOB: FOLKLORE AND FACT
Henry Mintzberg

If you ask a manager what he does, he will most likely tell you that he plans, organizes, coordinates, and controls. Then watch what he does. Don't be surprised if you can't relate what you see to these four words.

When he is called and told that one of his factories has just burned down, and he advises the caller to see whether temporary arrangements can be made to supply customers through a foreign subsidiary, is he planning, organizing, coordinating, or controlling? How about when he presents a gold watch to a retiring employee? Or when he attends a conference to meet people in the trade? Or on returning from that conference, when he tells one of his employees about an interesting product idea he picked up there?

The fact is that these four words, which have dominated management vocabulary since the French industrialist Henry Fayol first introduced them in 1916, tell us little about what managers actually do. At best, they indicate some vague objectives managers have when they work.

The field of management, so devoted to progress and change, has for more than half a century not seriously addressed the basic question: What do managers do? Without a proper answer, how can we teach management? How can we design planning or information systems for managers? How can we improve the practice of management at all?

Our ignorance of the nature of managerial work shows up in various ways in the modern organization—in the boast by the successful manager that he never spent a single day in a management training program; in the turnover of corporate planners who never quite understood what it was the manager wanted; in the computer consoles gathering dust in the back room because the managers never used the fancy on-line MIS some analyst thought they needed. Perhaps most important, our ignorance shows up in the inability of our large public organizations to come to grips with some of their most serious policy problems.

Somehow, in the rush to automate production, to use management science in the functional areas of marketing and finance, and to apply the skills of the behavioral scientist to the problem of worker motivation, the manager—that person in charge of the organization or one of its subunits—has been forgotten.

My intention in this article is simple: to break the reader away from Fayol's words and introduce him to a more supportable, and what I believe to be a more useful, description of managerial work. This description derives from my review and synthesis of the available research on how various managers have spent their time.

In some studies, managers were observed intensively ("shadowed" is the term some of them used); in a number of others, they kept detailed diaries of their activities; in a few studies, their records were analyzed. All kinds of managers were studied—foremen, factory supervisors, staff managers, field sales managers, hospital administrators, presidents of companies and nations, and even street gang leaders. These "managers" worked in the United States, Canada, Sweden, and Great Britain. In the [material that follows] is a brief review of the major studies that I found most useful in developing this description, including my own study of five American chief executive officers.

RESEARCH ON MANAGERIAL WORK

Considering its central importance to every aspect of management, there has been surprisingly little research on the manager's work, and virtually no systematic building of knowledge from one group of studies to another. In seeking to describe managerial work, I conducted my own research and also scanned the literature widely to integrate the findings of studies from many diverse sources with my own. These studies focused on two very different aspects of managerial work. Some were concerned with the characteristics of the work—how long managers work, where, at what pace and with what interruptions, with whom they work, and through what media they communicate. Other studies were more concerned with the essential content of the work—what activities the managers actually carry out, and why. Thus, after a meeting, one researcher might note that the manager spent 45 minutes with three government officials in their Washington office, while another might record that he presented his company's stand on some proposed legislation in order to change a regulation.

A few of the studies of managerial work are widely known, but most have remained buried as single journal articles or isolated books. Among the more important ones I cite (with full references in the footnotes) are the following:

- Sune Carlson developed the diary method to study the work characteristics of nine Swedish managing directors. Each kept a detailed log of his activities. Carlson's results are reported in his book *Executive Behavior*. A number of British researchers, notably Rosemary Stewart, have subsequently used Carlson's method. In *Managers and Their Jobs*, she describes the study of 160 top and middle managers of British companies during four weeks, with particular attention to the differences in their work.
- Leonard Sayle's book *Managerial Behavior* is another important reference. Using a method he refers to as "anthropological," Sayles studied the work content of middle- and lower-level managers in a large U.S. corporation. Sayles moved freely in the company, collecting whatever information struck him as important.
- Perhaps the best-known source is *Presidential Power*, in which Richard Neustadt analyzes the power and managerial behavior of Presidents Roosevelt, Truman, and Eisenhower. Neustadt used secondary sources—documents and interviews with other parties—to generate his data.
- Robert H. Guest, in *Personnel*, reports on a study of the foreman's working day. Fifty-six U.S. foremen were observed and each of their activities recorded during one eight-hour shift.
- Richard C. Hodgson, Daniel J. Levinson, and Abraham Zaleznik studied a team of three top executives of a U.S. hospital. From that study they wrote *The Executive Role Constellation*. These researchers addressed in particular the way in which work and socioemotional roles were divided among the three managers.
- William F. Whyte, from his study of a street gang during the Depression, wrote *Street Corner Society*. His findings about the gang's leadership, which George C. Homans analyzed in *The Human Group*, suggest some interesting similarities of job content between street gang leaders and corporate managers.

My own study involved five American CEOs of middle-to large-sized organizations—a consulting firm, a technology company, a hospital, a consumer goods company, and a school system. Using a method called "structured observation," during one intensive week of observation for each executive I recorded various aspects of every piece of mail and every verbal contact. My method was designed to capture data on both work characteristics and job content. In all, I analyzed 890 pieces of incoming and outgoing mail and 368 verbal contacts.

A synthesis of these findings paints an interesting picture, one as different from Fayol's classical view as a cubist abstract is from a Renaissance painting. In a sense, this picture will be obvious to anyone who has ever spent a day in a manager's office, either in front of the desk or behind it. Yet, at the same time, this picture may turn out to be revolutionary, in that it throws into doubt so much of the folklore that we have accepted about the manager's work.

I first discuss some of this folklore and contrast it with some of the discoveries of systematic research—the hard facts about how managers spend their time. Then I synthesize these research findings in a description of ten roles that seem to describe the essential content of all managers' jobs. In a concluding section, I discuss a number of implications of this synthesis for those trying to achieve more effective management, both in classrooms and in the business world.

SOME FOLKLORE AND FACTS ABOUT MANAGERIAL WORK

There are four myths about the manager's job that do not bear up under careful scrutiny of the facts.

1. *Folklore: The manager is a reflective, systematic planner.* The evidence on this issue is overwhelming, but not a shred of it supports this statement.

   Fact: Study after study has shown that managers work at an unrelenting pace, that their activities are characterized by brevity, variety, and discontinuity, and that they are strongly oriented to action and dislike reflective activities. Consider this evidence:

   Half the activities engaged in by the five chief executives of my study lasted less than nine minutes, and only 10% exceeded one hour.[1] A study of 56 U.S. foremen found that they averaged 583 activities per eight-hour shift, an average of 1 every 48 seconds.[2] The work pace for both chief executives and foremen was unrelenting. The chief executives met a steady stream of callers and mail from the moment they arrived in the morning until they left in the evening. Coffee breaks and lunches were inevitably work related, and ever-present subordinates seemed to usurp any free moment.

   A diary study of 160 British middle and top managers found that they worked for a half hour or more without interruption only about once every two days.[3]

   Of the verbal contacts of the chief executives in my study, 93% were arranged on an ad hoc basis. Only 1% of the executives' time was spent in open-ended observational tours. Only 1 out of 368 verbal contacts was unrelated to a specific issue and could be called general planning. Another researcher finds that "in *not one single case* did a manager report the obtaining of important external information from a general observation or other undirected personal communication."[4]

   No study has found important patterns in the way managers schedule their time. They seem to jump from issue to issue, continually responding to the needs of the moment.

   Is this the planner that the classical view describes? Hardly. How, then, can we explain this behavior? The manager is simply responding to the pressures of his job. I found that my chief executives terminated many of their own activities, often leaving meetings before the end, and interrupted their desk work to call in subordinates. One president not only placed his desk so that he could look down a long hallway but also left his door open when he was alone—an invitation for subordinates to come in and interrupt him.

   Clearly, these managers wanted to encourage the flow of current information. But more significantly, they seemed to be conditioned by their own work loads. They appreciated the opportunity cost of their own time, and they were continually aware of their ever-present obligations—mail to be answered, callers to attend to, and so on. It seems that no matter what he is doing, the manager is plagued by the possibilities of what he might do and what he must do.

When the manager must plan, he seems to do so implicitly in the context of daily actions, not in some abstract process reserved for two weeks in the organization's mountain retreat. The plans of the chief executives I studied seemed to exist only in their heads—as flexible, but often specific, intentions. The traditional literature notwithstanding, the job of managing does not breed reflective planners; the manager is a real-time responder to stimuli, an individual who is conditioned by his job to prefer live to delayed action.

2. *Folklore: The effective manager has no regular duties to perform.* Managers are constantly being told to spend more time planning and delegating, and less time seeing customers and engaging in negotiations. These are not, after all, the true tasks of the manager. To use the popular analogy, the good manager, like the good conductor, carefully orchestrates everything in advance, then sits back to enjoy the fruits of his labor, responding occasionally to an unforeseeable exception.

But here again the pleasant abstraction just does not seem to hold up. We had better take a closer look at those activities managers feel compelled to engage in before we arbitrarily define them away.

Fact: In addition to handling exceptions, managerial work involves performing a number of regular duties, including ritual and ceremony, negotiations, and processing of soft information that links the organization with its environment. Consider some evidence from the research studies:

A study of the work of presidents of small companies found that they engaged in routine activities because their companies could not afford staff specialists and were so thin on operating personnel that a single absence often required the president to substitute.[5]

One study of field sales managers and another of chief executives suggest that it is a natural part of both jobs to see important customers, assuming the managers wish to keep those customers.[6]

Someone, only half in jest, once described the manager as that person who sees visitors so that everyone else can get his work done. In my study, I found that certain ceremonial duties—meeting visiting dignitaries, giving out gold watches, presiding at Christmas dinners—were an intrinsic part of the chief executive's job.

Studies of managers' information flow suggest that managers play a key role in securing "soft" external information (much of it available only to them because of their status) and in passing it along to their subordinates.

3. *Folklore: The senior manager needs aggregated information, which a formal management information system best provides.* Not too long ago, the words total information system were everywhere in the management literature. In keeping with the classical view of the manager as that individual perched on the apex of a regulated, hierarchical system, the literature's manager was to receive all his important information from a giant, comprehensive MIS.

But lately, as it has become increasingly evident that these giant MIS systems are not working—that managers are simply not using them—the enthusiasm has waned. A look at how managers actually process information makes the reason quite clear. Managers have five media at their command—documents, telephone calls, scheduled and unscheduled meetings, and observational tours.

Fact: Managers strongly favor the verbal media—namely telephone calls and meetings. The evidence comes from every single study of managerial work. Consider the following:

In two British studies, managers spent an average of 66% and 80% of their time in verbal (oral) communication.[7] In my study of five American chief executives, the figure was 78%.

These five chief executives treated mail processing as a burden to be dispensed with. One came in Saturday morning to process 142 pieces of mail in just over three hours, to "get rid of all the stuff." This same manager looked at the first piece of "hard" mail he had received all week, a standard cost report, and put it aside with the comment, "I never look at this."

These same five chief executives responded immediately to 2 of the 40 routine reports they received during the five weeks of my study and to four items in the 104 periodicals. They skimmed most of these periodicals in seconds, almost ritualistically. In all, these chief executives of good-sized organizations initiated on their own—that is, not in response to something else—a grand total of 25 pieces of mail during the 25 days I observed them.

An analysis of the mail the executives received reveals an interesting picture—only 13% was of specific and immediate use. So now we have another piece in the puzzle: not much of the mail provides live, current information—the action of a competitor, the mood of a government legislator, or the rating of last night's television show. Yet this is the information that drove the managers, interrupting their meetings and rescheduling their workdays.

Consider another interesting finding. Managers seem to cherish "soft" information, especially gossip, hearsay, and speculation. Why? The reason is its timeliness; today's gossip may be tomorrow's fact. The manager who is not accessible for the telephone call informing him that his biggest customer was seen golfing with his main competitor may read about a dramatic drop in sales in the next quarterly report. But then it's too late.

To assess the value of historical, aggregated, "hard" MIS information, consider two of the manager's prime uses for his information—to identify problems and opportunities[8] and to build his own mental models of the things around him (e.g., how his organization's budget system works, how his customers buy his product, how changes in the economy affect his organization, and so on). Every bit of evidence suggests that the manager identifies decision situations and builds models not with the aggregated abstractions an MIS provides, but with specific tidbits of data.

Consider the words of Richard Neustadt, who studied the information-collecting habits of Presidents Roosevelt, Truman, and Eisenhower:

"It is not information of a general sort that helps a President see personal stakes; not summaries, not surveys, not the bland amalgams. Rather. . .it is the odds and ends of tangible detail that pieced together in his mind illuminate the underside of issues put before him. To help himself he must reach out as widely as he can for every scrap of fact, opinion, gossip, bearing on his interests and relationships as President. He must become his own director of his own central intelligence."[9]

The manager's emphasis on the verbal media raises two important points:

First, verbal information is stored in the brains of people. Only when people write this information down can it be stored in the files of the organization—whether in metal cabinets or on magnetic tape—and managers apparently do not write down much of what they hear. Thus the strategic data bank of the organization is not in the memory of its computers but in the minds of its managers.

Second, the manager's extensive use of verbal media helps to explain why he is reluctant to delegate tasks. When we note that most of the manager's important information comes in verbal form and is stored in his head, we can well appreciate his reluctance. It is not as if he can hand a dossier over to someone; he must take the time to "dump memory"—to tell that someone all he knows about the subject. But this could take so long that the manager may find it easier to do the task himself. Thus, the manager is damned by his own information system to a "dilemma of delegation"—to do too much himself or to delegate to his subordinates with inadequate briefing.

4. *Folklore: Management is, or at least is quickly becoming, a science and a profession.* By almost any definitions of science and profession, this statement is false. Brief observation of any manager will quickly lay to rest the notion that managers practice a science. A science involves the enaction of systematic, analytically determined procedures of programs. If we do not even know what procedures managers use, how can we prescribe them by scientific analysis? And how can we call management a profession if we cannot specify what managers are to learn? For after all, a profession involves "knowledge of some department of learning or science" (Random House Dictionary.)[10]

Fact: The managers' programs—to schedule time, process information, make decisions, and so on—remain locked deep inside their brains. Thus, to describe these programs, we rely on words like judgment and intuition, seldom stopping to realize that they are merely labels for our ignorance.

I was struck during my study by the fact that the executives I was observing—all very competent by any standard—are fundamentally indistinguishable from their counterparts of a hundred years ago (or a thousand years ago, for that matter). The information they need differs, but they seek it in the same way—by word of mouth. Their decisions concern modern technology, but the procedures they use to make them are the same as the procedures of the nineteenth-century manager. Even the computer, so important for the specialized work of the organization, has apparently had no influence on the work procedures of general managers. In fact, the manager is in a kind of loop, with increasingly heavy work pressures but no aid forthcoming from management science.

Considering the facts about managerial work, we can see that the manager's job is enormously complicated and difficult. The manager is over-burdened with obligations; yet he cannot easily delegate his tasks. As a result, he is driven to overwork and is forced to do many tasks superficially. Brevity, fragmentation, and verbal communication characterize his work. Yet these are the very characteristics of managerial work that have impeded scientific attempts to improve it. As a result, the management scientist has concentrated his efforts on the specialized functions of the organization, where he could more easily analyze the procedures and quantify the relevant information.[11]

But the pressures of the manager's job are becoming worse. Where before he needed only to respond to owners and directors, now he finds the subordinates with democratic norms continually reduce his freedom to issue unexplained orders, and a growing number of outside influences (consumer groups, government agencies, and so on) expect his attention.

And the manager has had nowhere to turn for help. The first step in providing the manager with some help is to find out what his job really is.

BACK TO A BASIC DESCRIPTION OF MANAGERIAL WORK

Now let us try to put some of the pieces of this puzzle together. Earlier, I defined the manager as that person in charge of an organization or one of its subunits. Besides chief executive officers, this definition would include vice presidents, bishops, foremen, hockey coaches, and prime ministers. Can all of these people have anything in common? Indeed they can. For an important starting point, all are vested with formal authority over an organizational unit. From formal authority comes status, which leads to various interpersonal relations, and from these comes access to information. Information, in turn, enables the manager to make decisions and strategies for his unit.

The manager's job can be described in terms of various "roles," or organized sets of behaviors identified with a position. My description, shown in Figure 1, comprises ten roles. As we shall see, formal authority gives rise to the three interpersonal roles, which in turn give rise to the three informational roles; these two sets of roles enable the manager to play the four decisional roles.

Interpersonal Roles

Three of the manager's roles arise directly from his formal authority and involve basic interpersonal relationships.

1. First is the *figurehead* role. By virtue of his position as head of an organizational unit, every manager must perform some duties of a ceremonial nature. The president greets the touring dignitaries, the foreman attends the wedding of a lathe operator, and the sales manager takes an important customer to lunch.

   The chief executives of my study spend 12% of their contract time on ceremonial duties; 17% of their incoming mail dealt with acknowledgments and requests related to their status. For example, a letter to a company president requested free merchandise for a crippled schoolchild; diplomas were put on the desk of the school superintendent for his signature.

FIGURE 1
THE MANAGER'S ROLE

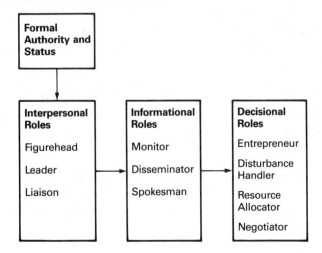

Duties that involve interpersonal roles may sometimes be routine, involving little serious communication and no important decision making. Nevertheless, they are important to the smooth functioning of an organization and cannot be ignored by the manager.

2. Because he is in charge of an organizational unit, the manager is responsible for the work of the people of that unit. His actions in this regard constitute the *leader* role. Some of these actions involve leadership directly—for example, in most organizations the manager is normally responsible for hiring and training his own staff.

    In addition, there is the indirect exercise of the leader role. Every manager must motivate and encourage his employees, somehow reconciling their individual needs with the goals of the organization. In virtually every contact the manager has with his employees, subordinates seeking leadership clues probe his actions: "Does he approve?" "How would he like the report to turn out?" "Is he more interested in market share than high profits?"

    The influence of the manager is most clearly seen in the leader role. Formal authority vests him with great potential power; leadership determines in large part how much of it he will realize.

3. The literature of management has always recognized the leader role, particularly those aspects of it related to motivation. In comparison, until recently it has hardly mentioned the *liaison* role, in which the manager makes contacts outside his vertical chain of command. This is remarkable in light of the finding of virtually every study of managerial work that managers spend as much time with peers and other people outside their units as they do with their own subordinates—and, surprisingly, very little time with their own superiors.

    In Rosemary Stewart's diary study, the 160 British middle and top managers spent 47% of their time with peers, 41% of their time with people outside their unit, and only 12% of their time with their superiors. For Robert H. Guest's study of U.S. foremen, the figures were 44%, 46%, and 10%. The chief executives of my study averaged 44% of their contact time with people outside their organizations, 48% with subordinates, and 7% with directors and trustees.

The contacts the five CEOs made were with an incredibly wide range of people; subordinates; clients, business associates, and suppliers; and peers—managers of similar organizations, government and trade organization officials, fellow directors on outside boards, and independents with no relevant organizational affiliations. The chief executives' time with and mail from these groups is shown in Figure 2. Guest's study of foremen shows, likewise, that their contacts were numerous and wide ranging, seldom involving fewer than 25 individuals, and often more than 50.

As we shall see shortly, the manager cultivates such contacts largely to find information. In effect, the liaison role is devoted to building up the manager's own external information system—informal, private, verbal, but nevertheless, effective.

Informational Roles

By virtue of his interpersonal contacts, both with his subordinates and with his network of contacts, the manager emerges as the nerve center of his organizational unit. He may not know everything, but he typically knows more than any member of his staff.

FIGURE 2

THE CHIEF EXECUTIVES' CONTACTS

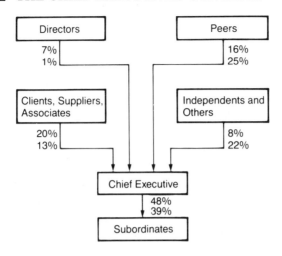

Note: The top figure indicates the proportion of total contact time spent with each group. The bottom figure indicates the proportion of mail from each group.

Studies have shown this relationship to hold for all managers, from street gang leaders to U.S. presidents. *In The Human Group,* George C. Homans explains how, because they were at the center of the information flow in their own gangs and were also in close touch with other gang leaders, street gang leaders were better informed than any of their followers.[12] And Richard Neustadt describes the following account from his study of Franklin D. Roosevelt:

"The essence of Roosevelt's technique for information-gathering was competition. 'He would call you in,' one of his aides once told me,' and he'd ask you to get the story on some complicated business, and you'd come back after a couple of days of hard labor and present the juicy morsel you'd uncovered under a stone somewhere, and *then* you'd find out he knew all about it, along with something else you *didn't* know. Where he got his information from he wouldn't mention, usually, but after he had done this to you once or twice you got damn careful about *your* information.'"[13]

We can see where Roosevelt "got this information" when we consider the relationship between the interpersonal and informational roles. As leader, the manager has formal and easy access to every member of his staff. Hence, as noted earlier, he tends to know more about his own unit than anyone else does. In addition, his liaison contacts expose the manager to external information to which his subordinates often lack access. Many of these contacts are with other managers of equal status, who are themselves nerve centers in their own organization. In this way, the manager develops a powerful data base of information.

The processing of information is a key part of the manager's job. In my study, the chief executives spent 40% of their contact time on activities devoted exclusively to the transmission of information; 70% of their incoming mail was purely informational (as opposed to requests for action). The manager does not leave meetings or hang up the telephone in order to get back to work. In large part, communication is his work. Three roles describe these informational aspects of managerial work.

1. As *monitor,* the manager perpetually scans his environment for information, interrogates his liaison contacts and his subordinates, and receives unsolicited information, much of it as a result of the network of personal

contacts he has developed. Remember that a good part of the information the manager collects in his monitor role arrives in verbal form, often as gossip, hearsay, and speculation. By virtue of his contacts, the manager has a natural advantage in collecting this soft information for his organization.

2. He must share and distribute much of this information. Information he gleans from outside personal contacts may be needed within his organization. In his *disseminator* role, the manager passes some of his privileged information directly to his subordinates, who would otherwise have no access to it. When his subordinates lack easy contact with one another, the manager will sometimes pass information from one to another.

3. In his *spokesman* role, the manager sends some of his information to people outside his unit—a president makes a speech to lobby for an organization cause, or a foreman suggests a product modification to a supplier. In addition, as part of his role as spokesman, every manager must inform and satisfy the influential people who control his organizational unit. For the foreman, this may simply involve keeping the plant manager informed about the flow of work through the shop.

The president of a large corporation, however, may spend a great amount of his time dealing with a host of influences. Directors and shareholders must be advised about financial performance; consumer groups must be assured that the organization is fulfilling its social responsibilities; and government officials must be satisfied that the organization is abiding by the law.

Decisional Roles

Information is not, of course, an end in itself; it is the basic input to decision making. One thing is clear in the study of managerial work: the manager plays the major role in his unit's decision-making system. As its formal authority, only he can commit the unit to important new courses of action; and its nerve center, only he has full and current information to make the set of decisions that determines the unit's strategy. Four roles describe the manager as decision-maker.

1. As *entrepreneur*, the manager seeks to improve his unit, to adapt it to changing conditions in the environment. In his *monitor* role, the president is constantly on the lookout for new ideas. When a good one appears, he initiates a development project that he may supervise himself or delegate to any employee (perhaps with the stipulation that he must approve the final proposal).

There are two interesting features about these development projects at the chief executive level. First, these projects do not involve single decisions or even unified clusters of decisions. Rather, they emerge as a series of small decisions and actions sequenced over time. Apparently, the chief executive prolongs each project so that he can fit it bit by bit into his busy, disjointed schedule and so that he can gradually come to comprehend the issue, if it is a complex one.

Second, the chief executives I studied supervised as many as 50 of these projects at the same time. Some projects entailed new products or processes; others involved public relations campaigns, improvement of the cash position, reorganization of a weak department, resolution of a morale problem in a foreign division, integration of computer operations, various acquisitions at different stages of development, and so on.

The chief executive appears to maintain a kind of inventory of the development projects that he himself supervises—projects that are at various stages of development, some active and some in limbo. Like a juggler, he keeps a number of projects in the air; periodically, one comes down,

2. While the entrepreneur role describes the manager as the voluntary initiator of change, the *disturbance handler* role depicts the manager involuntarily responding to pressures. Here change is beyond the manager's control. He must act because the pressures of the situation are too severe to be ignored: strike looms, a major customer has gone bankrupt, or a supplier reneges on his contract.

It has been fashionable, I noted earlier, to compare the manager to an orchestra conductor, just as Peter F. Drucker wrote in the *Practice of Management:*

"The manager has the task of creating a true whole that is larger than the sum of its parts, a productive entity that turns out more than the sum of the resources put into it. One analogy is the conductor of a symphony orchestra, through whose effort, vision and leadership individual instrumental parts that are so much noise by themselves become a living whole of music. But the conductor has the composer's score; he is only interpreter. The manager is both composer and conductor."[14]

Now consider the words of Leonard R. Sayles, who has carried out systematic research on the manager's job:

"[The manager] is like a symphony orchestra conductor, endeavouring to maintain a melodious performance in which the contributions of the various instruments are coordinated and sequenced, patterned and paced, while the orchestra members are having various personal difficulties, stage hands are moving music stands, alternating excessive heat and cold are creating audience and instrument problems, and the sponsor of the concert is insisting on irrational changes in the program."[15]

In effect, every manager must spend a good part of his time responding to high-pressure disturbances. No organization can be so well run, so standardized, that it has considered every contingency in the uncertain environment in advance. Disturbances arise not only because poor managers ignore situations until they reach crisis proportions, but also because good managers cannot possibly anticipate all the consequences of the actions they take.

3. The third decisional role is that of *resource allocator*. To the manager falls the responsibility of deciding who will get what in his organizational unit. Perhaps the most important resource the manager allocates is his own time. Access to the manager constitutes exposure to the unit's nerve center and decision-maker. The manager is also charged with designing his unit's structure, that pattern of formal relationships that determines how work is to be divided and coordinated.

Also, in his role as resource allocator, the manager authorizes the important decisions of his unit before they are implemented. By retaining this power, the manager can ensure that decisions are interrelated; all must pass through a single brain. To fragment this power is to encourage discontinuous decision making and a disjointed strategy.

There are a number of interesting features about the manager's authorizing others' decisions. First, despite the widespread use of capital budgeting procedures—a means of authorizing various capital expenditures at one time—executives in my study made a great many authorization decisions on an ad hoc basis. Apparently, many projects cannot wait or simply do not have the quantifiable costs and benefits that capital budgeting requires.

Second, I found that the chief executives faced incredibly complex choices. They had to consider the impact of each decision on other decisions and on the organization's strategy. They had to ensure that the decision would be acceptable to those who influence the organization, as decisions and on the organization's strategy. They had to ensure that the decision would be acceptable to those who influence the organization, as well as ensure that resources would not be overextended. They had to understand the various costs and benefits as well as the feasibility of the proposal. They also had to consider questions of timing. All of this was necessary for the simple approval of someone else's proposal. At the same time, however, delay could lose time, while quick approval could be ill-considered and quick rejection might discourage the subordinate who had spent months developing a pet project.

One common solution to approving projects is to pick the man instead of the proposal. That is, the manager authorizes those projects presented to him by people whose judgment he trusts. But he cannot always use this simple dodge.

4. The final decisional role is that of *negotiator*. Studies of managerial work at all levels indicate that managers spend considerable time in negotiations: the president of the football team is called in to work out a contract with the holdout superstar; the corporation president leads his company's contingent to negotiate a new strike issue; the foreman argues a grievance problem to its conclusion with the shop steward. As Leonard Sayles puts it, negotiations are a "way of life" for the sophisticated manager.

These negotiations are duties of the manager's job; perhaps routine, they are not to be shirked. They are an integral part of his job, for only he has the authority to commit organizational resources in "real time," and only he has the nerve center information that important negotiations require.

The Integrated Job

It should be clear by now that the ten roles I have been describing are not easily separable. In the terminology of the psychologist, they form a gestalt, an integrated whole. No role can be pulled out of the framework and the job be left intact. For example, a manager without liaison contacts lacks external information. As a result, he can neither disseminate the information his employees need nor make decisions that adequately reflect external conditions. (In fact, this is a problem for the new person in a managerial position, since he cannot make effective decisions until he has built up his network of contacts.)

Here lies a clue to the problems of team management.[16] Two or three people cannot share a single managerial position unless they can act as one entity. This means that they cannot divide up the ten roles unless they can very carefully reintegrate them. The real difficulty lies with the informational roles. Unless there can be full sharing of managerial information—and, as I pointed out earlier, it is primarily verbal—team management breaks down. A single managerial job cannot be arbitrarily split, for example, into internal and external roles, for information from both sources must be brought to bear on the same decisions.

To say that the ten roles form a gestalt is not to say that all managers give equal attention to each role. In fact, I found in my review of the various research studies that:

- Sales managers seem to spend relatively more of their time in the interpersonal roles, presumably a reflection of the extrovert nature of the marketing activity;
- Production managers give relatively more attention to the decisional roles, presumably a reflection of their concern with efficient work flow;
- Staff managers spend the most time in the informational roles, since they are experts who manage departments that advise other parts of the organization.

Nevertheless, in all cases the interpersonal, informational, and decisional roles remain inseparable.

TOWARD MORE EFFECTIVE MANAGEMENT

What are the messages for management in this description? I believe, first and foremost, that this description of managerial work should prove more important to managers than any prescription they might derive from it. That is to say, *the manager's effectiveness is significantly influenced by his insight into his own work.* His performance depends on how well he understands and responds to the pressures and dilemmas of the job. Thus managers who can be introspective about their work are likely to be effective at their jobs. The insert [at the end of the Reading] offers 14 groups of self-study questions for managers. Some may sound rhetorical; none is meant to be. Even though the questions cannot be answered simply, the manager should address them.

Let us take a look at three specific areas of concern. For the most part, the managerial logjams—the dilemma of delegation, the data base centralized in one brain, the problems of working with the management scientist—revolve around the verbal nature of the manager's information. These are great dangers in centralizing the organization's data bank in the minds of its managers. When they leave, they take their memory with them. And when subordinates are out of convenient verbal reach of the manager, they are at an informational disadvantage.

1. *The manager is challenged to find systematic ways to share his privileged information.* A regular debriefing session with key subordinates, a weekly memory dump on the dictating machine, the maintaining of a diary of important information for limited circulation, or other similar methods may ease the logjam of work considerably. Time spent disseminating this information will be more than regained when decisions must be made. Of course, some will raise the question of confidentiality. But managers would do well to weigh the risks of exposing privileged information against having subordinates who can make effective decisions.

   If there is a single theme that runs through this article, it is that the pressures of his job drive the manager to be superficial in his actions—to overload himself with work, encourage interruption, respond quickly to every stimulus, seek the tangible and avoid the abstract, make decisions in small increments, and do everything abruptly.

2. *Here again, the manager is challenged to deal consciously with the pressures of superficiality by giving serious attention to the issues that require it, by stepping back from his tangible bits of information in order to see a broad picture, and by making use of analytical inputs.* Although effective managers have to be adept at responding quickly to numerous and varying problems, the danger in managerial work is that they will respond to every issue equally (and that means abruptly) and that they will never work the tangible bits and pieces of informational input into a comprehensive picture of their world.

   As I noted earlier, the manager uses these bits of information to build models of his world. But the manager can also avail himself of the models of the specialists. Economists describe the functioning of markets, operations researchers stimulate financial flow processes, and behavioral scientists explain the needs and goals of people. The best of these models can be searched out and learned.

   In dealing with complex issues, the senior manager has much to gain from a close relationship with the management scientists of his own organization. They have something important that he lacks—time to probe complex issues. An effective working relationship hinges on the resolution of what a colleague and I have called "the planning dilemma."[17] Managers have the information and the authority; analysts have the time and the technology. A successful working relationship between the two will be effected when the manager learns to share his information and the analyst learns to adapt to the manager's needs. For the analyst, adaptation means worrying less about the elegance of the method and more about its speed and flexibility.

It seems to me that analysts can help the top manager especially to schedule his time, feed in analytical information, monitor projects under his supervision, develop models to aid in making choices, design contingency plans for disturbances that can be anticipated, and conduct "quick-and-dirty" analysis for those that cannot. But there can be no cooperation if the analysts are out of the mainstream of the manager's information flow.

3. *The manager is challenged to gain control of his own time by turning obligations to his advantage and by turning those things he wishes to do into obligations.* The chief executives of my study initiated only 32% of their own contacts (and another 5% by mutual agreement). And yet to a considerable extent they seem to control their time. There were two key factors that enabled them to do so.

First, the manager has to spend so much time discharging obligations that if he were to view them as just that, he would leave no mark on his organization. The unsuccessful manager blames failure on the obligations; the effective manager turns his obligations to his own advantage. A speech is a chance to lobby for a cause; a meeting is a change to reorganize a weak department; a visit to an important customer is a chance to extract trade information.

Second, the manager frees some of his time to do those things that he—perhaps no one else—thinks important by turning them into obligations. Free time is made, not found, in the manager's job; it is forced into the schedule. Hoping to leave some time open for contemplation or general planning is tantamount to hoping that the pressures of the job will go away. The manager who wants to innovate initiates a project and obligates others to report back to him; the manager who needs certain environmental information establishes channels that will automatically keep him informed; the manager who has to tour facilities commits himself publicly.

The Educator's Job

Finally, a word about the training of managers. Our management schools have done an admirable job of training the organization's specialists—management scientists, marketing researchers, accountants, and organizational development specialists.[18] But for the most part they have not trained managers. Management schools will begin the serious training of managers when skill training takes a serious place next to cognitive learning. Cognitive learning is detached and informational, like reading a book or listening to a lecture. No doubt much important cognitive material must be assimilated by the manager-to-be. But cognitive learning no more makes a manager than it does a swimmer. The latter will drown the first time he jumps into the water if his coach never takes him out of the lecture hall, gets him wet, and gives him feedback on his performance.

In other words, we are taught a skill through practice plus feedback, whether in a real or a simulated situation. Our management schools need to identify the skills managers use, select students who show potential in these skills, put the students into situations where these skills can be practiced, and then give them systematic feedback on their performance.

My description of managerial work suggests a number of important managerial skills—developing peer relationships, carrying out negotiations, motivating subordinates, resolving conflicts, establishing information networks and subsequently disseminating information, making decisions in conditions of extreme ambiguity, and allocating resources. Above all, the manager needs to be introspective about his work so that he may continue to learn on the job.

Many of the manager's skills can, in fact, be practiced, using techniques that range from role playing to videotaping real meetings. And our management schools can enhance the entrepreneurial skills by designing programs that encourage sensible risk taking and innovation.

No job is more vital to our society than that of the manager. It is the manager who determines whether our social institutions serve us well or whether they squander our talents and resources. It is time to strip away the folklore about managerial work, and time to study it realistically so that we can begin the difficult task of making significant improvements in its performance.

SELF-STUDY QUESTIONS FOR MANAGERS

1. Where do I get my information, and how? Can I make greater use of my contacts to get information? Can other people do some of my scanning for me? In what areas is my knowledge weakest, and how can I get others to provide me with the information I need? Do I have powerful enough mental models of those things I must understand within the organization and in its environment?

2. What information do I disseminate in my organization? How important is it that my subordinates get my information? Do I keep too much information to myself because dissemination of it is time-consuming or inconvenient? How can I get more information to others so they can make better decisions?

3. Do I balance information collecting with action taking? Do I tend to act before information is in? Or do I wait so long for all the information that opportunities pass me by and I become a bottleneck in my organization?

4. What pace of change am I asking my organization to tolerate? Is this change balanced so that our operations are neither excessively static nor overly disrupted? Have we sufficiently analyzed the impact of this change on the future of our organization?

5. Am I sufficiently well informed to pass judgment on the proposals that my subordinates make? Is it possible to leave final authorization for more of the proposals with subordinates? Do we have problems of coordination because subordinates in fact now make too many of these decisions independently?

6. What is my vision of direction for this organization? Are these plans primarily in my own mind in loose form? Should I make them explicit in order to guide the decisions of others in the organization better? Or do I need flexibility to change them at will?

7. How do my subordinates react to my managerial style? Am I sufficiently sensitive to the powerful influence my actions have on them? Do I fully understand their reactions to my actions? Do I find an appropriate balance between encouragement and pressure? Do I stifle their initiative?

8. What kind of external relationships do I maintain, and how? Do I spend too much of my time maintaining these relationships? Are there certain types of people whom I should get to know better?

9. Is there any system to my time scheduling, or am I just reacting to the pressures of the moment? Do I find the appropriate mix of activities, or do I tend to concentrate on one particular function or one type of problem just because I find it interesting? Am I more efficient with particular kinds of work at special times

of the day or week? Does my schedule reflect this? Can someone else (in addition to my secretary) take responsibility for much of my scheduling and do it more systematically?

10. Do I overwork? What effect does my work load have on my efficiency? Should I force myself to take breaks or to reduce the pace of my activity?

11. Am I too superficial in what I do? Can I really shift moods as quickly and frequently as my work patterns require? Should I attempt to decrease the amount of fragmentation and interruption in my work?

12. Do I orient myself too much toward current, tangible activities? Am I a slave to the action and excitement of my work, so that I am no longer able to concentrate on issues? Do key problems receive the attention they deserve? Should I spend more time reading and probing deeply into certain issues? Could I be more reflective? Should I be?

13. Do I use the different media appropriately? Do I know how to make the most of written communication? Do I rely excessively on face-to-face communication, thereby putting all but a few of my subordinates at an informational disadvantage? Do I schedule enough of my meetings on a regular basis? Do I spend enough time touring my organization to observe activity at first hand? Am I too detached from the heart of my organization's activities, seeing things only in an abstract way?

14. How do I blend in my personal rights and duties? Do my obligations consume all my time? How can I free myself sufficiently from obligations to ensure that I am taking this organization where I want it to go? How can I turn my obligations to my advantage?

Questions for Discussion

1. Are there certain skills that a manager can develop in order to be more effective?

2. What is the folklore about managerial jobs? Do most people believe the folklore?

3. Are there any similarities among the ten roles Mintzberg discusses or are they mutually exclusive?

4. Which of the ten roles are most important for top managers? Which for middle managers? Which for supervisors?

5. What use can a manager make of the self-study questions posed by Mintzberg?

Notes

1. All the data from my study can be found in Henry Mintzberg, *The Nature of Managerial Work* (New York: Harper & Row, 1973).
2. Robert H. Guest, "Of Time and the Foreman," *Personnel*, May 1956, p. 478.
3. Rosemary Stewart, *Managers and Their Jobs* (London: Macmillan, 1967); see also Sune Carlson, *Executive Behavior* (Stockholm: Strombergs, 1951), the first of the diary studies.
4. Francis J. Aguilar, *Scanning the Business Environment* (New York: Macmillan, 1967), p. 102.
5. Unpublished study by Irving Choran, reported in Mintzberg, *The Nature of Managerial Work*.
6. Robert T. Davis, *Performance and Development of Field Sales Managers* (Boston: Division of Research, Harvard Business School, 1957); George H. Copeman, *The Role of the Managing Director* (London: Business Publications, 1963).
7. Stewart, *Managers and Their Jobs*; Tom Burns, "The Directions of Activity and Communication in a Departmental Executive Group," *Human Relations* 7, no. 1 (1954): 73.
8. H. Edward Wrapp, "Good Managers Don't Make Policy Decisions," HBR, September–October 1967, p. 91; Wrapp refers to this as spotting opportunities and relationships in the stream of operating problems and decisions; in his article Wrapp raises a number of excellent points related to this analysis.
9. Richard E. Neustadt, *Presidential Power* (New York: John Wiley, 1960), pp. 153–154; italics added.
10. For a more thorough, though rather different, discussion of this issue, see Kenneth R. Andrews, "Toward Professionalism in Business Management," HBR, March–April 1969, p. 49.
11. C. Jackson Grayson, Jr., in "Management Science and Business Practice," HBR, July–August 1973, p. 41, explains in similar terms why, as chairman of the Price Commission, he did not use those very techniques that he himself promoted in his earlier career as a management scientist.

12. George C. Homans, *The Human Group* (New York: Harcourt, Brace & World, 1950), based on the study by William F. Whyte entitled *Street Corner Society*, rev. ed. (Chicago: University of Chicago Press, 1955).

13. Neustadt, *Presidential Power*, p. 157.

14. Peter F. Drucker, *The Practice of Management* (New York: Harper & Row, 1954), pp. 341–342.

15. Leonard R. Sayles, *Managerial Behavior* (New York: McGraw-Hill, 1964), p. 162.

16. See Richard C. Hodgson, Daniel J. Levinson, and Abraham Zaleznik, *The Executive Role Constellation* (Boston: Division of Research, Harvard Business School, 1965), for a discussion of the sharing of roles.

17. James S. Hekimian and Henry Mintzberg, "The Planning Dilemma," *Management Review*, May 1968, p. 4.

18. See J. Sterling Livingston, "Myth of the Well-Educated Manager," HBR, January–February 1971, p. 79.

EXERCISE 2
UNDERSTANDING MANAGERIAL JOBS

The ten roles described by Mintzberg are the basis of this exercise. Your assignment is to interview a manager and compare your findings with those of others in the class.

Find a plant manager, foreman, hospital administrator, store owner, or the like, whose job primarily involves supervising the work of other people or running an enterprise. (Your subject may be chosen from business, public or private agencies, schools, and so forth.) Your goal is to obtain the following information:

a. Which of the ten roles are most important—which contribute to effective performance by this manager?

b. Which of the ten roles are most time consuming?

c. What examples of the roles can be provided by this manager?

In conducting your interview, you may find the following questions helpful (but you may add your own):

1. What is your official title?

2. What do you do in a normal workday? For example, describe what you did yesterday.

3. What off-the-job duties are involved in your work?

4. Are you active in community or social clubs? Do they help you in your job?

5. What kinds of problems do you have to solve on the job? How do you handle the problems that arise?

6. With whom do you eat lunch? Do you entertain work associates?

7. How do you get subordinates to produce?

8. About how much time (percent) do you devote to your job?

Based on the information from your interview, complete the following manager role profile. Fill in Columns a and b and supply an example for each of the ten job roles. Arrange your interview so that you gather information on which to base the answers.

You might then examine your data to see if interpersonal roles, informational roles, or decisional roles are more important to effectiveness and which of them consume the most time.

You may be asked to report your findings for class discussion and comparison with others' findings about differences along such dimensions as job level in the hierarchy, type of firm, and so forth.

MANAGER ROLE PROFILE

(To be completed after interview)

Position: _____   Industry: _____

Level in hierarchy: _____   Size of Enterprise: _____
(top,middle,low)   (number of employees)

Roles the manager performs:

For each role, fill in the blanks under Columns a and b with the appropriate number from the following scale:

Column a. *How important is the role to effective job performance?*

1. Not important.
2. Of minimal importance.
3. Of some importance.
4. Of considerable importance.
5. Of very high importance.

Column b. *How time-consuming is the role?*

1. No time consumed.
2. Minimal time consumed.
3. Some time consumed.
4. Considerable time consumed.
5. Very large amount of time consumed.

	a	b
I. Interpersonal roles		
1. *Figurehead:* duties of a ceremonial nature; somewhat routine, little serious communication; (dinner, luncheons, dances, civic meetings, and so on) Example:	____	____
2. *Leader:* direct leadership; motivation and employee supervision; staffing and training; (develops people, selects personnel; influences employees) Example:	____	____

	a	b

3. *Liaison:* makes contacts outside the vertical chain of command; (staff meetings, luncheons with peers, clients, suppliers, government, and so on)
Example:

    a _____   b _____

II. Informational roles

4. *Monitor:* scanning the environment for information; nerve center for the organization; (interrogates liaison contacts and subordinates, reviews reports)
Example:

    a _____   b _____

5. *Disseminator:* passes along privileged information to subordinates (meetings, memos, letters, and briefings with subordinates)
Example:

    a _____   b _____

6. *Spokesman:* passes along information to people outside the organization (uses liaison contacts, speaks to groups, talks to suppliers and sales people, communicates to stockholders and directors)
Example:

    a _____   b _____

III. Decisional roles

7. *Entrepreneur:* adapts and changes organization to fit the environment; initiates project development; (cost reduction programs, reorganization of departments, public relations campaigns, development of forecasting systems)
Example:

    a _____   b _____

a   b

8. *Disturbance handler:* involuntarily responds
   to pressure; takes corrective action on
   problems (reacts to strike or grievance policy
   on bankrupt customer, responds to supplier
   who reneges on contract)
   Example:

   ____   ____

9. *Resource allocator:* decides what organizational units receive what resources; authorizes
   budgets and major decisions; (assigns personnel, sets objectives, makes capital expenditure
   decisions, schedules work)
   Example:

   ____   ____

10. *Negotiator:* represents organization in
    negotiating with employees, suppliers, cus-
    tomers; negotiates with other departments;
    (resolves jurisdictional disputes, hires key
    personnel, negotiates sale or union contracts)
    Example:

    ____   ____

CASE 3
SAMUEL I. SCHWARTZ

Si Schwartz had just finished talking to his son Paul who had called from college. Paul was considering changing his major to political science in the middle of his junior year. Paul really hadn't wanted to major in business, but his father had convinced him that this would be the best preparation for taking over the firm some day.

Si began thinking back about his own life and his dreams for his son. Si was the eldest of seven children of impoverished Jewish immigrants. His father had been fortunate to have a skill as a printer, and through hard work and sacrifice the elder Schwartz eventually scraped enough together to open his own small print shop.

Si finished grade school at the age of 14, enrolled in an evening high school, and went to work as an office boy for a newspaper. Since the paper had been unsuccessful, in a desperation move the owners gave control of it to Si, who was then 18. In lieu of salary, Si was offered half the newspaper's profits. By spending long hours at the office and studying merchandising techniques used in big city papers, Si quickly boosted advertising and made the paper profitable. Within two years the newspaper was in the black, and Si began earning a rather handsome salary. In the meantime, his father had died, leaving Si control of the print shop. By using some of the income from his job at the paper, Si began searching for ways to expand the print shop.

Within ten years, Si had built up a small publishing empire, expanding into magazine and book publishing as well as taking control of several failing newspapers in different cities.

Si seemed driven to assume control of a media giant. He began looking at and purchasing radio and television stations in the cities where his newspaper businesses were located. In thirty years, by pouring most of the money he earned back into the business, Si put together an empire from scratch, motivated by a phenomenal drive to build something of significance to leave to his children and family.

During this period, Si had some personal setbacks. His eldest son had decided to open his own law practice, and his daughter married a psychologist who had little interest in the family business. Now Paul was considering another career alternative. Because he had run a tight ship and refused to place responsibility in the hands of subordinates, Si knew he needed someone he could trust to take over the business.

Si rarely took vacations, preferring to spend his time at the office or traveling to his various business locations. He had planned a three-week trip to Europe one year, but he received so many calls from headquarters regarding business decisions that he flew back after only four days. During a recent business trip, however, chest pains forced him into the hospital where the doctors suggested he cut down his work schedule and take weekends off for trips to the mountains. But Si would have no part of that. He couldn't, or wouldn't, slow down.

Si's wife came into the den following Paul's phone call and noticed that Si was breathing rapidly and looked pale. She had just that day received a letter from the family physician urging her to have Si come in for a long-overdue checkup. When she asked if anything was wrong, Si snapped back, "I'd be all right if you would quit bothering me. I have lots of work left to do tonight."

Questions for Discussion

1. Is Si a typical entrepreneur?
2. Why isn't everyone like Si?
3. What motivates Si to keep running so hard?
4. If you were Paul, would you change your major?
5. If you were Si's wife, what would you do?

CASE 4
A DAY IN THE LIFE OF A MIDDLE MANAGER— SALLY BENSON

It was almost 6 p.m. and Sally Benson was still at her desk trying to tie up some "loose ends" with the hope that tomorrow might be a more productive day.

Sally is the western regional sales director, a middle management position in the Pro Line Company, a manufacturer of a well-known line of sporting goods. As she files away some mail she has answered and stacks the phone messages she still has to return, she wonders if being a middle manager is really "her kind of job." Actually, selling products, traveling, and interacting with clients and customers seemed much more to her liking than the tedious routine of her present job.

Take today, for example. She has come to the office early, so she can call Ted Lomax, the eastern regional sales director, to confer on a joint sales forecast they are trying to prepare. Working with Ted isn't the easiest of tasks. Compromise just isn't a word in Ted's vocabulary! She also needs to call the production managers of two of the company's eastern plants to find out what is causing the delay in the receipt of the new product lines. (Those production people just don't seem to realize that if we're to keep sales up we need a large variety of inventory in our warehouses.) These new product lines were promised two weeks ago and they still aren't here. The phone calls took longer than expected, but by mid-morning Sally is finally able to get settled into the major project she had planned for the day. After several days of laboriously perusing sales reports of the previous several years, she concludes that total sales, as well as productivity of individual salespersons can be improved if the region is redesigned and the territories of each salesperson adjusted. This is a major project and she needs to have at least a preliminary proposal ready to present to her district sales managers at her monthly meeting with them tomorrow afternoon.

A luncheon provides a pleasant interlude for Sally and gives her a chance to renew some old acquaintances from her days as this district's sales manager for Pro Line. Lunch keeps Sally away from the office a little longer than expected and when she returns she finds a half dozen phone messages, including an urgent call from the corporate vice president of personnel Bill Finley. She returns Finley's call and much to her dismay, she finds she is going to have to allocate a good portion of tomorrow's sales managers' meeting to presenting the company's new benefits program. Bill assured her all the materials she needs will arrive late this afternoon, and stressed the need for its immediate dissemination and explanation. After trying unsuccessfully to return several of the other phone calls, she returns to the territory redesign project she did not complete in the morning. She finishes that project just before the 3 p.m. appointment she has with a candidate for a district sales manager position that will open up next week. Sally spends over an hour with the candidate and is impressed enough with him to immediately make some follow-up phone calls to validate the accuracy of some of the information she received.

When 5 p.m. rolls around, she realizes she won't have much luck with further phone calls, and besides, the whole day has gotten away from her and she still has all the materials from Finley to review as well as having to prepare the agenda for tomorrow's meeting. Somehow she just has to figure out a way to motivate better performance from those sales managers. The redesign of the territory was only a partial solution. Sally wonders what else she can do. Well, since it is so late, at least the freeway traffic will have thinned out, so perhaps the 45-minute drive home will allow her to collect her thoughts and generate some creative innovations for tomorrow's meeting.

Questions for Discussion

1. Compare Sally's present job to what you think her previous job as a salesperson/sales manager might have been. How are they similar? How are they different?

2. What major roles of a middle manager are depicted in this case?

3. Why do you think Sally might be disenchanted with her present job?

4. Compare and contrast Sally's role as middle manager with that of entrepreneur Si Schwartz in the preceding case.

CASE 5
THE PERFECT PIZZERIA

Perfect Pizzeria in Southville, in deep southern Illinois, is the second largest franchise of the chain in the United States. The headquarters is located in Phoenix, Arizona. Although the business is prospering, it has employee and managerial problems.

Each store has one manager, an assistant manager, and from two to five night managers. The managers of each store work under an area supervisor. The specific criteria for being a manager or becoming a manager trainee are vague. The franchise has no training period for the manager. No college education is required. The managers for whom the casewriter worked during a four-year period were relatively young, (ages 24–27), and only one had completed college. The managers were chosen on their ability to perform the duties of the regular employees. Eventually they were promoted to a night managerial position. This is where they remained unless they expressed an interest in becoming part of the business.

The employees were mostly college students with a few high school students performing the less challenging jobs. Since Perfect Pizzeria was located in an area with few job opportunities, it had a relatively easy task of filling its employee quotas. All the employees, with the exception of the manager, were employed part-time. Consequently, they worked for less than the minimum wage.

Source: Adapted from a course assignment by Leland Neely for Professor J.G. Hunt, Southern Illinois University-Carbondale.

The Perfect Pizzeria system is devised so that food and beverage costs and profits are set up according to a percentage. If the percentage of food unsold or damaged in any way is very low, the manager gets a bonus. If the percentage is high, the manager does not receive a bonus, nor does he take a cut in salary.

There are many ways in which the percentage can fluctuate. Since the manager cannot be in the store twenty-four hours a day, some employees make up for their low paychecks by helping themselves to the food. When a friend comes in to order a pizza, extra ingredients may be put on the friend's pizza. Occasional nibbles by eighteen to twenty employees through the day at the meal table also raise the percentage figure. An occasional bucket of sauce may be spilled or a pizza accidentally burned. Sometimes the wrong size pizza may be made.

In the event of an employee mistake or a burned pizza by the oven man, the expense is to come from the individual. Because of peer pressure, the night manager seldom writes up a bill for the erring employee. Instead, the establishment takes the loss and the error goes unnoticed until the end of the month when inventory is taken. That's when the manager finds that the percentage is high and that there will be no bonus.

In the present instance, the new manager at Southville took retaliatory measures. Previously, each employee was entitled to a free pizza, salad, and all the soft drink he or she could drink for every six hours of work. The new manager, Ralph Samson, raised this figure from six to twelve hours of work. However, the employees had received these six-hour benefits for a long time. Therefore, they simply took advantage of the situation whenever Ralph or his assistant were not in the establishment.* Though the night manager, Paul Powell, theoretically had complete control of the store in the evenings, he did not command the respect that Ralph or the assistant manager did. That was because he received the same pay as the regular employees; Paul could not reprimand other employees; and he was basically the same age or sometimes even younger than the other employees.

Thus, apathy grew within the pizzeria. There seemed to be a further separation between Paul and his workers, which started out to be a closely-knit group.

Ralph made no attempt to alleviate the problem, because he felt it would iron itself out. Either the employees that were dissatisfied would quit or they would be content to put up with the new regulations. As it turned out, there was a rash of employee dismissals. Ralph had no problem in filling the vacancies with new workers, but the loss of key personnel was costly to the business.

With the large turnover, Ralph found he had to spend more time in the store, supervising and sometimes taking the place of inexperienced workers. This was in direct violation of the franchise regulations which stated that a manager would act as a supervisor and at no time take part in the actual food preparation. Employees were placed under strict supervision with Ralph or his assistant working along side. The operation no longer worked smoothly because of differences between the remaining experienced workers and Ralph, concerning the way in which a particular function should be performed.

Within a two-month period, Ralph was again free to go back to his office and leave his subordinates in charge of the entire operation. During this two-month period, the percentage had returned to the previous low level and Ralph received a bonus each month. Ralph felt that his problems had been resolved and that

*The assistant manager fulfills his or her role by working a two-hour shift during the luncheon period, five days a week. His or her primary function is to gain knowledge about bookkeeping or managerial aspects for a future managerial position in this or another unit.

store conditions would remain the same, since new personnel had been properly trained.

It didn't take long for the new employees to become influenced by the other employees. Immediately after Ralph had returned to his supervisory role, the percentage began to rise. This time Ralph took a bolder step. He cut out any benefits that the employees had—no free pizza, salad or drinks. With the job market at an even lower ebb than usual, most employees were forced to stay. The appointment of a new area supervisor made it impossible for Ralph to "work behind the counter," since the supervisor was centrally located in Southville.

Ralph tried still another approach to alleviate the rising percentage problem and maintain his bonus. He placed a notice on the bulletin board, stating that if the percentage remained at a high level, a lie detector test would be given to all employees. All those found guilty of taking or purposefully wasting food or drinks would be immediately terminated. This had no effect whatsoever on the employees, because they knew that if they were all subjected to the test, all would be found guilty and Ralph would have to dismiss all of them. This would leave him in a worse situation than ever.

Even before the following month's percentage was calculated, Ralph knew it would be high. He had evidently received information from one of the night managers about the employee's feelings toward the notice. What he did not expect was that the percentage would reach an all-time high. That is the state of affairs at the present time.

Questions for Discussion

1. Was Ralph functioning as you would expect a middle manager to do?
2. Does the store or company policy toward the selection of managers seem appropriate?
3. Are the different levels of management (manager, assistant manager, night manager) clearly defined and separable from the employees on the basis of salary, job duties, and authority?
4. Was Ralph properly motivated to solve the pizzeria's problem?
5. Did Ralph have the proper training to correct the problems that existed?
6. What needs to be done to raise the employees' and managers' morale and motivation?

READING 6
THE FUTURE OF PRIVATE ENTERPRISE INITIATIVES FOR THE 1980s
Kenneth Mason

Let me say right away how happy I am to be in Washington to speak at the invitation of someone other than the FTC or the SEC or the FCC. They are all

Source: Edited transcript of a lecture by Mr. Kenneth Mason, presented in the Caucus Room, Cannon House Office Building, Capitol Hill, on May 13, 1982. Mr. Mason is a Yale graduate and pursued a career in advertising before joining the Quaker Oats Company as Director of Advertising in 1962. He was elected President and Chief Operating Officer in 1976, and retired at the age of 57 in 1979 to undertake a program of study, writing, and speaking on management topics. He remains a director of Quaker Oats and of Rohm and Haas Company, Philadelphia.

fine folks in those agencies, but my experience—and I think the experience of almost everyone in industry—has been that, while their motives are superb, the understanding of basic business economics by Washington officials really leaves a great deal to be desired. In that regard, I have to tell you a true story about Washington and the Quaker Oats Company that occurred some years ago. It involves our Fisher-Price toy division, one of the world's leading toy companies. I am sure that those of you who have children, and certainly those of you who have grandchildren, are pretty familiar with Fisher-Price toys. Quaker acquired Fisher-Price back in 1969, when it was a very small company doing only about $35 million worth of business. Today it is a big company, doing close to $500 million worth of business.

During the early 1970s, as Fisher-Price was growing, their growth came from some very ingenious marketing efforts. In the early 1970s, Fisher-Price invented a toy called the "play family house". That is a very simple idea; it was simply a whole house with a fence around it and little tiny people that you could position around a little dog and a little cat. And this was a very successful device and sold a great many boxes. The next year Fisher-Price expanded that idea and came up with "play family farm". This was the same idea, except now instead of a suburban house, it was a farm and a barn; and instead of a dog and a cat, it had a cow and a goat. And the kids loved it and that was terribly successful. The next year Fisher-Price marketing people extended the idea one step further and came up with the "play family city parking garage". And this was a terrific little gadget. It had a little thing to wind; you put the little wooden car in the slot and you turned the handle, and the car went up and got parked on the second floor. The kids loved that.

Well, back when these were Fisher-Price's outstanding toys, the marketing director of Fisher-Price was invited by the Federal Trade Commission to come down and talk about some matters pertaining to the toy industry. It wasn't an investigation; they were just exchanging ideas. But since Fisher-Price is located near Buffalo, New York, and Quaker, the parent company, is located near Chicago, Quaker thought it would be smart to send one of their high-priced lawyers down to sit in with the Fisher-Price man just to make sure that everything was going to be all right. So these two fellows went down, one from Buffalo and one from Chicago, and met with the FTC in that wonderful building. And at the end of the day when they were finished with the meeting, they got on the elevator on the 6th floor there and started down. The day was over, and the lawyer from Chicago said, "Gee, Jack, we have been so busy all day long talking to the FTC that I haven't had a chance to ask you, how business is. How are things going?" And Jack said, "Well, despite the recession, business really isn't bad at all. So far this year, we have sold 600,000 houses, 500,000 farms and 450,000 city parking garages".

And at that moment, they noticed that there was another man in the elevator with them who was looking at them in a very curious manner. When the elevator reached the main floor and the doors opened and they got out, this fellow cleared his throat and said, "Gentlemen, I don't want to be rude, but I happen to be in the real estate business. . . ." He didn't need to finish his sentence.

We at Quaker took that story and put it into our regular lexicon. We use it to demonstrate the aphorism: When in Washington, expect to be misunderstood.

When you think of the very serious problems that are facing our nation today—the precarious state of the economy, the difficulty of getting agreement in the government, the escalating tension between the United States and a number of other countries, the belligerency right now in Latin America—you have to wonder why anyone would be attracted to a lecture on a subject of such apparently minuscule importance, at least in a global sense, as the philosophy of corporate management in the United States. Now—before you all decide I am absolutely right, and get up and leave—let me just quickly answer my own question by saying that in my opinion there are some very good reasons for anyone interested in the future well-being of this country to be concerned about what the American multinational corporation has become during the last 25 years and to ponder what this means for our society, our culture and our economy, during the remainder of this century.

Let me ask you first of all to consider briefly the financial power that is concentrated in a handful of American corporations. Just 500 companies do more than half of all the business done in this country. Fewer than 1,000 corporate entities control the use of $2 trillion in assets, and that is in an economy where the annual gross national product is only $3 trillion. There is a tremendous financial power in the American corporation.

Next, consider the social power of the American corporation. One thousand corporations provide the payroll for 20 million workers, and perhaps more important, they provide the work place for 20 million workers, their physical and intellectual environment for 40 hours or more a week. And these companies produce not only the products and services we use; they also produce the advertising which affects the way we think and feel about these products and services. And as psychologists have shown us, in some cases the advertising affects the way we feel about ourselves as well. And, of course, no one should forget that it is the American corporation that provides the financial support for commercial television in this country, the single most important cultural influence in America for the last 50 years.

So, you have tremendous financial power and you have tremendous social power. But in my view, the real key to corporate power in America, more important than the financial and social power, and the thing that makes the corporation the central institution of our time, is the rich and varied life-time career that it offers to young people from all walks of life. By "central institution" I mean like the church in the Middle Ages, like the army might have been in Roman times, like certain royal courts and certain great universities in various eras. Some of you may disagree with me, but I don't think there is a career in society today to compare with it. I don't think that ambassador or missionary, professor or military officer, or any other career that I can think of, offers a wider variety of intellectual challenge, or a greater opportunity to learn how the real world works, than a successful career in middle management in a typical multinational business corporation.

Let me just use our corporation, even one as modest in size as Quaker Oats, to give you an example of what I am talking about. Quaker is a company whose annual sales are less than $3 billion. We rank 161 on the Fortune 500. It is just an average, not an especially big or important multinational company. It is a company a lot of whose sales come from familiar brand names—Quaker Oats, Captain Crunch, Aunt Jemima, Kennel Ration, Flako, Puss N' Boots, Celeste Pizzas, names that are familiar. Those are things you know about. But what you don't know is that Quaker is also the largest sardine producer in Brazil and the largest chocolate company in Mexico. Quaker makes laundry bleaches in Venezuela and scouring pads in Colombia, in addition to food products. In Italy, Quaker sells more than $100 million a year in salad oil. In France, Quaker is a major factor in the pet food business. In Holland, Quaker is important in the manufacture of honey. Quaker's Fisher-Price toy division is the largest maker of pre-school toys in the world. Our Magic Pan restaurant division was one of the most successful restaurant developments in the 1970s. Our Brookstone division is one of the leading mail order houses in the country. Joseph A. Bank is also a Quaker subsidiary, and one of the best men's and women's clothing retailers and mail order companies in the East. We have a chemicals division which is the world's leading supplier of furfuryl alcohol which is a binding agent that is very important in the foundry industry.

I went through this list not to urge you to buy Quaker stock, but for another reason. It is to suggest to you what it might mean to be a manager in a company even as small and innocuous as Quaker Oats, because managers in companies like that spend most of their business lives on the very cutting edge of the major technological and social developments that occur all over the world. I am talking about developments in such areas as the genetic engineering of plants and chemicals, the improvement of nutrition for both humans and animals, the utilization of energy in manufacturing and transportation, the demographic trends and developing life styles in a dozen countries around the world. So a career in middle management, even in a company as small as Quaker, forces the development of expertise in very diverse and important subjects—subjects like new techniques of steel production, the chemistry of rice hulls, the creation of computer software, and the learning capabilities of children. Here you have corporations that, of necessity, are the very center of the latest technological developments in the world, and that have the financial resources and informational expertise to act on them. A moderately successful career, an average career, in a company like Quaker, can include managing people in a cereal plant, managing technology in a research lab, managing information in a corporate planning department, managing money in a financial department, or managing a self-contained operating unit in South America or in Europe. And you can have a career like that all within the space of a few years.

I don't think there has ever been an institution to equal the modern corporation in providing society with superb financial, physical, technological, and human assets all brought together under one management. And I don't think there is any equal for the opportunities it offers people with brains and ambition to develop and put to use skills and knowledge that used to be available only to the very rich and socially privileged. I think the case can be made that in all of human history there has never been an institution better equipped to do some tangible good in this world than the typical multinational corporation of today.

Now, when you think about the American corporation in this light—in the light of its economic power, its daily impact on our culture, its development of our best and brightest minds, and its bringing those minds into play on the major technological and social issues of the age—and when you add to that the belief of the current administration in Washington that the business of America is business, and that the business sector should begin to shoulder some of the social burdens that government would like to lay down, then I would submit to you that what the 500 chief executive officers of America's largest corporations think their responsibilities are as every bit as important to you and to me as what the 500 congressmen and senators who work here on Capitol Hill think their responsibilities are.

If you ask these 500 congressmen and senators what they think their number one responsibility is, you are going to get a number of different answers. You may get answers ranging from "My number one responsibility is to represent my constituency," to "Voting my conscience." But if you ask 500 chief executives what they think their number one responsibility is, you are going to get just one answer from all 500, and that answer is, "My number one responsibility is to bring a satisfactory number down to the bottom line".

Now, I want to say very quickly, I think that answer is absolutely right. I have given a number of talks around the country, and on occasion they have been reported in the business section of the newspaper the next day. Several times I have been astonished to see that a speech was given, so-and-so, and this fellow said he thought business was paying too much attention to the bottom line. All this proves is that people aren't listening. That is not what I had been saying. I think the bottom line is what business should be paying attention to. It is business' great distinguishing feature. It is what separates the private sector

from the public sector. It is what makes business people see that world differently from others—government people, for instance. It is what makes American executives so different from their European counterparts. It is a very important
concept, and I think it is and should be the number one concept of business. It
is a great compliment, not only to a manager but to anybody trying to get a job
done, to be described as "bottom-line oriented." That description means that the
person is perceived as someone who doesn't equivocate, isn't easily diverted from
his goals, and isn't likely to make excuses for his failures. I think those are great
qualities in any undertaking, not just business.

It is interesting to see the "bottom line" as a concept creep into our language.
Listen to Howard Cosell, for instance: "What's the bottom line on today's game,
coach?" Listen to Alexander Haig, in a televised Senate subcommittee hearing,
"Would you like me to bottom-line that for you Senator?" It is a part of our language; everybody understands what it means.

I am all for the "bottom line" as the definitive measure of performance in business. My quarrel with American corporate philosophy, and my great disappointment in the business leadership of my generation, is not that we have been too
concerned with the bottom line, but that we are drawing the "bottom line" in the
wrong place. We haven't kept pace with the important changes in where the
"bottom line" really is. In our society over the last 20 years, the "bottom line"
has continually moved lower and lower on the corporate income statement. I
think very few corporate chief executives have kept pace with that movement.

When I started in the business, the "bottom line" was net profit after taxes.
There just wasn't any other concept involved. The net profit after taxes was the
objective of all the plans that we worked on at Quaker, and everybody else that
we knew did the same. Then you said: Here is our net profit for the year, and
next year we've got to beat that. And we did; we beat our net profit figures, and
our net profit kept going up year after year, and that was just great. And then
one year came when our net profit went up, but our earnings per share went
down. The reason was that we had acquired some companies, and thus had put
out more stock than we had before. Our net profit total was going along fine,
but we had begun to dilute the stock.

All of a sudden the "bottom line" in our company changed. Our plans were no
longer focused on net profit after taxes, they were focused on earnings per share.
This involved a different calculation. Our "bottom line" dropped a notch. Now
we had this new target and so we said, "Okay, we are going to make our earnings per share go up every year." We did that for a while, and then one day the
financial man came in and he said, "Fellows, this is just terrific with these earnings per share figures up each year, but what you don't realize is that this is a
much bigger business now. You've got all these inventories over here, and all
those receivables over there; and you've got a lot more capital in this business.
It is nice that earnings per share keep going up, but the return on invested capital is going down, and we've got to do something about that."

Well, we suddenly had a new "bottom line" on the income statement, which
was return on invested capital, and that became the new name of our game. And
of course, no sooner did some of us operating guys, who weren't too smart to
begin with, get that through our heads and in comes the company's treasurer,
and he says, "Fellows, return on invested capital is indeed important; but what
the security analysts are looking for is return on equity. That is the number to
look for." So our "bottom line" dropped another notch, and return on equity became the key figure that we were building our plans around.

However, I don't think we came to the "bottom line" there either. The only
reason the company treasurer wanted return on equity was to please the security
analysts, and the reason he wanted to please the security analysts was to raise
our price/earnings ratio, so that the price/earnings ratio was what he thought
the "bottom line" was. But the price/earnings ratio itself isn't really what you

are after; what you are after is to make your stock price higher, so that the "bottom line" was actually the price of your stock on the stock market.

Well, that is just a rudimentary example of the bottom line falling lower and lower in the financial area. My point is that the bottom line is falling in other ways as well. All of those measures are clearly important. Net profit is important; return on invested capital, return on equity, stock market prices, etc. These all, of course, have to be taken into consideration by corporate managers. But I have come to the conclusion that there is another measure, more important than those. I think that farther down the page there is a *true* "bottom line" for business corporations, and I think it should be called "return on assets employed." By that phrase, "assets employed," I mean *all* the assets employed in the business, not just the financial assets, but the human assets, the intellectual assets, the physical assets, the technological assets, and the environmental assets.

Now the reason that I am convinced that I am right about this, that return on all assets employed is really the "bottom line," is that if it weren't, I think we would all be in the pornographic film business. In terms of net profit as a percent of sales, you simply can't beat a pornographic film. The same is true of return on capital, and of earnings per share (if there are shares in it), and return on equity. The initial investment in pornographic films is so low, and the earning life of a successful pornographic film is so long, that the return on investment of just a routinely successful pornographic film is practically astronomical. In addition to that, when you think of the rapidly increasing presence of video players in American homes, and you think of the increasing availability of cable television channels in cities all over the country, well, pornographic films may well be the fastest growing consumer market in America today.

Why aren't all the hot shot blue chip consumer goods companies in there fighting for a share of this new market? Aren't growth and high returns on investment exactly what every red-blooded chief executive officer is looking for? We think Quaker Oats is a hot marketing company; why didn't we go into the pornographic film business? Well, we are interested in growth and we are interested in high returns, but the reason we aren't interested in pornographic films is that we know, even if we haven't articulated it, that the pornographic film industry produces an unacceptably bad return on some of the most important assets corporations possess. Assets like brains, character, personal integrity, and the desire to do some good in this world; assets that most businesses, even though they don't state it openly, prize very dearly and are determined not to waste.

I think that the concept of "return on assets employed" as a "bottom line" for business operations really makes a great deal of sense. It maintains the crucial discipline of profit, because you can't get a good return on all assets without a return on the financial assets. At the same time, it reminds those of us who have been given the privilege of managing America's assets that there is a lot more to good management than turning in good profit figures.

The most glaring example I know of management turning in good profits but getting an incredibly bad return on assets employed is the commercial television industry in this country. It is one of the most profitable businesses in the world, by any kind of financial ratio, particularly the children's segment. Children's television delivers the highest profit margins that the networks get. Now I will defy any reasonable adult who is not currently employed in the television industry to sit down in front of a television set next Saturday morning for three or four hours, the way so many of our children do, and not be appalled at the way the United States of America, which is still the richest nation in the world, has chosen to use this incredible powerful medium on young children.

The question I keep asking is why is the intellectual and aesthetic quality of children's television in this country so disappointing? Certainly it isn't lack of money. American corporations spend well over $100 million a year just on Saturday morning television, just for those programs. Is it possible that what we see on the screen is the best that America's writers, directors, and producers can do with $100 million? Obviously it's not. We have seen what public television can do for children with much less money. Why is children's television the shame of the nation today? I think it is because television executives think that the huge profits they make on Saturday morning television mean Saturday morning television is a huge success. The truth of the matter is that much better programs could have been produced with the same amount of money, and when you factor in the equation at least some nominal value for the future potential a young child's attention represents, then I would submit that children's television in America is an economic disaster, and America's television executives are the most dismal failures in American business. I just don't see how anyone who really cares about the future of this country can fail to be concerned about the negative effect, as all the research tells us, that television is having on young minds.

The thing that kills me is that I would think those who would be most concerned would be the business community, those who have the largest stake in the free enterprise system, the large corporations. What all the research on television is telling us is that the commercial networks' preoccupation with crime and violence and sex is infecting the youth of the country with the very diseases that businessmen decry the most: Cynicism, apathy, lack of personal values, lack of respect for America and its political heritage. Who gets hurt the most by that kind of an attitude? American business corporations. I think the case can be made—in fact, I think it will be made in the future, by historians who write the business history of this era—I think the case will be made that the commercial networks' use of the television medium has been the most devastating and successful attack on the moral fiber of the nation ever conducted from within. The evidence mounts that the most serious threat to the continuing success of the free enterprise system is not that it may lose its freedom, but that it may lose its enterprise. If it does, I think that those business corporations who spend $5 billion a year to enable the networks to put this kind of programming on are going to have to accept a large portion of the blame.

You may think that in taking out after the networks I am getting far afield from the title of this lecture, but I don't think I am. I think I am still close to the point, because the misuse of this country's television medium, the failure of the business executives in television to get a good return on those very important assets, is just one example of many I think we could cite where American management is getting shockingly poor returns on very important resources.

Consider another example, the American labor force. For most of this century, it has been the best educated, best paid, and most competent labor force in the world. Now clearly, the labor force, the people who are going to work in your plant, are among the most important assets any company can possibly have. And this asset is not being managed by the government; it is managed by the free enterprise system. What kind of results has American management gotten from this country with the free enterprise system? Do workers in America understand and respect corporate problems and objectives? Do American workers take pride in their jobs and the products they make? The evidence suggests they don't.

Take the advertising industry. American corporations spend $60 billion a year in consumer advertising. It is still a lot of money. And what does this $60 billion a year expenditure get for American business? Well, for one thing, we get some help in selling merchandise that might not sell quite so well if it weren't advertised. But we also get, according to recent polls, the persuasion of more than 50% of all adult Americans that consumer advertising is misleading and untrustworthy. In a 1977 Gallup inquiry about the honesty and ethical standards of people in 20 different occupational groups, that included business executives, politicians, undertakers, car salesmen, the whole gamut of occupations, the advertising practitioner ranked dead last, 20th. Now, most of the ad agencies that created the advertising that has produced these results, both for the advertising industry and for the corporations, are quite profitable. But can you think of a worse return on investment for America's advertisers than to have made a $60 billion annual expenditure to convince the public that they are dishonest? If business had known in advance that this would happen, do you think they would still have hired those same agencies, and would those agencies have still been thinking of themselves as very successful businesses? I don't think they would.

Look at the environmental situation. The environment, we all admit, is a fairly important asset in any economy. And, in fact, it is the source of all economic activity. Now what have America's business leaders done to assure the public that we are going to manage this precious asset wisely? Well, mostly what the American business community has done is to dismiss those who raise environmental issues as kooks and cranks and bleeding hearts, who have no understanding of economics and who would throw millions out of work just to save a few trees in the woods or to fish in a river. This response can hardly give sober and concerned citizens the feeling that they're in good hands with American business.

There has been a great deal of discussion in recent years about the concept of corporate responsibility, and a great deal of progress, I think, in getting corporations to embrace that concept. It is now commonplace for the board of directors of most corporations to have a corporate responsibility committee that is chaired, almost always, by an outside director. That is a very good sign. The annual reports of corporations now almost without exception cite examples of how the corporation has performed as a citizen of the community; and we cite with pride how we give to charity, support the arts, and help the community to solve some problems. Recently the Business Roundtable, which is an organization of chief executive officers of 250 of the nation's most prestigious corporations, published a "Statement of Corporate Responsibility" which states unequivocally the belief of the Business Roundtable that business activities must make social sense.

This is a wonderfully healthy sign, and certainly ought to be applauded and encouraged. But supporting the arts isn't really what corporate responsibility is all about. It is what corporate philanthropy is about, and that is wonderful. But I don't think that true corporate responsibility is about the arts, giving charity, or helping the community solve problems. I think the real responsibility of corporations in our free enterprise system is to get good returns on all the assets we employ. Not just the assets we legally own, like the money, the land and the buildings and the machinery, but the assets that belong to somebody else, the assets that belong to the nation—people and air and water and things like that. It is my belief that if we don't get a good return on these assets, then the private enterprise system will have lost, not only its claim to fame, but also its reason for being. Then someone else, government or labor, will—and I think should—take over.

Of course, in this obligation to get a good return on assets employed, corporations are no different than any other organization, or any other organism, for that matter. They are no different from each of us in this room, and no different from any living entity. Because, whether we are managing a big business or a little one, or whether we have a big family or a small one, whether our health is good or bad, whether our IQ is at the genius level or just normal, there is really just one universal yardstick that measures all of us, whether we like it or not, and that is: How well did we do with whatever assets the good Lord happened to give us to work with? The quantity and quality of those assets varies enormously from individual to individual. It varies enormously from nation to nation, from species to species; it varies enormously from corporation to corporation. But I think the evidence is that we are all playing the same game.

We are all trying to get some kind of sensible return from the assets that are under our control. My career in business has convinced me that only a few institutions in the entire history of the world have been given so many magnificent assets to work with as the American business corporation, the large multinational has been given. And it is my belief that only to the extent that America's business leaders seek returns commensurate with the superb quality of those assets will the capitalism that has served this country so well in the past continue to serve it in the next century.

Question from the floor: How can we operationalize that concept for corporations and people who run them, since everything seems to be based on measurable and quantifiable performance? In other words, how do we get a handle on the return to all assets employed and on corporate responsibility in general?

Mr. Mason: That is an excellent question. I am impressed with how we have gotten a handle on corporate social responsibility in general. Now there is an unquantifiable concept, but the Business Roundtable Statement is an amazing step. Look at the oil companies and the power they have if they want to use financial power. But there isn't an oil company in the country today that is in the marketplace, in the media, saying, "I'm trying to make profits, that is my only responsibility." They don't brag about their profits. They are saying "I have to make this money because if I don't make the money I can't explore for oil, and I need to explore for oil because the country needs it." They have embraced the concept. They are afraid to come to the country and say "We have no responsibilities." They have accepted those. The Business Roundtable is the most prestigious organization in American corporate life today; and it has gone on record as saying, "We believe that business activity must make social sense." Now social sense may not be quantifiable dollars and cents, but once you have said "We must make social sense," it means that you are committed. So I am very hopeful. One of the key points I would make is I don't see the conflict with profits. I don't think it changes the fact that a company has profit obligations. You either make the money or you go out of business; there is no change in that. But I think there is general agreement in this country now that you can't get out there and just ignore the environment. And I hope we are going to get to the point where you just can't go on the air and ignore what television is doing to our culture. The fact that the concept can't be quantified, I think, doesn't mean that it hasn't been embraced. And I think we will see a lot of activity, a lot of changes, in corporations from what has already happened in this country. But probably not in my lifetime.

Question from the floor: What precisely is your criticism of advertising?

Mr. Mason: Well, I have two criticisms. One is the result. These surveys show that 50% of the adults interviewed believe that advertising is misleading. Those have to be very unproductive expenditures. With all that money to spend, how much more productive it would be if people didn't think it was misleading. I could run fewer ads, and my profits would be higher; or I could price my products lower, if one commercial would sell you. I think it has been a very bad expenditure of money, a very unproductive, lax expenditure. We criticize labor, the unions, and say, "You are feather-bedding, and there is a lot of unproductive activity." But here is a $60 billion expenditure that has been proven by surveys to be unproductive.

The second objection is that this country has been built, in my opinion, by two things, a fine system of government and a fine system of economic activity. And our free enterprise system really is wonderful; it is a magnificent thing. The thing that disturbs me is that since television came in it has lost its voice. The people of the United States don't hear from business, they hear from Hollywood.

The commercials, the exposure to business and business products in this country, comes from television; and what we are hearing is the voice of Hollywood. It's how Hollywood thinks we should talk about our soaps and our cereals and our cars. I think some of the lack of respect for business arises because business has treated its products in a very Hollywoodish fashion on the national media, rather than making sober, sensible comments about the products. I know the advertising people say, "Fine. That will be a very dull ad you want to write, nobody will listen to it and it won't work." I know the alternatives. I am not saying it is simple.

Those are my two complaints. That we abdicated our voice as business leaders to Hollywood script writers to write 30-second commercials, and that the results show that people don't really have much respect for advertising or its practitioners.

Question from the floor: What incentive do managers have to follow your advice?

Mr. Mason: Actually, what they have is a disincentive, because they have the great incentive for the reverse. The problem is that the stock market in America has become a speculative stock market, it is very interested in short-term results; and most corporation leaders are reluctant, to say the least, and maybe afraid in most cases, not to turn up short-term earnings as the market anticipates. I am very sympathetic with their problem. I think there are ways to change that. I won't give the lecture here, but one way would be to reduce the supposed dependence of American industry on security analysts' judgment of their performance. One way to do that would be to have a different taxation system for dividends, one which favored dividends over capital gains. This would enable corporations to give you a return on your money through dividends, and you wouldn't keep looking at the stock market thinking, "I've got to sell tomorrow because that is where most of my return is going to come."

Question from the floor: What difference do you see in the "bottom-line" concept, between foreign corporations and American corporations?

Mr. Mason: I think it is universally agreed that foreign corporations are in a position to take a longer range view than American corporations. They are not so wedded to the short-term effect of their price on the stock market. The foreign stock markets don't seem to be judging individual companies by market appreciation on a daily basis, so that they can take a much longer point of view. The real way to take a long range point of view is to look for return on all assets employed, but let's talk about the financial assets only, the return on financial assets employed over a period of time. If you are getting a good return overall, it shouldn't matter at all if your earnings vary from period to period. The American business leader has abdicated his leadership to security analysts in the brokerage firms, and he has let himself be locked into a rigid pattern of earnings increases with no deviation. This is a very bad way to run a business. It just adds one more hurdle and you have enough without that. There is no reason for business to have a rigid pattern. Businesses should have cycles. There is no reason for this year's first quarter necessarily to be over last year's fourth quarter. Doesn't mean a thing. Doesn't mean a thing if it is over; doesn't mean a thing if it isn't over. What matters is, are you getting a good return on your assets over any length of time and does your future look good? Have you brought the products along? Are you going to get a good return over a ten-year period? One quarter is meaningless. You have no idea the number of executives involved, and how much time they spend three days before that report goes out. Absolutely unproductive time. Foreign companies have it much easier.

What about the companies that are not publicly held; how do they compare with European companies? The publicly held company is at a great competitive disadvantage compared to the non-publicly held company. The non-publicly held company can make all kinds of short-term investment, can let its earnings grow on a cycled pattern, because it isn't reporting to the public. Its stock price is its own concern, and, if you run your own business, it doesn't matter what price your stock might be worth on any given day unless that is the day you plan to sell it. The American stock market has come up with an investment theory that doesn't make sense. It is that the return on your investment in stock should come in two forms, dividends and market appreciation, of which market appreciation is the greatest and most important. There are many theories which say corporations shouldn't pay dividends, that they should reinvest the money so that the market appreciation is greatest. This puts a short-term pressure on all executives to see that the stock price goes up, and that it never goes down. They are afraid to report lower earnings for fear that the market price will go down, even if it only goes down for three months. This is the short-term pressure that is causing bad business decisions.

Question from the floor: Why haven't you made your criticisms of advertising more effective?

Mr. Mason: I have expressed them as a person, and I have expressed them for the Quaker Oats company, which is not the largest advertiser but is a significant advertiser. But it is very difficult to move the broadcasting industry. One of the disappointments of my business career was that the people at Kellogg's and General Mills and General Foods—who are fine people, and I am not suggesting for a moment they aren't—missed a great opportunity to join in when Quaker, some years ago, was making a very strong plea for self-regulation in the cereal industry with respect to advertising. It would not violate the antitrust laws at all, but would enable us to almost force the networks to put on better programming and a better style of commercial for children. We made a very clear proposal and the other companies were reluctant to join us. I think self-regulation is the answer, and more business leadership and more business followership. It doesn't do any good to get business leadership if nobody comes along.

Question from the floor: I want to ask you a question about corporate growth, particularly by organizations.

Mr. Mason: I'm afraid the answer is equivocal. It varies by case. I don't think there is anything inherently wrong with one corporation merging with another, whether it's by acquisition or mutual agreement or whatever. I don't think there is anything wrong being a $70 billion company where there were once two $35 billion companies. I don't think it is automatically going to improve their return on assets, and those of us who have been in the merger and acquisition game have found to our great disappointment that the bigger we got the more our return on invested capital went down. I don't think there is anything wrong with the mergers if they don't violate the antitrust act, and that act is pretty well written. So if Du Pont and Conoco want to get together, or U.S. Steel and Marathon want to get together, and there is no law against it, I don't think it stifles anything. Big companies are awfully easy to compete with sometimes, because they are very worried about their stock price, and they are very worried about some other things, and they are very reluctant to do certain things that smaller companies can do.

Questions for Discussion

1. Think about a recent job experience you had. Did the management of the organization exhibit socially responsible behavior? How? What kind of impact did (does) the environment have on the business?

2. Think about the first post-college job you may have. Would you expect your superiors, co-workers, and subordinates to feel socially responsible? How might the environment influence this, either positively or negatively?

3. What is the "bottom line" for a business that you have been associated with?

4. In organizations, where does social responsibility come from: corporate culture, nature of industry, etc.?

CASE 7
TROUBLE IN TOYLAND

MINUTES OF THE ANNUAL MEETING OF THE STOCKHOLDERS OF RECORD—CHILDREN'S WORLD MANUFACTURING CORPORATION

President Waldo M. Tembler called the annual meeting of the stockholders, Children's World Manufacturing Corporation, to order at 3:07 p.m. at the Senator Hotel in New York. Although the meeting was scheduled to start at 2:00 p.m., persons representing themselves as the Committee to Spare Our Children from Needless Violence blocked the entrance to the main ballroom, barring stockholders and delaying the proceedings. When hotel security guards arrived, Mr. Tembler asked the protestors to step aside, stating that if they did, he would allow them to voice their feelings at the meeting.

Mr. Tembler welcomed the stockholders to the meeting and expressed confidence that Children's World would retain its title as the largest toy manufacturer in the world. A jibe of "bigness does not mean niceness" from the audience was shouted down by other stockholders. Mr. Tembler then completed his short opening remarks.

At 3:15, Roger V. Capp, Treasurer, reported gross corporate sales for the fiscal year (including all wholly owned subsidiaries in the United States, Mexico, Europe, and Asia) as 823 million dollars and consolidated net profits at 103.5 million dollars.

At 3:30, Arnold Ruttenberg, Corporate Director of Marketing, presented new toy items which would be ready for the wholesale trade well in advance of the Christmas season. Among these were Hector the Household Robot, the Astronaut Space Chase Game, and Black Lisa, the doll with the enchanting smile and a face everyone will adore. Ruttenberg was interrupted by a stockholder who identified herself as "Mrs. Ellen Trueblood, one of the black women in the New Jersey doll assembly plant."

Mrs. Trueblood claimed to have long ago suggested changes in the design profile of black Lisa which were totally ignored. Mrs. Trueblood went on to say that, as currently designed, Black Lisa was a young parody of the "old pancake lady" and would be an affront to the entire black community. Mr. Ruttenberg thanked her for her comments but said hers was only one opinion. He said Black Lisa was a design composite created after extensive market research with children of all colors, races, and nationalities.

Mr. Ruttenberg also answered questions from stockholders regarding suits filed by the Consumer Protection League of New York State alleging deceptive packaging of small toys. Mr. Ruttenberg noted that large protective boxes and

Source: Reprinted from Robert D. Joyce, *Encounters in Organizational Behavior,* 1972, with permission of Pergamon Press Ltd., Oxford, England.

related containers are often necessary to ensure damage-free product shipment, storage, and display.

Regarding the no contest plea entered by corporate attorneys in response to the federal suit filed under the Truth in Advertising Act, Mr. Ruttenberg stated that advertising agencies were often overzealous in their use of animation effects on television. Some toys do appear to be larger, faster, or better on television than they do in real life, said Mr. Ruttenberg, but it was a constant problem to place each toy in its best light considering the competitiveness of the industry. Mr. Ruttenberg added that a plea of no contest was not a guilty plea but merely a statement not to use such practices or methods in future advertisements.

At 4:10 p.m., Martin B. Prescott, Director of Corporate Design, spoke of future industry and company developments. He also re-emphasized the extensive design research which preceded the manufacture of Black Lisa. On the subject of product reliability, Mr. Prescott reminded the audience not to place too much importance on the long-running syndicated newspaper feature which condemned most toy manufacturers (and specifically Children's World) for purposeful and willful built-in toy obsolescence. Mr. Prescott added that product reliability in all toy and game lines had undergone major study in the last six months and only a few product adjustments were found to be required. These changes have already been incorporated into future production runs.

Responding to questions from a spokesman of the Committee to Spare Our Children from Needless Violence, Mr. Prescott stated:

1. Fewer war oriented toys were now being produced and fewer still were in the design stages due to changing public attitudes.

2. The company was currently reviewing its long sponsorship of the television program, Western Conflict, but no final decision, had, as yet, been made.

All planned presentations completed, President Tembler opened the podium to questions on any subject related to corporate activities.

Mr. Juan Alonzo argued that the E.E.O. (equal employment opportunity) agreements to which the company and the Union had agreed worked specifically in favor of women and blacks. He said unless something was done soon to improve job opportunities for Mexican-Americans, particularly in the office and professional areas, formal protests might well be invoked at the East Los Angeles and Phoenix facilities. Mr. Tembler replied that the E.E.O. provisions were fair to all but that he would personally instruct Darrin McCall, Personnel Manager, to review all promotions made in the last twelve months.

Sarah Fish of Queens called for a reduction of salaries and bonuses to officers but was ruled out of order, shareholders having previously authorized by majority vote the officers' salaries and bonuses to which she alluded.

John Ruskin Bench, a stockholder who described himself as "a proud American", accused the company of buying doll clothes and small mechanical parts from mainland China. The accusation was vigorously denied. Bench then asked if the company planned future procurements from Communist China. Mr. Tembler stated that world conditions were changing and the possibility did exist for the future. At this point Mr. Bench became very vocal and abusive and was escorted from the meeting by a security officer.

There being no further business to be discussed, the meeting was adjourned at 5:25 p.m.

Respectfully submitted,

Vernon T. Culhane
Corporate Secretary

1. What are the various issues that were discussed at this meeting?
2. Which of these issues should not have been discussed here?
3. Is corporate credibility important?
4. Were responses to stockholders adequate and credible?

**CASE 8
FLEXITHANE PAINT COMPANY**

Steve Sloan, sales manager for Flexithane Paint Company, was both pleased and concerned when his salespeople came to tell him about the alleged donations by their president, B. T. Scottman, to the Independent Political Party. These donations supposedly were given in exchange for a promise of unlimited access to PUR (polyurethane resin), a petroleum by-product considered to be the lifeblood of Flexithane. Sloan was pleased that his people had the sense of responsibility to bring the matter to his attention, but concerned that, when he appeared before the press tomorrow to answer questions about unfair trade practices, the issue would be raised.

Flexithane Company was founded in the late 1950s, after the Korean War, when plastic products were introduced into the U.S. economy. Initially, Flexithane manufactured plastic containers and bags as well as waxes, stains, and paint remover products. Because of the newness of plastic products and their lack of wide acceptance in the market, Flexithane's products were sold only to large distributors of paint and related products. As demand for plastic products became more prevalent and new uses for plastic were discovered, Flexithane responded to the demands and new uses through innovative research and development.

The culmination of its efforts was the development in the early 1970s of a highly profitable plastic-based paint manufactured from PUR. The product was water and mildew resistant as well as flexible after drying. The flexibility of the paint was an outstanding feature; it prevented cracking and crazing. The paint carried a ten-year guarantee.

As sales of the paint skyrocketed, Flexithane found itself in a production bind. Production at all four of its plants pushed full capacity, and management did not feel it was feasible to build another plant at the present time. Although the containers and bags helped round out the company's line of products, management, headed by the newly appointed president, B. T. Scottman, decided to limit the product line mainly to the new paint and their waxes and stains. Containers and bags still would be produced, but in only one of Flexithane's four production plants. That plant would allocate 40 percent of its production time to paint and 60 percent to the other products. The other three plants would produce paint only. Under Scottman's guidance, Flexithane became one of the country's largest manufacturers of flexible plastic-coated paints by 1981.

Scottman, who had an MBA, guided Flexithane in a stern but circumspect manner. He was highly oriented toward the company and, on several occasions, was heard saying that nothing would hinder his efforts to make Flexithane a giant in the industry. Scottman worked long hours and still found time for membership in his church, the country club, and the Independent Political Party. He was also on the board of the national bank, the local management executive club, and the county hospital.

Unfortunately, when the matter of the alleged donations came to Sloan's attention, Mr. Scottman was out of the country and could not be contacted for information. However, Sloan was able to obtain the following information from brief conversations with several corporate executives: The company records showed that two months ago a company check had been written to Wayne Watson, treasurer of the Independent Party and vice-president of Watson Oil Company. The amount of the check was $1,000, and it was designated as a political contribution. In the meantime, two large orders for PUR granules had been placed, one with Watson Oil Company and the other with another refinery. The unit price on each of these orders was commensurate with market quotes for the item. (Despite the national concern over prevailing oil uncertainties, there does not appear to be a current shortage of PUR).

With this limited information, Sloan was faced with a dilemma. What, if anything, should he say about the alleged donations?

Questions for Discussion

1. How should Sloan respond if the issue arises during the press conference?

2. Does this large, self-contained company need to be concerned about its environment? If so, what elements of the environment should it be aware of? Why?

3. How may Sloan use the concepts developed by Mintzberg (the roles of spokesperson and negotiator) in resolving his dilemma?

4. Is the $1,000 contribution legal? Is donating to a political party socially responsible corporate behavior? Why or why not?

EXERCISE 9
A UNIVERSITY'S ENVIRONMENT

Almost every organization, regardless of its type of nature, must be concerned with the external environmental influences that impinge upon it. This exercise is designed to provide you with an opportunity to evaluate the external environmental elements that influence an organization with which you are presently associated—your university.

Either individuals or small groups, as designated by your instructor, will be assigned the responsibility of interviewing one of the following persons in the university community to discuss the effects of the environment on university operations.

1. Vice-President for Academic Affairs.
2. Vice-President for Business Affairs (or a high-ranking financial officer).
3. Vice-President or Dean of Student Affairs.
4. Vice-President or Director of University Relations (such as the Public Relations Officer).
5. Purchasing Agent.
6. Director of Admissions.
7. Director of Alumni Association.

Your instructor may suggest additional or substitute persons to be interviewed. Questions you should focus on are:

1. What groups comprise a university's environment?
2. In what ways does each element of the environment affect the organization?
3. How does the environmental composition vary from a public school to a private school?
4. How do the internal variables of volatility, size, complexity, and objectives influence how critical external factors are to the school? Cite examples to substantiate your response to this question.
5. Based upon your research in this exercise, do university administrators act primarily as spokespersons or negotiators in their relationships with the environment?

Each person or group will be responsible for making a brief report to the class outlining its findings. The collective results should provide the basis for a complete evaluation of the environmental influences. Your instructor will give you additional specific instructions.

EXERCISE 10
EFFECTIVE MANAGERS

Below is a partial list of behaviors in which managers may engage. Rank these items in terms of their importance for effective performance as a manager. Put a 1 next to the item that you think is most important, 2 for the next most important, down to 10 for the least important.

_____ Communicates and interprets policy so that it is understood by the members of the organization.

_____ Makes prompt and clear decisions.

_____ Assigns subordinates to the jobs for which they are best suited.

_____ Encourages associates to submit ideas and plans.

_____ Stimulates subordinates by means of competition among employees.

_____ Seeks means of improving management capabilities and competence.

_____ Fully supports and carries out company policies.

_____ Participates in community activities as opportunities arise.

_____ Is neat in appearance.

_____ Is honest in all matters pertaining to company property or funds.

Bring your rankings to class. Be prepared to justify your results and rationale. If you can add any behaviors to this list which might lead to success or greater management effectiveness, write them in.

Save this exercise for use later on.

THE MANAGER'S INTERNAL WORLD

● LEARNING OBJECTIVES

This chapter exposes you to several concepts that will lead to a better understanding of:

1. Your attitudes about differences in human behavior.

2. Different motivation theories.

3. The importance of motivation to managers.

4. The factors that might account for good or bad job performance.

5. How people can perceive their environment and its impact on performance.

I f you talk to managers about their jobs, you will probably find that differences in jobs are partly determined by differences in people. We all realize intuitively that people are different, but how can we explain those differences?

People differ for many reasons. They have varied life experiences and work backgrounds, and different upbringings, physical abilities, and personalities, all of which lead to perceptual differences and varying aptitudes, abilities, and attitudes. People also have different motivations—and motivation is the major concept to be explored in this chapter. Abilities will also be examined, since they may affect performance. Because, as a manager, you will have to deal with people and their performance, an understanding of the above constructs should help you develop the perceptual skills crucial to the managerial tasks you will be asked to perform.

There are many motivation theories. Some have been around for a long time and others are relatively recent in origin. Managers sometimes are anxious to find the theory and apply it to every situation they encounter. In their rush to do so, they are uncritical of the theory and what it really says, and they ignore evidence that may challenge the theory and its application.

The reading in this chapter challenges you to examine theory and its application, particularly one aspect of motivation theory—incentive pay.

One of the ways to try to understand behavior is to examine our underlying assumptions about people and human nature. Our assumptions lead us to view the world in particular ways. We react to situations partly by how we think other people behave—that is, "where they are coming from." Perhaps you have been exposed to attitudes such as "people see work as demeaning and only as a means to an end" versus "people find work satisfying, enjoy it, and see it as an end in itself." McGregor has classified these assumptions as Theory X (man is lazy, incapable of self-control, has rational economic goals) and Theory Y (man tries to self-actualize, wants freedom and responsibility, is self-motivated and controlled, will integrate personal goals with goals of the organization). The effectiveness of management may depend on the degree to which actions based on these attitudes fit the reality of the situation. The exercise "Assumptions about People" is set up to help you see what your own attitudes are and how they might affect your own managerial behavior. To understand others, it is helpful to first understand ourselves.

One of the theories of motivation that managers sometimes try to use to understand human behavior is based on Maslow's hierarchy of human needs. This theory suggests that people are influenced by physiological needs, safety needs, social needs, esteem needs, and self-actualization needs. Some of them may vary in importance at different times. But there may be a general level of "needs distribution," and some of the needs are more important than others. Further, these needs may or may not be satisfied at the workplace. The exercise "Motivation by Maslow" is oriented to an examination of your own needs within Maslow's classification system. You will have a chance to see how your own needs compare to those of a national sample of managers.

There seems to be some confusion among managers and management students about the role of pay as a motivational factor and how important it is relative to other factors like responsibility, challenging work, sense of accomplishment, recognition, and so forth. Herzberg is one theorist who suggests that motivation can be looked at according to two factors—satisfiers and dissatisfiers (or hygienic factors). Satisfiers, according to the theory, are accomplishments that lead to feelings of growth in job competence. Hygienic factors (such as salary, working conditions, job security) must be minimally present to keep people from being unhappy but are not seen as positive motivators. One might characterize satisfiers as factors leading to self-actualization in Maslow's terms. The "Let There Be Light Corporation" case is included to help you explore the conditions under which this theory is helpful (or not) in explaining human behavior.

Have you ever wondered why some people seem to be successful and perform at high levels of skill and efficiency? Have you thought about how some days you seem to be able to work really well, while other days you can't do anything right? We have all experienced success and failure. What managers are interested in is how to encourage good performance and minimize poor performance. The earlier sections of this chapter deal mainly with one element—motivation. That, of course, is an important factor in performance. And as you've probably learned, it is a complex factor.

Other factors might help explain performance. For example, some people may have certain abilities which give them greater capability to perform certain kinds of tasks, but they may be less successful in other functions. Another factor that comes into play is our perceptions of how well other people are performing. We may have potential skills that we do not develop. Or we may think we are quite successful, while others see us in a different way. Sometimes, events in our environment serve to limit our effectiveness and don't allow us to perform at full potential. In "Unexpected Relief," you may find that the performance of an employee (or the perception of that performance) changed. What could account for that? Did the person change? Did the nature of the task change? Did motivation change? Which of these help the manager explain and understand performance?

The exercise "Good Performance" asks you to take a deeper look into your own performance. What you might be looking for is evidence that "performance equals ability times motivation." Does this equation hold true for you? Does it for others? Are there other parts to this equation? Which part is most important? What abilities are most crucial? Can managers use this equation in their work with other people? We hope you will find patterns of factors that distinguish good performance from poor performance. And you should recognize that motivation doesn't tell the whole story. ●

READING 11
WHATEVER HAPPENED TO INCENTIVE PAY?
Edward E. Lawler

Historically, the popularity of incentive pay has gone hand-in-hand with the popularity of the scientific management approach to work design. The 1920s and 1930s saw a tremendous growth in the installation of piece-rate and other individual incentive plans. For the last several decades, however, the popularity of incentive plans has been in steady decline. Fewer and fewer new ones have been adopted, and many of those that are in place are being eliminated. The impact of this trend has appeared in the attitudes of the American workforce: A 1983 study by the Public Agenda Foundation found that only 22% of American workers say there is a direct link between how hard they work and how much they are paid.

The movement away from incentive pay has had its costs, for there is considerable evidence that pay can be a particularly powerful incentive. Research shows productivity increases of between 15% and 35% when incentive pay systems are put into place. And there is some evidence that the absence of such pay is a *dis*incentive. The Public Agenda Foundation survey reports that 73% of American workers attribute their *decreased* job efforts to a lack of incentive pay. Given such effectiveness, the declining popularity of incentive pay systems is, at first glance, hard to understand. After all, there is a desperate need for management approaches that will increase productivity. So why not return to pay for performance?

There are important reasons for the decline of certain kinds of incentive pay—in particular piece rates—that need to be considered before we turn to what can be done to make better use of pay as an incentive.

PROBLEMS WITH PIECE-RATE PAY

The literature on incentive plans is full of vivid descriptions of the counterproductive behavior that piece-rate incentives produce. In many respects, this is caused not so much by the inherent nature of these incentives in themselves, but by the way they have been utilized in organizations. Nevertheless, it is difficult to separate the problems of implementation from the general nature of incentive pay. Here is a brief review of the major problems with piece-rate incentive plans:

Beating the System

Numerous studies have shown that, when piece-rate plans are put into place, an adversarial relationship develops between the designers of the system and the workers who participate in the plans. Employees play all sorts of games in order to get rates set in such a way that they can maximize their financial gains relative to the amount of work they do: They work at slow rates in order to mislead time study experts who come to set production standards; and they hide new work methods or productive procedures from the time study experts so that standards will not be changed. Additionally, informal norms tend to develop concerning how productive workers should be. In effect, workers set informal limits on their production, and anyone who goes beyond the limit may be socially ostracized (and sometimes even physically abused). Unfortunately for the organization, the informal standard is usually set far below what the workers are capable of producing.

Source: Reprinted by permission from *New Management,* Vol. 1, No. 4, 1984.

Other games include:

- producing at extremely low levels (when employees consider the official standards too difficult to reach), and
- using union grievance procedures to eliminate rates that are too difficult.

Finally, in order to gain leverage in negotiating piece-rates, employees may even organize unions so that they can deal from a more powerful base.

Often, unions are able to negotiate rates that allow workers to perform below standards—while being paid at a rate that represents their previous high level of performance. Thus, organizations end up with the undesirable combination of high pay and low performance.

Divided Work Force

Since many staff and non-production jobs do not lend themselves to production standards, an organization often ends up with part of its workforce on incentive pay and part of the workforce not on it. This leads to a we/they split in the workforce that can be counterproductive, and it leads to noncooperative work relationships. This split is not a management/worker split, but a worker/worker split. In its most severe form, this gulf can lead to conflict between the production people on incentives and those who are not—the people in materials handling, maintenance, and other support functions on whom production workers depend. This split can also lead to dysfunctions in the kind of career paths people choose—individuals may bid for, and stay on, incentive jobs even though these don't fit their skills or interests. The higher pay of incentive jobs also causes individuals to be inflexible when asked to change jobs temporarily, and causes them to resist new technology that might require a rate change.

Maintenance Costs

Because incentive plans are relatively complicated and need to be constantly updated, a significant investment needs to be made in the people whose job it is to maintain them. This maintenance problem is further complicated by the adversarial relationship that develops between employees and management. Since employees try to hide new work methods and to avoid changes in their rates (unless, of course, their rates are being raised), management needs to be extremely vigilant in determining when new rates are needed. In addition, every time a technological change is made, or a new product introduced, rates need to be adjusted.

Finally, there is the ongoing cost of computing wages relative to the amount and kind of work employees do. All this activity requires the efforts of engineers, accountants, and payroll clerks. Added together, the support costs of a piece-rate incentive system are thus significantly greater than those associated with alternative systems.

Organization Culture

The effect of dividing the workforce into those who are and those who are not on incentive pay—combined with the adversarial process of rate setting—can create a negative organizational climate. It produces a culture characterized by low trust, lack of information sharing, poor support for joint problem solving, inflexibility due to individuals protecting their rates, and the absence of commitment to organizational objectives.

In short, incentive pay is, at best, a mixed blessing. Although it may improve work performance, the counterproductive behavior that it generates, the maintenance costs, the splitting of the workforce, and the poor climate that it creates, may make it a poor investment. Hence, many organizations have dropped incentive pay (or decided not to adopt it) because they feel the negative effects outweigh potential productivity advantages. The decreasing popularity of incentive pay, however, cannot be understood solely from this perspective. Some important societal changes have taken place since Frederick Winslow Taylor first wrote about scientific management. These changes have also led to the declining popularity of piece-rate pay.

SOCIETAL CHANGES

The United States has changed dramatically since the first installations of incentive pay. The society, workers, and nature of the work itself have all changed. Let us see how these changes relate to the decline in incentive pay:

Nature of the Work

In the early 1900s, many manufacturing jobs involved the production of relatively simple, high-volume products. Today, the United States is moving rapidly toward a service-knowledge-information-high-technology-based economy. Many of the simple, repetitive jobs in manufacturing have been automated (or exported to less-developed countries). Instead of the traditional simple, stand-alone jobs that one individual could do, many jobs today involve the operation of complex machines, continuous process technologies, or the delivering of services which require the integrated work of many individuals.

Work in the United States today, therefore, is less amenable to individual measurement and to the specification of a "normal level" of individual production than it was in the past. Instead, performance can only be measured reliably and validly when a group of workers or an entire plant is analyzed. In many knowledge-based jobs, it is even difficult to specify what the desired product is until it has been produced. Work of this nature simply does not lend itself to incentive pay. Moreover, many jobs in services as well as manufacturing are subject to rapid technological change. This change conflicts directly with incentive pay because stability is needed to set rates and to justify start-up costs.

Finally, even in those situations where there might be simple, repetitive, stable jobs that would lend themselves to piece-rate pay, corporations are making these jobs more complex and creating conditions in which employees will be intrinsically motivated to perform them well. For example, in many companies, self-managing teams are being given responsibility for large chunks of work. Thus, the process of enriching jobs has made them less likely candidates for incentive pay because, first, a different kind of motivation is present and, second, the enrichment process has made the simple, measurable, repetitive, and individual nature of the jobs disappear. All told, then, the nature of jobs in the United States is less and less amenable to individual incentive pay.

Nature of the Workforce

When incentive pay was introduced in the United States, the manufacturing workforce was primarily composed of poorly-educated, immigrant workers who were entering factories for the first time. Today, workers are more highly educated and there is evidence to indicate that they have different values and different orientations toward their jobs than did their parents. For example, over 20% of today's workers have a college education and this, combined with a number of other social changes, has produced workers who are interested in influencing workplace decisions, who desire challenging work, and who seek to develop their skills and abilities. Piece-work pay plans tend not to fit the desires and interests of such workers.

Nature of the Society

During the last ten years, the United States has seen an expansion in employee rights, employee entitlements, and the kinds of legal avenues that are open to employees when they feel unfairly treated in the workplace. This has made incentive pay plans subject to grievances and to legal challenges which make them difficult and expensive to maintain.

In addition, the nation has seen increased international competition and the export of jobs to other countries. The consequent fear of job loss can lead to production restriction: Employees reduce production because they are afraid that, if they produce too much, they will work themselves or their co-workers out of a job. Hence, the long-term, macro need to be productive for purposes of international competitiveness gets lost in the short-term, individual struggle to maintain jobs.

CURRENT SITUATION

The net effect of these changes seems to have been to push the society toward pay practices that are more egalitarian and in which there is a smaller percentage of pay "at risk" that is, based on individual performance. Overall, the United States has become a society in which the profits of *companies* are at risk as a function of performance, but the pay of *individuals* is affected only at the extremes of performance. An employee only loses when the company is in such poor shape that it has to lay him or her off, and the employee only gains when growth is such that the employee has the opportunity to be promoted. The society seems to have evolved to where employees consider that they are *entitled* to a fair wage and extensive fringe benefits simply because they are employed. This kind of thinking is represented in union contracts that have eliminated piece-rate pay, and in companies that have offered high base wages to all employees in order to stay non-union.

FUTURE DEVELOPMENTS

Looking to the future, there are no indications of social or workplace changes in the offing that are likely to tip the scales in favor of incentive pay. Indeed, if anything, the trends that have led to the abandonment of incentives seem to be continuing. There is, however, one important trend which seems to call for the increased use of pay as a motivator—the lack of growth in national productivity and the worsening international competitive situation.

Given the international situation, it would seem foolish to abandon such a potentially powerful incentive as pay for performance. Just this point was made by the 1983 White House Conference on Productivity at which the increased use of pay as a motivator was recommended. The Public Agenda Foundation study also supports pay for performance. It found that 61% of workers surveyed want their pay tied to performance. Yet, my analysis so far has suggested that piece-rate and similar forms of incentive pay may be inappropriate. Moreover, the typical merit increase plan also has many drawbacks and is seldom an adequate motivator (because it fails to effectively tie significant amounts of pay to performance). What, then, is the answer?

There probably is no *single* answer, but for some companies a good strategy is to use some combination of profit-sharing, gain-sharing, and stock ownership. In proper combination, these approaches can dramatically increase the motivation of everyone in the organization. Not surprisingly, the use of these plans is showing a dramatic increase, and every indication is that they will continue to grow in popularity. Let us look at each of these three promising methods:

Gain-sharing Plans

The Scanlon Plan is the oldest and best known gain-sharing plan. More recently, a number of companies have adopted the Improshare plan and others have developed their own plans. The idea behind them all is to define a business unit—typically a plant or a major department—and to relate pay to the overall performance of that unit. Monthly bonuses are paid to all employees in a unit based on a pre-determined formula. Typically, bonuses are paid when there is a measurable decrease in such costs as labor, materials and supplies.

The Scanlon Plan was formulated by Joe Scanlon, a union leader in the 1930s, and has been in place in some companies for over 30 years. Until recently, it was used primarily in small, family-owned manufacturing organizations. During the 1970s, however, an interesting and important trend developed: such large companies as General Electric, Motorola, TRW, Dana, and Owens-Illinois began Scanlon-like gain-sharing in some of their manufacturing plants. This tendency of large corporations to subdivide into small units, each with its own bonus plan, seems to be spreading. The reasons for this are many and relate directly to the kinds of changes in the workforce and the society discussed above. Gain-sharing plans seem to fit current conditions better than piece-rate plans for five reasons:

- First, gain-sharing does not rely on individual performance measurement. This is important in workplaces where performance can only be measured objectively at the group or plantwide level, and where technology does not lend itself to the identification of individual output.
- Second, gain-sharing is typically developed and administered in a participative fashion. That is, employees have a say in the design of the plan and are able to participate in its ongoing maintenance and administration. This tends to significantly decrease the adversarial relationship between employees and management, and to fit better with a society in which workers want to be involved in business decisions.
- Third, gain-sharing affects everyone in the workforce: managers, production employees, and support people. Thus, it encourages the cooperation and teamwork that tends to produce an increase in overall organizational performance. The ability to include everyone in a plan can be an important advantage in almost all workplaces—since it means that the performance of the many can be increased, and not just the performance of a few.
- Fourth, gain-sharing meets the needs of organizations for increased productivity. Gain-sharing can positively affect organizational productivity payout to the individual—that is, situations are unlikely to develop where a bonus is paid and the organization performs poorly. Because the connection between individual performance and reward is less direct in gain-sharing, it may be a less powerful motivator than *individual* piece-rate incentives; nonetheless, in those workplaces where *cooperation* is the key to performance (e.g., where process production techniques are used), gain-sharing often leads to higher productivity.
- Fifth, gain-sharing requires less administrative support than individual piece-rate plans. While it still requires some administration, it does not require the setting of individual standards for each job, nor the calculation of pay for individual workers based upon their performance.

Thus far, gain-sharing has largely been limited to manufacturing organizations, but recently a few service organizations (such as banks and hospitals) have begun to experiment with it. My guess is that over the next five to ten years there will be increased use of gain-sharing plans, although a great deal remains to be learned about how they should be installed in non-manufacturing environments.

Profit Sharing and Stock Ownership

Profit sharing and employee stock ownership are better known, older, and more widely-practiced than gain-sharing. However, by themselves, they typically are less effective as motivators. This is particularly true in large organizations where the link between individual performance and corporate performance is poor, and the connection between individual performance and stock price is virtually nonexistent. Thus, particularly in large organizations, these pay systems are desirable primarily because of their symbolic value. Such approaches effectively tell all workers that they are part of a single organization and that their joint efforts are needed. Stock ownership, in particular, can emphasize the importance of long-term organizational performance (and, in very small organizations, they may make gain-sharing plans unnecessary because they have the same effect). In most organizations, however, these two systems should be thought of as symbolic and as balancing supplements to gain-sharing. The one exception is with top managers. For them, profit sharing and stock ownership plans should be thought of as the *major* motivators of performance.

Multiple Systems

Installing *multiple* pay systems that reward performance is potentially the most effective approach to improving organizational productivity and profitability. Yet, it is surprising how slow most organizations have been to use multiple bonus plans. Particularly in large organizations, many workers have lost a sense of the business and of their involvement in ongoing operations. As a result, they often become mere bureaucrats routinely carrying out tasks with little appreciation or concern for how their performance relates to the overall success of the business. Indeed, this type of relationship between individuals and organizations has contributed to both the stagnation in national productivity growth and, in many cases, to the manufacture of poor quality products.

Gain-sharing, profit sharing, and stock ownership are financial ways of getting people involved in their organizations. Such managerial approaches as quality circles, self-managing work teams, and individual job enrichment can also do this. But experience shows that the two tracks work best when they run parallel. Everything that is known about incentives clearly points out that motivation is greatest when people have both a psychological stake *and* a financial stake in the organization's success. The absence of a relationship between the success of the organization and the pay of the employee causes an important part of the business experience to be missed for the individual worker. Organizations that are "shot through with" a variety of participative and managerial systems produce this necessary link.

Questions for Discussion

1. What are the problems with piece-rate pay?
2. What are the societal changes that have affected the motivating factors of incentive pay?
3. What is the difference in approach when motivating employees with incentive pay plans such as piece-rate pay as opposed to gain-sharing, profit sharing, and stock ownership?
4. How do you feel about the future developments to increase motivation in workers? Will it work? Would it work for you?

EXERCISE 12
ASSUMPTIONS ABOUT PEOPLE

This exercise is designed to help you better understand the assumptions you make about people and human nature. There are ten pairs of statements. Assign a weight from 0 to 10 to *each statement* to show the relative strength of your belief in the statements in *each pair*. The points assigned for each pair must in each case total ten. Be as honest with yourself as you can and resist the natural tendency to respond as you would "like to think things are." This instrument is not a "test." There are no right or wrong answers. It is designed to be a stimulus for personal reflection and discussion.

1. It's only human nature for people to do as little work as they can get away with.   a. _____
   When people avoid work, it's usually because their work has been deprived of its meaning.   b. _____

2. If employees have access to any information they want, they tend to have better attitudes and behave more responsibly.   c. _____
   If employees have access to more information than they need to do their immediate tasks, they will usually misuse it.   d. _____

3. One problem in asking for the ideas of employees is that their perspective is too limited for their suggestions to be of much practical value.   e. _____
   Asking employees for their ideas broadens their perspective and results in the development of useful suggestions.   f. _____

4. If people don't use much imagination and ingenuity on the job, it's probably because relatively few people have much of either.   g. _____
   Most people are imaginative and creative but may not show it because of limitations imposed by supervision and the job.   h. _____

5. People tend to raise their standards if they are accountable for their own behavior and for correcting their own mistakes.   i. _____
   People tend to lower their standards if they are not punished for their misbehavior and mistakes.   j. _____

6. It's better to give people both good and bad news because most employees want the whole story, no matter how painful.   k. _____
   It's better to withhold unfavorable news about business because most employees really want to hear only the good news.   l. _____

Source: Adapted by permission from M. Scott Myers, *Every Employee a Manager* (New York: McGraw-Hill Book Company, 1970); and David A. Kolb, Irwin M. Rubin, and James M. McIntyre, *Organizational Psychology: An Experiential Approach,* 2d. ed. © 1974, pp. 241–242. Reprinted by permission of Prentice-Hall, Inc., Englewood Cliffs, New Jersey.

7. Because a supervisor is entitled to more respect than those below him in the organization, it weakens his prestige to admit that a subordinate was right and he was wrong.   m. _____
Because people at all levels are entitled to equal respect, a supervisor's prestige is increased when he supports this principle by admitting that a subordinate was right and he was wrong.   n. _____

8. If you give people enough money, they are less likely to be concerned with such intangibles as responsibility and recognition.   o. _____
If you give people interesting and challenging work, they are less likely to complain about such things as pay and supplemental benefits.   p. _____

9. If people are allowed to set their own goals and standards of performance, they tend to set them higher than the boss would.   q. _____
If people are allowed to set their own goals and standards of performance, they tend to set them lower than the boss would.   r. _____

10. The more knowledge and freedom a person has regarding his job, the more controls are needed to keep him in line.   s. _____
The more knowledge and freedom a person has regarding his job, the fewer controls are needed to insure satisfactory job performance.   t. _____

To get your scores, add up the points you assigned to the following:
Theory X score = Sum of a, d, e, g, j, l, m, o, r, and s.
Theory Y score = Sum of b, c, f, h, i, k, n, p, q, and t.

Recall the basic propositions of Theory X and Theory Y from the introduction to this chapter. With which set of attitudes do you most closely associate—Theory X or Theory Y? How is this likely to affect your behavior?

EXERCISE 13
MOTIVATION BY MASLOW

This exercise is designed to give you insights into your own needs and motivations based on Maslow's need theory. First complete the questionnaire. Your answers should be based on a job you currently have (either full time or part time). If you have no job currently, answer according to your feelings about the last job you did have. If you have never held a job, answer in terms of the job you expect to have when you start work. You will be asked to compute two scores after completing the questionnaire.

QUESTIONNAIRE   Given below are several characteristics or qualities connected with your job. For each characteristic, you will be asked to give three ratings:

   a. *How much* of the characteristic *is there now* connected with your job?
   b. *How much* of the characteristic do you think *should be* connected with your job?
   c. *How important* is this characteristic *to you*?

Each rating will be on a seven-point scale, which will look like this:

(minimum) 1   2   3   4   5   6   7 (maximum)

You are to *circle the number* on the scale that represents the amount of the characteristic being rated. Low numbers represent low or minimum amounts, and high numbers represent high or maximum amounts. If you think there is "very little" or "none" of the characteristic presently associated with your job, you should circle numeral 1. If you think there is "just a little," you should circle numeral 2, and so on. If you think there is a "great deal but not a maximum amount," you should circle numeral 6. For each scale, circle only one number. *Please do not omit any scales.*

   1. The *feeling of self-esteem* a person gets from being in my job position:
      a. How much is there now?   (min.) 1   2   3   4   5   6   7 (max.)
      b. How much should there be?   (min.) 1   2   3   4   5   6   7 (max.)
      c. How important is this to me? (min.) 1   2   3   4   5   6   7 (max.)
   2. The *opportunity for personal growth and development* in my job position:
      a. How much is there now?   (min.) 1   2   3   4   5   6   7 (max.)
      b. How much should there be?   (min.) 1   2   3   4   5   6   7 (max.)
      c. How important is this to me? (min.) 1   2   3   4   5   6   7 (max.)
   3. The *prestige* of my job *inside* the company (that is, the regard received from others in the company):
      a. How much is there now?   (min.) 1   2   3   4   5   6   7 (max.)
      b. How much should there be?   (min.) 1   2   3   4   5   6   7 (max.)
      c. How important is this to me? (min.) 1   2   3   4   5   6   7 (max.)

Source: Based on research and questionnaire developed by Lyman W. Porter. Questionnaire and data used by permission of Professor Porter.

4. The *opportunity for independent thought and action* in my position:
   a. How much is there now?   (min.) 1 2 3 4 5 6 7 (max.)
   b. How much should there be?   (min.) 1 2 3 4 5 6 7 (max.)
   c. How important is this to me? (min.) 1 2 3 4 5 6 7 (max.)

5. The *feeling of security* in my job position:
   a. How much is there now?   (min.) 1 2 3 4 5 6 7 (max.)
   b. How much should there be?   (min.) 1 2 3 4 5 6 7 (max.)
   c. How important is this to me? (min.) 1 2 3 4 5 6 7 (max.)

6. The *feeling of self-fulfillment* a person gets from being in my job position, that is, the feeling of being able to use one's own unique capabilities, realizing one's potentialities:
   a. How much is there now?   (min.) 1 2 3 4 5 6 7 (max.)
   b. How much should there be?   (min.) 1 2 3 4 5 6 7 (max.)
   c. How important is this to me? (min.) 1 2 3 4 5 6 7 (max.)

7. The *prestige* of my job position *outside* the company (that is, the regard received from others not in the company):
   a. How much is there now?   (min.) 1 2 3 4 5 6 7 (max.)
   b. How much should there be?   (min.) 1 2 3 4 5 6 7 (max.)
   c. How important is this to me? (min.) 1 2 3 4 5 6 7 (max.)

8. The *feeling of worthwhile accomplishment* in my job:
   a. How much is there now?   (min.) 1 2 3 4 5 6 7 (max.)
   b. How much should there be?   (min.) 1 2 3 4 5 6 7 (max.)
   c. How important is this to me? (min.) 1 2 3 4 5 6 7 (max.)

9. The *opportunity,* in my job, *to give help to other people:*
   a. How much is there now?   (min.) 1 2 3 4 5 6 7 (max.)
   b. How much should there be?   (min.) 1 2 3 4 5 6 7 (max.)
   c. How important is this to me? (min.) 1 2 3 4 5 6 7 (max.)

10. The *opportunity,* in my job, *for participation in the setting of goals:*
    a. How much is there now?   (min.) 1 2 3 4 5 6 7 (max.)
    b. How much should there be?   (min.) 1 2 3 4 5 6 7 (max.)
    c. How important is this to me? (min.) 1 2 3 4 5 6 7 (max.)

11. The *opportunity,* in my job, *for participation in the determination of methods and procedures:*
    a. How much is there now?   (min.) 1 2 3 4 5 6 7 (max.)
    b. How much should there be?   (min.) 1 2 3 4 5 6 7 (max.)
    c. How important is this to me? (min.) 1 2 3 4 5 6 7 (max.)

12. The *authority* connected with my job:
    a. How much is there now?   (min.) 1 2 3 4 5 6 7 (max.)
    b. How much should there be?   (min.) 1 2 3 4 5 6 7 (max.)
    c. How important is this to me? (min.) 1 2 3 4 5 6 7 (max.)

13. The *opportunity to develop close friendships* in my job:
    a. How much is there now?   (min.) 1 2 3 4 5 6 7 (max.)
    b. How much should there be?   (min.) 1 2 3 4 5 6 7 (max.)
    c. How important is this to me? (min.) 1 2 3 4 5 6 7 (max.)

SCORING

Compute your satisfaction scores in the Needs Satisfaction Table. This will indicate the degree to which your job satisfies your needs.

In each case, find your answers to Parts a and b of the appropriate item from the questionnaire (for example, 5a is how much feeling of job security there should be). Subtract a from b (b − a) and enter the score in the table below. Add up those scores and enter the sum; then divide by the appropriate number.

Compare this score to the national mean. If it is higher, your job provides *less* satisfaction for that particular need than jobs of a nationwide sample of manager. If it is lower, your job satisfies the need more than the jobs of the managers in the sample group.

Compute your score for each of Maslow's five needs categories in the Needs Importance Table. These scores are derived from Part C of each item on the questionnaire. Enter each score, find the sum for each need category, and divide by the number of questions in the total.

Compare your needs score to the national mean. If your score is higher, that need is more important for you than for the national sample of managers. Note that managers often have a lower need for esteem and a higher need for self-actualization. Do your need scores follow a similar pattern? You can also compare your scores with the results from the national sample by level of management.

NEEDS SATISFACTION TABLE

	Security	Social	Esteem	Autonomy	Self-Actualization
	5b − 5a =	9b − 9a =	1b − 1a =	4b − 4a =	2b − 2a =
		13b − 13a =	3b − 3a =	10b − 10a =	6b − 6a =
			7b − 7a =	11b − 11a =	8b − 8a =
				12b − 12a =	
Sum:					
Divide by:	1	2	3	4	3
Satisfaction score:					
National mean:[a]	0.43	0.33	0.61	0.78	1.05

[a]National means are from Porter's sample of 1,916 managers. The numbers are "grand means" for all levels of management combined.

NEEDS IMPORTANCE TABLE

	Security	Social	Esteem	Autonomy	Self-Actualization
	5c =	9c =	1c =	4c =	2c =
		13c =	3c =	10c =	6c =
			7c =	11c =	8c =
				12c =	
Sum:					
Divide by:	1	2	3	4	3
Satisfaction score:					
National mean:[a]	5.33	5.36	5.28	5.92	6.35

[a]National means are from Porter's sample of 1,916 managers. The numbers are "grand means"

Compare your Needs Importance Table with your Needs Satisfaction Table. Are your most important needs being satisfied? Are your need level and satisfaction scores close to top management or lower management? How do your results affect your behavior? Bring your results to class for discussion.

DISSATISFACTION AND IMPORTANCE OF NEEDS (BY LEVEL OF MANAGEMENT)

Mean dissatisfaction[a]

	Needs				
Level	Security	Social	Esteem	Autonomy	Self-Actualization
President	0.26	0.34	0.28	0.18	0.63
Vice-president	0.45	0.29	0.45	0.55	0.90
Upper middle	0.41	0.33	0.66	0.87	1.12
Lower middle	0.38	0.32	0.71	0.96	1.17
Lower	0.82	0.56	1.15	1.40	1.52

Mean importance[b]

	Needs				
Level	Security	Social	Esteem	Autonomy	Self-Actualization
President	5.69	5.38	5.27	6.11	6.50
Vice-president	5.44	5.46	5.33	6.10	6.40
Upper middle	5.20	5.31	5.27	5.89	6.34
Lower middle	5.29	5.33	5.26	5.74	6.25
Lower	5.30	5.27	5.18	5.58	6.32

[a]Dissatisfaction score is based on difference between obtained and expected fulfillment. Therefore, a difference score of 0 = complete satisfaction; a difference score of 6 = complete dissatisfaction.
[b]1 = lowest degree of importance; 7 = highest degree of importance.
Source: Reprinted by permission of the publisher, from *Organizational Patterns of Managerial Job Attitudes,* by Lyman W. Porter, copyright 1964 by American Foundation for Management Research, p. 17. Published by American Management Associations. All rights reserved.

CASE 14
LET THERE BE LIGHT CORPORATION

Let There Be Light Corporation (LLC) is a manufacturing firm that produces fluorescent lights for industrial, commercial, and consumer use. It consists of one plant located on the outskirts of a city having 60,000 residents. The company is divided into three major departments. They are the manufacturing department, assembly department, and the finished goods storage and shipping department. This case focuses on the situation existing in the manufacturing department.

The manufacturing department employs 40 people per shift, none having achieved higher than a high school education. The department is controlled by a department foreman, his assistant, and a management trainee. Of the 40 employees approximately 40% are black or from a minority group. The jobs in this department are divided into six major classifications: punch-press operators, material handlers, shearing machine operators, machine setup, welders, and painters.

The company runs three eight-hour shifts: day shift (7:00 to 3:30), a night shift (3:30 to 12:00), and a grave-yard shift (12:00 to 8:00). The grave-yard shift cleans, repairs, and lubricates the equipment. Each shift receives two ten minute breaks and a half-hour meal break. The ten minute breaks are taken by the whole shift at designated times before and after the meal breaks.

There are 22 punch presses each set up to perform a unique process. One person operates each machine while in a standing position. Pieces are fed into the machine, processed, and removed from the machine. An operator places each piece neatly on a rack so it can be sent to the next processing point. A typical piece may have to be processed on 6 to 8 different machines before it is sent to the painter and later to the assembly department. These employees have safety lines attached to their wrists to prevent them from getting their hands caught in the press.

Punch press operators are given a starting hourly wage of $3.25 per hour. They receive a raise every three months based on their performance. The company also offers a piece work incentive plan giving them an added bonus percentage of their hourly rate based on how many pieces an employee can produce above the company standards. The standards for a particular process are based on the individual's performance for new employees. A time and motion study is performed by the management trainee to determine the standard rate of production for each new employee. This rate is usually lower than the group rate applied to the senior employees of the plant. After the new employee has had ample time and experience at performing the different processes, he or she is expected to achieve the group standards set by the company.

The bonus rate is calculated by comparing the number of pieces processed on each machine against the standards set for that particular process. If the number of pieces processed exceeds the set standard, then the employee receives a bonus hourly rate. The bonus hourly rate is calculated by this equation:

Source: Adapted from a course assignment by Darwin Browne for Professor J. G. Hunt, Southern Illinois University-Carbondale.

$$\left(\frac{\text{Pieces Processed}}{\text{Hours Worked}} - \text{Standard Rate/Hour} \right) = \text{Excess}$$

$$\left(\frac{\text{Excess}}{\text{Standard Rate/Hour}} \times \text{Hourly Rate} \right) + \text{Hourly Rate} = \text{Bonus Hourly Rate}$$

For example, an employee is assigned a job to process 1,000 pieces on press #6. The standard rate is 200 pieces per hour and it takes 4 hours to complete the job. This employee has worked for the company for 6 months and earns an hourly rate of $3.50/hour. The bonus hourly rate would be $4.375.

$$\frac{1,000}{4} - 200 = 50 = \text{Excess} \left(\frac{50}{200} \times 3.50 \right) + 3.50 = 4.375 = \text{Bonus Hourly Rate}$$

If an employee is unable to achieve the individual or group performance standard, then he or she is paid the hourly rate. The worker is not penalized for inability or inexperience.

There have been many complaints to the foreman by the punch press operators about having to wait for material to be delivered to their machines and finished work taken to the next processing point. They claim that they should be given down time for these delays. Every minute that their production is delayed reduces the bonus time that they have built up. This is often a point of conflict between employees and the foreman. Punch press operators have also complained about the length of time they have to wait in line at the recording office. When they start or end a job they have to get their time card punched at the recording office. Sometimes they have to wait as long as ten minutes before the secretary gets their cards punched. This also contributes to increases in their production time which decreases the bonus time they have earned by one minute for every minute of delay. There is no effort by management to subtract the break time of the time required for safety checks. A safety check is necessary each time the worker starts a new job or comes back from a break. There is a high turnover of help for this position and a high level of scrappage. The punch press operators, in general, seem to be apprehensive towards management.

Material handlers are paid a flat starting rate of $4.35 per hour. They get steady raises based on their performance. Their performance is basically a value judgment made by the foreman. They drive a lift truck and are responsible for supplying the punch press operators with materials when necessary and moving the processed material to the next processing point. There are two material handlers that are responsible for the 22 punch presses.

Arguments often flair up between the punch press operators and the material handlers. The press operators argue that they are not getting the material fast enough. The material handlers claim that they are getting the material to them as fast as they can. Sometimes they have to wait for punch press operators to finish a rack of material on one machine before it can be taken to the next processing point. The material handlers have to estimate when a particular machine will run out of material and try to get the material to the punch presses before they run out. In a sense, they coordinate the flow of materials between the different punch presses. There is not a great turnover in this position, because it is one of the higher paying jobs in the plant.

The foreman of this department is highly production oriented. His major concern is getting the work done. He seldom compliments any of the employees for their performance. In general, he communicates with his employees only when it is necessary. He limits his communication to assigning different tasks to be performed and answering complaints of the workers. He rarely gives down time to the punch press operators. He feels that down time should only be applied when a machine breaks down and should not be applied toward delays in the flow of materials.

Upper management of Let There Be Light Corporation is faced with costly problems stemming from low morale among the punch press operators. There is a high level of scrap and employee turnover is high among these operators.

Questions for Discussion

1. Should the punch press operators receive a low hourly rate with a bonus rate calculated based on their productivity?

2. Is it fair to the punch press operators to limit their productivity and bonus pay by not including a certain time period allocated especially to safety checks, down time, and machine breakage?

3. Does the foreman communicate properly with all divisions of the manufacturing department?

4. How should the firm introduce new employees without lowering the productivity of the experienced employees?

5. What appears to be the primary method of motivation in this case?

6. Is the above method of motivation a good one in this case? If not, why?

CASE 15
UNEXPECTED RELIEF

A new rate schedule from Medicare that required an unusual service-charge breakdown caused an overload in the insurance claims office of Regional Hospital. Even by scheduling all the overtime allowed by the budget, the section head was unable to keep the work from piling up. Mr. Barker, accounting division director, requested a procedure change as soon as possible to reduce the burdensome workload. In response to his request, Mr. Marks, an assistant hospital administrator whose specialty was conversion to computer operations, was assigned to analyze the problem. On the recommendation of Mr. Marks, a special project unit was set up near the insurance office to convert the problem procedure to data processing. Mr. Marks took charge of the special project, assisted by staff personnel and one claims supervisor. Completion of the special conversion project within six months was necessary in order to meet audit requirements and to qualify for a federal hospital grant.

On Wednesday, the day after the special unit was set up, Mr. Marks asked Mr. Barker to send three reliable clerks from his division. General supervision of the clerks would be retained in the division from which they had been borrowed, but the clerks would receive technical supervision in the special project unit.

Source: John M. Champion and John H. James, *Critical Incidents in Management* (Homewood, Ill.: Richard D. Irwin, 1975). Copyright 1975 by Richard D. Irwin, Inc.

One of the clerks selected for the special project unit was Ms. Lin Buxby, who had graduated from high school one year ago with a good achievement record. She had near-point vision corrected by contact lenses, a fact that was reflected on her personnel record. The supervisor to whom she was first assigned called personnel about the matter but he was assured that Ms. Buxby's eyesight problem should not handicap her for general clerical work. At her first formal appraisal six months after being hired, Ms. Buxby's overall performance was rated as "good" by the supervisor. Partly for this reason, she was selected as one of three clerks to go to the special project unit.

On Thursday, the three clerks were told about their temporary reassignment by Mr. Barker shortly before they were to undertake their new duties. The type of work was not mentioned in his brief announcement. The reassignment was unexpected by them. Two of them readily accepted the reassignment with comments such as "Our pay will be the same" and "We can still have lunch with our friends here because we're just going across the hall."

Lin Buxby, however, was noticeably upset by the turn of events. She asked Mr. Barker, "Why can't I stay here? When can I return?" Her questions went unanswered.

When the three clerks arrived at the special project unit on Friday, one of the staff members explained the work to be done, desks were chosen, and work was assigned. During the first coffee break Lin rushed back across the hall. Bursting into tears, she implored Mr. Barker to let her return and continue training in her original assignment. She said, "The confusion and pressure are too much. And we don't know what to expect next." Mr. Barker explained that the situation would soon settle down, that the experience would help her when she returned to her original training position, and that she might be able to make some overtime wages. Lin seemed convinced and went back to work in the special project unit.

Two working days later Mr. Marks called Mr. Barker and demanded that Lin be replaced immediately. Mr. Marks said that Lin was too slow, that she couldn't do anything right, and that Mr. Barker had sent an incompetent clerk for a top-priority project. This attracted Mr. Barker's attention because he did not want to make that kind of an impression on the assistant hospital administrator. He was upset and surprised and convinced that Lin's poor performance was intentional. A replacement for Lin was selected.

The next morning, Mr. Barker took Lin's replacement to the special project unit, brought Lin back, and talked to her. It appeared that Lin didn't know why she had been replaced. When he referred to her being so slow and making so many mistakes, Lin said, "No one said anything to me about making mistakes. But I know I was slow. The lines on the data sheet ran together due to the columns on the coding sheets being only 1/4-inch wide. Everything seemed to swim in front of my eyes. Trying to make sure I didn't make mistakes slowed me up. I told the supervisor about my trouble and she said, 'I'll see what I can do.' The next thing I knew was that you came over and brought me back."

Mr. Barker could not avoid the conclusion that everyone connected with the Lin Buxby incident was partially responsible.

Questions for Discussion

1. What should Mr. Barker have done?
2. Is Barker right that everyone was responsible?
3. What should be done with Ms. Buxby now?

EXERCISE 16
GOOD PERFORMANCE

1. Think back in your work or school experience to a time when you were performing your *very best*. Check (✓) the items below and indicate if they were present or absent in that situation. Also list other items not on the list which may have accounted for the high performance.

2. Now try to remember a time when you were performing poorly or at less than your best. Check (✓) the factors that were present or absent. Can you add any factors that may have led to poor performance?

   What can you conclude about your own performance and past successes and failures? Does this suggest anything to managers concerned about performance of subordinates?

Factor	High Performance		Low Performance	
	Present	Absent	Present	Absent
Past experience with the task	_____	_____	_____	_____
Interest in the task	_____	_____	_____	_____
Expectation of reward for success	_____	_____	_____	_____
Helpful co-workers on the task	_____	_____	_____	_____
Previous training for the task	_____	_____	_____	_____
Strong identification with the task	_____	_____	_____	_____
Knew specifically what was expected	_____	_____	_____	_____
Superior who was interested and helpful	_____	_____	_____	_____
Felt responsible for doing the task	_____	_____	_____	_____

PLANNING

M

● **LEARNING OBJECTIVES**

The experiences in this chapter should:

1. Help you understand the elements in the planning process.

2. Suggest how planning might be done.

3. Help you understand the limits and usefulness of planning.

4. Give you an appreciation of the problems in setting objectives, analyzing environments, making strategic choices, and implementing plans.

any managers don't like to plan. They are action oriented, and planning is not an activity that leads to *immediate* and tangible feedback. However, planners usually outperform nonplanners. Planning doesn't guarantee success, but it does give you a competitive edge. It gives you a way to cope with change. It focuses your activities on objectives. And it provides you with a way to gauge and compare progress. For these reasons, we hope this chapter will encourage you to plan and help you find ways to improve planning.

Planning involves several interrelated steps:

- Determining goals and objectives.
- Examining the environment and forecasting change.
- Selecting the means to achieve the ends.
- Analyzing the results (which feed back into this process).

Objectives are important because they define the organization and its environment, help to coordinate decisions, and provide performance standards. Objectives are influenced by the environment, the enterprise's resources, and values of top management. Useful objectives are those that are measurable, attainable, and consistent with the internal and external environment.

The environment is examined by managers who look for threats and opportunities. Forecasts of changes in the environment (competition, economy, resources, and so on) are important in this analysis. Predictions of the future are made so that plans to deal with it may be formulated.

The plans flow from objectives and environmental analysis. Different levels of management are involved in different ways. Top managers do strategic planning, defining basic missions and strategies, and top-level budget allocation. Middle managers use these plans as a guide for developing policies, rules, procedures, and quarterly plans. Supervisors then are involved with schedules, short-run budgets, and daily and weekly plans, which are monitored by middle managers.

Finally, results are analyzed to measure progress toward the objectives. Should this progress be insufficient or should environmental conditions change, new plans must be established so that the process can begin again.

Elements of Effective Corporate Planning," the reading in this chapter, deals with the factors that seem to trigger top management's perception that the organization has a need for planning. The problems encountered and the conditions necessary for effective planning are also presented. The case "Don Smith's Objections to Objectives" gives you an opportunity to examine the difficulty of setting good objectives. The case also introduces the idea that a Management by Objectives (MBO) approach to help in planning may not be ideal for all organizations or units in an enterprise.

The "Consolidated Movie Theatres" exercise allows you to play the role of planners who need to decide what sorts of information might be useful to their task. The exercise shows the importance of environmental scanning to the planning process.

The "Planning under Crisis Conditions" case shows you that planning can be difficult for a manager when time pressures exist. As part of that case, you are asked to make short-term plans for scheduling the activities of a manager.

The "Strategic Planning for the Gantry Company" exercise exposes you to a decision-making situation in which you make a choice of strategic alternatives for accomplishing long-run objectives of the firm. You will find that factors of risk and group consensus may be involved in arriving at strategies to accomplish the goals of the firm, thus influencing plans for the firm's future.

Of course, planning must be translated into action—it is not an independent managerial task. In the exercise "Planners and Operators," you will have a chance to see some of the problems of translating plans into results. The exercise combines elements of planning, communicating, and intergroup relationships when one group plans a task and then instructs another group how to carry it out. This will give you a more realistic idea of how some elements of management are interconnected.

READING 17
ELEMENTS OF EFFECTIVE CORPORATE PLANNING
Ronald J. Kudla

This study is concerned with strategic, or long range, corporate planning where the planning horizon is greater than one year. Corporate planning is defined as a formalized, structured process which includes the establishment of corporate goals and objectives and the development of divisional plans as a means to achieve them. Specific areas of concern in the study include the perception of a need for planning, analysis of planning from a process viewpoint with particular emphasis on organizational structure, and elements of effective corporate planning.

Although corporate planning is a relatively new activity that emerged in the past 10–15 years, limited data are available on how executives came to perceive a need for this type of planning in their organizations. This study seeks to provide this data by determining what events were associated with perception of a need for planning.

Source: Long Range Planning, 9 (August 1976): 83–93. Reprinted by permission.

Many authors including Ansoff, Ackoff, and Andrews[1] have taken a conceptual planning approach with little attention given to how the planning effort is organized and how the planning process is conducted. Practitioners are more concerned with how planning is actually done rather than how it ought to be done. This study attempts to describe the planning activity in process terms by identifying key elements in the planning process and answering the question, "Who does what and how?."

Although much has been written about planning, surprisingly little has been written about effective planning. Do some firms do planning more effectively than others and why? Hence, another concern of the study is the identification of the elements of effective planning and discussing their importance to various types of planning systems.

STUDY OBJECTIVES

Specific objectives of the study were to:

1. Determine what factors led to perception of a need for corporate planning.

2. Determine how firms currently plan by taking a process viewpoint rather than a conceptual approach.

3. Determine how the planning effort is organized with particular emphasis on organizational structure and functional responsibility relationships.

4. Identify the most important factors in effective planning as reflected by planning executives.

5. Determine what criteria are used to evaluate the plans and the planning process.

6. Idenify current planning weaknesses.

7. Identify any trends that appear to be developing in the corporate planning area.

NATURE OF THE SAMPLE

In-depth interviews were conducted with key planning executives in 14 large corporations in the Pittsburgh Metropolitan area. A profile of these corporations is shown in Table 1.

As shown in Table 1, the sample included 11 manufacturing firms, 2 public utilities, and 1 engineering and construction firm. Most of these firms are large, broad-based, multidivisional companies operating in mature industries including aluminum, steel, chemicals, oil, and capital equipment. They sell a wide range of products to numerous, well-identified and relatively stable markets. Table 1 provides more detailed information.

These sample firms reflect several built-in biases, in addition to the obvious geographic bias, that should be recognized. A "big business" bias exists because most of the firms are large corporations. These firms are conservative in how they conduct their businesses and how they plan. They stay primarily in their area of competence with little diversification activity. Although some of the largest industrial concerns in the United States are in the sample, care must be taken in making any broad generalizations concerning planning because of the biases previously cited.

TABLE 1

CORPORATE CHARACTERISTICS

Name of Company	Principal Line of Business	Approximate 1973 Annual Sales Volume ($ Millions)
Allegheny Ludlum Industries	Manufacturer of stainless and specialty steels	763.0
Aluminum Company of America	Integrated producer and fabricator of aluminum	2,180.0
Calgon Corporation (Subsidiary of Merck & Co.)	Diversified producer of water treatment chemicals, water softeners, and related water purification equipment	70.2[a]
Duquesne Light Company	Public utility providing electric energy	247.6
Gulf Oil Corporation	International firm engaged in exploration, production, transportation, refining, and marketing of petroleum products	10,000.0
H. J. Heinz Company	Major food processor including condiments, tuna, and potatoes	1,438.0[b]
Heyl & Patterson	Designs, procures, and erects coal processing and bulk material handling transfer equipment	25.0
Jones & Laughlin Steel Corp.	Fully-integrated steel manufacturer	1,530.0
Joy Manufacturing Company	Manufacturer of heavy capital goods including coal and hard rock mining machinery, drilling equipment, and industrial compressors and pumps	396.0
Koppers Company, Inc.	Diversified manufacturer of forest products, plastics, road materials, and pollution control equipment	723.0
Mellon-Stuart Company	Contracting and engineering consulting firm	120.0
Peoples Natural Gas Company (Subsidiary of Consolidated Natural Gas Co.)	Gas distribution company	118.0
PPG Industrial, Inc.	Manufacturer of coatings, resins, paints, flatglass, continuous fiberglass, and agricultural chemicals	1,510.0
United States Steel Corporation	Large, diversified, fully-integrated steel manufacturer	7,000.0

[a]1966.
[b]1974.
Source: Annual reports.

PERCEPTION OF A NEED FOR PLANNING

Although the firms participating in this study have done planning in one form or another for years, more formalized, structured planning focusing on long-range strategy selection has evolved only in recent years. Long-range corporate planning systems were designed to meet the specific needs of the firm as perceived by key executives. One of the objectives of this study was to determine what events triggered perception of need for this type of planning.

The most prevalent event associated with perception of a need for more formalized planning was a change in top management. The situation in each of these firms was much the same. Typically, the newly appointed President or Chairman of the Board asked where the company was and where it was going, and where the firm ought to be going and how should it get there. The emphasis on planning arose from three sets of factors—organizational, external, and performance.

The major organizational factor was growth in size and complexity of the firm and its business resulting in a need for improved decision making, planning, and control. External factors included the accelerated pace of technological, economic, political, and social change which created a need for a flexible, more responsive organization. Both the need to cope with change and coordinate, ap praise, and plan an enterprise of expanding size and complexity led to adoption of a more formalized planning system. Key executives felt that a formalized corporate planning system would ensure that the planning of divisions was in the interest of the corporation as a whole.

Performance factors also played a role in installation of some corporate planning systems. For example, PPG Industries experienced a precipitous decline in earnings mainly due to several strategic errors. These errors included diversification into unrelated areas, inappropriate pricing policies, and short-sighted capital expenditure programs. To prevent their future occurrence, the new management team instituted a corporate planning system.

Other trigger events cited include major reorganizations, membership of a key executive in a professional association that stressed planning and participation of a key executive in an advanced management seminar that emphasized planning. McKinsey & Company, an international management consulting firm, was retained to perform an organizational study of Calgon Corp. One of the results of the subsequent organization proposed by McKinsey and adopted by Calgon management was the installation of a formal, long-range planning system. At Heyl & Patterson, a major designer of coal processing equipment, the President was a member of the Young Presidents' Organization which stressed long-range planning.

In Alcoa, an advanced management seminar sponsored by the Alcoa Training Department was attended by 24 key general managers. In this seminar, a week was devoted to planning. As a result of this seminar, one of the participants recommended that a task force be formed to study the company's planning needs. This step was the beginning of Alcoa's first corporate plan.

An analysis of all trigger events showed that many of them were external to the firm. This finding raises the question of why more events were not internal and more specifically, why a change in top management was required before long-range planning was given a new emphasis. Why couldn't incumbent management take the necessary action? Although a complete answer to this question is beyond the scope of this study, some insight can be provided.

According to respondents, executives have a great tendency to concentrate on current operations and maintain the *status quo*. The prevailing attitude is as long as the firm does well today the future will take care of itself. Moreover, long-range planning is a difficult activity involving a systematic examination of

TABLE 2

PHASES OF A DECENTRALIZED PLANNING PROCESS

Establish corporate goals and objectives.

↓

Set environmental premises.

↓

Collect information and forecast.

↓

Establish divisional goals and objectives.

↓

Develop divisional plans.

↓

Revise objectives and plans if objectives are not met.

Source: Field interviews.

TABLE 3

PPG INDUSTRIES—CORPORATE OBJECTIVE

Type of Objective	Abridged Statement of Objectives
Financial (primary)	Return on stockholders' equity—14.5 percent. Sales growth—6 to 10 percent.
Human resources	Employ least number and highest quality of people to accomplish financial objective.
Corporate image	Have the company accepted as a profit-oriented, responsible firm with the ability to meet future economic and social challenge.
Communications	Have all of public relations and advertising directed in varying degrees toward the corporate image objectives.
Field of business	Exploit strength and avoid diversification into unrelated areas.
Geographical	Conduct operations on a global basis.
Nature of business	Preserve current strength and upgrade specialty and proprietary products.
Specific business target	Secure substantial and rewarding position in selected growth areas.
Operating divisions	Have all divisions operating at satisfactory level of profits and feed available resources into the most deserving and profitable operations.
Technological objectives	Concentrate R&D effort on fields having good potential for success and reward.
Management	Effectively manage managers.
Profit	Have everyone in the organization strongly profit-oriented.
Public responsibility	Discharge this responsibility to all publics.

Source: PPG Industries, Inc.

an uncertain future. This effort requires a substantial block of time, money, and energy. Some respondents felt that forecasting is an imprecise science of limited value and therefore planning beyond one year is also of marginal value. More will be said about this subject in subsequent sections.

TABLE 4
TYPICAL FINANCIAL OBJECTIVES

Type of Objective	Quantification (Percent)
Returns	
Return on capital employed	12.0
Return on invested capital	
Pre-interest	10.0
After interest	8.2
Return on equity	13.6
Capital Structure	
Cost of capital	10.0
Debt/equity ratio	66.6
Shareholder equity	60.0

CLASSIFICATION OF PLANNING SYSTEMS

Planning systems encountered in this study can be classified into three categories—centralized, decentralized without a corporate planning department, and decentralized with a corporate planning department. The nature and type of planning varies with the size and complexity of the firm's organization, the nature of the firm's business and the personal values of key executives.

Generally, large, multinational companies do decentralized planning where the planning is done at the divisional and departmental level rather than by a centralized corporate group. Each operating division is large enough to support its own planning activities. Whether a corporate planning department exists or not depends on the need for such a department which is partially determined by the complexity of the firm's planning process and the ability of the divisions to plan efficiently.

DESCRIPTION OF A DECENTRALIZED PLANNING PROCESS

A decentralized planning process is described in terms of a simplified model, key elements and a supportive data base.

A Simplified Model

Although considerable variation existed in the planning processes encountered in this study, there were, nevertheless, several major phases in common. These phases are listed in Table 2.

As shown in Table 2, the first stage of a decentralized planning process is the establishment of corporate goals and objectives. This phase sets the firm on a specific direction by clearly defining the company's intent in all aspects of its business. Clearly defined corporate goals and objectives are important because they focus all of the firm's planning activities in the same direction and have motivational value as well. An example is PPG Industries' statement of corporate objectives shown as Table 3.

From Table 3, note that:

1. Seven of the thirteen objectives are directly related to profits which underscores the primary importance of financial objectives.

2. Recognition of environmental influences is reflected in the corporate image, communications, and public responsibility objectives.

Typical financial objectives are shown in Table 4.

TABLE 5

OUTLINE OF A BUSINESS PLAN

   I. Description of Business
   II. Objectives/Goals
      A. Achievements sought
      B. Quantification of A
   III. Environmental Considerations
      A. Economics
      B. Consumers
      C. Competitors
      D. Government/Political
      E. Social
      F. Technological
      G. Market Research
   IV. Internal Assessment
      A. Strengths/Weaknesses
      B. Requirements for Success
   V. Strategy
   VI. Evaluation of Alternatives
   VII. Tactics
      A. Marketing, Supply/Demand Analyses
      B. Manpower, Skills
      C. Raw Materials
      D. Capital
      E. Operations
      F. R and D
   VIII. Economic Projections/Results
      A. Basic assumptions underlying plan and economics
      B. Economics—Revenues, Costs, Profit, Returns, etc.
      C. Sensitivity/Risk Analyses
   IX. Monitoring
      A. Measurement
      B. Control
   X. Contingency Plans

Financial objectives are the only ones that are quantified. A review of other objectives including social responsibility is provided in a subsequent section.

In reviewing the remaining phases of the planning process shown in Table 2, it should be recognized that considerable overlap exists. These phases are not performed stepwise but rather the process is continuous with activities within two or more phases oftentimes being done concurrently by the same department.

The second phase of the planning process is setting environmental premises. This phase includes an analysis of all environmental factors that could significantly impact the firm's business. Specific factors included are the economic environment, consumers, competitors, governmental and political influences, technological make-up, and market research findings.

Collect information and forecast, the third phase, has to do with forecasting sales and demand and analyzing the economic consequences of a specific sales volume forecast. Pro-forma financial statements are prepared which include projected revenues, costs, profits, returns, and related data.

While data is collected and forecasts made, divisional management set their specific objectives and goals. These objectives are similar to the corporate objectives but have a more divisional relevance.

Divisional plans are developed in parallel with divisional goal and objective formulation. The plans observed in this study had many different formats but had the same basic data. An example of a typical plan outline is shown as Table 5. This table is the outline of a major firm's business plan. The plan includes

TABLE 6

RELATIVE IMPORTANCE OF PLANNING PROCESS ELEMENTS

	Degree of Importance		
Element	**Very Important**	**Moderately Important**	**Not Very Important**
Top management support	X		
Managerial participation	X		
Opportunity/competence match	X		
Comprehensive and complete		X	
Feedback and control		X	
Flexible		X	
Simplicity		X	
Facilitative organizational structure		X	
Multiple objectives			X
Includes all organizational levels			X
Includes all time periods			X
Explicit consideration to risk and uncertainty			X

an evaluation of alternative strategies, selection of a preferred strategy and delineation of action plans or tactics that will be used to implement the preferred strategy. Specific tactics are defined in terms of manpower, raw material and capital requirements, and R & D and operations support. An interesting part of the outline is a set of contingency plans. These are plans that are put in effect if variations in some sensitive factor significantly alter forecasted operating results.

An adaptive mechanism, the main element of the last phase, is needed to revise objectives and plans if objectives are not met. This mechanism is normally provided through monthly, quarterly, and annual reviews.

Key Elements

Key elements of the planning process and their relative importance are shown in Table 6.

Broad generalizations cannot be made based on this data primarily because of the small sample size and several other factors. Respondents answered according to their personal values and their planning knowledge *vis-a-vis* their unique organizational contexts. Semantics difficulties were also prevalent such as in defining a facilitative organizational structure. Nevertheless, a few comments are worth noting. The following paragraphs discuss the elements in terms of their degree of importance.

1. *Very Important.* According to respondents, top management support is vital in creating a planning atmosphere within the firm. Subordinates pursue planning activities more creatively and vigorously when top management is committed to planning. The importance of managerial participation is almost axiomatic in the sense of a self-evident truth. Individuals who will ultimately be held responsible for implementing plans must do the planning.

2. *Moderately Important.* These factors are desirable elements of a planning process but are not of paramount importance. Feedback and flexibility are important because of constantly changing environmental factors. An organization conducive to planning facilitates the planning process.

3. *Not Very Important.* Despite the growing emphasis on social responsibility as a corporate objective, multiple objectives were not rated as very important. The financial objective is the primary objective with all other objectives having secondary importance. Several respondents stated that the social responsibility objective is difficult to quantify. This objective usually enters the planning process at the top management level.

Not all organizational levels are included in the planning process. For example, a plant manager normally is included but a plant foreman might not be. Nor are all time periods reflected in the planning process. The planning horizon ranged from 3 to 10 years with a typical planning period of 5 years. Periods beyond 10 years were rarely treated in the planning process.

Risk analysis was rated as not very important. The common method of analysis is subjective estimates and range forecasts. Range forecasts involve making optimistic, pessimistic, and probable estimates. This unsophisticated treatment of risk is primarily due to a lack of analytical tools at the divisional level, the high cost and time resources required for statistical analyses and a general lack of faith in the ability to assess an uncertain future with sufficient precision to improve current decision making.

Data Base

None of the firms uses a management information system as a planning data base. The approach taken in data collection is that information is where you find it. Divisional managers might request information from salesmen, the market research department, the corporate planning group, corporate library or other knowledgeable group or person in the firm. Each manager gathers data in his own style.

FACILITATIVE ORGANIZATION-AL STRUCTURE

A facilitative organizational structure is one that is conducive to planning and is not necessarily the same as the firm's basic organizational structure. Illustrative of the most sophisticated versions of such an organizational structure are the "planning organization" of Cleland and King[2] and Zand's "collateral organization."[3]

To facilitate understanding of the planning (or facilitative) organizational structure to be presented, a brief review or the organizational structure of a decentralized firm will be made.

Firm's Organizational Structure

A multidivisional structure is characterized by a decentralized vertical-type organizational structure with several levels of management. Departmentation is according to function and product. A typical structure is shown in Table 7.

Table 7 shows there are four major types of positions. At the top is the general office which consists of top management and staff groups which coordinate, appraise and plan goals and policies, and allocate resources for the quasi-autonomous divisions. One of these staff groups is corporation planning which will be discussed at greater length in the next section.

Each division's central office, headed by a divisional general manager, administers a number of departments. Each of these departments is responsible for a major function such as sales, market research, manufacturing, and engineering. The departmental headquarters in turn coordinates, appraises, and plans for a number of field units. At the lowest level, each field unit runs a plant, a branch or district sales office, an accounting office, and so forth.

TABLE 7

THE MULTIDIVISIONAL STRUCTURE

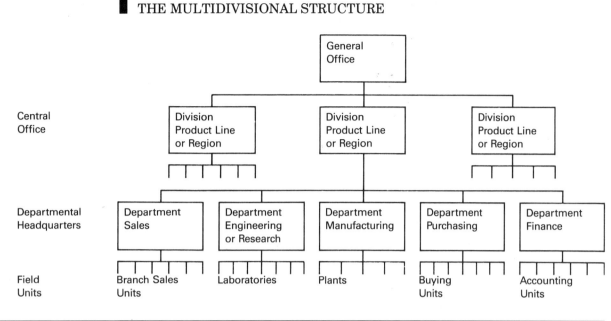

Source: Alfred D. Chandler, Jr., *Strategy and Structure*, MIT Press (1962). Reprinted by permission.

Planning Organization

One of the objectives of this study was to determine how the planning effort is organized by identifying who is functionally responsible for each of the several planning tasks. Although differences existed in functional responsibility in individual firms because of differences in size of firm, nature of business, and type of planning system, functional responsibilities were the same in most of these firms. Table 8 is a display of functional responsibility relationships that was representative of the firms visited. A brief review of the table is made in the following paragraphs.

1. *Top Management.* Top management normally is comprised of the Chairman of the Board, President, and several key Vice-Presidents. Typical titles for this group were Management Committee, Operating Committee, and Policy Committee. This group's responsibilities included establishing corporate goals and objectives, setting the planning horizon, reviewing and approving divisional plans, and allocating resources to the divisions.

2. *Corporate Planning Department.* This department provides overall coordination of the planning effort, assists in the development of corporate goals and objectives, makes environmental assumptions, reviews divisional plans, makes a financial consolidation (integration) of divisional plans, and evaluates plan effectiveness.

3. *Divisional General Management.* The divisional general manager is totally responsible for his division's plan. He normally delegates planning tasks to his staff groups, and reviews and approves their recommendations subject to his modifications. Specific tasks he performs include setting the planning horizon, selecting alternative strategies, and measuring progress against the plan.

4. *Divisional Staff Groups.* These groups make environmental forecasts, collect strategic information, assist in the development of divisional goals and objectives, formulate alternative strategies, and develop specific tactics.

TABLE 8

FUNCTIONAL RESPONSIBILITY RELATIONSHIPS

| | Functional Responsibility | | | | |
| | Corporate | | Divisional | | Other |
Planning Activities	Top Management	Corporate Planning Department	Divisional General Management	Divisional Staff Groups	Intermediary Planning Groups
Phase					
Establish corporate goals and objectives	▲				
Establish corporate goals and objectives	●	●			
Set planning horizon	●		●		
Organize and co-ordinate planning effort		●			●
Make environmental assumptions					
Make environmental assumptions	▲	●	▲	●	
Collect information and forecast					
Forecast sales	▲		▲	●	
Assess firm's strengths and weaknesses			▲	●	
Evaluate competitive environment			▲	●	
Establish divisional goals and objectives					
Establish divisional goals and objectives	▲		▲	●	▲
Develop divisional plans	▲	O	▲		▲
Formulate alternative strategies		O		●	
Select alternative strategies		O	●		
Evaluate and select projects			▲	●	
Develop tactics			▲	●	
Revise objectives and plans if objectives are not met	▲				
Integrate plans		●			
Allocate resources	▲				
Review progress against the plan	●		●		
Evaluate plan's effectiveness		●			

Key ▲ Approves
   O Reviews, evaluates and counsels
   ● Does the work

Source: Field interviews.

5. *Intermediary Planning Groups.* These groups, found in large corporations having numerous operating units, facilitate the planning process by improving communications and providing specific coordination. In Alcoa, each major operation has a Planning Board which reviews and evaluates the 5-year plans of Industry Managers and then presents a planning overview to top management, the Operating Committee.

Gulf has two major intermediary planning groups—the Planning Council and the Planning Task Force. The Planning Council coordinates and appraises the plans of the operating divisions and monitors progress against the plans. The Planning Task Force is a working group which generates new ideas and analyzes the impact of various resource allocations on the firm. This task force is also concerned with assessing the interactions among divisions accompanying various strategies.

CONDITIONS FOR EFFECTIVE PLANNING

Effective planning may be conceptually defined as planning that results in capturing tomorrow's opportunities and avoiding tomorrow's problems by making correct decisions today. While this definition is fairly straightforward, it has inherent difficulties when applied operationally. The crux of the problem is: Given today's decisions, a decision-maker can never know the future consequences of different decisions because today is gone and bygones are bygones. This lack of an operational definition makes it difficult to measure planning effectiveness. An example will more clearly illustrate the problem.

Assume the firm has available three strategic opportunities, diversify into market A, B, or C. In light of today's information, suppose the firm diversifies into market A. Assume further that the firm will not fully know if it made the right decision until years hence. Suppose that the firm then learns the diversification into market C would have been a better decision using any evaluation criteria. But what if diversifying into market D would have been an even better decision? Market D, however, was not perceived at the time of the initial decision to be an available opportunity. Accordingly, perceiving all relevant strategies and choosing the correct one in light of today's information appears to be one of the goals of effective planning.

Although we can never know beforehand with certainty if today's decision is correct, we can, however, increase the likelihood that the correct decision will be made. Four conditions necessary for more effective planning were identified in this study—planning knowledge and skills, a planning climate, psychological commitment and effective group behavior. Note that these conditions are not presented as guaranteeing effective planning, but do increase the likelihood that planning will be effective.

There is a well-defined body of knowledge concerned with planning that should be made available to key participants in the planning process. This information can be disseminated through various company training programs or can be acquired externally. This body of knowledge should not be confined to one individual or group such as the Corporate Planning Department. A long-range corporate planning system was delayed for years at Allegheny Ludlum partly because knowledge was not widely distributed in the operating divisions.

Planning skills are more difficult to acquire. The ability to conceptualize and creatively envision a large number of alternative strategies is not widely distributed in the management population. Some people are much more intuitive than others. The strength of key planning executives in this area is a major determinant of planning effectiveness as previously defined.

A planning climate is necessary for effective planning.[4] This climate is created in two major ways, through top management support and managerial participation. Top management support should take the form of executives establishing clearly defined corporate goals and objectives and taking an active role in the planning process. Managerial participation is needed because planning must be done by those individuals who will ultimately be held responsible for implementing plans. At United States Steel Corporation, top management's emphasis on steel operations and facilities planning has had a debilitating effect on long-range planning in substantial non-steel operations. Nearly all respondents cited the importance of top management support and managerial participation in effective planning.

Commitment to planning at all organizational levels greatly enhances planning effectiveness but is difficult to attain. As in any field but particularly in planning, great concentration is required that can only exist with a deep psychological commitment to this activity. Commitment should exist at three levels—commitment to the planning process, commitment to the firm's goals, and commitment to implementation of plans.

Effective group behavior also emerged as a critical factor in effective planning. At H. J. Heinz Company, the Director of Corporate Planning studied the long-range plan of one of the firm's major divisions and concluded that departments in that division appeared to contribute to the divisional plan with little if any interaction among other divisional and corporate departments. This situation may well be symptomatic of a serious deficiency in the division's planning process. Interestingly, the process is not evaluated at Heinz, only the final result, the plan, is evaluated. Several other respondents commented that being open and a sensitive listener is important to effective planning. These qualities are characteristic of effective group behavior.

PLANNING WEAKNESSES

During the course of the study, a number of planning weaknesses were identified.

1. *Inability to Forecast Accurately.* The rapidity and number of changes in environmental factors have made it difficult to forecast accurately. Some firms such as Joy Manufacturing Company have concluded that long-range planning is an academic exercise of limited value because of the inability to forecast accurately economic factors impacting the capital goods market. Their philosophy is if you can't forecast well, forecast often.

2. *Too Routinized and Mechanical.* A tendency exists for planning to become too mechanical thus defeating the purpose of planning which is to make critical evaluations of strategic opportunities available to the firm. Managers lose their vigorous, questioning attitudes.

3. *Overemphasis on Short Term.* There is too much emphasis on the first 1 or 2 years of a 5-year plan partially due to top management parochialism. The result, commonly termed the hockey stick effect, is that plans in years 3, 4, and 5 are not well thought out; the objectives are clear but the means to achieve these objectives are not.

4. *Inability to Track Performance.* Firms face a continual problem in trying to track a division's performance *vis-a-vis* their plans. The problem arises because of outside factors beyond the control of managers and because of management promotions which result in the new manager reaping the benefits or problems of planning that preceded him.

5. *Lack of Planning Process Evaluation.* None of the firms in this study evaluate the planning process. Although guidelines for planning are normally available, managers are free to do planning in their own style. Some managers perform this task more effectively than others. Plans are usually evaluated on the basis of degree of attainment of goals and objectives and top management opinion. These evaluation criteria are not entirely adequate for reasons previously cited.

TRENDS IN PLANNING

Specific trends in planning depend on the maturity of the planning system. Virtually all the firms expect to do more planning. Frequently cited planning trends are listed below.

1. *More Top Management Participation.* Although planning is primarily bottoms up, more top down planning is expected with greater top management participation in all phases of the planning process.

2. *Growing Emphasis on Environmental Factors.* Environmental factors are expected to receive increased attention because of their rapid change and significant impact on the firms' business.

3. *Extension of the Planning Horizon.* Firms plan to do more long-term strategy selection even though some have expressed an inability to forecast accurately.

4. *Increased Delegation of Planning Responsibility.* Planning should become more decentralized. The expected benefits of decentralization include accelerated personnel development, better communication, improved decision making, and greater commitment to planning as an important corporate activity.

5. *Greater Attempt to Evaluate Plans and Managers.* Several firms are placing greater emphasis on measuring manager against their plans. Incentives are being tied to how well managers plan. The anticipated result is a greater commitment to planning. To better evaluate plans, some firms are comparing different 5-year plans on a year-by-year basis.

6. *More Changes in Plan Content.* More simplification of detail and uniformity of format is expected. However, long-term resource requirements are expected to be more detailed.

7. *Greater Planning Sophistication and Efficiency.* Planning should become more sophisticated and efficient. The scientific approach to problem-solving is becoming more widespread in firms with the development of computer models and systems analysis. Efficiency is expected to increase as managers become more proficient in planning.

SUMMARY OF FINDINGS AND CONCLUSIONS

This study sought to investigate what factors led to perception of a need for corporate planning, how the planning effort is organized, and what are the conditions for effective planning. The principal findings and conclusions are:

1. The most frequently cited event associated with perception of a need for corporate planning was a change in top management. A formal, long-range planning system was designed to cope with rapidly changing environmental factors and increased firm size and complexity and to avoid serious strategic errors.

2. Planning systems can be classified into three categories—centralized, decentralized with a corporate planning department, and decentralized without a corporate planning department. Large, multidivisional firms do decentralized planning where the planning is done by divisions and departments rather than by a centralized corporate group. The existence of a corporate planning department depends on the complexity of the firm's planning process and the degree of coordination and communication that is needed.

3. The decentralized planning process consists of six stages—establishing corporate objectives and goals, setting environmental premises, collecting information and forecasting, establishing divisional goals and objectives, developing divisional plans, and revising objectives and plans if objectives are not met.

4. The key elements of the planning process are top management support and managerial participation. Top management support should take the form of taking a more active role in the planning process. Subordinate pursue planning activities more creatively and vigorously when top management is committed to planning. The importance of managerial

participation is axiomatic because planning must be done by those individuals who will be held responsible for implementing plans.

5. There are five major participants in the decentralized planning process—top management, corporate planning department, divisional general management, divisional staff groups, and intermediary planning groups. Specific tasks typically performed by each group are summarized as follows:

   a. *Top management*. This group establishes corporate goals and objectives, sets the planning horizon, reviews and approves divisional plans, and allocates resources to the divisions.

   b. *Corporate planning*. This department provides overall coordination of the planning effort, assists in the development of corporate goals and objectives, makes environmental assumptions, reviews divisional plans, makes a financial consolidation of the plans, and evaluates effectiveness of the plans.

   c. *Divisional general management*. This group delegates planning tasks to staff groups, and reviews and approves their recommendations subject to modifications. This group also sets the planning horizon, selects alternative strategies, and measures progress against the plan.

   d. *Divisional staff groups*. These groups make environmental assumptions, collect strategic information, make forecasts, assist in the development of divisional goals and objectives, formulate alternative strategies, and develop tactics.

   e. *Intermediary planning groups*. These groups, found in large organizations having numerous operating units, facilitate the planning process by improving communications and providing specific coordination. They appraise divisional plans and oftentimes present a planning overview to top management.

6. Four conditions necessary for more effective planning were identified—planning knowledge and skills, a planning climate, psychological commitment, and effective group behavior. These conditions do not guarantee effective planning but do increase the likelihood that planning will be effective. Each condition is discussed in the following paragraphs.

   a. *Planning knowledge and skills*. A well-defined body of knowledge concerned with planning should be made available to key participants in the planning process. This information can be disseminated through various company training programs or can be acquired externally. Planning skills are more difficult to acquire. The ability to conceptualize and creatively envision a large number of alternative strategies is not widely distributed in the management population. Some managers are more intuitive than others. The strength of key executives in this area is a major determinant of effective planning.

   b. *Planning climate*. A planning climate, necessary for effective planning, is created in two major ways—through top management support and managerial participation. Both of these ways were discussed previously.

   c. *Psychological commitment*. Commitment to planning at all organizational levels greatly enhances planning effectiveness. As in any field but particularly in planning, great concentration is required that can only exist with a deep psychological commitment to this activity.

d. *Effective group behavior*. This factor emerged as a critical factor in effective planning. The level and quality of departmental interactions as well as the open-mindedness and sensitive listening of key planning executives influences the quality of the planning.

7. A number of planning weaknesses were identified including inability to forecast accurately, too routinized and mechanical planning, overemphasis on short term, inability to track performance, and lack of plan and planning process evaluation.

8. Specific trends in planning depend on the maturity of the planning system. Virtually all of the firms participating in this study expect to do more planning. Frequently cited trends include more top management participation, growing emphasis on environmental factors, extension of the planning horizon, increased delegation of planning responsibility, greater attempt to measure managers against their plans, greater planning sophistication and efficiency and more changes in plan format and content.

Several areas appear to merit further study including value of a planning data base, use of planning ability as a criterion for promotion, improved decision making through risk analysis and planning process evaluation.

As previously mentioned, none of the firms surveyed in the study use a management information system as an integral part of the planning process. Managers gather information in different ways according to their unique modes of interaction. Because managers do not necessarily gather all the information that is available and relevant to their planning, a centralized information exchange center might improve information flow by evaluating, storing, and retrieving information. One approach to designing an information exchange center is to form a task force to study present informational arrangements and needs. Based on this study, a new system could be designed and implemented to meet these needs.

Planning ability might be a useful criteria for promotion because planning skills are a determinant of effective planning. Instead of building a planning system around existing managers, attention might be given to selecting managers for promotion on the basis of their inherent planning skills such as the ability to conceptualize. After a satisfactory method is devised to measure planning ability, managers can be tested and ranked according to their planning ability. In addition, training programs can be designed to improve managers' planning skills.

To make the proper trade-offs between alternative strategies and payoffs, management needs a better handle on risk and uncertainty. Risk analysis is a more advanced science than is practiced by firms participating in this study. The use of statistical techniques in the major operating divisions should complement a manager's judgment which is supreme, resulting in improved decision making. The first step might be to determine the specific needs of divisions in regards to risk analysis. Once this determination has been made, steps can be taken to make risk analysis available to all divisions.

Although some managers plan more effectively than others, how managers actually plan is rarely evaluated. A study of how managers plan may have merit because process factors might be identified which could explain variations in planning effectiveness and improve the quality of planning. One approach might be to have a trained individual observe the behavior of several key managers during the planning process with particular emphasis on frequency and quality of departmental interactions, information sources and inputs, and group behavior.

Questions for Discussion

1. What factors seem to trigger top management perceptions that there is a need for planning in their organization? Why do these factors necessitate strategic planning?

2. In a decentralized planning process, who are the major participants and what do they do? How does this differ from a centralized process?

3. What problems are encountered by firms trying to do long-term planning?

4. What conditions are necessary before effective planning can be carried out?

5. As a firm matures, how might its planning process change?

6. Does the sample lead to possible bias in results found? If so, how do you think the conclusions might differ for a different sample?

Notes

1. H. I. Ansoff, *Corporate Strategy*, New York: McGraw-Hill (1965); R. L. Ackoff, *A Concept of Corporate Planning*, New York: Wiley (1970); K. R. Andrews, *The Concept of Corporate Strategy*, New York: Dow-Jones Irwin (1971).
2. D. I. Cleland and W. R. King, "Organizing for Long Range Planning," *Business Horizons*, August (1974); and "Developing a Planning Culture for More Effective Strategic Planning," *Long Range Planning*, June (1974).
3. D. C. Zand, "Collateral Organization: A New Change Strategy," *Journal of Applied Behavioral Science*, 10, no. 1 (1974).
4. See D. I. Cleland and W. R. King, "Developing a Planning Culture for More Effective Long Range Planning," *Long Range Planning*, June (1974).

CASE 18
DON SMITH'S OBJECTIONS TO OBJECTIVES

You are Stan Stuart, plant personnel manager for Countrywide Manufacturing Company's local plant in Jamestown, Ohio, a city of about 17,000 people. The plant is the principal employer in the area.

During the past two years the Personnel Division in the central headquarters of Countrywide has been quite successful in helping line managers learn and implement a new Management by Objectives (MBO) program throughout the company. The vice-president for personnel of Countrywide was recently embarrassed when the company president asked him, "If MBO is improving effectiveness in the line divisions throughout all the plants, why haven't you used it more in your own personnel area?" This resulted in a directive to you and all plant personnel officers to come up immediately with a five-year plan applying the MBO approach. You wrote a memorandum to your branch chiefs asking them to submit a first draft of a plan to include objectives and how they are to be implemented and evaluated. This would provide data for a planning conference of your branch chiefs.

Don Smith is the chief of your counseling branch. He was hired two years ago to replace an employee who was retiring. Don was right out of college, having completed a Masters in counseling. He has proved himself to be highly successful in getting the line managers in the plant to use counseling services. The

Source: James Lau, *Behavior in Organizations* (Homewood, Ill.: Richard D. Irwin, 1975), pp. 213–214. Copyright 1975 by Richard D. Irwin, Inc.

quality of his branch's service is recognized throughout the plant. Last year Don recruited Donna Maier, who had just completed her undergraduate work. Don has trained her well, and the two of them are a great team.

In addition, Don employed on a part-time basis three counselors (they work full-time for the local public health office but are allowed to work for Country-wide in their free time). Don and Donna are the only regular employees in the branch.

The following is an informal memorandum you received from Don in answer to yours:

Dear Stan:

I am scheduled to leave on my two-week vacation tonight so I am writing you my views on MBO. I am sure you will understand when I say MBO seems to apply to production areas very well and to areas of personnel like wage and salary administration, but it really does not apply to counseling services. Last week, Donna and I saw a total of twenty-five employees for counseling and had eight interviews with supervisors about problem people. The three part-time counselors each worked two hours last week and their case load was four each for a total of twelve. Compare this with the situation two years ago when I came aboard and the one-man counseling service was handling only four to five cases a week.

Our business is so pressing that the obvious objective is to get another full-time counselor. We find that more and more we have to book appointments for a week to two ahead. The people who need several sessions with a counselor because of the seriousness of their cases are being assigned to the part-time guys from Public Health whenever possible. We are getting more and more calls from supervisors asking for help in handling nonproductive employees. One has asked us to work with him on a motivation program for his section which would help raise the production of all eight of his people. We have been able to do nothing so far on the program to help alcoholics and problem drinkers which central headquarters thinks we should be doing. I am really not sure this is a problem here; we have had no referrals. Supervisors seem more interested in problems of pregnant girls than social drinkers.

Do you agree with me when I say that in a service area like counseling, the main objective is to get enough qualified counselors to handle the employee problems that already exist? So the objectives of my branch are (a) more personnel, and (b) a bigger budget. If you need anything else on MBO for our branch, ask Donna. She knows our work as well as I do.

See you in two weeks,

Don Smith

Don's answer is the first you receive from your branch chiefs. You are a little taken aback and wonder if the rest of your team is going to be as flippant, and apparently perplexed, in trying to formulate their objectives. The chiefs of your medical and training branches were making snide remarks about MBO at lunch yesterday. This could prove embarrassing because the vice-president for personnel is the executive who brought MBO programs into the organization. You become vaguely aware that you are not sure how Don should go about defining his objectives. You decide, in view of Don's vacation, to write his objectives yourself.

Questions for Discussion

1. Should you write Don's objectives for him? If so, what would you include? If not, how do you explain this to your supervisor?

2. Are Don Smith's objectives for his branch adequate?

3. Do you think the rest of the branch chiefs will react as Don Smith has?

4. Does the personnel division need objectives? Can it plan its activities as other units can?

EXERCISE 19
CONSOLIDATED MOVIE THEATRES, INC.

INSTRUCTIONS

This exercise is designed to gauge your skill in formulating corporate strategy.

After reading the case below, assume the role of a newly elected director of the Consolidated Movie Theatres, Inc. (CMT) and describe the corporate strategy you would suggest for the firm. Please include in your statement an assessment of the main considerations that led to your conclusion.

To help you formulate your corporate strategy, pieces of information are available to you pertaining to the CMT situation. A listing of these pieces of information is provided below. In fifteen minutes your instructor will indicate that you can take as many as three of these items of information from the front desk. Subsequently, the instructor will invite you to the desk three more times at five minute intervals for additional pieces of information—a maximum of three each time. The largest total number of pieces of information which you can select is twelve. However, you are not required to take any.

Before approaching the desk, rank your preferences for the information by numbering the pieces you will choose on the lines provided in the listing. Place the number 1 beside the piece you will pick up first, should you choose any; 2 beside the second most preferred, etc., up to the number 12, if necessary.

You will be allowed forty-five minutes for this assignment and may begin to write at any time. Please read the following case, then complete the form regarding information you desire. Proceed to consider your strategy recommendations, to be completed by 45 minutes from now.

CONSOLIDATED MOVIE THEATRES, INC.

Consolidated Movie Theatres, Inc. (CMT) is composed of twenty-eight largely autonomous, previously independent theatres located throughout central Pennsylvania. Several years ago the manager-owners of privately-owned operations exchanged their theatre ownerships for CMT stock and the right to continue as theatre managers with the corporation. They believed that this freeform conglomerate arrangement would result in increased profits for all. Their corporation is run by five fulltime directors, elected by the stockholder and entrusted with the responsibility of formulating corporate strategy and directing the overall corporate activities.

Since their incorporation, CMT theatres had restricted their film offerings to those movies rated G (general audiences), PG (parental guidance suggested), and R (restricted to persons over 18), with rare exceptions when X-rated—and never pornographic-type—films were shown.

During the past year, CMT's seventh of operation, profits of the CMT theatres dropped almost 14 percent from the previous year, even though the profits of the theatre industry at-large had reached all-time high levels during the same period.

In reviewing the performance of their offerings in the past year, the CMT directors discovered that the few X-rated films that they had shown had far-and-away been the most profitable, followed by those rated R. Further, competitors of CMT who had occasionally shown pornographic-type films had outdrawn the CMT theatres on the dates when this type of film was shown.

Source: Prepared by John A. Pearce II, Eakin Endowed Chair in Strategic Management, George Mason University. Used by permission of the author.

Recently, a major film distributor approached the CMT directors with an offer to supply them with a selection of top quality X-rated and pornographic-type films for the following 12 months, the minimum contract period. These films, if ordered, would constitute approximately one-third of the films shown at any single theatre during the year, with the remaining two-thirds being supplied by the corporation's present distributor.

In discussing the possibility of contracting for films from a second distributor, the CMT directors foresee an opportunity for increased business by attracting a new segment of moviegoers. On the other hand, they fear a twelve-month commitment to a moderately risky venture and they have expressed concern regarding the long-run impact of a rather drastic change in their film offering.

The next page contains information sources from which you may choose. Again, you need to propose a strategic recommendation, and may or may not choose up to 12 additional pieces of data when offered the opportunity.

CMT Information Available

This page contains information available to CMT directors. You may select up to 12, 3 at a time. Rank order the top 12 pieces you wish to receive, then pick up the information from the instructor when indicated.

___ 1. Labor Union Considerations

___ 2. CMT's Perceived Role in the Competitive Environment

___ 3. Concession Stand Operations

___ 4. Technological Factors

___ 5. Return-on-Investment Information on CMT and the Industry

___ 6. Inventory Control Concerns

___ 7. Manager's Commitment to a Revised Strategy

___ 8. Social Factors Affecting CMT Theatres

___ 9. Overhead Cost Changes

___10. CMT Ideals and Long-term Goals

___11. Impact on Media Advertising

___12. CMT Theatre Locations

___13. Theatre Ticketing Pricing and Film Costs

___14. Political and Legal Factors

___15. In-theatre Promotions at CMT

___16. CMT Corporate Performance Targets

___17. Theatre Hours

___18. Activities Valuable to the Customer

___19. Desired Benefits from a Revised Film Offering

___20. Likelihood of Success with X-rated Films

___21. Employee Attitudes Toward a Revised Strategy

___22. Economic Conditions in CMT Theatre Areas

___23. CMT Corporate Abilities

___24. Distribution Channels

___25. Other (Please specify at the desk)

CASE 20
PLANNING UNDER CRISIS CONDITIONS

Juan Carlos is the general manager of the Houston plant of Perfect Plastics Corporation. It is 1:30 p.m. on Tuesday, November 3. Juan has been tied up most of the morning in an executive committee meeting making final arrangements for the annual plant inspection that is to be conducted by a visiting group of officers from corporate headquarters. Juan goes to lunch with Sue Owens, customer services representative, where they discuss her plans, which have led to improved delivery time to their largest account, the Erb Drug Company. Juan congratulates Sue on her efforts to better service this account. Right after returning from lunch, he remembers that he hasn't yet had a chance to vote in the general election.

The morning mail is waiting for Juan when he returns, along with a telegram and several interoffice memos and notices of phone calls. (See Figure 1). Juan's secretary has placed them at the top of his communications in-basket because they appear to be the most urgent ones.

As Juan reads through this material, he realizes that he needs to respond quickly because conferences with members of the visiting plant inspection team will occupy virtually all his time for the next two days. The team is arriving at 5:00 p.m., and Juan must leave the office by 4:00 p.m. to be sure he will be at the airport on time to meet them and escort them to the hotel at which dinner has been arranged.

Juan knows he has to plan his time carefully; therefore, he wonders how he should dispose of the messages during the next couple of hours.

Questions for Discussion

1. Which of the six messages is most urgent? Why?

2. Can Juan delay a response to any of the messages? If so, which ones and for how long?

3. Can Juan delegate action on any of these communications? To whom? What should his instructions be?

4. How would you recommend that Juan spend his next two hours in the office?

5. Can managers plan their schedules to avoid problems like the ones Juan is facing?

FIGURE 1

Interplant Memo

Monday, Nov. 2
4:30 p.m.

To: Juan Carlos

From: Al Larsen, Maintenance Supt.

We have just received a call from the Houston Power Company telling us that all power to the plant will be off from 7:00 a.m. until 9:00 a.m. on Wednesday morning in order for emergency repairs to be made on the high-voltage transformer serving the plant. I urged them to change the time, but they said that this was the only time they could do it without causing an even longer shutdown. I tried to reach you by phone, but you were in a meeting. We need to get together with the people in production as soon as possible to figure out how we are going to handle the power outage.

Telegram

Nov. 3
10:45 a.m.

Mr. Juan Carlos
Plant Manager
Perfect Plastics Corporation

A number of the prescription containers in your last shipment did not meet our specifications. We request immediate cancellation of remainder of order until you make satisfactory adjustments.

J. L. Erb, President
Erb Drug
Company

Phone Call

Offset Printing Company called while you were out.

( ) will call back
(x) please call

Message: The page proofs for the Houston Management Club Conference a week from Saturday are ready for checking. Since you are the Conference chairperson, they would like you to take a look at the proofs as soon as possible. They wanted me to be sure and remind you that if the programs are to be printed in time for mailing, the printing of them must start not later than tomorrow morning.

Interplant Memo

Nov. 3
11:00 a.m.

To: Juan Carlos

From: Hal Barnes, Personnel Dept.

We received a call from the Town House Hotel saying that there has been a foul-up in reservations for our people arriving from headquarters. They could not provide the suite of rooms in the rear of the hotel that headquarters requested. The only thing available is a suite of rooms on the third floor, street side, which would be rather noisy. What shall I do?

Phone Call

John Davey, Assistant Plant Manager, called while you were at lunch.

( ) will call back
(x) please call

Message: Quality Control has discovered a problem with one of the molding machines used in plastic bottle manufacture. Repairs may require rescheduling production runs and delays on several orders.

Phone Call

Your wife called at 1:15 p.m.

( ) will call back
(x) please call

Message: The wife of the president is traveling with the visiting team. She wants your wife to have dinner with her. Your wife was planning to go to the play at the high school tonight where your son has the lead role.

EXERCISE 21
STRATEGIC PLANNING FOR THE GANTRY COMPANY

This exercise is designed to help you learn how individuals and groups might plan strategy for their organization.

First, read the background information of the Gantry Company on your own. Then, individually, complete Table 1, Individual Resource Distribution. Next, read the section on strategic alternatives, and complete Table 2, Individual Strategic Resource Distribution. Finally, meet with your team to make decisions about Table 3, Group Strategic Resource Distribution.

After you have completed these tables, work on the Analysis Section.

Gantry Company: Background Information

The Gantry Company is a well-regarded medium-size food processing company located in central Ohio. Its major orientation is the production and marketing of jams, jellies, and ice cream toppings in the United States and Canada. Gantry is fairly well established in about two thirds of the major markets, and sells through food and discount wholesalers and retailers. Gantry maintains one plant in Ohio and has contracts for fruit and other raw materials (e.g., sugar, syrup, glass containers, and so on) with a variety of suppliers.

The company has justifiably earned a reputation for producing high-quality food products. Over the past few years, Gantry has enjoyed a 10 percent annual gain in sales and earnings in the products and markets they now serve. This has been accomplished without significant investments in research and development, new products, or production improvements for the past ten years.

The Gantry family, owners of the company, have indicated a willingness to explore a number of alternative growth possibilities for the future. They have hired you as a consultant to assist them in making strategic decisions with regard to how they should invest in the future. The feeling is that to sustain growth, the company is at the point where some investment needs to be made.

Capital is not a constraint. Through retained earnings and a good line of credit, Gantry is capable of investing in several projects. The owners, however, do wish to use their capital wisely, such that they produce a greater return on capital than what can be achieved now.

As a consultant, you have been asked to plan the priority of investment projects that you think the company should pursue. The owners suggest that you consider allocating funds to the following five strategic alternatives:

1. Increase penetration of existing markets.
2. Increase number of markets served.
3. Extend vertically forward (closer to the final consumer).
4. Extend vertically backward (closer to the basic raw materials).
5. Expand production capacity.

Given these five strategic alternatives, you should indicate in Table 1 how you would prefer to allocate the resources available to the Gantry Company. Assuming that total resources equal 100 percent, distribute your allocation to each of the five alternatives in any manner you prefer, such that they add to 100 percent. You must allocate something to each alternative. Your distribution should reflect the importance you feel each should have in terms of its contribution to overall development and goals of the company.

TABLE 1
INDIVIDUAL RESOURCE DISTRIBUTION

Strategic Alternative	Resource Allocation
1. Increase penetration of existing markets	_____%
2. Increase number of markets served	_____%
3. Extend vertically forward	_____%
4. Extend vertically backward	_____%
5. Expand production capacity	_____%
Total	100%

Your consulting firm has explored the five strategic alternatives in greater detail with company executives and industry experts. Two options (I and II) have been identified as potential ways to implement each of the five strategic alternatives. After reading each option for each alternative, indicate how you would allocate resources among each option on Table 2. You may allot 100 percent to I and 0 percent to II, or vice versa; or you may use any combination of resources (e.g., 50–50, 70–30, 15–85, and so on) so long as the resources allocated to the two options equal 100 percent for each alternative.

If you allocate less than 100 percent to either option, it may result in less than optimum returns for that particular option. The returns are assumed to be relatively proportional to the amount invested. However, 100 percent allocation to either option does not necessarily automatically assure full accomplishment of that option.

Option I	**Option II**
1. Increase penetration of existing markets	
Add sales personnel and promotional efforts in existing markets. Focus on those products (jams and jellies) that contribute greatest profit margin. There is a high probability that this effort can increase demand for currently profitable products.	Introduce new lines of products (honey, peanut butter, jelly combination) into existing markets. The company image may lead to consumer acceptance and, if successful, high profitability. Consumer acceptance of these higher priced convenience products is subject to uncertain economic conditions.
2. Increase number of markets served	
Using existing product lines, invest in promotion in major domestic markets not now served.	Using existing product lines and possibly one new line, begin processing and promotion in selected foreign markets. The returns of this strategy are likely to be high with relatively low volume. However, the instability in the countries involved may result in takeover or control of processing plants.
Market research suggests demand in some major markets may justify this activity and would help growth in sales. Return on investment will be roughly the same as in current markets, but volume will be higher.	

3. Extend vertically forward (closer to the final consumer)

Invert in small retail outlets (24-hour convenience stores) which handle limited product lines including Gantry products. This could result in increased sales, but future growth potential of these outlets is limited.

Buy out or merge with some of the wholesalers who deal in Gantry products as well as products of other food processors. Expertise in wholesaling is not currently one of Gantry's strengths, but control over these distributors could result in a considerably higher rate of return.

4. Extend vertically backward (closer to basic raw materials)

There is an opportunity to invest in the development of three or four of the orchards owned by major fruit suppliers used in toppings and jellies and jams. Gantry currently employs inspectors who have technical competence in cultivating and harvesting these fruits. Control of these raw materials would help smooth fluctuations in product availability and cost.

Acquire or merge with the major glass works that provides jars and bottles for packaging jams and jellies. Very significant cost savings could be achieved in total product cost with control over this resource. Technology and management know-how in this field are not possessed by Gantry, and the glass company has been owned by the same family firm for eighty years.

5. Expand production capacity

Some processing efficiencies could result from investment in more modern processing equipment and procedures in the production of jams and jellies. A reduction in amount of product inspection would also result in increased plant output without significant losses in product quality (although the "Grade A Fancy" rating from USDA may become only "Grade A").

Invest in new plants located closer to sources of raw materials (orchards). There is some concern that if an orchard fails due to unfavorable climatic conditions, severe inefficiencies and plant closings could result. (Crop failure occurs every four or five years). At the same time, transportation costs can be significantly reduced yielding much higher profitability.

At this point, you should meet with a study group and make group decisions about how you would allocate resources *among* the strategic alternatives. And, within each alternative, decide how your group wants to allocate resources between the two options. Discuss each alternative and option completely before deciding on your allocation. Follow the procedures you used individually, and place your decisions in Table 3.

TABLE 2

INDIVIDUAL STRATEGIC RESOURCE DISTRIBUTION

Strategic Alternative	Option I	Option II	Total
1. Increase penetration of existing markets	_____ %	_____ %	100%
2. Increase number of markets served	_____ %	_____ %	100%
3. Extend vertically forward	_____ %	_____ %	100%
4. Extend vertically backward	_____ %	_____ %	100%
5. Expand production capacity	_____ %	_____ %	100%

TABLE 3

GROUP STRATEGIC RESOURCE DISTRIBUTION

Strategic Alternative	Resource Allocation among Alternatives	Option I	Option II	
1. Increase penetration of existing markets	_____ %	_____ %	_____ %	100%
2. Increase number of markets served	_____ %	_____ %	_____ %	100%
3. Extend vertically forward	_____ %	_____ %	_____ %	100%
4. Extend vertically backward	_____ %	_____ %	_____ %	100%
5. Expand production capacity	_____ %	_____ %	_____ %	100%
	100%			

ANALYSIS

Do a little introspection about yourself. When confronted with decision situations, are you a risk seeker or risk averter? Do you seek out and make decisions that expose you to a high degree of risk in situations you are uncertain about? In these instances, there might be a high payoff or high loss. Are you willing to take such a chance? Or do you seek to minimize loss and play it "close to the vest?" For example, if you play poker, are you often willing to gamble on a bluff or draw to a hand that has a low probability of success but possibly high payoff (risk seeker); or would you fold the hand and not risk further losses (risk averter)?

In the space below, indicate whether you are a risk seeker or risk averter. If you avoid risk in most or all situations, pick a number closer to 0. If you are a high risk taker, choose a number closer to 100. Circle the number that best describes your approach to risky situations.

Risk Averter   0   10   20   30   40   50   60   70   80   90   100   Risk Seeker

This is your "individual risk estimate."

To help you analyze your actual attitudes toward risk taking, complete Tables 4 and 5.

In Table 4, enter in Column 1 the values you individually decided upon for each strategic alternative in Table 1. In Column 2, enter the values you decided upon for Option II in Table 2. Multiply Columns 1 and 2 and enter the product in Column 3. At the bottom of that column, add the column total, then divide by 100 for your "individual risk attitude." In Column 4, enter the values your group decided upon (from Table 3) for allocation among the strategic alternatives. In Column 5, enter the values your group chose for Option II in Table 3. Column 6 is the product of Columns 4 and 5. At the bottom of Column 6 total the values, then divide by 100 for your "group risk attitude." You may have noted that Option II for each strategic alternative was more risky than Option I.

In Table 5, for each member of your group, enter the "individual risk estimate" in Column 1 and enter the "individual risk attitude" (from Table 4, Column 3) in Column 2. Find the average for these two columns. At the bottom of Column 2 enter the "group risk attitude" (from Table 4, Column 6).

You might wish to explore what differences exist within your group, and why these occur.

TABLE 4

ATTITUDES TOWARD RISK

	INDIVIDUAL		
	Col. 1 **% Alloc. to** **Alternative**	**Col. 2** **Option II** **Alloc.**	**Col. 3** **(1) x (2)**
1. Penetrate existing markets	————	————	————
2. Increase number of markets	————	————	————
3. Extend vertically forward	————	————	————
4. Extend vertically backwards	————	————	————
5. Expand production capacity	————	————	————
		Sum =	————
		Individual risk attitude	
		Sum/100 =	————

	GROUP		
	Col. 4 **% Alloc. to** **Alternative**	**Col. 5** **Option II** **Alloc.**	**Col. 6** **(1) x (2)**
1. Penetrate existing markets	————	————	————
2. Increase number of markets	————	————	————
3. Extend vertically forward	————	————	————
4. Extend vertically backwards	————	————	————
5. Expand production capacity	————	————	————
		Sum =	————
		Group risk attitude	
		Sum/100 =	————

TABLE 5

RISK ESTIMATE AND ATTITUDE COMPARISONS

Group Member	**Col. 1** **Individual** **Risk Estimate**	**Col.2** **Individual** **Risk Estimate**
———————————	————	————
———————————	————	————
———————————	————	————
———————————	————	————
———————————	————	————
———————————	————	————
———————————	————	————
———————————	————	————
———————————	————	————
Average	————	———— (A)
Group risk attitude	————	———— (B)

EXERCISE 22
PLANNERS AND OPERATORS

This experience combines elements of planning, communication, group dynamics, and managerial interrelationships into one exercise. Clusters of ten or so people will be formed and divided into three subgroups. Four persons will serve as "planners," four as "operators," and the remaining participants will serve as "observers."

The planners will be separated and conduct a conference to decide how to instruct operators to do a task. The operators will then carry out the task as best they can while the observers watch the process, making notes of efficiencies and difficulties.

Your instructor will give you directions for completing this exercise.

Source: Adaptations from "Intergroup Exercise: Planners and Operators," R. A. Schmuck, et al., *Handbook of Organization Development in Schools* (Palo Alto, Calif.: National Press Books, 1972), with permission of The Center of Educational Policy and Management, University of Oregon.

DECISION MAKING

●LEARNING OBJECTIVES

To sum up, this chapter has as its objectives:

1. To promote your understanding of the decision-making process.

2. To help you understand what style of decision making is appropriate and under which conditions.

3. To help you develop decision-making skills in order to become an effective decision maker and manager.

4. To understand the unique problems associated with the group decision-making process.

D

ecision making takes place in all organizations, and most other aspects of management involve this process. A decision-making situation exists when there are two or more alternatives for doing something and you must choose which one to use. Typically, the choice is made on the basis of which alternative is likely to reach the objective in the most efficient way. That sounds simple, doesn't it? It's not.

Before a decision takes place, four conditions must be satisfied.

1. A gap must exist between a desired state and the existing condition.
2. The gap must be large enough to be noticeable.
3. The decision maker must be motivated to reduce the gap.
4. The decision maker must believe some action can reduce the gap.

Note that some problems might be completely ignored. If a person thinks fate or luck is involved, then there may be a "decision" not to make a decision.

If a decision is to be made, then we must decide how to make it. Here is where you start getting into debates. Many new techniques have been devised to make decision making more rational—trying to find "optimal" solutions to problems. Yet practicing managers have resisted these for several reasons:

- They may be afraid the technique will outperform them.
- They may not understand the value of the technique, or how to use it.
- They may feel the technique is inappropriate for their problem, or too restrictive in its scope of application.
- They may believe the technique is too costly.
- They may prefer to rely on their own intuition.

In some cases these reasons are valid. For example, extremely complex and unique kinds of problems may require creativity and judgment that techniques cannot provide. In other instances, however, these reasons are unfounded or invalid. For routine, programmed decisions, these tools may provide valuable inputs to decision makers or, in a few cases, may even provide the decision. The reading "Managers without Management Science?" discusses this problem. What is the conflict and possible compromise between reliance on intuition and judgment versus the use of sophisticated scientific, mathematical models?

Before reading that article, we hope you understand that decisions can take place under three conditions:

1. *Certainty*—the environment is completely known, as are all outcomes of all possible alternatives.
2. *Uncertainty*—the environment is completely unknown.
3. *Risk*—probabilities of different outcomes for alternatives can be calculated or assumed, although not all possible outcomes are known.

In practically all business situations, if not all decision situations, the decision maker deals with risk and uncertainty. In the case of uncertainty, the decision maker attempts to move to a position of risk by considering a more limited set of alternatives and assuming some probability of outcomes for them. Decision making also often involves tradeoffs. This is sometimes done using cost benefit analysis. One of the cases in this chapter and an exercise introduce elements of risk and trade-offs in decisions. The "Cost-Benefit Decision at Bluebird Smelter" case shows the conditions necessary before a decision is made and addresses tradeoffs. The "Alcon Canning Company" exercise deals with two alternative choices, possible outcomes given different risk assumptions, and you are asked to make a decision. Your discussion about this approach will hopefully point out some of the limitations to this decision mode.

Of course, there are many other aspects of decision making. For example, you should recognize that decision makers don't have complete freedom to act on their own at all times. Decisions affect others who will sometimes try to influence the decision so it's more favorable for them. Politics exist in all organizations. Furthermore, there are often conflicts between short-term and long-term decisions. The case "Like an Old Penny" points out some of these difficulties associated with decision making.

Another component of decision making is that managers make decisions ranging from the use of highly rational approaches to highly creative approaches and styles. These issues and others are addressed by the exercise "A Quiz for Decision Makers." We hope you will take this "test" and discuss your answer with others. You may find out that there are conflicting attitudes about what constitutes "good" decision making.

Finally, you should be aware that decisions made by groups could differ from those made by individuals. The "Decision by the Group" case and "Prestigious Occupations" exercise should give you an understanding about how group decisions might differ from individual decisions. The "Whom Do You Let Go?" exercise will give you a chance to examine the dynamics of a group decision you must make.

You probably still want to know, "How do I make a decision?" Assuming you use a rational approach, the usual prescription is to follow the "scientific method."

1. Recognize and define the problem.
2. Search for information and describe alternatives.
3. Estimate probabilities of certain outcomes resulting from each alternative.
4. Choose the alternative with the best outcome (expected) in light of the objective.

Again, this is a rational approach and is subject to the vagaries of politics, compromise, and nonrational approaches described above. The comprehensive case "From Disequilibrium to Disequilibrium" suggests how the various decision factors might work together in a particular situation. ●

READING 23
MANAGERS WITHOUT MANAGEMENT SCIENCE?
Milan Zeleny

Since scientific methods simply exhibit free intelligence operating in the best manner available at a given time, the cultural waste, confusion, and distortion that results from the failure to use these methods, in all fields in connection with all problems, is incalculable.

John Dewey,
Logic, The Theory of Inquiry

INTRODUCTION

In a recent article, C. Jackson Grayson, Jr. states that he used absolutely *none* of the management science tools explicitly.[1] Yet, to the question whether he might have done better by using *some* management science models his answer is *no*. How does he know?

That question is the main subject of this note. Can a decision maker do better without science, models, computers, etc.? In other words, can we rely exclusively on experience, intuition, expert judgment, hunch or genius? The answer is *no*. Or, *more precisely*, it all depends on the decision maker, the problem and the environment.

The arguments are structured according to the following sequence of problems:

- How reliable is human intuitive judgment in simple as well as complex decision situations?
- Can a scientific, mathematical, computerized model outperform human decision makers?
- How crucial is the quantity and the quality of information for intelligent decision making?
- What is intuition and counterintuition in a good decision?

TESTING THE EXPERTS

Most important business decisions occur under conditions of uncertainty, and thus the intuitive assessment of probability must be part of any judgment, implicitly or explicitly.

Amos Tversky and Daniel Kahneman[2] have conducted some interesting experiments on judgmental evaluations of probabilities. The results are not encouraging. Take for example *anchoring*.

Humans usually make estimates by starting from some initial value which is *then* adjusted to yield the final answer. In one experiment those initial values were determined by spinning a wheel of fortune in the subjects' presence. The subjects were instructed to indicate whether the value was too low or too high, and then they were asked to make their estimate by a proper adjustment. Different groups were given different initial values. These "roulette" values had a marked effect on the estimates—e.g., the percentages of African countries in the U.N. were estimated as 25% and 45% by groups which received 10% and 65% as initial values respectively. Even a monetary reward for accuracy did not reduce the anchoring effect!

Source: Reprinted by permission from Milan Zeleny, "Managers without Management Science?" *Interfaces*, 5, no. 4, August 1975. Copyright 1975, The Institute of Management Sciences.

Also, the researchers have shown that human decision makers demonstrate remarkable *insensitivity to prior probability* of outcomes. Subjects were shown brief personality descriptions of several individuals from a group of 100 professionals—engineers and lawyers. They were asked to assess, for each description, the probability that it belonged to an engineer rather than to a lawyer. One group was told that the sample group consisted of 30 engineers and 70 lawyers and the other group was given the reversed ratio. The subjects in the two different situations produced essentially the same probability judgments. Even when the personality description was intentionally made irrelevant to either engineers or lawyers!

In another experiment, subjects assigned the *same* probability of obtaining an average height greater than six feet for samples of 1,000, 100, and 10 men. Moreover, subjects *failed to appreciate the role of sample size* even when it was emphasized in the formulation of the problem.

Another important conclusion of Tversky-Kahneman is quoted directly:

> *Given input variables of stated validity, a prediction based on several such variables can achieve higher accuracy when the input variables are independent of each other than when they are redundant or correlated. Redundant input variables generally yield input patterns that appear internally consistent, whereas uncorrelated input variables often yield input patterns that appear inconsistent. The internal consistency of the pattern of input (e.g., a profile of scores) is one of the major determinants of representativeness, and hence of confidence in prediction. Consequently, people tend to have greater confidence in predictions based on redundant input variables than in predictions based on uncorrelated variables. Because redundancy among inputs usually decreases accuracy and increases confidence, people tend to have most confidence in predictions that are very likely to be off the mark.*

This observation can have an enormous impact on our view of the value of information as we shall discuss later.

Consultants and other experts are often called upon to predict the future value of a stock, the demand for a commodity, the Dow-Jones average or future profit. These predictions have been shown to be insensitive to the *reliability of the information* used and to the *expected accuracy of the prediction*. For example, if the descriptions of various companies (favorable or unfavorable) are unrelated to their profits, the same value should be predicted for all companies. But in reality, very high profit will be estimated if the description is most favorable. Similarly, the prediction of a remote value (e.g., future profits) was found to be identical to the evaluations of the information on which the prediction was based (e.g., previous year profits).

Another phenomenon which usually escapes most decision makers is *regression toward the mean*, i.e., the successful performance is likely to be followed by a deterioration in performance and vice versa. Still, rewards are typically administered when performance is good and punishments are administered when performance is poor. Because of regression toward the mean, behavior is most likely to improve after punishment and most likely to deteriorate after reward. Therefore, one is most often rewarded for punishing others and most often punished for rewarding them!

We could go on describing the experiments of Tversky and Kahneman. Let us state their conclusions in a summary:

> *Reliance on heuristics and the presence of common biases are general characteristics of intuitive judgment of both laymen and experts.*
>
> *It is astonishing that experts fail to infer from life-long experience such fundamental statistical rules as regression toward the mean or the effect of a sample size.*

> *Most judgmental errors are systematic and predictable. People do not usually detect them because events are not normally coded in terms crucial for grasping statistical rules.*

"BOOTSTRAP-PING"

Let us turn to the work of Robyn M. Dawes.[3] His main concern is what role the human judge *should* play in prediction and decision making. Let us state his main conclusion, based on extensive experimental work:

> *If a reasonable sample of cases exists for which the output values are known, the best way to make the predictions is to derive rational weights for the input variables on the basis of multiple regression; human judges should be ignored.*

Dawes goes even further. What if we do not have a reasonable sample from which to derive regression weights? Can anything be done which would still be superior to human judgment? His answer is yes.

Experiments have shown that many linear models did a better job of predicting the outcome the decision maker was trying to predict than did the decision maker himself. The paramorphic representation of a decision maker's behavior may be more predictive of the outcome than is the decision maker himself. This phenomenon is called *"bootstrapping."*

In general, linear models seem to be superior to human decision makers under certain conditions. Actually, linear models whose weights were randomly selected *on the average* outperformed the linear models whose weights were selected on the basis of experts' judgments!

Another researcher, Paul Slovic,[4] has supported most of Dawes' findings and demonstrated them on examples of stock market "decision makers." First, he discusses the finding that the decision maker's *length of professional training* and *experience* often showed little relationship to accuracy of judgments. Similarly, the amount of information available to the decision makers was not necessarily related to the accuracy of their inferences.

As for the weights entering linear regression models it has been found that the longer a broker has been in the business, the less accurate was his insight into his weighting policy. Slovic also suggests that the algebraic model captures the judge's weighting policy and applies it more consistently than the judge. Substitution of the model for the manager, under certain conditions, can produce decisions superior to those the manager made on his own.

It is implied that the current role of the human decision maker could be misplaced. Man simply cannot take proper account, simultaneously, or various multiple attributes (and their complex interactions) of existing alternatives. Essentially a man should "tell" the computer *how* he wants decisions made, and then let the machine make the decisions for him, i.e., a man decides which variables should be included in the input, performs elementary comparisons with respect to subjective attributes, decides what kind of information will be gathered and how much, but mainly is concerned with the criteria of decision, goals, and objectives. These have to be defined and human judgment always will be essential here.

In an article by Yntema and Torgerson[5] one source of misunderstanding between managers and management science is identified:

> *. . .in business it is now common to use computer programs to calculate how to maximize some quantity or other; linear programming is the prime example. As the mathematics becomes more sophisticated and computers become more powerful, the success of these methods will depend less and less on the number of variables and the complexity of the relations that can be considered. Planners will find themselves paying even more attention than they do now to the precise definition of the quantity to be maximized.*

We are still witnessing management scientists paying more attention to the problems of handling large numbers of variables and constraints and to the sophistication of algorithms and managers still refusing to use them. Both sides should concentrate on *what* and *why* rather than *how* to optimize.

Finally, some managers argue that they cannot use linear models because the reality is nonlinear. So they push for even more complex mathematical models (nonlinear) and thus encourage management science and the scientist to move further away from being useful to them. Would a manager accept the decision of a complex nonlinear model if he has rejected that of a simple linear model?

There is no sufficient evidence that nonlinear models are superior to linear models. Actually the opposite might be true. Linear models are usually extremely robust approximations to nonlinear monotone functions. Linear models are of greater practical value in decision making. Dawes describes an experiment in which the linear model constructed of every single one of 80 judges did a better job than the judges themselves.

HOW MUCH INFORMATION IS ENOUGH?

It is probably safe to state that the current manager's view of a man-computer interaction is that a computer, with all of its mathematical models, is supposed to provide a sufficient amount of information on which a decision maker can base his decision. Another view of this interaction is the reverse, i.e., man should decide about the information and the criteria and let the model make the final decision.

Man is a bad processor of information generated by computer—he is a bad processor of information in general. Then why this craving for more information, for MIS, data banks, and other expensive tools believed to improve a decision maker's decision?

S. Oskamp[6] describes a study of 32 judges, including 8 professional clinicians, who were given background information about a patient's case. The information was divided into four sections. After reading each section of the case, the judges established their diagnoses. The correct diagnosis was known only to the investigator. Oskamp found that, as the amount of information about the case increased, accuracy remained at about the same level while the clinicians' confidence increased dramatically and became disproportionately great!

This finding supports the conclusions of Tversky and Kahneman, namely that people tend to have most confidence in predictions that are very likely to be off the mark.

The current boom in Management Information Systems (MIS) is directed toward obtaining as much information as possible. Additional information boosts managers' confidence and helps their decisions to be more forcefully implemented; it does not necessarily improve the quality of their decisions. Only some minimum threshold level of information is actually utilized in forming a decision—all the rest of this expensive information is used to increase the decision maker's confidence. Actually information in excessive doses is harmful since it increases confidence where caution and doubt should be exercised. But one doesn't make it as a manager by being cautious and modest. One must appear aggressive and confident. Therefore managers reject management science which is intended to improve their decisions but are inclined to accept management information systems which tend to increase their confidence, though the decisions might stay inferior.

Tversky and Kahneman found that people respond differently when given no information and when given *worthless information*. When no specific information is given people tend to employ statistical laws; when worthless information is given—they use it and ignore the laws!

It is not necessary to concur with "bootstrapping" and to advocate replacing decision makers by machines. But managers should realize what management science has to offer and that the managers should make necessary steps in bridging the gap between them and management scientists. This rather complex recommendation might appear to be counterintuitive.

INTUITION, COUNTER-INTUITION, AND ACCEPTABILITY

Complex systems tend to behave counterintuitively and thus their models (if they are correct) tend to suggest counterintuitive answers. Consequently, management science models are not likely to be accepted because they give different solutions from what an expert would expect intuitively.

We find again and again that acceptability is the ultimate criterion of a successful model (and of its creator). It does not really matter whether the model is correct or incorrect or whether the decision maker is right or wrong. In both cases the intuitive preconception must be satisfied as a necessary condition for acceptance. This is a very serious *dilemma:* A correct model (possibly counterintuitive) will probably be unacceptable because it does not support intuitive judgment. Yet, an incorrect model has a better chance of acceptance because it tends to be less counterintuitive and thus more appealing to intuition of top executives. It is therefore "useful."

C. West Churchman[7] supports the point that the acceptance by managers should be the ultimate test of management science. He says: "If the manager doesn't act as the model says he should, then something is wrong, and until the error is explained the model cannot be accepted." And later he concludes that: ". . .we *can* say that acceptance is an ultimate test of the validity of a model." In view of what has been stated about the reliability of intuitive judgments it looks as though management science models are utilized for what they are not designed: to support managers' intuition and to improve their confidence. Whether they provide correct or incorrect answers seems to be irrelevant.

Churchman actually knows the answer: "If we could accomplish a fuller understanding of the process of acceptance, we would create a very beautiful thing to behold. The manager and the scientist would 'work together' in a very intricate and elegant way." But he is quite skeptical about its feasibility because ". . .ignorance may be of value to the manager. The manager may want to be ignorant, i.e., to ignore knowledge." Although the manager's ignorance should be taken into account, management scientists should help to remove it.

As Peter Drucker[8] observes: "Managers, by and large, have failed to take managerial responsibility for management scientists and management sciences. They have left the management sciences unmanaged—and are therefore largely responsible for their degenerating into a bag of tricks, a 'management gadget bag' of answers to nonexisting questions in many cases."

Managers are responsible, responsibility is their profession. They should understand the limitations of intuitive expert judgments. They must understand what the management sciences can do, that they are the manager's tools, and not the tools of the management scientist. They have to realize the limitations of management science, caused by its origin and history. Management sciences (and scientists) can change but they must be stimulated and led in proper directions by managers. They must be managed.

CONCLUSIONS AND IMPLICATIONS

We have shown how unreliable managers' judgment could be in dealing with well-structured and well-defined problems of analytical nature. It is quite tempting to conclude that if human performance is inferior in dealing with simple problems, not much should be expected from its encounters with complex and messy problems.

There is a catch. Complex problems are not simple collections of simpler problems; they are not decomposable. We often confuse largeness with complexity. Large, combinatoric problems are usually well-structured, decomposable into simpler subproblems and thus can be entrusted to computers and models. They are not complex in the sense of being messy, fuzzy, ill-structured, qualitative, etc. Thus, the conclusions of judgmental psychologists are not transferable to all types of human problem solving. No experiments have yet been conducted to evaluate human performance in dealing with true complexity.

To find a product of, say, 1,000 numbers is a well-structured, although a large, problem. It is not complex but we can learn that finding the answer by intuition could be a misplaced effort. On the other hand, to find a solution to a traffic mess at a busy intersection should better be entrusted to the sure and fast functioning of the human mind. Even a model involving velocities and masses of all objects, probabilities of their trajectories, and expectations of subjects' states of mind, even such models could not compete with human grasp of totality, simultaneity, and gestalt of the situation.

There are essentially two modes of human problem solving; analytic and intuitive. Both these modes are the endpoints of the same continuum of thought. The analytic end can be characterized as having explicit, sequential, and recoverable attributes, while the intuitive end has implicit, nonsequential, and nonrecoverable attributes. Analytic thinking relies on logical sequences, symbolic structures, componentwise decomposition, and vertical reasoning. Intuitive thinking relies on holistic impressions, visual and spatial images, impulsive synthesis, and lateral reasoning.

As managerial concerns advance from simple, well-structured, static, and deterministic problems toward more complex, fuzzy, dynamic, and stochastic problems, the *optimal* working framework of the human mind changes from logical, rational, sequential, and quantitative, to perceptive, intuitive, simultaneous, and qualitative. To approach the problems of reality in their full complexity of an analytical-intuitive unity requires a conscious enhancement of both ends of this ever shifting continuum of thought.

Most problems of management are neither purely analytic, nor purely intuitive; rather, they combine both components in an intricate interaction. Information might be processed according to explicit rules, but the conclusions reached through such transformations are often checked, revised, and even distorted by past experience, expert judgment, and intuition. In this sense the problems are mixed or "messy" and cannot be effectively approached within either purely analytic or purely intuitive framework of thought.

Both modes of thinking are optimal, both are equally important. They are used interchangeably in dependency on the properties of a particular problem. To solve a well-structured problem by intuition is as suboptimal as to solve ill-defined problems by analytical simplification.

Management Science has been successful where it enhanced man's analytical faculties in dealing with analytical problems. It has been less successful in trying to approach complex problems via analytical decomposition. It has not even tried to enhance man's intuitive faculties in dealing with intuitive problems.

The continuous refinement and sharpening of existing analytical tools help to delegate an increasing number of human tasks to human contrivances such as computer models, decision rules, or automatic devices. The effect is that it allows more and more problems to be transferred from the realm of intuition into that of analysis. The outcome should be the development of new analytical tools permitting intuition to be set free to develop its capability to deal with additional problems.

Management Science has neglected the intuitive factor of managerial decision making. It tends to replace intuition by analysis rather than to enhance intuition. Peter F. Drucker[9] offers the following view:

Insight, understanding, ranking of priorities, and a "feel" for the complexity of an area are as important as precise, beautifully elegant mathematical models—and in fact usually infinitely more useful and indeed even more "scientific." They reflect the reality of the manager's universe and of his tasks.

Questions for Discussion

1. How reliable is intuitive judgment for decision making?
2. Can management science models outperform human decision makers?
3. How much information is necessary for good decision making?
4. Can management scientists be managed?

Notes

1. C. Jackson Grayson, Jr., "Management Science and Business Practices," *Harvard Business Review*, July–August 1973, pp. 41–48.
2. Amos Tversky and Daniel Kahneman, "Judgment under Uncertainty: Heuristics and Biases," *Science*, 185, pp. 1124–1131.
3. Robyn M. Dawes, "Objective Optimization under Multiple Subjective Functions." *In Multiple Criteria Decision Making* (USC Press, 1973), pp. 9–17.
4. P. Slovic, "Psychological Study of Human Judgment: Implications for Investment Decision Making." *Oregon Research Institute*, 11, no. 1.
5. D. B. Yntema and W. S. Torgerson, "Man-Computer Cooperation in Decisions Requiring Common Sense." *IRE Transactions on Human Factors in Electronics*, 2 (1961), pp. 20–26.
6. S. Oskamp, "Overconfidence in Case-Study Judgments," *Journal of Consulting Psychology*, 1965, 29, 261–265.
7. C. West Churchman, "Reliability of Models in the Social Sciences." *Interfaces*, 4, no. 1, November 1973.
8. P. Drucker, *Management, Tasks, Responsibilities, Practices* (New York: Harper & Row, 1973), p. 513.
9. Drucker, *Management*, p. 516.

CASE 24
COST/BENEFIT DECISION AT BLUEBIRD SMELTER

Bluebird Smelter is owned by a large, national mining company and located in Bluebird, a town of 12,000 in western Montana. The smelter, which has been operating profitably for 35 years with 125 employees, processes copper ore arriving by railroad. Its most distinguishing feature is a tall, brick stack, visible for miles and used as a landmark by nearby residents, which emits a visible plume and often leaves a faint, smudgy pall over Bison Valley, the geological basin in which Bluebird is located.

Bucolic Bison Valley has about 25,000 residents and attracts retirees from big city life and wealthy weekenders who build retreats or buy small farms in the area. The economy of Bison Valley has been primarily agricultural but tourism is an important—if small—component, as is Bluebird Smelter.

Source: From *Casebook for Business, Government and Society,* Second Edition by George Steiner and John F. Steiner. Copyright © 1975, 1980 by Random House, Inc. Reprinted by permission of the publisher.

Bluebird Smelter is the only major industrial pollution source in the valley. Fugitive and stack emissions from the smelter include sulfur dioxide (SO_2), sulfuric acid, inorganic arsenic, particulates from copper and iron dust, asbestos, nitrogen oxides, aromatic hydrocarbons, and traces of other potentially injurious chemicals. On sunny days when the air is still and during periods of temperature inversion over the valley the action of the sun on smelter emissions contributes to photochemical smog similar to that in urban areas. Auto emissions and agricultural activities are also sources of photochemical oxidants, but smelter emissions are far more important.

Because of its conspicuous presence, dramatized by the tall stack, visible plume, and a lingering odor from SO_2 emissions, a small, local environmental group called the Earth Riders made the plant a target in the mid-1960s. Lawsuits and political pressures by the Earth Riders led to installation in 1972 of costly pollution control equipment at the smelter that reduced emissions by 75 percent from an uncontrolled state. This brought improved air quality, but visible pollution, adverse health effects, and crop damage continued.

Later in the 1970s Bluebird Smelter was granted a series of variances from federal and state air quality standards when the company let it be known that further pollution control expenses would force closure of the plant. From the 75 percent control level, costs escalated rapidly and further controls—say to the 90 percent level—would cost more in total than the original 75 percent reduction. Bluebird Smelter could not afford it. The massive expenditures required would push the plant into long-term financial loss.

Many townspeople told reporters from big-city papers that they wanted jobs and were willing to tolerate a little dirty air. Local observers thought that closure of the smelter would throw Bison Valley into an economic recession. Despite opposition and organized protest by the Earth Riders, the Bluebird City Council passed five resolutions asking for deviation from air quality standards for the smelter and sent them to state and federal agencies. When several Earth Riders chained and locked themselves to railroad tracks leading to the smelter, demanding that ore shipments cease and the plant close down, the mayor of Bluebird, a veterinarian, placed a placard in his office window offering "Free Rabies Shots to Earth Riders. No Appointment Necessary."

In 1980 a state public health official conducted an epidemiological study of the region because it offered the unique opportunity to observe the health effects of a single, major source of industrial pollution. Using standard mortality tables the official determined that there had been 25 "excess" deaths in Bison Valley over the five-year period between 1974 and 1979. These were deaths from emphysema, lung cancer, tuberculosis, pneumonia, and ischemic heart disease over and above those naturally occurring in a population not exposed to similar industrial pollution. Such results were not surprising given the existing SO_2 and particulate levels. The unique element in the situation was that the cause was a single source rather than a collection of sources mixing together as in most industrial and urban areas. What could not be determined, of course, was which deaths were the "excess" ones. The extra five fatalities averaged each year were part of a group of several hundred deaths, most of which were statistically "expected."

Also, a group of economists from a prestigious research institute in another city picked the Bluebird Smelter as a test case for a research project on the health effects of pollution. The figures they produced led to debate among the various local groups involved in the controversy. The researchers looked at the operation of Bluebird Smelter in terms of costs and benefits to the community and to society. The following table shows their basic calculations.

The Earth Riders seized upon the study, arguing that if total costs of smelter operation exceeded benefits, then a clear-cut case had been made for closing the plant. It was already operating at a loss; in this case a net social loss of $730,000.

ANNUAL BENEFITS AND COSTS OF BLUEBIRD SMELTER

Benefits		Value
Payroll for 125 employees at an average of $15,000 each		$1,875,000
Benefits paid to workers and families at an average of $1,000 each		125,000
Income, other than wages and salaries, generated in the valley by the company		4,600,000
Local taxes and fees paid by the company		100,000
Social services to community and charitable contributions		20,000
	Total	$6,720,000

Costs		
Excess deaths of 5 persons at $1 million each[a]		$5,000,000
Other health and illness costs to exposed population		450,000
Crop and property damage from pollutants		1,000,000
Reduction of aesthetic value and quality of life		500,000
Lost revenues and taxes from tourism		500,000
	Total	$7,450,000

[a]Calculated on the basis of recent court decisions compensating victims of wrongful death in product liability cases in Western states. The figure reflects average compensation.

Thus, in the eyes of the environmentalists Bluebird Smelter was in social bankruptcy.

The smelter's managers and members of the Bluebird City Council, on the other hand, ridiculed the study for making unrealistic and overly simplistic assumptions. They questioned whether the costs were meaningful, citing estimates of the value of a human life that were much lower than $1 million, made by other economists. They argued that health risks posed by the smelter were less than those of smoking cigarettes, drinking, or riding motorcycles and that benefits to the community were great. They even suggested that important costs had been left out of the calculations such as sociological and psychological costs to workers who would be laid off if the plant closed.

The debate raged and the smelter continued to operate.

Questions for Discussion

1. Do you believe that the costs to society of smelter operation outweigh the benefits?

2. Do you believe that the cost figures in the researcher's calculations, particularly those representing human life, are accurate?

3. Are any important benefits or costs not included in the analysis of the smelter's operation? What are they?

4. List and explain several alternative solutions to this controversy. Which is best and why?

Notes

1. Michael D. Bayles, "The Price of Life," *Ethics*, Vol. 89, No. 1 (October 1978), pp. 20–34.
2. Baruch Fischhoff et al., "Weighing the Risks," Environment, May 1979, pp. 17–38.
3. William Lowrance, *Of Acceptable Risk* (Los Altos, California: William Kaufmann, Inc., 1976).
4. Walter Oi, "Safety at Any Price?" *Regulation*, November–December 1977, pp. 16–23.
5. Steven E. Rhoads, "How Much Should We Spend to Save a Life?" *The Public Interest*, Spring 1978, pp. 74–92.
6. Max Singer, "How to Reduce Risks Rationally," The Public Interest, Spring 1978, pp. 16–23.

EXERCISE 25
ALCON CANNING COMPANY

The Alcon Canning Company opened its doors for business in April 1967. The organization has grown from its relatively small beginnings to a fairly large operation; however, the canning process initiated in Alcon's early days has remained essentially unchanged by them. Technological innovations in recent years have begun to make some of Alcon's equipment and processes obsolete, and management is now considering the possibility of modernizing, d_1, or not modernizing, d_2, its operations. This decision depends upon the uncertain events of future demand for its output. According to the estimates of the company's research staff, the payoffs (in millions per annum) net of modernization costs, of modernization or no modernization, relative to a high (s_1) or a low (s_2) demand, are as follows:

			States of Nature	
			High Demand	Low Demand
			s_1	s_2
Decision	Modernizing	d_1	4.0	1.5
Alternatives	Not Modernizing	d_2	3.0	2.5

Furthermore, it is the judgment of the research staff and sales personnel of the company that the odds are .55 in favor of a high demand. With these data, the management can decide whether or not to modernize now. However, the sales manager suggests it is possible to continue production with the existing process for another year and then decide on modernization, when it will be known whether a high or a low demand will actually result. The drawback of this decision postponement is that modernization will then cost $25 million more—i.e., net profits for modernization will be reduced by this amount from previous estimates.

Questions for Discussion

1. If management is to decide on modernization now, what is the optimal act?
2. If management is to adopt a sequential decision procedure, how would it go about it?
3. Which decision procedure is the best in terms of expected profits for this problem?
4. What other factors might the decision makers need to consider?
5. What is the place of probability theory in decision making?

CASE 26
LIKE AN OLD PENNY

Carl Herman, a marketing vice president, viewed his job as consisting of three distinct planning states: short, intermediate, and long-range. Working from the future to the present, Carl and the other top executives would determine where the company should be within the next decade and then attempt to formulate plans to get it there. When Carl pondered the matter, he felt that it was interesting the way people plan for the distant future without worrying but become extremely concerned about what will happen within the next couple of days or weeks. For example, just that afternoon the company executives had been talking about product planning and what the future would hold. It was noted that, in the industry, 70 percent of all current products on the market were never even contemplated ten years earlier. Thus, long-range planning was very important. The company had to keep abreast of the changing market conditions. Research and development, coupled with good market research, were vital ingredients in the long-range plan.

When it came to intermediate planning, the executives were also pretty sure of the course the company should take. Most of the time was spent talking about resource allocation and how the company had to ensure itself not only of a good market share but also of adequate production capability. This stage of the planning meeting took a little longer than the time devoted to long-range planning and there was more caution.

The final part of the meeting dealt with short-range planning. Here the executives appeared to be in disagreement with some of the plans being implemented. Part of this disagreement was brought about by the fact that the company was not doing as well as it expected in some areas. However, there was also some concern over performance in the areas where the company looked good. A couple of the executives felt that there might be unwarranted optimism and that a good, close, conservative look should be taken before the company plunged on any further. Others felt that the firm had a winning hand in some areas of the market. The company's reputation was good and the product was of high quality. If the public wants our product, they reasoned, we should sell it to them. Why should we feel guilty about our success? We knew we were going to do this well and we did. What is causing all the argument?

It was at this point that the president, Phil Kommer, interrupted. For most of the meeting he had been sitting quietly at the head of the table. This was generally the approach he liked best, only taking the floor if he had something important to say. The president was brief and to the point:

"Gentlemen, I've been sitting here listening to the discussion about short- and long-range planning with great interest. There is one thing I find disconcerting. When we discuss long-range planning, everyone seems to be in agreement about where we should be going and how we can get there. When we get to intermediate planning or resource allocation, there is some disagreement, but we generally iron out all the problems. However, when we get to short-range planning, the fat really hits the fire. We spend most of the meeting arguing over things that we decided a couple of years ago. We set long-range plans and when it comes time to implement them, we disagree. There is tremendous bickering over what we agreed upon long ago. Now what I'm wondering is, how come we are so quick to make long-range decisions but so unwilling to implement them the way we said we were going to? How come we didn't get all this argument years ago when the matter was first broached?

Questions for Discussion

1. Why is there conflict about decision making in the long and short term? Is risk a factor?
2. Is the conflict in this case natural, or a problem that requires solution? When is conflict good?
3. How can firms deal with this problem? Suggest specific steps.

EXERCISE 27
A QUIZ FOR DECISION MAKERS

Circle the answer you feel is most correct to complete the statement:

1. The effective manager
   a. is constantly making important decisions.
   b. makes relatively few important decisions.

2. Good business decisions
   a. are usually formulated to apply to a number of situations, both present and future.
   b. are formulated to apply to specific problem situations because the wise manager realizes that no two situations are exactly alike.

3. Effective decision makers
   a. always try to put a decision on the highest conceptual level.
   b. forget about abstract thinking and concentrate on the specific situation at hand.

4. In reaching an important decision, the manager should
   a. keep in mind the compromises and concessions that are inevitable before a decision can be implemented.
   b. reach a decision as he sees fit and iron out the compromises later.

5. A good decision maker
   a. encourages his subordinates and associates to disagree with him.
   b. quashes all disagreement.
   c. encourages people to disagree with him before a decision is made, but does not tolerate disagreement after a decision is reached.

6. For every problem situation, there is
   a. one correct decision.
   b. any number of right decisions.

7. As every good manager knows,
   a. there are some situations in which it is best to do nothing.
   b. any problem can be solved at any time by forceful decisions.

8. Faced with a great deal of disagreement over a particular decision, the manager should
   a. keep everyone happy by sending the problem back for further study.
   b. make a decision and stick with it.

9. Managers with outstanding decision-making ability
   a. usually have a technical background.
   b. come from all sorts of backgrounds.

Source: Reprinted with permission from *Plant Administration/Engineering,* 30, no. 7, copyright 1971 by Maclean-Hunter, Ltd.

CASE 28
DECISION BY THE GROUP

John Stevens, plant manager of the Fairlee Plant of Lockstead Corporation, attended the advanced management seminar conducted at a large midwestern university. The seminar, of four weeks' duration, was largely devoted to the topic of executive decision making.

Professor Mennon, of the university staff, particularly impressed John Stevens with his lectures on group discussion and group decision making. On the basis of research and experience, Professor Mennon was convinced that employees, if given the opportunity, could meet together, intelligently consider, and then formulate quality decisions that would be enthusiastically accepted.

Returning to his plant at the conclusion of the seminar, Mr. Stevens decided to practice some of the principles which he had learned. He called together the twenty-five employees of Department B and told them that production standards established several years previously were now too low in view of the recent installation of automated equipment. He gave the men the opportunity to discuss the mitigating circumstances and to decide among themselves, as a group, what their standards should be. Mr. Stevens, on leaving the room, believed that the men would doubtlessly establish much higher standards than he himself would have dared propose.

After an hour of discussion the group summoned Mr. Stevens and notified him that, contrary to his opinion, their group decision was that the standards were already too high, and since they had been given the authority to establish their own standards, they were making a reduction of 10 percent. These standards, Mr. Stevens knew, were far too low to provide a fair profit on the owner's investment. Yet it was clear that his refusal to accept the group decision would be disastrous. Before taking a course of action, Mr. Stevens called Professor Mennon at the university for his opinion.

Questions for Discussion

1. Does Mr. Stevens have to abide by the decision of the employees?
2. Was the original proposal to give the group authority over standards a good one?
3. What could Stevens have done to avoid the mess he is in?

Source: John M. Champion and John H. James, *Critical Incidents in Management*, 3d ed., (Homewood, Ill.: Richard D. Irwin, 1975), pp. 62–68. Copyright 1975 by Richard D. Irwin, Inc.

EXERCISE 29
PRESTIGIOUS OCCUPATIONS

Below is a list of fifteen occupations of possibly varying prestige. We want your opinion on how a national sample of U. S. adults ranked the occupations as to prestige. Your individual results will be compared with those of others in your class and with the national sample of the U. S. adult population. First, read the directions below and complete the form independently.

Directions

A national sample of adults ranked the following fifteen occupations as to their prestige. Your task is to rank the occupations in the same order of prestige as the sample did. Place the number 1 by the occupation that you think was ranked as the most prestigious, place the number 2 by the second most prestigious occupation, and so on through the number 15, which would be your estimate of the sample's idea of the least prestigious of the fifteen occupations.

Remember, do not give your own opinion of how prestigious the occupations are; tell how you think the sample of the U. S. adult public ranked them. You will compare your answers with the actual rankings.

Priest _____

Nuclear physicist _____

Author of novels _____

Banker _____

Member of the board of directors of a large corporation _____

Carpenter _____

Owner of a factory that employs about 100 people _____

Physician _____

Electrician _____

Lawyer _____

Architect _____

College professor _____

Official of an international labor union _____

State governor _____

Undertaker _____

Your instructor will ask you to form into small groups and give you directions to complete this exercise. Leave this page blank until you receive instructions for its completion. It is to be used for a group decision.

Carpenter	_____
Owner of a factory that employs about 100 people	_____
Physician	_____
Electrician	_____
Lawyer	_____
Architect	_____
College Professor	_____
Official of an international labor union	_____
State governor	_____
Undertaker	_____
Priest	_____
Nuclear physicist	_____
Author of novels	_____
Banker	_____
Member of the board of directors of a large corporation	_____

EXERCISE 30
WHOM DO YOU LET GO?

The following problem is designed to give you an understanding of how groups might go about making a difficult decision and what factors might affect that decision. There is no "correct" answer to this problem—only what each member of the group thinks is the right thing to do.

You should form into small study groups for this exercise and read the company background and employee descriptions. Then decide how you are to solve the problem facing the company.

BBF, INC.: COMPANY BACKGROUND

Better Business Forms, Inc. is a small manufacturer of specialty paper products used by small business firms. Their major product is printed sales vouchers custom made for retail and dining establishments. Initially, BBF had grown quite rapidly, thus increasing production capacity and personnel. As a result of a paper shortage, BBF has had difficulty getting long-term contracts with its suppliers, and customer dissatisfaction with backlogs has increasingly become a problem. Thus, some production cutbacks are going to be necessary in the near future.

BBF is a nonunion company located in an urban area where equal employment lawsuits had become quite prevalent. BBF has not had any lawsuits in this area to date, but management feels that the company is potentially vulnerable even though the most recent employee additions have been mostly women and minority candidates.

On the following page are brief descriptions of six employees of BBF. Your group should make a recommendation about who should be laid off if the production cutbacks eventuate. Rank them in order of who you would let go first, second, and so on. The last person who would be laid off in this group would be ranked sixth.

BBF, Inc.—Employee Descriptions

- Charles Jefferson—Black male; age 43; veteran from Vietnam; married, wife pregnant; with company one year; good work record so far; capability to be better performer.
- Naomi Smith—White female; age 45; recently divorced; supports three children; with company five years; number of recent absences; fairly good work record otherwise.
- Robert Boyd—White male; age 20; unmarried; with company three years; good performance record; wants to start own business some day.
- Ralph Ball—White male; age 45; married, no children at home; with company ten years; erratic work record; reputed to be alcoholic.
- Sarah Field—Black female; age 36; husband recently disabled, two children; on the job two months; too early to evaluate performance.
- Carmelita Valiquez—Hispanic female; age 41; six children; husband employed intermittently; with company nine months; steady worker; not too bright.

CASE 31
FROM DISEQUILIBRIUM TO DISEQUILIBRIUM

At the close of the Jackson Regional Medical Center's (JRMC) monthly board meeting, Mr. Bibbins, the hospital administrator, brought out what he felt was the most important issue on the meeting's agenda.

"Gentlemen, and of course you too, Ms. Dixon, recently I have given a great deal of thought to our upcoming facility expansion. As you know, this move into our new facility is going to take a tremendous amount of coordination and cooperation on the part of our entire organization. The staff has mentioned to me on several occasions that the employees and supervisors are becoming increasingly restless and apprehensive as a result of the anticipated move. After some preliminary investigation and considerable thought, we have decided to recommend to the board that JRMC contact a consultant to assist us in adapting to the ongoing expansion program."

The board was aware of the hospital's past instability, and the need for outside management assistance was acknowledged. After a brief discussion, the members unanimously recommended to Mr. Bibbins that he contact the local university for assistance. Members of the university management department had previously provided consulting assistance.

HISTORY OF JRMC

JRMC is a 160-bed general hospital in northeastern Arkansas. The American Hospital Association classifies JRMC as a short-term ambulatory hospital. In 1975, the hospital officially became a regional facility and adopted the name of Jackson Regional Medical Center. The community in which JRMC operates was expanding, primarily due to the influx of retired individuals and a growing university community. Due to this expansion in the immediate area, demand for medical services had increased significantly. A major physical facility expansion program had been adopted in 1972, and a projected completion date of June 1977 was set. Construction began and has been progressing on schedule. The project is scheduled for completion in eighteen months.

The Medical Center presently employs approximately 500 persons. This employment figure is to be increased by approximately 22 percent when the expansion program is completed. The expanded facility will have 240 beds. The structure of JRMC management also has changed. Prior to the initiation of the physical expansion program, there was only one assistant administrator. When the program is completed, there are to be three assistant administrators. All functional departments anticipate expanding employment rosters, with the need for additional nurses to be particularly critical.

JRMC has had four administrators in the past eight years. The present administrator, Mr. Bibbins, has been with JRMC for less than one year. The previous three administrators were asked to resign for various reasons. Mr. Bibbins seems to have established his credibility with department heads and general employees. However, an aura of uncertainty continues to surround the administrator's position. This uncertainty has been a contributing factor to one present departmental dilemma—that of departmental autonomy. Various departments throughout the Medical Center tend to segregate themselves into

Source: Daniel Cochran, Donald Latham, and Donald White, University of Arkansas. By permission of the authors.

autonomous groups rather than working closely with one another. Many persons familiar with internal conditions at JRMC believe that permanent leadership emanates from department heads, rather than from the administrator's office.

CONSULTANT'S MEETING WITH JRMC

Two weeks after the monthly board meeting, Dr. Harold and Dr. Black, from the university's management department, met with Mr. Bibbins, his assistant administrator, Mr. James, and the Director of Personnel and Training, Mr. Arnold. The men discussed their organization's problem of trying to adapt to the organization's facility change. Mr. Bibbins and his staff quickly briefed the two management professors on their facility's expansion situation and stressed the "disequilibrium" which existed within the hospital as a result of this organizational change.

"Dr. Harold and Dr. Black, I feel that I must warn you before we go any further that our employees, including our supervisors, are extremely suspicious when it comes to 'outsiders'! They are even suspicious of anyone outside of their particular department, and especially the administration. In fact, I'm confident that by this afternoon, rumor will have it that 'the administration' has just hired two New York psychologists to analyze our organization."

After additional discussion, Dr. Black concluded the meeting by suggesting that after the consultants' intervention, the administrator provide some feedback to the hospital employees about the nature, purpose, and worth of the consultants' assistance. Mr. Bibbins and his staff agreed to this suggestion.

INTERVENTION STRATEGY

As a result of the first meeting, it was concluded that obtaining inputs from employees in the form of either ideas or suggestions might clarify those real and imagined problems that the employees believed were related to a major building program. This was thought to have the advantages of enumerating real problems and also providing an awareness of the perceived problems at various employee levels. It was hoped that a free flow of uninhibited responses could be generated.

Group meetings rather than the questioning of individuals through opinion surveys were decided upon as the information-gathering approach to be used. It was agreed that "group think" would probably yield better results than isolated individual reactions to printed questions and would be more efficient, timewise, than face-to-face interviews. Harold and Black informed Mr. Bibbins that they currently were involved in the study of a number of such group decision-making processes. They were convinced that any of the group processes they had been working with would be beneficial to the Medical Center. However, they saw in the hospital's present situation an opportunity to study the performance of three specific group techniques in a field setting. Consequently, they requested that Mr. Bibbins allow them to conduct a series of group meetings using these three information-gathering processes.

Harold explained to Mr. Bibbins, "We are agreed that the group approach to gathering this information will no doubt be superior to obtaining employee inputs on an individual basis. I think that Dr. Black and I can safely say that the information we will gather from your employees will be beneficial to JRMC no matter what group technique we use. However, this will afford us an excellent opportunity to determine for future use which technique might be best in this type of setting and/or situation." After a brief discussion between Bibbins and Harold, the administrator gave his consent to the joint consulting-research effort.

The three group decision-making processes utilized in the project included: nominal group technique (NGT), brainstorming, and interacting group. The employee groups were administered all three technologies, while the supervisors were administered the NGT and brainstorming technologies. Each technique utilized the same beginning question, "What significant personnel and/or organization factors (or changes) must be taken into account in connection with a hospital expansion program?" It was felt that this question would generate relevant ideas that would help the hospital better adapt to changes resulting from its present expansion program. The actual ideas generated from these techniques are included in the Appendix.

METHODOLOGY

A separate systematic random sample was drawn from a computer printout of pay records for daytime employees and supervisors. Five groups of six individuals each (three employee and two supervisor groups) made up the sample; however, additional individuals were selected and utilized as alternates. The names selected were examined by departments to insure that the sample was representative.

A brief orientation meeting for the participants was concluded a week prior to the actual experiment. The purpose of this introductory meeting was to help insure that the employees could participate at the scheduled time and to generate favorable interest in the project.

To minimize interviewer bias, one consultant conducted both NGT sessions and one consultant conducted both brainstorming sessions and the interacting group session. Each group meeting was conducted at approximately the same time of day in the same surroundings (JRMC library).

Anonymity was a prime concern, and each group interviewed was told the importance of keeping the session private until all groups had met.

FINAL REPORT AND FOLLOW-UP

After all of the group meetings were held, the results were analyzed by the consultants and submitted to Mr. Bibbins. The report was accompanied by a request that a subsequent meeting be held by the three men to discuss its content after the findings were reviewed by him. However, unexpected problems with the building program occurred during the same week in which the report was transmitted. Mr. Bibbins became involved in extensive negotiations with the contractor and failed to get back to Harold and Black. Six months later Mr. Bibbins still had not acted on the consultants' report.

APPENDIX GROUP NO. 1 (NGT) SUPERVISOR

1. Need more personnel.
2. Priorities on purchasing equipment.
3. Priorities on equipment requirements prior to even planning.
4. Adequate expansion for meeting public needs.
5. Communication coordination among departments.
6. Creation of new status among present personnel.
7. How to perform effectively while in the midst of moving.
8. Communication with employees to make them feel they are a part of the program (expansion).
9. Inadequate preplanning—resulting in inadequate facilities.
10. Versatile and open-minded staff.
11. Satisfying personnel remaining in old building.
12. Different functions as a result of moving.

13. New facilities may not be adequate.
14. Coping with financial increases—all internal cost increases.
15. Only one walkway between old and new building—problem of.
16. Concern with physical movement of patients to new facility.
17. Uncertainty of move for some departments.
18. Insufficient number of elevators for number of supplies, visitors, patients.
19. Salary increases.
20. Scattered centers of attention due to layout.
21. Mental adjustment from small to large operation.
22. Through improvement of serious nursing services, the quality of care given will be improved.
23. Dealing with hostilities in departments that have been overlooked during expansion.

APPENDIX GROUP NO. 2 (BRAIN-STORMING) SUPERVISOR

1. Well planned (exceptionally).
2. Temporary confusion.
3. Leadership changes.
4. Decision-making process (changes).
5. Lacking continuity of concepts.
6. Communications.
7. Employees' understanding.
8. How will it be financed?
9. Priorities of financing.
10. Priorities in planning total project.
11. Changes in staff?
12. Informal power structure changes.
13. Coping with the change (people).
14. Quality control changes.
15. Lines (levels) of communications will change.
16. Responsibility will change (institution).
17. Internal responsibilities will change.
18. Employee auto.
19. Need to be more competitive (patients, personnel, services, and wages).
20. Change of community image.
21. Expectations of hospital by community will change.
22. Depersonalization among employees and community.
23. Maple trees cut down!
24. Parking?
25. Security of facility (internal and external).
26. Promoting urbanization!
27. Outpatient facilities.
28. Longer hours for employees.
29. Escort services.
30. No salary increases as a result of expansion (money drained away).

31. Physical layout problems (directional).

32. Competition for expansional space (internal-departmental).

33. Handling of disappointment due to poor planning (i.e., not getting what wanted or needed).

34. Work flow problems.

35. Recruitment of personnel.

36. Training and retraining (in-service education).

37. Regulatory standards change.

38. Safety problems.

39. Public orientation to availability of services.

40. Better facilities for specific diseases.

41. Public reactions to health care changes (cost!).

42. Present inconvenience.

43. Need tolerance until more complete.

44. Present fatigue of staff (mental and physical).

45. Disbelief in eventuality of results.

46. Insecurity about jobs, personal space, job description, and loss of familiar surroundings (community included).

47. Increased opportunity for employment (positive).

48. Need of bad debts (patients) to decrease to help finance new building.

49. Inflation problems.

50. More job satisfaction (positive).

51. Prestige of working in a medical center (positive).

52. Disillusionment.

53. Now have a greater teaching capacity (positive).

54. Can now draw more from university due to size (in-service education, etc.).

55. Expansion is a good idea! Necessary.

56. Expansion is a continual process.

57. Lack of consultation with personnel involved prior to decision making.

58. Employee turnover.

59. Cost of high turnover.

60. Hidden cost of education (financial resources not available for needed training).

61. Hidden cost of donation.

62. Administrative continuity.

63. Need for internal socialization and recreation.

64. Lack of support from administration and medical staff.

APPENDIX GROUP NO. 1 (INTERACTING) EMPLOYEE

1. Probably bother nursing more.

2. Major problems with switchboard!

3. Dietary—only one lab.

4. Very little known about expansion program.

5. Purchasing problems (when order, kind of service, maintenance contracts).

6. New personnel techniques.

7. Size of departments will increase.

8. Will have to learn more.
9. Training new personnel.
10. Recruiting new personnel.
11. Changed telephone system (but we don't know about the new system, Centrex!).
12. Need training on new system (telephone).
13. Apprehensive about new telephone system.
14. Personnel, supply, and new equipment problems.
15. Parking problems.
16. Moving supplies a problem.
17. Reorder points (supply) will change.
18. New dietary facilities will be better (more room).
19. Haven't been told anything about the move!

APPENDIX GROUP NO. 2 (NGT) EMPLOYEE

1. We are here for the good of the patient and the public and all personnel should work toward that end.
2. Personnel shortages now and in the future more obvious.
3. Re-evaluate what we are doing—jobs.
4. Need for more administrative people.
5. Building safety.
6. Need for additional parking—place for employees.
7. Need for additional personnel after expansion.
8. Needs for additional compensation to "live" needed additional personnel.
9. Financial responsibility to the public.
10. Need for employees to see what is going on.
11. New employees need a job description.
12. Need for more doctors.
13. Employee training—present.
14. Communication between administration and employees.
15. Need for new and better equipment for patients.
16. Need for new and better equipment for employees.
17. Need for more efficient food processing.
18. Need for food that patients would like.
19. Need for larger cafeteria.
20. Need for free parking for employees.
21. Need nursery for visitors (keep them out of lobby).
22. Mandatory insurance needs to be done away with.
23. Present care is good.
24. Priority system for employee duties.
25. Need for isolation floor (only).
26. Need for psychiatric facilities.
27. Need for separation of patients due to illness.
28. Employee safety—diseases in hospital.
29. Need more patient accessory—linen, etc.
30. Need additional day-care facilities.

31. Need for better laundry.
32. Need for specialized training for employees.
33. Employees need better understanding with supervisors.
34. Need for employees to know what's being built.
35. Need for new facility to be more efficiently designed than old.
36. Need recreation facilities for patients.
37. Lounge for patients.
38. Need prayer room.
39. Present prayer room is inadequate.
40. Need new administrative system.
41. Need more work clerks.
42. Need employee pool (all departments).
43. Need additional security.

APPENDIX GROUP NO. 3 (BRAIN- STORMING) EMPLOYEE

1. Orientation to new facility.
2. Parking problems.
3. Need for more space.
4. Noise!
5. More elevators.
6. Work flow (uniform) from old to new hospital.
7. Traffic flow.
8. Visitor control.
9. Security control.
10. Proper staffing for new facility.
11. Lack of equipment.
12. Dining room space!
13. Education of personnel.
14. Immediate community concern.
15. Automobile traffic control around hospital (narrow streets and congestion).
16. Financing of new facility.
17. Bigger waiting room for visitors.
18. Separate surgical waiting area (with hostess).
19. Bathrooms (more)!
20. Overnight facilities for family of seriously ill.
21. Orientation (tours) for child patients.
22. Playroom facilities for pediatric patients.
23. Separate pediatric patients by age (rooms—teenagers and children).
24. Communications between departments.
25. Telephone system. (Is it adequate?)
26. How will departments work while moving to new building?
27. Time allotted for moving.
28. Control of utilities while moving.
29. Personal relationships during move (tempers!).
30. Are architects familiar with hospital design needs?

31. Never consulted with employees concerning expansion!

32. Concerned about emergency room facilities (enough?).

33. Separate emergency room entrance (not lobby).

34. Better emergency transportation (helicopter and pad).

35. Faster emergency care (so patients don't have to wait so long).

36. Need signs to direct people to hospital.

37. Special facilities for prisoner patients.

38. Fire prevention (regulations, etc.)

39. Adequate storage facilities.

40. Need to anticipate future needs (expansion—buy land).

41. Heating and air-conditioning control (separate or master control).

42. Linens (more).

43. All supplies (more).

44. More adequate control supply.

45. Is pharmacy going to be adequate?

46. Security of drugs!

47. Servicing of facility.

48. Need oxygen and suction in new surgical holding area.

49. Lounges for employees (locker space, eat lunch, and secure personal gear, and resting area beds).

50. Attitudes of patients during move.

51. Remodeling of old hospital.

52. Concern for phasing out old jobs and entrance of new.

53. Enforcing smoking regulations (positive!).

54. Control of safety regulations.

55. Fire drills (actual).

56. Need a full-time safety director.

57. Necessary emergency power?

58. Disaster drills (actual!).

59. Enforce ID regulations (especially doctors).

60. Is there an alarm system to alert security personnel?

Questions for Discussion

1. Analyze and group the participants' responses to pinpoint the problem areas JRMC faces with its planned expansion—for example, patient-care problems, public relations, supplies/equipment problems, and so on. Which areas do you think are most important?

2. What steps should Mr. Bibbins have taken to follow up on the study? How do you think the employees and supervisors who took part in the survey reacted to the lack of feedback on their effort?

3. Make some recommendations based on the study's findings which would improve the communications and the organizational climate at JRMC.

CHAPTER 5

ORGANIZATION DESIGN AND CHANGE

● **LEARNING OBJECTIVES**

When you have finished this chapter, you should:

1. Have a better understanding of job design strategies.

2. Understand how to diagnose variables important to organization structure.

3. Understand the conditions under which different organization designs are appropriate.

4. Appreciate the relationships among structure, climate, decision making, and effectiveness of an organization.

5. Understand the change process and reasons for human resistance to it.

6. Understand reasons for conflict and how change can be managed.

This chapter is designed to help you understand how a firm is organized or structured. When managers decide on a plan to accomplish their objectives, they need to decide whether their current organization is capable of performing the necessary functions in an efficient and effective way. In order to get work done, people are assigned to jobs. Specific tasks are assigned, and jobs are designed such that the tasks are interrelated to one another and oriented to the goals of the enterprise. First we will look at job design (how the jobs are broken down) and then how they are brought together and organized.

Job design has two essential components—technical aspects (the work to be done) and human aspects (the employees who do the work). Your previous experiences should help you understand how various human factors may help or hinder employees in their jobs. The technical aspects also can influence this.

Jobs differ along many dimensions:

- Variety—number of motions and operations.
- Cycle time—the time it takes to complete the job.
- Task identity/wholeness—whether the job is seen as splintered or whole.
- Knowledge/skill required—amount of knowledge or skill necessary to do the job.
- Human interaction—jobs range from team efforts to lonely "lighthouse keepers."
- Freedom/control—do employees control the job or is it machine paced?
- Responsibility/autonomy—does the employee have responsibility or is he told exactly what to do and when to do it?
- Physical exertion—jobs can be fatiguing or not require physical labor.
- Environmental pleasantness—physical working conditions vary from pleasant to unpleasant.
- Locations of work—inside/outside; single location/many locations.
- Time of work—long hours of less difficult work, or short hours of intense work.

For each dimension, jobs differ and employees' perceptions of what they like vary. Don't assume that everyone wants freedom and responsibility; some want to be told what to do and when to do it.

There can be some real efficiencies with specialized jobs. But there has been much written about overspecialization of jobs and how demeaning it can be to workers. Many job design observers have focused on ways to reverse this approach through:

- Job rotation—specialized jobs are rotated among employees.
- Job enlargement—simplified jobs are combined for more diversity.
- Job enrichment—job depth is increased by increasing employee responsibility, freedom, and control.

Basically, the argument for these proposals is that what is lost in efficiency will be gained back by greater effectiveness of employees. There are differences of opinion here, of course, particularly from the perspective of considering individual differences and what employees want from their jobs. The field exercise, "Job Design," may allow you to discover for yourself some of the problems.

Of course, when jobs are designed, they must be linked together to accomplish overall goals. This is usually done by putting together an organization chart. Of course, as the reading suggests, "What's Not on the Organization Chart" may be more important than what is.

Several choices need to be made when considering the type of structure that can accomplish organizational objectives. The basic form of departmentation is one of these—whether to pursue a primitive, functional, divisional, or matrix form. A second set of choices deals with how broad or narrow various design features should be. Some examples are:

- Jobs can be specialized and simplified or broad and more vaguely defined. (specialization)
- Policies, rules, and job descriptions can be written and well defined, or nonexistent or unused. (standardization and formalization)
- Power and authority can be centralized at the top, or spread throughout the organization. (locus of control)
- Spans of control can be wide or narrow, with flat or tall hierarchies, respectively. (hierarchy)

Some argue that there is one best way—use a functional structure with narrow design features (a typical bureaucracy). Critics of this approach suggest a broader approach is more desirable with divisional or matrix departments.

Before accepting one design or the other, you should consider that prescriptions made by physicians are not identical for all illnesses. Physicians who treat pneumonia the same way they treat high blood pressure are considered quacks. They need to diagnose causative effects of different symptoms before prescribing an organizational solution. Some of the variables to be considered are:

- Dependence on external forces—customers, suppliers, governments, and so on.
- Technology—machines, methods, and processes used to do the work.
- Volatility—the degree of change in markets and technology.
- Complexity—number of factors that affect the environment.
- Size of the organization.
- Personnel—characteristics of the people working for the firm.

Flowing from these, predictions are made about which organization design is appropriate for each variable. For example, if technology is routine, volatility and complexity low, size large, or dependence high, narrow design characteristics might be most effective. If personnel have high intelligence and education, are from urban environments and were reared in permissive atmospheres or have a great deal of experience, then broader designs would be called for.

We have included several cases and exercises to help you explore various design dimensions. The "S & C Electric Company" case explores questions about what organizational and job design is best for its situation. "The Seventeenth National Bank" case indicates how *designing jobs* and relating them structurally directly relates to strategy of the organization. The exercise on "Organization Climate" might suggest how the *social system* within an organization is related to its *structural design*.

There are two exercises that you can use to tie all this together. "Studying an Organization" can be used to help you diagnose and analyze an enterprise of your own choice. You can use it to help you decide how the enterprise is structured and whether that structure is appropriate for the environment in which it exists. "Sears vs. Kmart" asks you to compare and contrast two similar organizations and note how structure and climate aid in their effectiveness.

Usually, when managers go about redesigning organizations, they must start with the existing structure and climate and change it. The second major subject of this chapter deals with organization change and development.

Resistance to change is a frequent and natural occurrence. Four of the most common reasons for resistance are: (1) parochial self-interest, (2) misunderstandings and lack of trust, (3) different assessments, and (4) low tolerance for change. There are a variety of approaches for overcoming resistance to change. Six methods include: (1) education and communication, (2) participation and involvement, (3) facilitation and support, (4) negotiation and agreement, (5) manipulation and cooptation, and (6) explicit and implicit coercion.

Several experiences in this chapter are provided to help you understand the nature and problems associated with organization changes. The "Resistance to Change" case asks you to recommend a policy change dealing with employee compensation. And the "Get Rid of Franklin!" case deals with the problems change creates when some employees get jobs that others wanted. In many cases like these, change results in conflict, and you are asked to suggest approaches for dealing with resistance to change. How managers deal with these problems can be important to their own success. ●

EXERCISE 32
JOB DESIGN

This field exercise will help you understand how jobs are designed and what this may mean to people working in them.

Find a work group in your community that will allow you to observe people at work and talk to them about their jobs. It may be in an office, a factory, a school, or the like. Using the guidelines below, come up with a profile of the jobs within one of the work groups of the organization you visit. You should attempt to measure the jobs through observation of the employees' performance such that you can complete the job profile. If different jobs exist in the group, pick one or two that seem to be more specialized.

JOB PROFILE

Job Title_____Organization_____

Circle the most appropriate number

Number of motions performed	Large number of motions	7 6 5 4 3 2 1	Small number repeated often
Number of operations performed	Large number of different operations	7 6 5 4 3 2 1	Small number repeated often
Number of different tools used to do the job	Large number	7 6 5 4 3 2 1	Small number
Human interaction	High	7 6 5 4 3 2 1	Low
Freedom and control	High	7 6 5 4 3 2 1	Low—machine
Responsibility, autonomy	High	7 6 5 4 3 2 1	Low
Degree of physical exertion	High	7 6 5 4 3 2 1	Low
Environment	Pleasant	7 6 5 4 3 2 1	Unpleasant
Numbers of places work performed	Single location	7 6 5 4 3 2 1	Many locations
Location of work	Inside	7 6 5 4 3 2 1	Outside
Timing of work	Continuous, intense	7 6 5 4 3 2 1	Intermittent

After completing the job profile, ask several of the employees how they feel about their jobs—if they are satisfied or would like to see their jobs changed in some way.

Ideally, you should ask if you can come back to talk to the employees after you do some further analysis, explained below. If that is not possible, after you have observed the work group for some time, ask the employees how they feel about their jobs. For example, you could ask:

- Do you like your job?
- Do you think your job is routine/dull/monotonous/repetitious?
- Do you find ways to add variety to your job? What are they?
- If your job were to be enriched or enlarged, how would you like that? (Give examples of additional functions workers might be able to perform.)
- If your job were changed in this way, would you expect to be paid more?

Again, ideally, this should be done on a second visit, if possible. Before that visit, find a job profile (if you have observed more than one kind of job) that appears to be very narrow in scope (more specialized, fewer motions, repetitive, few operations, few tools, machine paced). Develop a job redesign strategy to enlarge that person's job and reorganize the work of the work group you studied. Then make the second visit with this redesign strategy to find out employee reactions to it as outlined above. If that is not possible, you should still create a design strategy of enlargement or enrichment based on the information from your first visit.

Bring your job profiles, redesign strategy, and employee reactions (to current design and proposed redesign) to class for discussion.

READING 33
WHAT'S NOT ON THE ORGANIZATION CHART
Harold Stieglitz

Organization charts come in various sizes, colors, and even textures. Most are black and white and printed on paper. Some are affixed to office walls—and made of materials that are easily changed. Some charts are highly detailed; some are very sketchy. Some are stamped confidential and secreted in the desks of a chosen few; others are broadly distributed and easily available. Despite these and other variations that might be noted, all organization charts have at least one thing in common: they don't show how the organization works. Or, as some people say, they don't show the real organization.

Such a statement, which usually emerges as a criticism of organization charts, goes beyond the fact that the organization chart, like milk, may be dated but not fresh. For it is increasingly understood that no organization chart is 100 percent current. Rather, the criticism is that even the most current chart is utterly inadequate as a diagram of the organization.

Few organization planners, even those whose major preoccupation is drawing charts, argue too vehemently against this criticism. They just go on drawing their charts. Most often, the charts they draw are of the conventional type made up of boxes and lines. These usually end up in a pyramidal shape with a box (generally larger) at the top to represent the chief executive.

However, behind the preparation and issuance of the chart, there is, presumably, this basic understanding: An organization chart is not an organization. And there is far more to an organization—even in the limited sense of an organization structure—than can ever be put on a chart.

But while the chartist himself may be aware of it, this knowledge is seldom pervasive. Some companies recognize this and attempt to underscore the fact that a chart is just a two-dimensional representation by placing the following caution at the bottom of the chart:

> *Level of boxes shows reporting relationships and has no significance with regard to importance of position or status.*

Such a caution of demurrer is seldom sufficient to quiet the critics or unruffle ruffled feathers, and is quite often taken with a large grain of salt—sometimes because the chart does show some of the very things that the demurrer may say it doesn't. If nothing else, for example, the head of a unit that doesn't appear on an organization chart can be reasonably sure that his unit is not rated important enough to merit inclusion.

Actually, the conventional organization chart (see Figure 1) shows very little. It implies a little more than it shows. But the inferences that are drawn from it are limited only by the experience, imagination and biases of the beholder—in or outside of the company. In other words, one of the troubles with charts seems to be the people who read them.

WHAT IT SHOWS

1. Division of work into components. These components may be divisions or departments or they may be individuals. Boxes on the conventional chart represent these units of work.

Source: Reprinted with permission from *The Conference Board Record,* November, 1964, pp. 7–10.

FIGURE 1

A CONVENTIONAL ORGANIZATION CHART

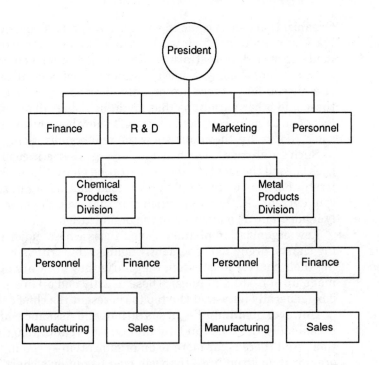

2. Who is (supposed to be) whose boss—the solid lines on the chart show this superior-subordinate relationship with its implied flow of delegated responsibility, authority and attendant accountability.

Implicit in these two are several other things that the chart is designed to show:

3. Nature of the work performed by the component. Depending upon the descriptive title placed in the box, what this shows may be specific (Facilities Engineering), speculative (Planning) or spurious (Special Projects).

4. Grouping of components on a functional, regional or product basis. This is also conveyed to some extent by the labels in the boxes.

5. Levels of management in terms of successive layers of superiors and subordinates. All persons or units that report to the same person are on the one level. The fact that they may be charted on different horizontal planes does not, of course, change the level.

It is rather difficult to pinpoint anything else about a structure that is actually shown on an organization chart. Some may argue whether, in fact, even the few items above can be read directly from any or some charts.

WHAT THE CHART DOESN'T SHOW

What an organization chart doesn't show is often the most interesting part of the chart—at least to the internal personnel. And it is the inferences that arise from what's missing which companies attempt to deal with in their demurrers or cautions. The demurrers, as already suggested, don't always scotch the inferences. In many cases, the warnings may be erroneous or incomplete.

Degree of Responsibility and Authority

Take, for example, this caution: "Size and position of boxes do not indicate degree of responsibility or authority." Well, it is quite possible that they do. Indeed in the mere process of showing superior-subordinate relationships, the chart does clearly imply varying degrees of responsibility and authority. This is implicit in the process of delegation.

A possibly more accurate demurrer might be "any relationship between size and position of boxes and degree of responsibility and authority may be coincidental, accidental or just plain odd." For what the chart clearly does not show is the degree of responsibility and authority exercised by positions on the same management level. Two persons on the same management level may have vastly different degrees of authority. A man on the third level may have more or less authority than a second-level manager in a different chain of delegation.

Of course, because the chart cannot adequately begin to depict varying degrees of authority, it cannot show the degree of decentralization. Decentralization, organizationally speaking, has relevance only in terms of delegation of decision-making authority. Almost by definition, it refers to the level at which decisions are made.

Inferences about decentralization are often drawn from charts; the company chart that shows activities grouped into product divisions or regional divisions as opposed to a purely functional grouping is often referred to as decentralized. That may or may not be the case. The view from the top may be of a highly decentralized company; the view from the bottom or intermediate layers may be quite the opposite. And a functionally organized company can be as highly decentralized as a divisionally organized company. It all depends on the level at which decisions are being made. The chart cannot depict that, nor can it depict the extent of the restrictions—in the form of policies, budgets, procedures, reports, audits—that make for more or less decentralization.

Staff and Line

Distinguishing between staff and line is an arduous, hazardous, and so far as some organization planners are concerned, an academic chore. Attempting to determine line and staff from an organization chart presents similar hazards. Titles or functional labels alone won't do it. What one company considers line may be staff to another. Again, it depends on the responsibility and authority delegated to the units.

Of course, the nature of the company's business may give clues to what is staff or line. In a manufacturing company, for example, certain functions are traditionally viewed as staff: personnel administration, public relations, legal and secretarial, and finance are examples. In a services company the arrangement may be quite different. But reliance on the nature of the business can be misleading. In manufacturing, for example, divisionalization has brought into being staff units with labels such as manufacturing and marketing—labels that typically would belong to line components in a functionally organized firm.

In some companies, charting methods are used to attempt to distinguish what these firms consider to be line and staff (or service and operating) units. Sometimes the so-called staff units are charted on one horizontal plane, one line on another. Other companies use skinny little lines to connect staff, healthier looking lines to connect line or operating units. Still others add labels to underscore this visual aid.

With all these visual distinctions, a chart reader might readily infer what is obviously being implied: there is a difference between the two types of units. To try to interpret these differences in terms of line-staff responsibilities, authorities, and relationships presents the same difficulties as reading the degree of decentralization from the chart.

Status or Importance

To some people, inclusion on the organization chart is, in itself, a status symbol. The physical location on the chart—the linear distance from the chief executive—is viewed as a measure of importance. And there's the rub. Given the limitations of a piece of paper, not everyone can be charted equidistant from the chief executive. Reassurances like "size and position of boxes do not reflect importance or status" are seldom reassuring enough. The incumbent charted in a particular spot may realize the truth of this statement; but he may fear that the "other fellows may not," or vice versa.

There is little question but that position on an organization chart, in some companies, does imply relative importance and status. But it has the same limitations in implying (or covering up lack of) importance as do size of office, titles, parking lot space, etc. Most people still rely on the pay envelope as a more accurate reflection of relative importance. And the organization chart just isn't designed to reflect the pay structure of the company.

In short, the organization chart may imply relative importance or status, but, to rephrase a caution that might appear on a chart, "Any inferences drawn from this chart regarding relative importance or status may or may not be correct."

Lines of Communication

Another caution that shows up is: "This chart does not indicate channels or contact." Actually it does. What it doesn't show is *all* the channels of contact or communication. Possibly a more appropriate warning might be: "This chart indicates a few of the major channels of contact—but if the organization sticks to only these, nothing will get done." For it is a truism of organization that no one unit or individual operates in isolation from all the others. All are linked by an intricate network of communication. (Maze may be a more apt term than network). Proper organization performance relies on this network and on each unit and individual becoming party to it. To chart the total network is practically impossible. To attempt to chart it—and thus introduce certain rigidities into it—might easily frustrate its workings.

Relationships

In a real sense, lines of communication are really relationships. "You can't have one without the other"—and the picture of either that shows up on the chart is that of only a few key links in the total network.

Any organization is a hotbed of relationships. Not all of them, of course, necessarily grow out of the nature of the work of the company. Even those that do, however, do not show up on the conventional or even unconventional organization chart.

On occasion a company has noted: "This chart shows relationships only and does not represent levels of management." The caution may have been on the wrong chart, for on the chart in question the opposite seemed true.

More frequently the company notes: "This chart shows reporting relationships only. . ." Even this seems questionable—it is accurate only if the phrase "reporting relationships" is understood to mean superior-subordinate reporting relationships.

Organizational relationships—as opposed to social, etc., relationships within a company—grow out of the division of work and delegation of responsibility and authority. A number of functional relationships, authority relationships, staffline relationships, and just plain work relationships may come into play in reaching any decision or in completing any given piece of work. Most companies long ago gave up any attempt to even begin to show all of these relationships on a chart.

The "Informal" Organization

To some people, that mystical entity known as the "informal" organization is the *real* organization. *It* is how things really get done.

The *it* referred to, however, may be any number of things, depending upon the point of view. To narrow it to just two types—there is the "informal" organization and the *informal* organization.

The "informal" organization, in this makeshift dichotomy, encompasses all relationships and channels of communication that mature, reasonable people are expected to develop and use in order to meet organizational objectives. As mature, reasonable people, they are expected, of course, to also respect their superior's need to be kept informed of matters affecting his area of accountability. This "informal" organization is viewed as a logical and necessary extension of the formal organization. It is informal only in the sense that nobody has found it necessary to inundate the organization with memorabilia that fully spell out its workings.

The *informal* organization, on the other hand, encompasses all the relationships, communication channels, and influences or power centers that mature, reasonable people develop because a lot of other people in the organization are not mature and reasonable—"especially the bosses who needn't be informed because they'll only say 'no'." Rather than being a logical extension of the formal organization, it comes into being because the formal organization is viewed as being illogical or inflexible or inefficient or just plain inconsistent with the personal and possibly organizational objectives being worked toward. This *informal* organization, according to "informal" organization specialists, gets work done in spite of the formal organization.

Neither shows up on the organization chart: the "informal" because it's too complex to be reduced to a two-dimensional chart; the *informal* because that would make it formal—a heresy that would immediately give rise to another *informal* organization.

For those not fully satisfied with this dichotomy, there may be a third type— the INFORMAL organization. It includes parts of the "informal" and *informal*. By definition, it covers everything not shown on the organization chart; by definition, it can't be charted.

THE INADEQUATE CHART

Attempts to revamp the conventional organization chart in order to overcome these and other limitations have produced many examples of modern, nonobjective art (Alexander Calder's mobiles have been mistaken for organization charts). There is the circular chart (and its variants) designed to better convey internal relationships and to better camouflage "status." There is the chart with the vertical lines between boxes stretched to reflect similar levels of responsibility or similar levels of pay (scrapped after first attempt–required too long a sheet of paper). There is the chart with the pyramid up-ended to reflect the true flow of authority—from subordinates to superiors (scrapped after first attempt— "That's rubbing it in").

Despite all its limitations, the conventional chart is increasingly used to depict the skeletal structure of the organization. For more complete documentation of what this chart means, companies rely on position guides, linear responsibility charts, statements of general responsibilities and relationships—indeed, the whole organizational manual.

The essential value of the chart seems to lie in the fact that it does strip the organization to the skeletal framework. In so doing, it serves a useful purpose both as a tool of organizational analysis and a means of communication.[1] As a complete picture of the organization, it is recognized as being completely inadequate. But it evidently is less inadequate than most substitutes.

Note

1. See "Charting the Company Organization Structure," *Studies in Personnel Policy,* no. 168, for detailed description of charts and their uses.

Questions for Discussion

1. What are the two major things explicitly depicted by all organization charts?

2. What are several other factors often implicit in organization charts?

3. The article suggested a number of things which organization charts do not show. Is it really true that organization charts don't show these factors? *Explain.*

4. What is the difference between the "informal" organization and the *informal* organization?

5. Overall, is the organization chart an adequate representative of the organization? Why or why not?

CASE 34
M & M ELECTRIC COMPANY

M & M Electric Company is located in Atlanta. It is a maker of high voltage interruption equipment. This includes switchgear used by utilities, factories, and institutions for the supply and distribution of their electric power.

Since its founding in 1910, M & M has expanded several times. The president, John Murphy, recently moved the company to a new plant in a semiresidential area of Atlanta. It had a railroad siding for receipt and shipment of large, heavy equipment. Most employees lived close to this location.

Since the move to the new plant, the company has grown at a faster rate, largely because of the additional capacity of the new location. Sales over the last two and a half years have averaged approximately $45 million per year. Periodically backlogs of orders have accumulated, but up until about a year ago, these backlogs were dissipated within two months. Since that time, however, a backlog of $9 million in accepted orders has continuously been on the books.

M & M products require a high degree of accuracy and dependability. They must be durable, for they are typically housed outside. The company's primary function is to serve as a custom assembler of electrical switchgear and transmission gear. It does very little original equipment manufacturing per se.

The firm has been long established as a medium-sized company with the highest quality product. Its prices for heavy equipment are high by industry standards. It's prices do not reflect changes in industry prices due to upswings or downswings in the construction or utility business, due to the high quality.

Mr. Murphy owns 70 percent of the stock of M & M, and there is no public ownership. Murphy lives three blocks from the plant and works 60–70 hours per week. He is 55 years old. His wife has worked as an executive secretary at M & M for 15 years. She is intimately familiar with company operations and serves as a frequent consultant. She is 48 years old.

Mrs. Murphy is regarded by many of the office employees as being loud, brash, and "taken" with her grandeur as Executive Secretary. She makes it a point to

Source: Adapted from a course assignment prepared by John C. Ferguson for Professor J. G. Hunt. Used with permission.

informally interview each new office employee and to openly voice her interpretation of the M & M code of conduct for employees. It is commonly thought that Mrs. Murphy "compensates" for Mr. Murphy's generally friendly, non-regulatory manner.

The various departments of M & M include accounting with the controller as its head; engineering and research with a vice president for research, and a vice president for engineering; manufacturing, with its department head also serving as the executive vice president of the firm; purchasing, whose vice president also serves as vice president of public relations; sales, whose vice president serves as head of the sales, personnel, market planning, and services department.

THE MANUFAC-TURING DEPARTMENT

The manufacturing and purchasing departments are of special interest. Prior to the new plant move, the functions of purchasing and production control (manufacturing) were considered one department with a single vice president. However, each is now a separate department.

When the two departments were separated, an additional vice presidential opening was filled with a subordinate who had worked for the firm for 15 years, and had "come up through the ranks." The other vice president, however, had been with the company for over 25 years. Both of these men were well qualified for their positions, although their personal philosophies of management differed greatly. Both departments, although now separated, must still work together closely.

The manufacturing department is run by Mr. C. C. Franke, 47, who is the vice president. Mr. Franke is also executive vice president of the firm and a long standing friend of John Murphy. Because of the scope of this department, Mr. Franke has an assistant who is the director of manufacturing administration, Mr. M. J. Paul, 43. Both Franke and Paul are college graduates. Under Mr. Paul there are managers of the various operations of the department. These are:

- Manager—Fabrication and Tooling—F. Franklin
- Manager—Plant Engineering—C. K. Jefferson
- Manager—Maintenance—G. J. Klause
- Superintendent—Material Services—J. R. May
- Manager—Metal-Enclosed Gear—L. R. Worth

The function of the manufacturing department is to combine the purchased component parts and the M & M manufactured parts into the final product for job order electrical systems, send it to the construction site, and if in the contract, supervise its installation.

Mr. Paul is mainly concerned with the output function of his department, and is in effect, an assistant to the vice president in the area of fabrication, inventory, and metal-enclosed gear output.

Paul and Franke work closely together and share the same philosophy that a day's work is worth a day's pay. Both however, seem to consider a day's work as a measured amount without regard for the employee time required to complete these assigned tasks. Although the switchboard and offices are not officially open on Saturday, it is considered standard procedure for manufacturing office employees (not secretaries or staff help) to work at least part of a day on Saturday. Work loads are adjusted to make this mandatory for the job executives to keep up with assignments. These executives are paid a straight weekly salary. The plant is operative all day Saturday.

The atmosphere in the department has been likened to the military in that all desks are arranged in a row, with all desk equipment located in the same places for each desk. Job executives are specifically assigned to jobs in progress and are required to directly supervise the collection of inventory items and record work progress in relation to shipping deadlines. They are not permitted to leave the manufacturing office without first checking out with the head secretary. They must return immediately after tending to their out-of-office business. The turnover rate in this department for executives and for secretarial help is the highest in the entire company, including the plant.

Mr. Franke is rarely seen in the office and Mr. Paul seems to be the implementor of Mr. Franke's policies. Mr. Paul is an ex-Marine and frequently displays his temper when delays on shipments arise. This pressure on the job executives has led to such practices as inventory shifting from one person to another, faked reports, falsified delivery time reports from purchasing, and other such activities to avoid conflicts with Mr. Paul. Paul has, on occasion, fired job executives and secretaries on the spot, contrary to the overall M & M policy of a two-week notice.

This management philosophy seems acceptable to Mr. Franke, and is allowed to continue since this unit is the "crucial" link in the output chain, with its direct control of the productivity of the company plant. Apparently this philosophy is also acceptable to Mrs. Murphy. Her office is located adjacent to this department. Both Mr. Franke and Mr. Paul account for this philosophy by explaining to the rest of the job executives how the problem of the backlog is being placed directly on their shoulders, and that any mistakes during this crucial time will only magnify the backlog problem.

THE PURCHASING DEPARTMENT

Purchasing contributes to productivity in just one area—that of procurement. Yet this area of procurement has within it many problematic operations and a diversity of conditions just as sweeping as those of the manufacturing department.

This department has as its vice president, Mr. Alfred A. Anderson, 62. As purchasing agent and second in command for the purchasing department, Mr. George Geoff, 58, supervises the actual buyers in the department. Mr. Geoff has been with M & M for two weeks longer than Mr. Anderson, both having started to work with the firm 22 years ago after military service. Mr. Anderson owns some share of the company stock, and has a liberal arts college degree. He is also a personal friend of John Murphy's. The buyers in purchasing each handle one group of materials as follows:

- George Geoff—Castings, office equipment, scrap sales, steel structures.
- W. J. Wallace—insulating materials, metals, paint, printing, stationary, and office supplies.
- L. J. Morehouse—forgings, glass, turned parts, contacts, springs, stampings, and fastenings.
- G. W. Waters—connectors, insulators, nameplates, molded plastics, and shipping supplies.
- B. J. Black—metal-enclosed switchgear components, fuels, maintenance materials for buildings and equipment, outside processing, tools, manufacturing and plant engineering supplies.

The turnover in purchasing is very low, and even the secretaries have stayed with the department amid offers to change to manufacturing, with more salary. The buyers have been with the company eight, five, sixteen, and two years, respectively. Each aids the other during vacation periods.

The function of the purchasing department is to procure components and other non-productive supplies that are to be charged to the respective departments. Prices of items purchased are therefore a consideration when approving purchase orders for other departments.

Lead time and availability of productive goods is an area in which the manufacturing department and purchasing must communicate. Changes in the dates for delivery (especially when required earlier than originally estimated) is a problem for purchasing. Inventory space for large items such as transformers, which make up the largest proportion of component items, is not sufficient for order scheduled more than one week ahead of assembly.

The major supplier for a couple of key components are Westinghouse and General Electric. Both of these vendors are highly independent and difficult to work with. Neither is dependable for original delivery estimates, and shipment of M & M products without these components is out of the question. Many departmental conflicts arise because of late delivery from these two vendors. Occasionally substitute products are available, although many contracts specify Westinghouse or GE components.

Mr. Anderson and Mr. Geoff both agree that their department is not to be run with tension or fear. Accuracy is required and no detail is too small to be overlooked. Saturday work for buyers is not required, for most vendors do not accept orders on Saturdays. Some buyers prefer to use Saturdays to maintain their paperwork while others work this into their five-day routine. The purchasing department is small, and for this reason unity, friendship, and cohesion are emphasized by Anderson and Geoff. Buyer assistance is readily available from Mr. Geoff, who has had experience ordering all of M & M product needs. Mr. Anderson largely handles his upper management affairs through Mr. Geoff. He is out of the office several hours a day as his duties of public relations vice president demand his presence at many community functions.

Purchasing keeps very complete records of orders and material requisitions from manufacturing. This file system has revealed the actual cause for assembly and inventory readiness delays in many cases. This file system is often used by the job executives of the manufacturing department since their overall department files are not adequate for these people to use effectively. Cases of record falsifications and other time falsifications from manufacturing have been discovered this way. Purchasing has been "blamed" for many production delays by Mr. Murphy through Mr. Franke. This filing system was instituted to refute or substantiate these statements.

The purchasing function is subject to delays from outside economic effects and labor strikes. For example, ceramic insulator lead time for ordering stands at one year. With this in mind, the buyer must anticipate likely needs and order these items without specific manufacturing requests. Castings for some of the M & M manufactured parts are custom order jobs from vendors. When a casting breaks on a machine, it may be several months before a similar casting can be received. In this case, duplicates are ordered for frequently used castings, although inventory costs for idle castings and duplicates is carefully controlled by accounting. Thus, purchasing also faces the task of judgmental ordering—a system that has only intuition and past performance as justifications.

THE PRESENT SITUATION

John Murphy has expressed his displeasure with the continuing backlog of sales to manufacturing output. He is concerned about increasing output with the present facilities. The plant now operates three shifts but is not assumed to be at maximum efficiency. The solution appears to Mr. Murphy to have to come from the manufacturing and purchasing departments, either with a speed up of assembly and inventory readiness, or a shortening of delay figures.

The relationships between the two departments become even more critical as both try to shift responsibility for delays to the other department. Upper management has not yet agreed to step in and reorganize, yet the hint of combining the departments has been spread. A further hint of computerization for the long-run operation of the firm seems inevitable, although as yet unapplied to purchasing. At the very least, a short-run solution is necessary as soon as possible for sales are continuing to be made at a high rate and the rates of cancellation for orders on "hold" have also started to rise.

Questions for Discussion

1. Has the company's growth and increased sales had an effect on its structure?
2. Are these changes frequently encountered as a firm grows? Explain.
3. Could "grapevine" communication between Mrs. Murphy and Mr. Murphy be a part of the company's problem?
4. Does the friendship between John Murphy and Mr. Franke interfere with the managerial practices of the company?
5. How could the problems between the management department and the purchasing department be corrected?
6. Is the division of a managers duties a good idea? (Mr. Anderson is divided between the production department and the public relations department.)

CASE 35
SEVENTEENTH NATIONAL BANK, DATA PROCESSING DEPARTMENT

BACKGROUND

Described here is a computer programming department in an aggressive bank located in the Dallas-Fort Worth metroplex. Overall, the bank is experiencing moderate growth now and forecasts better than moderate growth in the future in both the data processing department and other operations. The objectives of bank management are to make the bank competitive with the largest banks in the area and to expand the data processing department into a service bureau to handle the computer processing functions of banks and other financial outlets in addition to those of Seventeenth National (SN).

The exact goals of the data processing department as a service bureau have not been established. Currently, the department acts as a small service bureau and is doing computer processing for four banks other than SN. One of the four banks has already indicated that it intends not to renew its contract with the service bureau because the bank is getting its own computer and feels the work can be performed in-house less expensively.

Of the four banks being serviced, the three that will remain generate little revenue for the service bureau. One of the three is very small and is being serviced only because of its name. The service bureau uses it as bait to attract new customers.

The revenue earned from servicing outside companies is used by the service bureau to help offset the costs of doing its own bank's computer processing. In the future, management would like the data processing department to become a significant revenue source and, possibly, even separate from the parent bank acting as a subsidiary.

Source: Adapted from a course assignment prepared by W. D. Lincoln for Professor J. G. Hunt, University of Texas, Arlington. Copyright 1980, R. N. Osborn, J. G. Hunt, and L. R. Jauch.

The data processing department employs people in three major departments: keypunch (15); computer operations (10); and programming (10). The department, as a whole, is managed by one person who has a private secretary. This gives the data processing department a total of 37 people, as shown in Figure 1.

Prospective clients of the data processing department are interviewed by its manager to determine feasibility and profitability of the venture. If both sides agree to a contract, a date is set indicating when services will begin. The date chosen must conform to existing workloads and schedules of keypunch, operations, and programming. Work capacity for these departments is usually scheduled at least six months ahead of time, since new people may have to be hired and trained or new machinery purchased to accommodate servicing customers. The six-month schedule is revised frequently to adjust priorities of jobs.

The first major service performed by the data processing department for a new customer is to design the computer system that satisfies the client needs. Meetings are held between experienced programmers, the data processing manager, and the new customer to determine which programs and procedures will be required to meet those needs.

After the system is designed and agreed upon by all parties, programmers write the programs in the system. Depending on the size of the system, a staff of programmers will be chosen to manage the work on the project. Since most systems designed by this data processing department are usually small, one person is assigned the job of managing the project. The title given to this person is "project leader"; he or she will be responsible for making sure that programs are written to conform to design specifications and that the project will be completed on time.

People selected to work on new systems are chosen by the data processing manager and the manager of systems and programming. Even though a person may hold a specific title assigned as a result of a promotion previous to this project (e.g., systems analyst, project leader, or programmer), this person may occupy one of several positions while working on this system. A "programmer" may be assigned as the leader of this project with other programmers working for him or her. This is done to train the person for a project leader position should he or she be promoted to that position later on.

The time that it takes to design and implement a system ranges anywhere from a few days to several years. Most major systems in this particular data processing department take three months to a year to complete. During this time, the programmers will write and test new programs, while the project leader coordinates their activities, answers their questions, monitors time and

FIGURE 1

DATA PROCESSING DEPARTMENT STRUCTURE

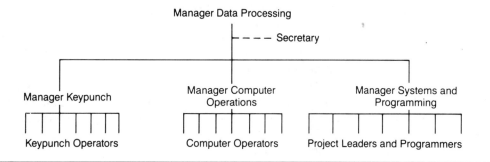

resources spent on the project, and initiates any changes required to the baseline design. People on the project are allowed much flexibility in the hours they work as long as milestones needed for the system are completed on time.

Frequently, small program maintenance jobs are given to project leaders and programmers while these people are assigned to a project. These maintenance jobs are usually unrelated to the project and need to be performed because an existing program was not set up to handle it, or the problem may be that a customer has requested that a change be made to comply with a new law. The reasons why program maintenance jobs originate are numerous, but nevertheless they require attention and completion.

Too many program maintenance jobs assigned to people working on projects can cause the original and estimated project completion date to be missed. This happens quite frequently, and customers get very upset when they are told that their system won't be ready for another three weeks, or even longer.

Writing a new system for a customer is similar to constructing a bridge or a building. Much planning is required before any work actually takes place. After the workers are hired, a great deal of coordination and additional planning is required to keep the job on schedule and to make sure that the job is done according to engineer's specifications. Without the right controls, the final product can be a total disaster, and sometimes is.

SUMMARY CHARACTERISTICS

Size

The total size of this bank is 600 to 700 employees. At the first and second levels in the data processing department, the number of employees is 32 and 5, respectively. Overall, the bank is experiencing 10 to 15 percent annual growth and predicts that this growth will continue in the future.

Work Flow

Work flow in the data processing department is highly specialized in keypunch and computer operations, but the opposite is true in programming. Programmers perform a variety of tasks such as writing new programs, correcting problems in existing programs, documenting procedures, keypunching small amounts of data, meeting with customers, and teaching classes to customers and other programmers on technological changes and enhancements. Regardless of the task performed, it is almost always interdependent with the work of someone else.

Tasks

Task outcome predictability in programming is high in the long-term sense, but not necessarily so in the short term. Programmers usually (but not always) know what the eventual product of their work will be. A programmer must test programs that he or she writes or modifies before letting the program be used on customers' "live" data. Programs do not always function as intended at first. Different data are processed by the programmer through the program to test as many conditions as possible. Sometimes a program will malfunction because it handles a certain condition differently than intended. This is called a "bug" by computer people, and it results from not testing the program properly.

Even though a programmer may consult a more experienced programmer about how to handle a problem, the programmer is still not assured that the advice given is always reliable in all situations. There are usually many different ways to handle the same condition in a program, but many times each method depends on such things as the size of the computer, its speed, the amount of data being processed, and how often it is processed. Each time advice is given, these factors should be considered by all concerned.

Physical Surroundings

The programmers are all in one room and all of the project leaders are in another. Visual barriers in each room are strategically placed to reduce eye contact, but no barriers exist to prevent or reduce noise. Interruptions take place constantly, and some programmers have even had to take their work home in order to have enough peace and quiet to concentrate.

Delegation

Much discretion is given to programmers on how to handle a particular problem. Programmers are required to research certain topics selected for them by the programming manager and give a two-hour class to the rest of the programmers. The intent of the education program is to keep the programmers informed about new ways of handling program problems, technological enhancements that eliminate certain other problems, or a refresher course in selecting the best way among existing resources to handle them. The method chosen to handle the problem is left up to each programmer, and very few of the decisions are ever referred outside of the department.

Standards and Rewards and Penalties

Standards for programmers are set very high. They are exceptionally clear and can be measured quite accurately. Sometimes classes are held to let the programmers modify existing standards or add new ones. The programming department is very "standards" oriented and strongly encourages that each person follow these when writing programs.

Rewards and penalties are directly related to performance. Programmers are given salary reviews every six months. If the programmer did a good job during the previous six months, he or she is given a raise and possibly a promotion. Those who perform poorly get no raises or promotions and may be discharged if their performance continues to be less than satisfactory.

Supervision

Supervisory rule enforcement is strict only when actually writing programs; other rules are not strictly enforced. Close direction is usually given to all people in the department. Deadlines for work must be made and quality of work must be satisfactory. Inducements are usually in the form of rewards, with penalties used primarily for poor performers.

CURRENT CONCERN

The bank president has recently talked to the data processing manager about organization of the department. She (the president) is wondering if the department is organized as well as it should be, given its current internal and external data processing mission and other crucial variables. She is also wondering what the structure should look like two and five years from now if the bank and department growth-estimates are even approximately correct. She expects the department to aggressively pursue the outside business mentioned earlier and is willing to grant the department head as much authority as needed to accomplish his external and internal missions. She also has said she will grant reasonable budget increases if they can be justified. The department head knows she didn't get the name "Iron Nell" for nothing. She is a bear on efficiency and doesn't like high turnover even among programmers, who are known for their notoriously high turnover rate. The data processing manager knows that he must put together a report for her in the near future if he is to be able to get the increased budget he feels he needs.

Questions for Discussion

1. How would you characterize the nature of the jobs in the data processing department?
2. How would you characterize variables such as size, technology, diversity, and personnel?
3. What organizational style would you recommend at this time?
4. If you were the department head, what would you tell Iron Nell?

EXERCISE 36
ORGANIZATION CLIMATE

In this exercise you will have a chance to analyze an organization's climate and how it might be related to structure.

First complete the climate questionnaire. When making your responses, your answers should be based on an organization you currently work for (either full or part time). If you have no job currently, answer according to your knowledge of the last organization you worked for. If you have never had a job, answer in terms of the kind of organization you expect to work for when you start to work or one that you feel you know fairly well from previous study or knowledge of a close relative who works for the organization.

Answer each item as best you can according to the following scale:

1—If you *definitely agree* with the statement.

2—If you are *inclined to agree* with the statement.

3—If you *neither agree nor disagree* with the statement.

4—If you are *inclined to disagree* with the statement.

5—If you *definitely disagree* with the statement.

CLIMATE QUESTIONNAIRE

_____ 1. Sometimes I have difficulty knowing who has the authority to make decisions in this organization.

_____ 2. Most employees in this organization take responsibility for doing their jobs; supervisors mainly set guidelines.

_____ 3. Competent people here are the ones who are rewarded by the promotion system.

_____ 4. Our business has been built up by taking calculated risks at the right time.

_____ 5. This organization has a pretty relaxed and easygoing atmosphere.

_____ 6. Managers in our organization are really interested in helping us out in our career development.

_____ 7. Our organization expects pretty high standards of performance from us.

_____ 8. The best way to make a good impression around here is to make your position clear and well known and argue for its acceptance.

_____ 9. People take pride in belonging to this organization.

_____10. The red tape and bureaucracy in this organization are kept to a minimum.

_____11. If you want to get ahead in this organization you have to be willing to stick your neck out sometimes.

_____12. The threats and criticism we get from supervisors are minimal; they try to use positive encouragement instead.

_____13. Our managers are usually willing to take a chance on a good idea.

_____14. It's very easy to get to know people in this organization.

Source: Adapted from George H. Litwin and Robert A. Stringer, Jr., *Motivation and Organizational Climate,* Boston: Division of Research, Harvard Business School, 1968. Copyright © 1968 by the President and Fellows of Harvard College. Adapted and reprinted by permission.

_____15. People in this organization really trust each other.

_____16. Our managers believe that we can always do a better job than we do now.

_____17. Competition is seen as healthy by our managers.

_____18. I feel that I am a member of a well-functioning team.

_____19. In some of the projects I've worked on, I've had difficulty knowing who is in charge.

_____20. The philosophy of our organization is that people should solve their own problems.

_____21. People in our organization are rewarded in proportion to their job performance.

_____22. Occasionally we have to take some pretty big risks to keep ahead of the competition.

_____23. Relationships between managers and workers in our organization are warm and friendly.

_____24. I can usually count on help from my boss and co-workers when I have a difficult problem.

_____25. There is a feeling of pressure to improve our performance around here.

_____26. We are encouraged to express our opinions on issues even if it means disagreeing with superiors.

_____27. People around here are very loyal to the organization.

KEY FOR SCORING ORGANIZATION CLIMATE

Find your responses to each of the items below and sum across the row. Then divide by 3 to give you an average score for each climate dimension.

Structure	1___	+ 10___	+ 19___	= ___	/3 = ___
Responsibility	2___	+ 11___	+ 20___	= ___	/3 = ___
Reward	3___	+ 12___	+ 21___	= ___	/3 = ___
Risk	4___	+ 13___	+ 22___	= ___	/3 = ___
Warmth	5___	+ 14___	+ 23___	= ___	/3 = ___
Support	6___	+ 15___	+ 24___	= ___	/3 = ___
Standards	7___	+ 16___	+ 25___	= ___	/3 = ___
Conflict	8___	+ 17___	+ 26___	= ___	/3 = ___
Identity	9___	+ 18___	+ 27___	= ___	/3 = ___

Do all nine dimensions tend to be closer to 1 or 5? Are the climate items consistent with the structure of the organization? (That is, are climate dimensions closer to 1 oriented to less structure, closer to 5 oriented to more structure?)

EXERCISE 37
STUDYING AN ORGANIZATION

Your task is to examine an organization by measuring the external and internal variables influencing its structure. Choose an organization that is willing to give you information—perhaps you are employed there, perhaps it will allow you to observe its behavior or will give you interviews, or perhaps the information is available from published or private sources. Compare all possible data and recommend a structure for the firm.

1. First examine the enterprise so that you can characterize the predictor variables. The first three of these factors are internal; the last three environmental.

   A. Size of the firm:

   How large is the firm at the location you are studying?

   Is the firm:

   (1) Small (under 250 employees).

   (2) Medium (251–1,000 employees).

   (3) Large (1,001 or more employees).

   B. Diversity of products and services:

   A firm has high diversity if the number of products/services it offers is large and if these products/services span more than one standard industrial classification code (SIC Code). Diversity is also large if the firm sells in a large number of markets, faces a large number of competitors, and uses many sources of material and human resources.

   Does the firm have:

   (1) Low diversity.

   (2) Moderate diversity.

   (3) High diversity.

   C. Employee characteristics:

   Characterize the employees as predominantly persons with

   (1) High levels of education, high intelligence, and a great deal of experience.

   (2) Moderate levels of education, moderately intelligent, and with moderate experience.

   (3) Low levels of education, lower levels of intelligence, and experience.

   Note: High level of education means that the typical employee has attended college. Moderate means the employee is a high school graduate. Low means the employee did not graduate from high school.

   D. Stability of technology:

   Technology consists of the techniques (such as equipment, computers, and so on) used on inputs to the enterprise (such as materials) to accomplish the company's objectives.

   Is the technology:

   (1) Stable—very slowly changing (over many years) as in metals manufacturing.

TABLE 1

RELATIVELY INDEPENDENT AND DEPENDENT ENTERPRISES

Dependence Factor	Relatively Independent Enterprise	Relatively Dependent Enterprise
Resource Suppliers		
Stockholders (Business)	AT&T	Hallmark
Unions	IBM	Chrysler
Suppliers: Subparts	A&P	Local Clothing Store
Regulators		
Government	Ace Hardware	New York Life Insurance Co.
Community	New York Life Insurance Co.	Small Textile Manufacturer
Clients/Customers	General Foods	McDonnell Douglas
Competitors	IBM	Small Textile Manufacturer

(2) Moderate—in between 1 and 3.

(3) Volatile–changing rapidly, as in electronics.

E. Stability of market:

Stability of the market (which includes competitors, customers, pricing, styles) is a condition in which the marketplace for the firm's products or services changes very little and very slowly.

Is the market:

(1) Stable—like those for vegetable oil, auto parts, candy.

(2) Moderate—in between, such as that for toys.

(3) Volatile—like those for ethical drugs, chemicals, office and business equipment, photography.

F. Dependence:

Dependence is the relative loss of flexibility in choice of organizational structure or enterprise strategy because of external pressures. Independence is freedom to choose a strategy and organizational structure without the need to consider the requirements of resource providers (suppliers, unions, stockholders), regulators (government, community), and clients and customers.

Table 1 provides a few examples both of companies that are relatively dependent and of companies that are independent of external forces. With its diversified ownership, AT&T is not as dependent on the wishes of the owners as Hallmark's management is on the wishes of the Hall family.

Scale the firm on the following types of dependence:

Suppliers	Very Dependent (=3)	Dependent (=2)	Independent (=1)
1. Stockholders			
2. Unions			
3. Materials			
4. Competitors			
5. A few customers			
6. Government			

Weight Dependence Index:

Add up scores and divide by six. The higher the number, the more dependent the organization. The scale is as follows:

Weighted Index

Very dependent	18–13
Dependent	12–7
Independent	6-0

2. Now that you have scaled the firm, see if you can assign it in an appropriate structure. Table 2 displays the four stages of structural development: the primitive structure, the functional structure, the divisional organization, and the matrix. In general, if firms follow a growth strategy, they appear to move from primitive to functional to divisional and will go to matrix if necessary.

Briefly, a matrix structure is one that uses a dual command system for many or most managers. A typical middle or supervisory manager would report simultaneously to two superiors: a permanent boss in the functional part of the organization and one or more temporary bosses in the project (or divisional) part of the organization.

Note (in Exhibit 1) that a subproject manager (SPM) reports to a lab manager within the operations/technical group and also to an assistant project manager (APM)—or, to put it otherwise, is part of two work groups and divides his energy and time between them. In sum, matrix is a compromise organization serving the needs of the customer and the company. Matrix tends to evolve in organizations rather than be imposed as a new approach. A typical evolution might be:

- To temporarily add project managers to a functional organization for several short-term but important jobs.
- To then make the project manager system permanent for parts of the organization.
- Finally, to extend it throughout the organization in a firm that is in effect a mature matrix organization in which a majority of managers belong to two groups and are responsible to two superiors.

Here are some additional guidelines for assessing how the predictor variables can affect which structure should be used.

The first three variables we will look at are internal variables: size, diversity, and employee characteristics.

TABLE 2

THE RELATIONSHIP BETWEEN STRATEGY AND STRUCTURE
(DEPARTMENTATION) IN EFFECTIVE FIRMS

Strategy	Structure (Departmentation)			
	Primitive	Functional	Divisional	Matrix
Small single product/service line firm; stable growth, growth, or retrenchment	X			
Medium single product/service line firm; stable growth, growth, or retrenchment		X		
Medium single product/service line firm; growth			X	
Large single product/service line firm; stable growth, growth, or retrenchment		X		
Large single product/service line firm; stable growth, growth, or retrenchment			X	
Large several product/service line firm; stable growth, growth, retrenchment			X	
Large multiple product/service line firm; stable growth, growth, or retrenchment				X

A. Size:

Research indicates that as a firm increases in size, primitive organizations are no longer effective. What organization evolves then?

If the firm grows in size by increasing sales in the same line of business, it can be very effective with a functional organization or, in special cases, with a divisional organization.

EXHIBIT 1

TRW SYSTEMS GROUP—THE APM-SPM-WPM CHAIN

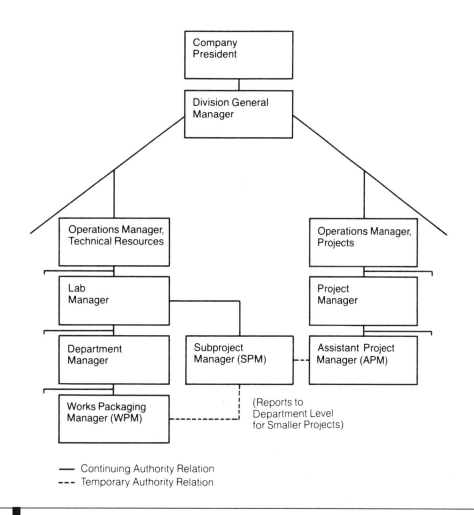

— Continuing Authority Relation
--- Temporary Authority Relation

So it can be seen that size influences structure. Primitive structure loses its effectiveness because a top manager can only interact with so many people. Functional structure loses its effectiveness because of size interacting with the next variable—diversity.

B. Diversity:

Diversity will affect the organization structure, for functional structures do not respond well to diversity. The more diversity, the greater the move toward divisional structure or, in special cases, matrix structure.

C. Employee Characteristics:

Some variables do not affect the form of departmentation directly, but influence the way in which other structural design features are configured. Table 3 examines these relationships.

TABLE 3

THE RELATIONSHIP BETWEEN TWO EXTERNAL AND INTERNAL
FACTORS AND STRUCTURAL DESIGN FEATURES

	Breadth of Structural Design Features[a]	
Predictor Variable	**Narrow**	**Broad**
Employee Characteristics		
Education	Low	High
Rearing	Authoritarian	Nonauthoritarian
Location of rearing	Rural	Urban
Intelligence	Low	High
Experience	Minimal	Wide
Dependence	High	Low

[a]The structural design features include:

	Narrow	**Broad**
Job design	Work simplification	Job enlargement
Job definitions	Specialized	General
Height of hierarchy	High	Low
Span of control	Small	Wide
Decision-making locus	Centralized	Decentralized

Refer to your data on the organization's employee characteristics and to Table 3 to see what approach is most appropriate. In general, higher education and intelligence are correlated with a preference for broader design features (e.g., enlarged jobs, decentralized decision making).

The next factors discussed are external ones: technology, market stability, and dependence.

D. Technology:

Stable technology is effectively structured as functional. Volatile technology is more effectively structured as matrix or divisional.

E. Market stability:

How does market stability affect structure? The more stable, the less information to be processed. As noted in Table 2, highly stable industries indicate either primitive or functional structures. Volatile industries indicate matrix or divisional structures. But some highly specialized, volatile companies are run by entrepreneurs who are well-attuned to the market.

As volatility increases (as change accelerates), it is harder to effectively systematize and thus harder to organize traditionally. Generally, volatile market conditions also lead to broader design features.

F. Dependence:

You have already rated the organization on dependence. You will see from Table 3 that low dependence leads to a preference for broader design, while a highly dependent organization is likely to be narrower in these other design features.

3. Decision-Making Grid

   After the six variables have been examined, which choice should be made?
   Fill in the grid that follows.

Predictor Variable	Primitive	Most Likely Structure Functional	Divisional	Matrix
1. Size				
2. Diversity				
3. Stability of technology				
4. Stability of market				

Predictor Variable	Job Design and Definition	Most Likely Design Height of Hierarchy	Span of Control	Decision Locus
1. Employee characteristics				
2. Dependence				

If all the predictor variables indicate a single form of structure, that will be your choice. But often, different variables give conflicting signals, especially with six variables. Some variables are stronger influences than others. Here is our estimate of their relative strength.

Very Strong	Strong	Weaker
Size		
Market stability	Technology	Dependence
Diversity		Characteristics of employees

Rules of thumb might be:

1. If five or six variables point to a single structure or design, adopt that structure or design.

2. If four or more variables point to one structure or design and the others to another structure or design, then examine the first four. If three of them are listed above as strong variables, stay with the predominant structure.

3. If the strong variables are mixed, structure your organization in a compromise of design features.

   I. Choice of structure is _____

   II. Choice of design is _____

   III. Explanation/justification for choice _____

   _____

   _____

   _____

   _____

   _____

   _____

   _____

EXERCISE 38
SEARS VS. KMART

Here is a field exercise you can do the next time you go shopping. It is designed to help you explore the significance of various aspects of organization structure on effectiveness and goal accomplishment.

You will be asked to analyze two different establishments in the same line of business. You will compare and contrast these firms as carefully as you can to see what makes them really work. Since you've probably visited one or both of these stores, you already know something about them. But try to place yourself in a position of seeing them for the first time. Then try to integrate what you have learned in this chapter and from other experiences in this book about how firms are managed.

Form into groups of about four and read your assignment. As a group, visit each store (preferably in the same general location). You might want to evaluate service, quality, price, and so on.

YOUR ASSIGNMENT

Your group, Fastalk Consultants, is known as the shrewdest, most insightful, and most overpaid management consulting firm in the country. You have been hired by the president of Sears to make recommendations for improving the motivation and performance of personnel in their operations. Let us assume that the key job activity in store operations is dealing with customers.

Recently, the president of Sears has come to suspect that his company's competitor, Kmart, is making heavy inroads into Sears' market. He has also hired a market research firm to investigate and compare the relative merits of products and prices in the two establishments, and has asked the market research firm to assess the advertising campaigns of the two organizations. Hence, you will not need to be concerned with marketing issues, except as they may have an impact on employee behavior. The president wants you to look into the organization of the two stores to determine the strengths and weaknesses of each.

The president has established an unusual contract with you. He wants you to make your recommendations based upon your observations *as a customer.* He does not want you to do a complete diagnosis with interviews, surveys, or behind-the-scenes observations. He wants your report in two parts.

1. Given his organization's goals of profitability, sales volume, and fast and courteous service, he wants an analysis that will compare and contrast Sears and Kmart in terms of the following concepts:

Organizational Goals	**Horizontal Division of Labor**
Conflict?	Formalized Policies?
Charity?	Departmentalization?
	Standardization of Rules?
Environment	
Stable/Changing?	**Vertical Division of Labor**
Simplex/Complex?	Number of Levels?
Certain/Uncertain?	Span of Control?
	Centralization?
Size	
Large?	**Communication**
Medium?	Direction?
Small?	Openness?

Personnel	**Leadership Style**
Knowledgeable?	Task Oriented?
Well Trained?	People Oriented?

Jobs	**Employee Motivation**
Variety?	Type?
Wholeness?	Intrinsic/Extrinsic?
Interaction?	Rewards?
Freedom?	Support?
Time of Work?	Coordination?
Location of Work?	Decision Making?

How do Sears and Kmart differ in these aspects? Which company has the best approach?

2. Given the corporate goals listed under point 1, what specific actions might Sears' management take in the following areas to achieve these goals (profitability, sales volume, fast, and courteous service)?

- Job design and workflow
- Organization structure (at the individual store level)
- Employee incentives
- Leadership
- Employee selection

3. Having completed your contract with the president of Sears, prepare a report for presentation to class. This should include:

a. Specific recommendations you have considered in 2 above.

b. Reasons for these suggestions based on your knowledge of leadership, motivation, job design, organization, and so on.

CASE 39
RESISTANCE TO CHANGE

The Central Distributing Company (CDC) is a wholly owned subsidiary of the Reiter Company, a manufacturer of a wide variety of work gloves and caps. With headquarters in Davis, Illinois, CDC markets the gloves and caps, as well as related products (jackets, vests, sport shirts, etc.).

CDC currently employs twenty salesmen in seven states in the northern midwest region. Salesmen contact merchants and take orders, with all shipments of goods from a central warehouse in Davis. Salesmen's territories are such that they are able to see each customer at least once every eight weeks. The territories were originally divided so that the salesmen could call upon each customer every four weeks, but orders were often too small. Sales territories are not considered in terms of sales potential. The owner of Reiter and the sales manager for CDC both agree that the potential of an area is dependent upon the salesman serving the territory. Recent sales records are indicated in Table 1.

Salesmen are compensated on a salary plus quota-bonus system. They receive a "guaranteed draw" of $600 monthly, with car furnished and a personal travel allowance of up to $100 weekly. A quarterly quota of $30,000 was established, and salesmen receive 5 percent of sales over this quota as a bonus. The quota is the same for all salesmen regardless of territory. The bonus is cumulative. If, for example, a salesman sells only $28,000 worth of merchandise one quarter, he receives a bonus only on any amount over $32,000 in a subsequent quarter.

Lee Edwards, the sales manager for CDC, feels that a uniform quota would possibly stimulate sales in some of the less productive territories. However, he has been receiving complaints by some of the salesmen indicating that a reevaluation of the plan was needed. Some salesmen were also upset because when busy periods occur, production can't keep up with demand and shipments are allocated based on the weekly percent of a salesman's annual total. Thus, at a time when all salesmen can sell more merchandise than they can obtain, salesmen having better records are favored. Mr. Edwards feels that this provides an added incentive for the poorer salesmen.

As a result of increasing complaints, Mr. Edwards was considering several alternatives:

   a. Allocate variable quotas based on the previous year's sales by territory.

   b. Set quotas based on per capita income by territory.

   c. Reallocate territories such that better salesmen are placed in territories which are generating fewer sales currently.

   d. Drop the cumulative bonus feature.

   e. Allocate shipments in peak demand-low supply periods to territories where sales are lowest.

He sent a memo outlining these alternatives to all the salesmen and was waiting for replies before he made a decision.

Source: Adapted from "The Reiter Company," William F. Glueck, School of Business and Public Administration, University of Missouri, Columbia, Missouri, Copyright 1970 by William F. Glueck.

TABLE 1

CENTRAL DISTRIBUTING CO., SALES RECORD FOR MONTH OF JUNE

Territory	Salesman	Sales
Galesburg, Illinois	Gene Hodges	$17,865.21
Freeport, Illinois	Walter Erskine	13,804.68
Warsaw, Indiana	Ray Fenton	11,308.38
Oskaloosa, Iowa	Bud Stone	11,216.79
Vandalia, Illinois	Bruce Williams	11,052.95
Clearlake, Iowa	Russel Palmer	10,964.23
Macon, Missouri	Richard Robertson	10,168.27
Lincoln, Illinois	Douglas Winnear	10,071.31
Fort Dodge, Iowa	Jack Forsythe	9,267.38
Bedford, Indiana	Stan Abel	9,133.64
Virginia, Illinois	Robert Walkley	9,127.92
Sullivan, Missouri	John Keenan	8,064.62
Taylorville, Illinois	Bill Rodli	8,008.28
Connersville, Indiana	Mike Evans	7,280.47
Van Wert, Ohio	John Hulett	6,680.53
Lafayette, Indiana	James Delbert	6,264.41
Mankato, Minnesota	Bill Durk	6,216.83
Princeton, Missouri	Alfred Cummings	5,452.35
Greenville, Ohio	Harold Gibbons	5,296.89
Wilmar, Minnesota	Mike Stewart	4,720.86

Questions for Discussion

1. Consider each alternative one at a time. What replies will Mr. Edwards likely receive from the top five salesmen? What replies would he likely get from the bottom five salesmen?

2. Assuming he decides on alternative b, how would he overcome the resistance he is likely to receive?

3. What would happen if he chose alternative c?

4. What would you do if you were Mr. Edwards?

CASE 40
GET RID OF FRANKLIN!

The Franklin problem apparently started about the time that Harold Newland, president of Newland Electronics Corporation, issued this memorandum:

Source: Reprinted from Robert D. Joyce, *Encounters in Organizational Behavior,* 1972, with permission of Pergamon Press, Ltd., Oxford, England.

December 2

To: Staff

From: H. Newland

Subject: Organizational Changes

As you are all well aware, growth at Newland Electronics Corporation this past year has exceeded our planned estimates. Sales of our unique microswitches and relays have risen above the 15 million dollar level with anticipated sales to reach 18.5 million next year. This is a credit to our entire organization.

This growth will require several organizational changes if we are to continue our success pattern. Our new organizational structure will reflect additional specialization within our existing functional groups. For some it will be a blessing, since many persons will not be required to "wear as many hats as before."

Effective immediately, I will personally intensify our efforts in long-range product and market planning. Mr. Charles Murphy will become Executive Vice President, responsible for overall plant management. Mr. Martin Brown will now devote full time to our sales effort as Vice President—Marketing. We are now seeking a qualified person to assume the position of Vice President—Finance.

Dr. Arnold Wilson, who has provided much of our recent technological growth as Supervisor of the New Products Group, will become Vice President—Operations.

Additional changes at other levels will be announced by Mr. Murphy as they are effected.

H. NEWLAND

The next memorandum was released two weeks later:

December 18

To: Staff

From: A. Wilson

Subject: Changes in the Operations Department

The following promotions are announced effective immediately:

Edward Bellman—Director of Manufacturing

Robert Maxey—Director of Engineering

Matthew Doyle—Supervisor of Product Engineering

Thomas Carlson—Supervisor of New Products

Harry Pleasant—Manufacturing Superintendent

The attached organization chart will now apply [see Figures 1 and 2].

A. WILSON

Approved: C. MURPHY

It was March. Dr. Arnold Wilson had only been Vice President—Operations for two months, but it had seemed like a year. It was one thing to solve technical problems as he had been doing as former head of the New Products Group. Lately, however, it seemed as if all he did each day was listen to "people" problems. Now he had another problem.

Wilson was aware that there was some friction between Bill Franklin of Engineering Services and Matthew Doyle of Product Engineering. Apparently the situation had worsened because both Doyle and Bob Maxey, the new Director of

FIGURE 1

NEWLAND ELECTRONICS CORPORATION (BEFORE ORGANIZATIONAL CHANGES)

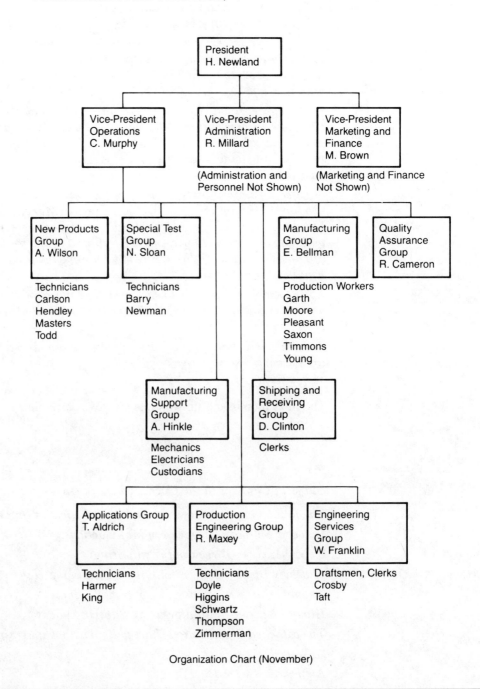

Organization Chart (November)

Engineering, came to Wilson's office this morning and demanded that Franklin be terminated.

FIGURE 2

NEWLAND ELECTRONICS CORPORATION (AFTER ORGANIZATIONAL CHANGES)

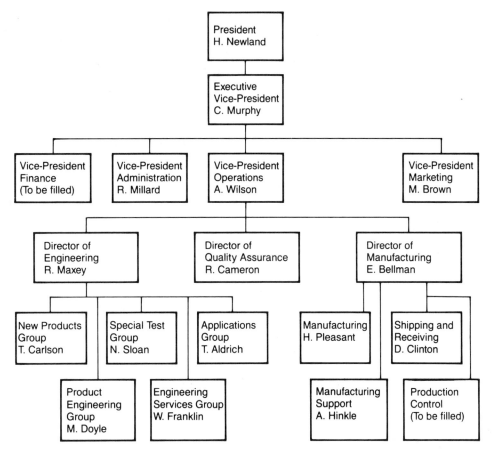

Organization Chart (January)

Maxey and Doyle brought two charges against Franklin:

1. Franklin was not cooperating with Doyle's Product Engineering Group (production engineering). Drafts and technical writing support requests were constantly ignored. Projects were falling behind schedule.

2. Franklin personally was too young and inexperienced to handle this responsibility in a growing organization. He also was lacking in technical electronics know-how and preferred drinking coffee to learning his job. He ran his group like a kindergarten—all for fun and no effort.

Their proposal was to terminate Franklin or transfer him out of the Engineering Department. Maxey did not have authority to terminate a group supervisor and had brought the problem to Wilson.

Bill Franklin was twenty-nine and an Industrial Management graduate. He had spent two years in the Army and had been at Newland for three years. He started as an engineer in Product Engineering when the supervisor there was Milt Henry. Henry had liked Franklin, and when Henry decided to leave Newland, he suggested the creation of a new Engineering Services Group to provide technical writing, drafting, and related services to both the engineering and manufacturing areas. It was to be a talent pool on call when needed. Henry suggested young Franklin to head this new group and Franklin got the job.

Henry was not replaced from within. Instead, Charles Murphy selected Robert Maxey, a senior engineer from another small firm within the industry. Maxey was well qualified. He had a B.S. and M.S. in Electrical Engineering and twelve years experience. Maxey later brought in three engineers who had worked with him before. . .Doyle, Higgins, and Zimmerman. From almost that point on there was constant conflict between Franklin and Product Engineering, particularly Maxey and Doyle.

When Maxey and Doyle left, Wilson called Bill Franklin to his office. Franklin was enraged, but not surprised at the charges. He said that Maxey and Doyle told him they were taking the problem to Wilson.

Franklin claimed that over 70 percent of his technical writing and drafting effort was already being supplied to Product Engineering. The remainder was spread out thinly to all other user areas. He agreed he could use more draftsmen, but felt the problem was deeper than that. In Franklin's opinion, Maxey and Doyle just had to have everything their own way. They were demanding a complete change in the drawing and specification numbering system. Franklin felt they wanted specifications systems like those used in their prior company. They were also purposely hypercritical of errors, and vastly exaggerated this as supposed incompetence. They really wanted control of drafting and specs by making it part of Product Engineering. Franklin felt this was coming and would not tolerate it.

He stressed his management ability as supervisor of the largest engineering group and felt his people were extremely loyal and hardworking, citing the facts that he had the lowest turnover and absentee rates in the entire plant.

Wilson suggested the possibility of a transfer to manufacturing but Franklin was cool to the idea. He felt it would be a demotion. Franklin offered his solution to the problem. "I'm doing my job like always. Get Maxey and Doyle off my back!"

Wilson decided to get more information from other likely sources. Ed Bellman had an opinion:

"Franklin is a bright young man. We all like him out here. I've heard he is technically weak, but he seems to be a good supervisor. I would consider him in floor supervision or for a spot in our new Production Control Group. I talked with him a few weeks ago, but he didn't seem very interested."

Wilson (to himself)—

Bellman is still miffed at being passed over for Vice President—Operations. He is a good production man but lacks formal education. He would have difficulty managing my technical people.

Bellman (to himself)—

So, Ph.D. Wilson develops a product or two and they start grooming him for the top. I wonder how long he can work these problems out on his slide rule. The men's room scuttlebutt has it that the prima donna engineering types are looking to this Franklin decision as a test of Wilson's management ability. Good luck, Doctor Wilson.

Wilson conducted several additional discussions.

Carlson said:

"I've had no problems with Franklin, but then you (Dr. Wilson) did most of the liaison with him before your promotion. I don't think he fully carries his share though."

Sloan said:

"My complaint is a lack of technical writing. Franklin says it's getting diverted to Product Engineering. The work quality seems all right though. Mr. Maxey and Mr. Doyle are pretty sharp guys and are real assets to our company."

Aldrich said:

"Franklin is a friendly guy, but as an Industrial Management graduate, he just doesn't have enough technical background in electronics. Perhaps night school courses would help. I think the feelings of a new Engineering Manager should be given special consideration."

Cameron said:

"Franklin works relaxed. . .perhaps too relaxed. But he has management organization and personnel ability that puts most of us to shame. Several months ago I tried to talk two of his men into a transfer to Quality Assurance. I thought they would jump at the opportunity even though no raises were involved. Neither one left."

Wilson had been trained to be a logical person and was disturbed by the emotional way almost everyone had responded when the Franklin situation was discussed. Wilson wished he had more facts to work with but felt he had to take some type of action very soon.

Questions for Discussion

1. What would you do if you were Wilson?
2. What comments can you make about the behavior of:
   (a) Maxey? (b) Doyle? (c) Franklin? (d) Wilson?
3. Discuss the personnel effects of the organizational changes.
4. Is another organizational change in order?

CHAPTER 6

STAFFING

T he staffing function deals with the effective management of human resources both to achieve the objectives of the enterprise as well as to provide for the satisfaction and development of its employees. Thus, staffing encompasses all those activities necessary to ensure that the right people are in the right jobs at the right time. Implicit in the staffing function are the activities of planning, recruitment, selection and placement, orientation, evaluation, training and development, and compensation. This chapter helps you look more closely at some of these topics.

One of the most significant trends in recent years has been the post-World War II baby boom and the resulting movement of this generation into managerial positions. The rapid advances of earlier generations can affect the careers of younger men and women; therefore, the implications of these advances should be understood. The reading "When Ambition Is No Asset" gives you some ideas about how both women and men might be affected, as well as personal and personnel approaches for dealing with the impact of career "plateaus."

Of course, affirmative action programs have created a lot of pressure on management. In the case "The Derailed Career," you can explore whether affirmative action programs might have made a difference for one young manager.

With or without affirmative action programs, you will find that there are techniques useful in developing your own career. The "Personal Development" exercise is included here to give you some insights into your career preparation. Of course, there will be problems and readjustments along the way; at different stages of one's career certain problems appear. For example, young managers often experience anxiety and have difficulty making expectations fit with reality. Middle managers experience crises related to their personal lives and dreams. Recognizing and planning for these problems may help ease them.

Another important aspect of the staffing function is that of performance appraisal and promotion. The "Gobdel, Lee, and Page" case assesses the various factors underlying performance appraisal systems and the relative importance of these factors on promotions.

Effective staffing involves dealing with recruitment, training, and appraisal of personnel as well as peer and subordinate relationships. The "Brown Shoe and Volar Armies" case illustrates some of the difficulties an organization can face in these staffing activities when it shifts its goals and approach. Clearly this case points out that objectives of the organization can be accomplished through the staffing function, but that needs of employees must also be considered as training, recruiting, and appraisal programs are established to meet organizational goals. The case also shows how subordinate-superior relations can be affected when an organization makes major shifts in its staffing function.

In order for the staffing function to be performed effectively, firms must begin thinking of their employees as assets rather than only as costs. The last case in this chapter, "Aztec's Approach to Human Resource Accounting," provides you with an opportunity to gain some insights into this concept.

READING 41
WHEN AMBITION IS NO ASSET
Judith M. Bardwick

I'm 44. I think that's young. The prime of life, as a matter of fact. But right now I seem to be getting some kind of message. Oh, nobody has said anything outright. But, hell, Bob just got promoted to the head of the section, and he's only 36. I hate to have a kid over me. I have to admit that he is good. Real good. But I could have done that job. The truth is, I was sure I was going to get that spot. I've been in this job for over six years. The guy before me was promoted after only three. . .

There's talk about giving me a slot in San Francisco, but Marjorie and the kids would be really upset if we left New York. You know, they said it would be a "terrific opportunity" but I'm not really sure it's a promotion. There's more money in it, but the truth is, the work would be just the same—only in another city. . .

When I joined this company, it was terrific. I was promoted every few years, faster than anybody who started with me. I made more money than anybody my age. The sky was the limit. And I worked. Did I work! Nights, weekends. We moved four times in the first ten years. And it was worth it. . . .

Was it? Was it worth it? Hell, I don't know. Is this it? Am I on the shelf? Forty-four and gone as far as I'm going. I don't feel too good. As a matter of fact, I feel lousy.

This man is plateaued. What does that mean? If you are *structurally plateaued,* it means that promotions have ended. While your job may change, there will be no significant increases in responsibilities, status, money, or power as long as you remain in the same organization. Any future moves will be horizontal at best (and demotion is even a possibility). If you are *content plateaued,* it means that your work doesn't change much—it doesn't challenge you or require that anything new be learned.

In workshops on plateauing I have run for managers, there are moments when the tension is palpable. The room is silent, no one moves, and no one looks at

Source: Reprinted by permission from *New Management,* Vol. 1, No. 4, 1984.

anyone else. People sit rigidly as they think, "My God, they're talking about me." Closet fears—often expressed as hostile jokes—come out in the open.

Being plateaued is the cause of widespread (but generally unacknowledged) stress for people whose self-esteem depends upon success. The fear (or the fact) of being plateaued can result in hard times, especially for those whose careers were once fast-track, those who were once assured that they were the best and the brightest. Those are the people who may feel plateaued not only at work, but plateaued in life in general. Without the exhilaration of triumph at work, *nothing* feels exciting. Instead, life seems to be made up of routines, none of which provides any sense of vivid pleasure.

MANAGERIAL INTERVENTION

As the manager of plateaued people, when do you need to do or say something? You need to intervene whenever someone's productivity, involvement, and creativity fall off significantly. That often happens when people are under great stress, because when people are truly upset they have trouble managing anything other than their own emotions.

When being plateaued is the source of stress, then symptoms of the condition are likely to emerge at work. These symptoms can include coming late, leaving early, absenteeism, and frequent illness. Other symptoms are irritability and hypersensitivity to criticism. Sometimes people drink or smoke excessively. . .they may eat or sleep a lot or very little. . .their dress can change. Perhaps the most serious symptom is withdrawing from the job or from people. Any marked change in personality or behavior can be a symptom of major stress—for example, a sudden interest in philosophic questions such as "the meaning of life," or in pop-psychology. Classically, men have love affairs, usually with younger women. Currently, athletics has become a way of coping with stress. When it is used as a way of coping with life, it can lead to excessive behavior. We all know 50-year-old men who suddenly become marathon runners, transforming their frustrated competitiveness from work to the road.

Some symptoms of stress are easy to identify. But not everyone who is plateaued will be stressed, and plateauing is not the only cause of stress. And, in many cases, neither the stressed individual nor the person's superior is likely to recognize the most common and psychologically-efficient response to the chronic pain of being plateaued: The person increases the amount of time spent at work. Depressed and angry, the person works long hours—but doesn't work well.

WHAT THE BOSS NEEDS TO KNOW

Ambition is no asset when it cannot be fulfilled. Instead, it can become a burr, resulting in chronic dissatisfaction and feelings of frustration. Hence, those managers who regard promotion as the only significant reward are likely to become frustrated, because promotions end long before retirement for almost everyone. This structural plateauing is virtually inevitable because of "the Rule of 99%": Less than 1% of the people in an organization make it to the highest level of decision-making.

While most people know these odds, some persist in pursuing promotion right to the end of their careers. Such people tend to think of themselves as exceptions. That is, because they were successful at the beginning of their careers, they developed expectations that they would continue to climb. Very few of these managers will accept the fact that it is much easier to be promoted on the lower rungs of the organizational pyramid, because there are many more opportunities for promotion nearer the base, and a much greater breadth of ability among those with whom one is competing. The higher a manager climbs, the harder it becomes to look outstanding.

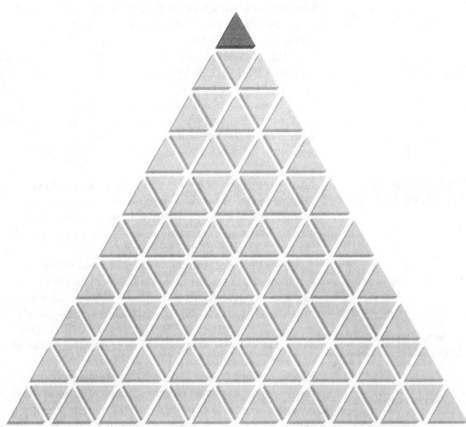

The Rule of 99%: Less than 1% of managers make it to the top of an organization

Further, promotion became the most important organizational reward during the past three decades because of a unique set of circumstances. Those who are now 45–60 years old were born around the time of the Great Depression. At that time, America had the lowest birth rate in its history. And when the Depression Kids went to work after World War II, they participated in the longest sustained economic boom America has ever had. As organizations expanded during this boom, a large number of promotional opportunities were created for a small number of people. As a result, managers were promoted at an unusually rapid pace. In addition, since prosperity continued for about 25 years, these unusual conditions came to be perceived as typical. Thus, a career of abnormally swift promotions came to be seen as normal.

Plateauing is now increasing because conditions in the 1980s are exactly the opposite. There are too many managers. By 1985, there will be a 45 percent increase in the number of people aged 30–39 (as compared with the preceding generation). While some members of the current generation have non-traditional values that are less dominated by the need for career success, that trait is *not* characteristic of those who have chosen to work in competitive organizations. In addition to the sheer number of people in their 30s, the number of managers in actual competition has increased greatly because of the reduction in discrimination against women and blacks. While members of these two groups did not constitute a significant part of the pool of managers before the mid-1970s, 20 percent of the MBA degrees that will be granted in 1985 will be earned by women and 5 percent by blacks.

Given the increasing number of those in the managerial pool—and the fact that the ranks of management are not expanding in most organizations—competitive pressures are likely to increase. Hence, while the average age of those who became structurally plateaued was about 45 in the late 1970s, today there are managers in their early 30s who are plateaued.

The population increase, the rising number of educated people, the stagnant economy, and certain aspects of technological change dictate that the high rates of promotion that once existed will not exist in the near future. Although promotions have been the major organizational reward for outstanding performance in expanding organizations, in the future promotions will be the exception rather than the rule.

One of the first traumas for those who were once successful in the promotion game is the realization that they are no longer regarded as exceptional. For those who were once treated as exceptions, being regarded as ordinary can be shattering. For those once regarded as promising, being seen as merely dependable and competent is a tremendous come-down.

PLATEAUED MEN

If the plateaued individual is an executive, his negative emotions may be increased by the responses of those he manages. A plateaued manager who occupies the same slot for a long time is often viewed as a "road block" by his subordinates. Plateaued managers are also frequently seen as powerless because they aren't able to do anything to help themselves. Put yourself in the shoes of such an executive. If the people who work for you think that you block their promotions, see you as powerless, and don't want to work for a loser—then their resentment will add to your negative self-esteem.

The managers who are most likely to become seriously alienated when promotions end are those who have been so well rewarded by the organization in the past that they let their lives become dominated by work. These people have no other emotional resources or significant activities from which they can derive good feelings about themselves. This typically happens to men in upper-middle to upper-level management—almost all of whom are married and are fathers and have a comfortable and comforting relationship with their wives and children. Psychologically, they *need* their families. But, for many, *passion* is restricted to work.

Most men whose work has dominated their lives inevitably come to feel that they gave less time and less emotional involvement to their wives and children than would have been ideal. It is very common for men to feel guilty about this. Guilt is especially likely if their children's lives did not turn out as they had hoped, if their marriage is comfortable but somewhat boring, or if their wives are unhappy. As men contemplate how they have spent their lives, it is no doubt the case that very few children or marriages or wives fulfill early expectations. Thus, adding disappointment with personal accomplishments to disappointment associated with work, a man may feel that he has failed in all the important aspects of his life.

Men have a special vulnerability when they can no longer feel successful through work. Masculinity is normally gained through success in competition, and work is the most important competitive arena for middle-class men. Masculinity has to be earned; it is not a quality that we attribute to men simply because they are male. In this society, the gut-level fear of plateaued men is that they are no longer men.

One of the most dramatic indications of the relationship between success at work and how men experience themselves can be found in their perceptions of how old they are. In interviews with men whose ages range from 36 to 59, I find that chronological age is *not* significant. Instead, the men who say, "I am plateaued," are the ones who say, "I am middle-aged." No matter what their actual age, those who are not plateaued and who expect further promotions usually say they are not middle-aged.

In my workshops, I often ask corporate managers how they spend their days. They usually say that they get to the office between 7:30 and 8:00 in the morning and return home at 7:00 or 7:30 at night. They frequently bring work home and, whether they do anything with it or not, work is on their minds. So even when they are not at work, they continue to think about it. What, then, is home? Home is the haven to which they repair before they go back into competition; home, which includes family, is terribly important, even when little attention is paid to it.

PLATEAUED WOMEN

In this regard, women managers are likely to have a vulnerability which most men do not. When I ask corporate men how many are married, about 95 percent will raise their hands. When I ask the same question of corporate women who are in middle management or above, the percentage who are married is very low. Census data tell us that the rates of "never marrying," "divorcing," and "remaining childless" are highest for women who are economically successful and who have five or more years of college. In brief, the chances are good that the plateaued, successful woman will realize that the cost to her of success was not, as it is for men, a *less-fulfilling* family life than might have been but, rather, *no* family at all. The gut-level fear of these women is that they might not be women.

Women who combine marriage, maternity, and a career are usually less vulnerable to the stress of plateauing. Women who continue to have their traditional home as well as job responsibilities do not focus on work as exclusively as men and unmarried women. Still, their lives are hardly free from stress. Since the social rules governing dual-career marriages are not really established, such marriages require continuous compromise and endless discussion about the division of responsibilities. That is a tense way to live. Thus, while these women are less likely to feel as angry as unmarried women when they plateau, the quality of their home lives will nonetheless have been affected by the demands of work. Like married men, married women, too, are likely to question the value of how they have spent their lives when they realize they are plateaued.

PLATEAUING AND SUPPORTIVE RELATIONSHIPS

Since most of the people in middle management and above are men, I've had more exposure to the problems of plateaued men than women. I find that those men who have emotionally-sustaining personal relationships do not necessarily have less need for recognition and success on the job. On the other hand, the absence of emotionally-affirming relationships usually relates to a very intense need for confirmation from the organization. Those men who seem unable to be emotionally close to anyone—wives, children, or friends—ask the organization for the good feelings about themselves they don't get elsewhere. Hence, while a workaholic may look like an organizational asset in the short run, in the long haul the organization will not be able to meet his emotional needs. Managers have to realize that meeting the needs of a workaholic requires more than a promotion—he needs insight into his problem and new sources of esteem and fulfillment.

WHAT CAN BE DONE?

While plateauing is a painful subject, it must be taken out of the closet. That's the responsibility of the manager of the plateaued individual. Being open about plateauing means encouraging managers at all levels to accept the reality that promotions do not go on forever. When confronted with this reality, it is possible that some very good people may decide to leave the organization. That is not a problem. The problem in most organizations is that there are too many good people to promote them all. The organization can afford to lose some good people. The organization can't afford to lose its stars. But there are very few stars, and they can be retained if they are well rewarded.

One way to reward them (everyone, really—not just stars) is to value their professionalism and competence. Since they must find pride in mastering their work and in learning new tasks without seeing this as an instrumental step to a promotion, their knowledge, wisdom, perspectives, skills, and experience have to be esteemed for themselves. In essence, corporations must be careful not to couple structural *and* content plateauing. Opportunities for the expansion of experience have to be available in the absence of opportunities for moving up in the hierarchy.

When managers are asked what is important to them in their jobs, their most frequent answers are "challenge and change." People say that they need to learn, to grapple, and to cope with *difficult* new problems that are important to the organization. The opportunity to do that is a major reward. Therefore, plateaued people should not be confined to the same task for so long that feelings of boredom replace their sense of mastery.

Plateaued managers should be encouraged to think about job changes. While an organization cannot promise that their wishes will always be granted, the objective should be to replace their passivity with activity. Passivity increases the sense of powerlessness, depression, and resentment. Activity generates a sense of mastery and optimism—as long as some positive change does, in fact, occur. For that reason, plateaued managers should be encouraged to think about what work alternatives might exist for them, what they might prefer to do, and how those changes could be created.

Organizations can use lateral transfers to alleviate the stress of content plateauing. In addition to the stimulation that such transfers generate, these job changes also assure people that the organization is confident that they can handle different responsibilities. Although changing people's jobs always involves some loss of productivity while new tasks are being mastered, the possibility of significantly increasing their involvement because of new challenges far outweighs this loss.

Lateral transfers should be thought of on three dimensions: horizontal, vertical, and in terms of time. The simplest changes are horizontal; people are transferred from one job to another.

More complex horizontal changes involve altering jobs. This can be designed so that new positions involve a combination of old and new responsibilities.

More elaborate changes can involve vertical as well as horizontal positions (if status differences are not great).

Finally, horizontal or vertical changes can vary from short-term assignments to permanent new positions.

In some organizations, it is appropriate to create teams to handle projects. Since members of a team have both common and unique skills, the group can handle a broader range of projects than can the same number of individuals working singly. Working in teams is a way to increase the amount of change in the content of tasks all group members do.

Organizations often choose to increase the rate of promotions by increasing the number of levels in the hierarchy. The alternative, of course, is to reduce the importance of promotions by reducing the number of levels in the hierarchy. The latter is usually a better strategy—for when there are fewer levels, power is distributed more horizontally than vertically and this lessens the importance of promotion. For example, a team is a small unit in which power is essentially horizontal. Being a member of a team can reduce the individual's need for promotion and for solo success.

It is crucial to pay constant attention to plateaued people, especially those who are so dependable that they tend to be taken for granted. To this end, an annual or biannual performance evaluation is inadequate in terms of frequency of feedback. Worse, performance reviews are often inadequate because many supervisors are uncomfortable conveying criticism, and thus they avoid saying anything negative. We all understand that people resent too much criticism. Less easily understood is the fact that people also resent it when they feel that they do not get *enough* criticism. They wonder: "If I am praised so much, and I'm as good as people say I am, why haven't I been more successful?"

Mostly, people feel anxious when they don't get critical feedback. Because they know they are not perfect, the absence of criticism leaves them uncertain about how they are really regarded. Most people want to know how they are really being judged and what their future is likely to be. Plateaued people, too, need that information.

Given the vulnerability of those whose psychological investments are restricted to work, corporations should be prepared to counsel people about personal issues, particularly if that can be done within the context of work. While management should not probe into personal lives, personal problems can easily affect the quality of work. For example, corporate counselors might give advice on participation in community organizations, in athletic activities, or on making more time for family and friends.

Organizations can prepare people financially and psychologically for early retirement. Since an enforced early retirement often generates bitter resentment, it is most desirable for people to volunteer to retire. That will only happen when there is a supportive program that enables people to see early retirement as an opportunity to begin a second career or to start a new life.

In essence, the organization can reduce the negative feelings of managers by giving them information about plateauing that lessens their sense of failure. Their uncertainty can be reduced by giving them candid evaluations. They can be remotivated by giving them challenging new work assignments that tell them the organization has confidence in their abilities. They can be encouraged to increase other involvements. All of this gives them the message that they are valued.

Those who are depressed about being plateaued are trying to redefine ambition. The decline of ambition is usually seen in the negative—as giving something up. This has to be transformed into the positive—as the possibility to gain aspects of the self and of life which one didn't have before.

Since plateauing is inevitable for all but the one percent, the organizational climate has to change so that it becomes permissible to say, "I like my job and I do it well. I'm willing to work hard, but work won't run my life any more. I've got some other things I need to do."

Organizations benefit when they remove (or prevent) the stigma of failure and the despair of frustration among their plateaued managers. The necessary first step is for the organization to acknowledge the problem. Only then can the issues be confronted and resolved. I have never held a workshop on plateauing that didn't begin with palpable tension. But then, I never held a workshop that didn't end optimistically—with great relief.

Questions for Discussion

1. What does it mean to be plateaued? What is the difference between being structurally plateaued and being content plateaued?

2. What are the similarities and differences between plateaued men and plateaued women?

3. Why are promotions not as frequent in the 1980s as they were thirty years ago?

4. What can corporations do about plateaued managers who are considered needed by the organization?

CASE 42
THE DERAILED CAREER

Joanne Bradwell, 28 years old, obtained her MBA degree from a prestigious midwestern university about three and one-half years ago. Soon after her graduation she was hired by a medium-sized, highly profitable investment banking firm. She, along with five other recent graduates, was assigned to a management training program to work in problem areas with trained managers who would direct their program and supervise their work. Initially, the experienced managers were concerned about whether Joanne would work out well in an environment consisting of an all-male managerial staff. Their concerns were quickly allayed as Joanne's peers and supervisors grew to respect her capabilities, and even the female secretaries, who originally resented her managerial role, came to like and respect her. It seemed obvious to everyone that Joanne was headed for success.

When the training program was completed, Joanne was assigned as assistant to Jim Holland, the manager of the acquisitions department. Joanne was pleased with the assignment as she had particularly enjoyed working in this department during her training period, and Jim had evaluated her work very positively during that time.

However, in less than a year Joanne began to have serious doubts about her potential for future advancement in this organization. Conversations with some of her colleagues from the training program indicated that they had continued to receive challenging assignments and that the decisions that they were making were giving them significant visibility in the company. One of the five had already been promoted to a department manager and two others had received transfers to other parts of the organization where promotional opportunities seemed imminent.

Looking back, Joanne thought to herself, "All I've done in this year is analyze data and generate voluminous reports which allow others to make the decisions critical to the organization. I've got to talk this situation over with Jim," she thought, "but he's become so distant over this past year I'm just not sure how to broach the situation."

Jim, meanwhile, was having some thoughts of his own about Joanne as he sat at his desk preparing annual performance reviews. "Joanne is an extremely competent assistant. She's a real pro at generating and synthesizing all the data I need to make decisions. Some of her recommendations even have a lot of merit, but I'd sure be hesitant to have her interact with important customers. I just don't think she'd come across well with them. I suppose I ought to talk to her about that but maybe it's not worth mentioning to her since it's doubtful she's really serious about a career with us anyway. Rumor has it she'll be getting married soon and then it's only a matter of time until children come along."

Questions for Discussion

1. Is Joanne being discriminated against? If so, how?
2. Where did Jim, Joanne, and/or the organization go wrong in this situation?
3. Would affirmative action programs have helped Jim and Joanne?
4. If you were Joanne, what would you do in this situation?

EXERCISE 43
PERSONAL DEVELOPMENT

The purpose of this inventory is to give you an outline for looking at your life goals systematically. Your concern here should be to describe as fully as possible your aims and goals in all areas of your life. Consider all goals that are important to you, whether they are relatively easy or difficult to attain. Be honest with yourself. Having fun and taking life easy are just as legitimate life goals as being president. You will have a chance to rate the relative importance of your goals later. Now you should try to just discover all of the things that are important to you.

LIFE GOAL INVENTORY

To help make your inventory complete, we have listed general goal areas on the following pages. They are:

1. Career satisfaction
2. Status and respect
3. Personal relationships
4. Leisure satisfactions
5. Learning and education
6. Spiritual growth and religion
7. Others

These categories are only a general guide; feel free to change or redefine them in the way that best suits *your own life*. The unlabeled area is for whatever goals you think of that do not seem to fit into the other categories.

Directions: First fill out your own goals in the various sections of this inventory, making any redefinitions of the goal areas you feel necessary. Ignore for the time being the three columns on the right-hand side of each page. Directions for filling out these columns follow goal set G.

A. Career Satisfaction
General Description: Your goals for your future job or career, including specific positions you want to hold:

Individual Redefinition:

Specific Goals	Importance (H,M,L)	Ease of attainment (H,M,L))	Conflict with other goals (yes or no)

Source: From Kolb, Rubin, and McIntyre, *Organizational Psychology: An Experiential Approach,* 2d ed. © 1974, pp. 277–290. Reprinted by permission of Prentice-Hall, Inc., Englewood Cliffs, New Jersey.

B. Status and Respect
   General Description: To what groups do you want to belong? What are your goals in these groups? To what extent do you want to be respected by others? From whom do you want respect?

Individual Redefinition:

Specific Goals	Importance (H,M,L)	Ease of attainment (H,M,L))	Conflict with other goals (yes or no)

C. Personal Relationships
   General Description: Goals in your relationships with your colleagues, parents, friends, people in general.

Individual Redefinition:

Specific Goals	Importance (H,M,L)	Ease of attainment (H,M,L))	Conflict with other goals (yes or no)

D. Leisure Satisfactions
   General Description: Goals for your leisure time and pleasure activities—hobbies, sports, vacations; interests you want to develop.

Individual Redefinition:

Specific Goals	Importance (H,M,L)	Ease of attainment (H,M,L))	Conflict with other goals (yes or no)

E. Learning and Education
   General Description: What would you like to know more about? What skills do you want to develop? To what formal education do you aspire?

Individual Redefinition:

Specific Goals	Importance (H,M,L)	Ease of attainment (H,M,L))	Conflict with other goals (yes or no)

F. Spiritual Growth and Religion
General Description: Goals for peace of mind, your search for meaning, your relation to the larger universe, religious service, devotional life.

Individual Redefinition:

Specific Goals	Importance (H,M,L)	Ease of attainment (H,M,L))	Conflict with other goals (yes or no)

G. Others

Definition:

Specific Goals	Importance (H,M,L)	Ease of attainment (H,M,L))	Conflict with other goals (yes or no)

I. Directions for Rating Goals

Goal Importance: Now that you have completed the inventory, go back and rate the importance of each goal according to the following scheme:
H—Compared to my other goals, this goal is very important.
M—This goal is moderately important.
L—A lot of other goals are more important than this one.

Ease of Goal Attainment: According to the following scheme, rate each goal on the probability that you will reach and/or maintain the satisfaction derived from it.
H—Compared with my other goals, I easily reach and maintain goal.
M—I reach and maintain the goal with moderate difficulty.
L—It would be very difficult to reach this goal.

Goal Conflict: In the last rating space, write whether or not (Yes or No) the goal is in conflict with any of your goals. Then fill out the Goal Conflicts form.

II. Goal Conflicts

List the goals that are in conflict with one another. Which ones are the most serious? Which will require your personal attention to be resolved?

1.

2.

3.

4.

5.

III. Life Goal Focus

1. At this point, see if you can focus on a single, top priority goal for your future. To do this, develop a fantasy about your future life. You might use one of the following formats:

   a. Write your own eulogy. This should not be a newspaper obituary, but a eulogy spoken at your funeral by a friend who knew you well.

   b. Describe a newspaper or magazine article written about you five or ten years from now.

2. Identify the major goal that is expressed by your fantasy. Now examine these goals in terms of the following issues:

   a. How realistic is the goal given your abilities and resources?

   b. What are the key subgoals required to achieve the long-term goal?

IV. The Goal Achievement Plan

1. From the inventory pick the goal you most want to work on in the *next six months*. In choosing this goal, you should consider the following issues. [See the ratings you made of goals and goal conflict (I, II).]

   a. Importance of the goal

   b. Ease of attainment

   c. Whether the goal is in conflict with other goals (and would therefore require working on those other goals)

2. The goal you choose to work on may include two or three of the goals you listed on the inventory. The main thing is to get clearly in mind what future state you are striving for. To do this, complete the goal definition form.

GOAL DEFINITION FORM

State as exactly as possible what goal you want to achieve in the *next six months*.

_____

_____

_____

Now think about your goal in terms of the following questions. How important is it that you achieve your goal?

_____

_____

_____

How does this goal relate to your long-term goals? What conflicts are there?

_____

_____

_____

What do you think about your chances of succeeding? What will happen if you do succeed? What will happen if you fail?

_____

_____

_____

How will you feel when you attain this goal? (Try to imagine yourself with the goal achieved. What are your feelings?)

_____

_____

_____

How will you feel if you do not attain this goal? (Try to imagine again. What are your feelings?)

_____

_____

_____

3. Now that you have defined your goal, the next step is to plan how to achieve it. There are four issues to be examined.

   a. Personal shortcomings to overcome
   b. Obstacles in the world to overcome
   c. Actions that you can take to achieve your goal
   d. Help you can get from others

The first two categories refer to things which can prevent you from reaching your goal. The last two categories refer to things which you and others can do to achieve your goal.

The diagram that follows illustrates how these fit into the goal achievement plan. At the top of the diagram is your goal. The circle in the middle of the diagram represents your self now. Your personal shortcomings and obstacles in the world are forces that are keeping you

My Goal
How important is it?
How does it relate to my long-term goals?
How will I feel if I attain it?
How will I feel if I do not attain it?
What are my chances of success?

Personal Shortcomings

Obstacles in the World

My Self Now

Your Actions

Help from Others

from moving toward your goal. Your plan should try to accomplish two things:

- To reduce the personal shortcomings and world obstacle forces which keep you from your goal.
- To increase the force of your actions and help from others.

The questions on the Removing Obstacles Form and the Planning Action Form which follow are designed to help you accomplish this.

REMOVING OBSTACLES

What personal shortcomings will keep me from achieving my goal?

1.

2.

3.

4.

What obstacles in the world will keep me from achieving my goal?

1.

2.

3.

4.

What can I do to eliminate or lessen the effect of any of these obstacles or shortcomings? (Note that you need not eliminate the block entirely. Anything you can do to lessen the force of the obstacle will start you moving toward your goal).

Obstacle   What can I do about it?

_____   _____

_____   _____

_____   _____

_____   _____

_____   _____

_____   _____

_____   _____

**PLANNING
ACTION**

What specific things can I do which will move me toward my goal?

1. _____

_____

_____

2. _____

_____

3. _____

_____

_____

4. _____

_____

_____

5. _____

_____

_____

Circle the one which you are going to emphasize the most.

Who can help me achieve my goals? What will I ask of them?

_____

_____

_____

_____

1. _____ _____

_____

_____

_____

_____

2. _____ _____

_____

_____

_____

_____

3. _____ _____

V. Achievement Progress Record Form

Now that you have made your plan, the next thing to do is to put it into effect. The Achievement Progress Record is designed to help you keep a weekly record of your progress toward your goal. This record has two purposes:

1. It will give you an indication of where you stand; whether you are ahead or behind schedule in achieving your goal.

2. It will serve as a constant reminder of your goal and your desire to achieve it.

MEASURING YOUR PROGRESS

To accomplish the first purpose it is necessary that you define for your self just how you can *measure* progress toward your goal. The graph on the following page lists the next twenty-five weeks along the bottom line. The left-hand side of the graph is anchored at the base by your position now. The top of the line represents your goal. You need to decide what units will indicate your progress up to this line toward your goal. For some goals this is easy, e.g., if your goal is to get better grades you might want to indicate hours of study per week on the graph. Other goals are more difficult to measure.

For these you may want to indicate each week what percent of the total plan you have completed. You may want to keep more than one graph to record each of the actions you plan to use in achieving your goal. *Record in the space on the left of the chart how you plan to measure progress toward your goal.*

ACHIEVEMENT PROGRESS RECORD FORM

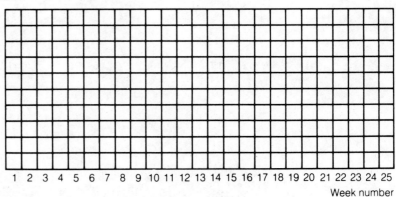

My achievement goal
is fully accomplished

1 2 3 4 5 6 7 8 9 10 11 12 13 14 15 16 17 18 19 20 21 22 23 24 25

Distance
from my goal
when I started to
work toward it

Week number

CASE 44
GOBDEL, LEE, AND PAGE

This incident and case takes place in Honolulu, Hawaii. Gobdel, Lee, and Page (GLP) is an international public accounting firm and, as such, has offices and affiliates located throughout the world. Larger firms such as GLP audit 80 percent or more of the firms listed with the U. S. Securities and Exchange Commission.

Certified public accounting firms have a number of functions. Usually, 60 percent of their business is auditing; that is, the firm independently examines the records and other supporting documents which companies have used to prepare their financial statements. As a result of their investigation, they offer an opinion of the financial statements, that is, on their preparation in accordance with generally accepted accounting principles applied on a consistent basis. The remaining 40 percent of the business involves accounting services such as the installation of computerized accounting systems and preparation of tax returns. The Honolulu office has its personnel divided into three areas: audit (60 percent), administrative services (accounting systems) (15 percent), and tax (25 percent). One third of the audit division specializes in small business auditing and managerial advice.

While GLP has offices worldwide, its home office is located in New York. It has about 50 offices in the United States (one of which is in Honolulu) and 50 outside the United States. All offices operate similarly, offering the same services and the same quality. The firm has a standardized set of operating procedures and rules which are set by the home office. GLP is a partnership. There are about 500 partners around the world.

Most public accounting firms have four professional levels: partners, managers, seniors, and juniors. The Honolulu office has the following number of professionals: 4 partners (one of whom is designated managing partner), 8 managers, 10 seniors, and 14 juniors. Each partner has absolute authority and responsibility over "his" clients. Every partner of the firm is a general partner and participates in the firm's managerial decision. The more responsibility and seniority, the more influence individual partners tend to have.

Although there are exceptions, public accounting firms do not normally grow in size by merger of CPA firms, as often happens in industry. In contrast, they grow as their clients grow. Many clients "outgrow" their local CPA firm's services and switch to larger regional or international firms such as GLP.

Firms such as GLP are compensated by their clients based on a fixed fee; that is, the firm estimates the number of hours it will take to perform the audit and charges a fee based on these hours times a billing rate per hour. To reduce the fee, clients put pressure on the firm to perform the audit in shorter periods of time. Lurking in the background is the possible loss of the account. However, a few major clients do, in fact, switch CPA firms.

This client pressure plus the desire of the partnership for greater profitability translates into a general awareness and concern for time in CPA firms. Time pressure becomes a pressure to reduce the time officially spent on the job by juniors and seniors who do most of the field work. Time budgets expressed in terms of hours per step are set for each step of the audit. Often, these budgets are "ideal" times and leave no margin for unexpected problems. Because of

Source: By Kurt E. Chaloupecky, Department of Accounting, Southwest Missouri State University, and William F. Glueck. From W. F. Glueck, *Cases and Exercises in Personnel.* Copyright Business Publications, Inc. 1978. All rights reserved.

career pressures, no one admits that the time budgets are "challenging." When an accountant gets behind, he often works overtime without charging for it. Charging for it would be an admission that one could not meet the goals. Unofficially, some seniors expect juniors, while charging a normal eight-hour day, to work from eight until six o'clock, with as little time off for lunch as possible.

The time pressure becomes most serious during the first four months of the calendar year because of audit report and tax return deadlines. It is not atypical for a senior to accumulate (over and above overtime not charged) 600 hours of overtime per year. The majority of these hours are accumulated during the busy season. It is not uncommon for seniors and juniors to work 80 hours per week to complete audit and tax reports on time. Twelve-hour days, seven days a week, become burdensome by April 15. Overtime expectation is reinforced by values associated with being a "professional accountant." This takes professional dedication indeed.

GLP's concept of professionalism includes total dedication to the profession and the firm. Hours of work are not to be questioned because such questions are considered unprofessional. Preparation for training meetings is expected to be done by the employee on his own time. He is also expected to prepare for the CPA examination on his own time. Overtime or out-of-town assignments are made with little or no advance notice. Personal inconvenience is not important to a truly professional individual.

GLP'S PROMOTION ARRANGEMENT

Professional accountants are recruited by GLP at college campuses. All except a few lawyers and computer specialists have degrees in accounting. International firms such as GLP pay handsome salaries. Indeed, GLP considers a portion of the salary paid during the first three years of employment to be an investment which hopefully will provide future dividends. Smaller local or regional firms cannot afford to make such an investment.

To assure that only the best accountants are promoted to partner, an "up or out" system has been developed. It is expected that anyone who is to remain with GLP must pass the CPA examination. Roughly 25 percent of the candidates sitting for the exam pass. Secondly, a time frame for each level is set. Unless you make partner by age 35, or shortly thereafter, you will basically never make it. Thus the upwardly mobile accountant must pass through all four levels in about 13 years. Although all promotions come from within, GLP prides itself on not being tied to seniority. Merit alone is rewarded. Typically 25 percent of newly hired juniors are weeded out within two years. Salaries generally reflect the evaluation of the accountant. If one does not get a good raise, one is being told something. Over an eight-year period, less than 20 percent of those hired are retained by the firm.

Professional development continues at all levels as all experiences are considered to be learning experiences. Juniors are assigned to a variety of seniors to aid in the audit. This allows the junior to receive wide experience and to be widely evaluated. His or her work is reviewed by the senior, then the senior's manager, and finally by the partner in charge of the client. At each level a point sheet is prepared indicating additions or corrections needed, as seen by each level of the hierarchy. These corrections or additional comments are returned to the lower levels of the hierarchy to be cleared and thus become a learning experience. Corrections and additions are reviewed and approved through the same chain of command.

After each assignment, the supervising senior and manager write a written evaluation of the work of the junior or senior under his or her immediate supervision. This evaluation covers not only technical competence, but also subjective factors such as judgment, imagination, leadership, and resourcefulness.

Thus the firm creates multiple evaluations of each person. However, part of these evaluations are indeed subjective.

The subjectivity may be reinforced by the social system at GLP. Juniors and seniors work primarily in the field at the client's office. They go to lunch together, and when on out-of-town assignments, it is expected that one take dinner with the group and afterwards have a few drinks with the others. Partners and, to a lesser extent, managers, work primarily in the firm's office. They, therefore, spend more time together, go to lunch together, and so forth.

HARRISON HAMILL

The case of Harrison Hamill who experienced such a promotion system is worth considering. Harrison Hamill graduated from a mainland private college in accounting with an A average. Wishing to specialize in tax accounting, he took his first job with the Internal Revenue Service for two years. He visited at GLP whenever home in Honolulu, and it became clear that he would like to work with them. They offered him a position. At age 23, he was hired by GLP.

Hamill worked very hard. At age 25 he was made a senior. He helped bring in a fair amount of tax business, but most of it was small business, not the prestigious accounts the partners usually seek. He moved ahead reasonably well and passed his CPA exam at age 26. He was concerned that he might not make partner, for tax accounting is off the mainstream of auditing. However, he socialized with others in the firm as much as he could, worked hard, and minded his own business.

Hamill kept his options open, however. He went to many events—alumni and others—to broaden his circle of friends. But at age 34 he knew he wasn't going to make it. Little signs were given: office size, raises, invitations not extended. Quietly, he visited smaller firms and eventually joined one that made him a partner. There were two other partners and a few juniors. Hamill actually took a compensation cut to do this, but he felt he had no real choice. At best he could have stayed on as a "lesser being," a manager with only cost of living raises. However, even this position could not be considered permanent.

Hamill wondered where he had gone wrong. Was it when he turned down a transfer opportunity to Los Angeles? Did he unintentionally send a signal that he wasn't willing to pay the price? Should he have transferred to the auditing division? Was tax accounting too far off the mainstream? He wondered why there had to be an up-or-out system and why at age 35. To his nonaccountant friends, he explained that he wanted to strike off on his own and stop being an organization man. But his accountant friends knew what really happened.

Hamill was told, when he asked, that he was pleasant, competent, and a good tax man. But that his evaluations indicated he lacked complete dedication to GLP.

Questions for Discussion

1. Do rigid up-or-out cutoffs make sense in promotions?
2. Does GLP consider its cost of turnover, or are they really exploiting these juniors to save money?
3. How can firms avoid allowing irrational personnel factors to influence their promotion decisions?
4. What did Harrison Hamill do wrong?

CASE 45

THE BROWN SHOE AND VOLAR ARMIES

PREFACE

This case describes the transition in training and disciplinary methods that the Army followed between 1971 and 1973. The transition came about as a result of President Nixon's effort to have an all Volunteer Army by 1973. The changes began in June of 1971, and were still being carried out at the training centers, and military installations throughout the country as of the time of this case, 1973.

The casewriter was involved in the change, being introduced on April 7, 1971, and taking basic training under the "old style" training, and then in June of 1971, he was assigned to an Advanced Infantry Training company that was taking part in the new approach that was being called the "Volar Concept," which was an abbreviation for Volunteer Army.

PART I—THE BROWN SHOE ARMY

The term "Brown Shoe Army" comes from career non-commissioned officers (NCO) to the type of training that was formerly used. This term is very appropriate, because it encompasses all of the exercises a soldier was required to do. Some of these were long forced marches, low crawling through sand and dirt, or running from place to place in sandy, rocky terrain. All of these had the effect of turning a soldier's boots brown.

Under the Old Army training doctrine, a recruit was nothing, and should be treated as such. In many training centers they were required to wear a white tag over their name tag to denote them as a new "trainee." This was called a "maggot tag." The Drill Sergeants referred to individuals as maggots, and treated them as such. They would only talk to maggots when the maggots did something wrong, and then only at the top of their lungs. Many recruits were afraid of their Drill Sergeants, as it was not uncommon to "fall down the stairs" if there was disfavor with a Drill Sergeant. To "fall down the stairs" referred to getting roughed up, or beaten up. This used to be a common occurrence in the army. If a recruit were to blame a Drill Sergeant, the recruit would only be asking for more trouble. Drill Sergeants were not authorized to touch a soldier, but the rule was seldom enforced by an officer. This fear, or respect for authority, was the desired effect of this threat of punishment. The sergeants wanted the recruit to do whatever they said, no matter how inconsequential it might seem at the time the order was given.

Life in the barracks, as was the entire military, was very structured. Everything had a place, and everything must be in that place. Each locker had to be set up in the prescribed military manner. This was called the SOP, or Standard Operating Procedure. The military had a SOP for everything that could ever possibly occur. The lockers were subject to inspection at all times. All socks, t-shirts, underwear, and handkerchiefs were to be an exact size, and occupying a certain portion of a locker. The rest of a recruits clothes were to hang in a certain order, and all of the field gear was to be arranged in a precise manner. All of this was subject to inspection, and if a locker was not found in order, the unlucky recruit was usually assigned extra duty of some sort: Kitchen police (KP

Source: Adapted from a course assignment prepared by Daniel McGill for Professor J. G. Hunt. Used with permission.

meant working in the kitchen for one additional day over the required days), guard duty, or C.Q. runner (the Charge of Quarters runner who stayed up all night with the Charge of Quarters NCO). This NCO was in charge of the company in the absence of the company commander.

The meals were very good, or at least tasted good to the trainee. During the first eight weeks, the trainee was allowed no "snacks" from home, or the Post Exchange (PX), or anything but army food. The discipline in the dining hall was very strict, with no idle conversation or smoking allowed after the meal. The theme was get in, eat, and get out, as quickly as possible. Some soldiers had to stand at parade rest (a military position) while waiting in line, although this was the exception, not the rule.

The training received in the army was a type of programmed learning. The periods were broken down into blocks of instruction, each aimed at bringing the recruits to a certain level of achievement. As an example, in three hours a recruit could be taught to disassemble and assemble an M-16 rifle in three minutes. Until the time of the class, the recruit was unfamiliar with the rifle. One drawback was that there was no room for the individual to show creativity, or excel above the class. Any behavior of this type resulted in punishment, rather than reward. Many individuals resented this type of instruction because they were used to learning at a faster rate and under a different system.

All learning was task related, and many people wondered whether it was the instruction that they learned from, or the constant repetition. Again, there were the pressures by the Drill Sergeants for the trainee to perform the tasks as required, nothing more, and nothing less.

The casewriter was only trained in the use of infantry equipment. However, from talking to other recruits, it was learned that the training for any of the army's MOS's (Military Occupation Skills) from heavy equipment to dental assistant, was conducted in this manner. Another facet of training was that wherever the company went, the soldiers walked, ran, or forced marched. This was a part of the physical training that recruits went through to get in top shape. There were approximately two-hours per day devoted to physical training, and the running and walking were an added touch. At the end of the eight-week cycle, a soldier was in excellent physical condition.

There were many times during the training cycle when an individual was put to a stress test. This could come in many ways, such as keeping a troop up all night training, and then continuing training the next day. The usual tension, coupled with the fatigue would make people react in different ways than they normally would. Then the troops were watched, and if anyone made a mistake, that person was singled out, reprimanded, or pushed a bit. The instructors were looking for the soldier who relaxed, and then couldn't react under stress. This was to weed out many people that were unable to cope with army life, or should definitely not be assigned to a position of responsibility.

During the long eight weeks of basic training, the recruits were not allowed off the post. This was never explained to the soldiers, it was just an accepted fact. Recruits could go to movies on post, but not off post. This did not bother most trainees, but some would try to sneak off post, and this resulted in severe punishment. All punishment came from a soldier's company commander, after apprehension by the Military Police (MP).

The role of the officer and NCO's in the army was somewhat similar. Both were task-oriented, but the methods used to achieve this task were the main difference. The enlisted recruits had more contact with the NCO's than the officers. This follows the pattern of the entire army. The officers were there to see that the procedures were followed, but had little contact. The NCO's had the job of training the recruits. The mannerisms of the NCO's were very gruff and "hardcore" to use an army term. Many of the NCO's were not too much older than the recruits, but really tried to throw their weight around. This similarity in ages has plagued the Army for many years, with no solution in sight.

The basic training in the "old army" was hard, but when a soldier completed it, that soldier had a good knowledge of the army, how it functioned, and was ready to proceed on to the next training assignment.

PART II—THE VOLAR ARMY

The phrase "VOLAR" comes from the new Volunteer Army program the army embarked upon in early 1971. Under this program, there was the idea that a recruit should be treated as a soldier immediately upon entry into the army. The trainee recruit, and the recruit's rights were respected, and the "maggot" tags were done away with. The recruits, or trainees as they were now called, were still told to do things, but often there was an explanation offered. At this time the army was instituting a new motivation program, along with other programs in related areas. A trainee's effort and performance was evaluated each day by a Drill Sergeant. There was a point system to reward the soldier for making his bed, going to training, and performing the assigned tasks. The maximum number of points for one week was twenty-five, and various rewards were given for set point values. As an example, 23 points would earn the trainee a two-day and night pass. It would start on Friday after training, and run until 10:00 P.M. Sunday night, with unlimited restrictions on travel. If the trainee earned 19 points there was only a one day and night pass. This appeared to change the attitude of many of the people in the casewriter's company. Before this addition, they did things because they were told directly to do them, and were afraid of the consequences. Now, they did the same tasks, but because of a new inward motivation, and the possibility of a reward. A lot of the complaining and griping stopped, and was replaced with talk about the weekends and what each person was going to do with time off. The instant respect of authority, and discipline seemed to suffer under this approach, but morale appeared higher. Now, the only motivating factor for the trainees was the points to be earned. No longer did they react because of orders from higher ranking individuals, trainees became concerned with the benefits in terms of points.

Life in the barracks, under the VOLAR system was quite different from the system used in basic training. The locker inspections and SOP were replaced by the phrase, "must be clean and orderly." There were no locker inspections at all, so it really didn't matter. Most lockers were pretty messy under this rule. The areas that were lived in still had to be kept clean, but since the points that were earned were dependent upon this, there was no problem. One addition to the barracks' day room was a beer machine. This was called the "VOLAR" machine by most recruits, and was used quite heavily during the course of an evening. There were also soft drink and candy machines added. These appeared to increase morale, but also appeared to decrease the physical condition of the users.

The meals were essentially the same under the VOLAR system, but the atmosphere in the dining hall was now relaxed. The rule of eating in military attire only was dropped, and the no-smoking rule was dropped. The only change in the menu was the addition of hamburgers and hotdogs to the noon meal. This was the army's idea of giving the trainee what it was thought was wanted. This was warmly accepted by the recruits.

The training methods remained essentially the same. The only addition was more breaks during the training sessions. Class would be held for one hour, and then a fifteen minute break would be given. During the breaks, snack trucks, or "hoagie" trucks would come by selling drinks and sandwiches. The only other change was in the method of getting to and from the training site. Recruits were repeatedly bussed, or trucked to the same areas they had walked to in earlier days. Also, the rule of running from place to place was dropped. The whole atmosphere seemed to change from rigid military to hard Boy Scouts.

The individual soldier was still put to the stress test, but was given a much easier time than before. The role of the Drill Sergeant changed from being an unapproachable, figure of authority, to that of a counselor who would talk to recruits, and try to help them with their problems. With this change many people who were not able to cope with the stress, or responsibility went by unnoticed.

In talking to many of the people who had gone through this new system of training, the casewriter found that a number of them did not feel qualified to act as a combat soldier. This thought was echoed by the career NCO's whom the casewriter worked with and talked to during his time in the army. These people indicated that the soldier that was trained in an atmosphere as permissive as VOLAR didn't perform in a combat situation. These career NCO's had been in Vietnam, and had seen both types of soldiers in action. The view given to the casewriter by them was that this type of training is all right for a loose, peacetime army, but for an army to go to war, we will need a highly trained, cohesive group of men, who will obey orders and not question them. The problem of questioning orders came up quite often during the latter years of the Vietnam war. In a close situation, the lives of all the men might depend on one man carrying out a specific order.

The opinion of the career NCO's, and officers is that the army will have to revert to the former standards and training methods if it is going to be an effective deterrent to a foreign power. Presently, the army is yielding to the pressure to be all volunteer. Is the army too lax? Did it make a mistake in pursuing the VOLAR course of action?

Questions for Discussion

1. How can the army improve its training and development techniques?
2. Is performance evaluation a major issue in this case?
3. How can the army overcome its problem of similarity in ages between its recruits and non-commissioned officers?
4. How should the army motivate its new recruits?
5. Should the army relax its training method in order to improve recruitment of new soldiers?
6. Is the stress test a good method for selection and placement of personnel?

CASE 46
AZTEC'S APPROACH TO HUMAN RESOURCE ACCOUNTING

The Aztec Corporation, founded in 1965, manufactures cosmetics and hair products for men and women. The corporation experienced substantial growth during the 1970s, opening numerous branches and subsidiaries throughout the United States. Realizing the significance of its "people," Aztec became interested in the concept of human-resource accounting. The accompanying Figure 1 is an excerpt from the corporation's 1985 annual report and is supplementary to the usual audited financial statements. The annual report explains:

FIGURE 1

AZTEC CORPORATION AND SUBSIDIARIES

Balance Sheet	1985 Conventional and Human Resource	1985 Conventional Only
Assets		
Total current assets	$16,830	$16,830
Net property, plant, and equipment	4,300	4,300
Excess of purchase price over net assets acquired	1,555	1,555
Deferred financing costs	210	210
Net investments in human resources	2,004	—
Prepare income taxes and other assets	260	260
	$25,159	$23,155
Liabilities and Stockholders' Equity		
Total current liabilities	$ 4,005	$ 4,005
Long-term debt, excluding current installments	6,923	6,923
Deferred compensation	150	150
Deferred income tax based upon full tax deduction for human resource costs	1,002	—
Stockholders' equity:		
Capital stock	1,725	1,725
Additional capital in excess of par value	5,499	5,499
Retained earnings:		
Financial	4,853	4,853
Human resources	1,002	—
	$25,159	$23,155
Income Statement		
Net sales	$45,221	$45,221
Cost of sales	29,541	29,541
Gross profit	$15,680	$15,680
Selling, general and administrative expense	11,653	11,653
Operating income	$ 4,027	$ 4,027
Interest expense	628	628
Income before taxes	$ 3,399	$ 3,399
Net increase in human resource investment	208	—
Adjusted income before income taxes	$ 3,607	$ 3,399
Income taxes	1,828	1,828
Net income	$ 1,779	$ 1,571

(000s deleted, so totals may appear slightly inaccurate.)

Human-resource accounting is an attempt to identify, quantify, and report investments made in recruiting, acquiring, training, familiarizing, and developing people. Outlay costs connected with these activities are accumulated and capitalized where they are expected to have value beyond the current accounting period. The basic outlays in connection with acquiring and integrating new people are amortized over their expected tenure with the company. Investments made for training or development are amortized over a much shorter period of time. Total write-off of an individual's account occurs upon his departure from the company.

Questions for Discussion

1. Were there more write-offs of human assets during 1985 than new investments? Explain, using the numbers given in the exhibit.

2. Why do you think that advocates of human-resource accounting prefer such a formal approach instead of less formal measures like employee-attitude surveys, employee-turnover measures, absenteeism, and similar measures?

3. Do you support the use of human-resource accounting? Explain your position.

LEADING AND INTERPERSONAL INFLUENCE WITH GROUPS AND INDIVIDUALS

W

hat makes some people great leaders? Are they born leaders? Does the environment spawn them to fill a gap? Such ideas have generally been dismissed. How, then, do people become leaders?

Leadership, or influencing people effectively, is a function of the leader, the work group, and the situation. It is defined as a set of interpersonal behaviors designed to influence employees to cooperate in the achievement of objectives. We might try to explain it as an influence derived from sources of power the individual may possess including:

- **Legitimate power**—formal authority conferred by the organization.
- **Monetary/reward power**—granting or withholding financial reward.
- **Skill/expertise power**—influence based on skill and competence.
- **Affection power**—ability to get others to like you.
- **Respect power**—influence based on respect.
- **Rectitude power**—influence based on setting a moral example.
- **Coercive power**—physical, often negative, influence such as threatening to fire an employee.

The more sources a leader can draw on, the more influence that person will have. The exercise "Power and Influence" is included here to help you examine your own attitudes about power and to determine whether you respond to some of these sources of power more than others. The "Joe Schultz" case also gives you a chance to analyze a problem situation from the perspective of power and influence. This is one important aspect of leadership. Another is the selection of a leadership style.

The reading by Tannenbaum and Schmidt gives you a classic description of "How to Choose a Leadership Pattern." No doubt you have heard many professors use the phrase "It all depends. . ." That is not just the easy way out when the answer is unknown. There are several styles of leadership, and no one way is best under all conditions. The trick is to know what will determine the "best

● LEARNING OBJECTIVES

Leadership will be important to your managerial career. We hope this chapter will:

1. Give you an understanding of how different sources of power aid in developing influence and leadership.

2. Provide an understanding of the various leadership styles.

3. Develop an awareness of the conditions under which each style is appropriate.

4. Give you personal insight into developing a leadership style under which you will work most effectively.

5. Help you deal with superiors.

6. Suggest ways of relating to colleagues and work groups.

way." Tannenbaum and Schmidt give you some ideas about the possible continuum of leadership behavior and conditions under which each behavior tends to be more appropriate. What they call "subordinate-centered" leadership is sometimes referred to as a democratic, participative style. What they call "boss-centered" leadership—at the opposite end of the continuum—is referred to as an autocratic, traditional style in which individual decision making and control are favored. And, of course, many variations exist between the two extremes. Some of the middle-ground styles are variously referred to as "laissez-faire," "consultative," "mixed," and so forth.

One of the elements underlying leadership style is the leader's attitude toward employees. If you did the exercise in Chapter 2, "Assumptions about People," take it out and look at it again. If your assumptions about people tended toward a Theory X point of view, you would be characterized as being closer in your preferences to the conservative, autocratic leadership style; if you tended toward Theory Y, you probably prefer democratic styles.

Another exercise, more specifically oriented to pinning down your ideal, is "Leadership Style and Philosophy." When you complete that exercise, you should have a deeper understanding of how you think leaders should act. This may be important not only for developing your own leadership style but also for recognizing the kind of leadership you may want to work for in the future. The "Building the Hotel San Francisco" exercise also gives you an opportunity for firsthand experience with, or exposure to, different leadership styles. You might be surprised at your reaction to different styles and to which style seems to yield the best results.

A significant point in management thought today is that any leadership style is effective if it matches the needs of the situation, the work group, and the leader. One of the problems leaders face is whether they should change their style to fit the situation or try to change the situation to meet their style. In "The Secret of Bradford's Warehouse" you are shown a leader whose style appears at times to be inconsistent. Yet he seems to be effective. You might consider the importance of consistency versus flexibility.

Of course, managerial interrelationships are influenced by perception; that is, different management levels view problems from different perspectives. The "Metro City Health Department" case presents such an example. Concepts you have learned from leadership theory, influence theory, or motivation theory may be applied in analyzing and resolving perceptual differences.

Another important aspect of your job will be interrelationships with other managers, both peers and superiors. Some suggestions for relating to colleagues in your organization include:

- Providing for their need satisfaction: help satisfy or reinforce needs of the colleague.
- Interacting frequently with them: get to know your colleagues and their problems.
- Sharing information with them: give information useful to colleagues so they may do their job better.
- Exerting peer pressure on them: political efforts and coalitions of peers are sometimes necessary to influence peers.
- Reorganizing work: redesign work flow to avoid troublesome colleagues.
- Appealing through the hierarchy: get rules established and hierarchical pressure put on the peer.

The first three methods of relating to colleagues tend to be preferred, the others being reserved for more difficult problems of uncooperativeness. In the case "The Troublesome Boss at Worldview Travel," you will encounter a problem of relating to a superior. You might consider what approaches you would follow to deal with "the boss."

No experiences involving the line and staff difficulties, which crop up in many organizations, are presented here. However, we would prescribe similar remedies for them. That is, staff should:

- Frequently and regularly interact with the line.
- Build exchange relationships.
- Satisfy needs (by giving credit to the line, for example).

Line executives may then begin to appreciate that the staff is there to help, and they will probably begin to operate on an exchange basis by trying to satisfy staff needs.

Leadership also requires knowledge of work groups. Work groups exist in all work organizations. There are formal groups, designed to achieve purposes assigned to them, and informal groups, which usually decide their own objectives. A group can provide for its members' need satisfaction, and can perform useful functions for the organization of which it is a part or it can be dysfunctional for an organization. One key to leadership success is understanding how groups function and how to use them advantageously.

One of the more important features of groups and how they function is expressed by the term *cohesion*. What some call *esprit de corps* can be generated if managers use such techniques as assigning homogeneous members to the group, keeping the group small, providing for frequent communications, giving it high status, and maintaining its stability. Even outside pressure on the group can serve to strengthen its cohesion.

Managers are concerned about group effectiveness since work is often accomplished in groups. In addition to cohesiveness, size, and so on, managers should recognize that groups often develop powerful norms of behavior used to socialize and control members, or expectations shared by group members of how they ought to behave under a given set of circumstances. These norms can work for or against management goals.

Individuals within groups often assume roles. Some group members tend to be task oriented; they are concerned with getting the job done. Functions such as opinion or information seeking and giving, coordinating, energizing, or evaluating are performed by these members. Others serve group maintenance roles; they tend to be supportive, helping individuals who defend the group and its members. Functions they might perform include encouraging, compromising, expediting, observing and commentating, or following. They promote favorable relationships within a group by emphasizing social-emotional issues. Of course, not everyone fits one of these roles. Some may prefer an isolated role. Others may try to perform both roles.

Status within a group is often important to individuals. To the extent that members perform task and maintenance roles and uphold the norms of the group, to the extent that they are similar to many other group members or are judged to be more competent because of their knowledge or experience, or to the extent that they possess other characteristics highly valued by the group, they will possess more status and power—they are likely to be informal leaders.

The "Uris Hall Dormitory Kitchen" case also exposes you to some of the elements of group functioning. You may also gain insight into ways in which groups function by observing the groups you will join when acting out the cases and exercises in this chapter and others. ●

EXERCISE 47
POWER AND INFLUENCE

A. Power

A number of people have made statements about power and winning (e.g. P. T. Barnum, Mao Tse-tung, Leo Durocher, Lord Action, Vince Lombardi). Some of them are listed in the table that follows. Indicate how you feel about each of the statements by circling number 1 if you strongly disagree, number 5 if you strongly agree, and so on.

	Strongly Disagree	Disagree	Neutral	Agree	Strongly Agree
Winning is everything.	1	2	3	4	5
Nice guys finish last.	1	2	3	4	5
There can only be one winner.	1	2	3	4	5
There's a sucker born every minute.	1	2	3	4	5
You can't completely trust anyone.	1	2	3	4	5
All power rests at the end of the gun.	1	2	3	4	5
Power seekers are greedy and can't be trusted.	1	2	3	4	5
Power corrupts; absolute power corrupts absolutely.	1	2	3	4	5
You get as much power as you pay for.	1	2	3	4	5

B. Influence

During the past week or so you have come in contact with many people. Some have influenced you positively (turned you on), some negatively (turned you off). Try to recall recent experiences with employers, peers, teachers, parents, clergy, and the like who may have influenced you in some way. Then try to think about how and why they influenced you as they did.

1. On the following table, list the names of all those who influenced you during the past week or so according to the kind of power that person used. The same person's name may appear under more than one type of social power if that person used multiple power bases. Also, indicate whether the influence was positive (+) or negative (–).

Social Power Base	Names and Whether (+) or (–)
Coercive	
Monetary	
Legitimate	
Skill/expertise	
Affection	
Respect/rectitude	

2. After examining your list, check (✓) the questions below.

	Yes	No
a. Was there one person who had + marks appearing under several social power bases?	_____	_____
b. Was there one person who had – marks appearing under several social power bases?	_____	_____
c. Did you find that most of the people with + marks tended to fall under the same power bases?	_____	_____
d. Did you find that most of the people with – marks tended to fall under the same power bases?	_____	_____

3. From your answers to the last two questions list which social power bases you found to be positive (+) and which you found to be negative (–).

+	–
_____	_____
_____	_____
_____	_____
_____	_____

Do you think you personally prefer to use those power bases you listed under + when you try to influence people? Do you actually use them?

C. Power and Influence

From the table in Part B, find the one person who you think had the strongest positive influence on you (Person 1), and the one who had the strongest negative influence (Person 2). These are most likely the persons whose names appear most frequently.

In the following table, place a 1 on the line for each statement that best indicates how you think Person 1 would respond to that statement. Put a 2 on the line for each statement that reflects how you think Person 2 would respond to that item.

	Strongly Disagree	Disagree	Neutral	Agree	Strongly Agree
Winning is everything.	_____	_____	_____	_____	_____
Nice guys finish last.	_____	_____	_____	_____	_____
There can only be one winner.	_____	_____	_____	_____	_____
There's a sucker born every minute.	_____	_____	_____	_____	_____
You can't completely trust anyone.	_____	_____	_____	_____	_____
All power rests at the end of the gun.	_____	_____	_____	_____	_____
Power seekers are greedy and can't be trusted.	_____	_____	_____	_____	_____
Power corrupts; absolute power corrupts absolutely.	_____	_____	_____	_____	_____
You get as much power as you pay for.	_____	_____	_____	_____	_____

Now compare your responses in Part A to those in Part C. Do you more closely resemble Person 1 or Person 2? Do you prefer to use the kinds of power that person uses? Which kinds of power do you use most frequently? Which do you use least frequently? When do you feel you have the greatest power? When do you have the least power? How do these answers compare to what you found in Part B3?

CASE 48
JOE SCHULTZ

Joe Schultz was a first-line supervisor of a group of assembly line workers at the Supreme Manufacturing Company. With a high school education, he had been with Supreme in this department as an assembly worker himself, and had been promoted to supervisor five years ago. His leadership style had been what might be called "active, controlling, and task oriented;" he was of the same ethnic group as many of his subordinates (German); he would often "kid" with them in Germanic slang; and would on a few occasions join them at the local Hofbrau after work on Fridays. He was well liked by his subordinates and their work performance was among the best in the company.

Joe was recognized as being highly intelligent and mechanically expert and had been encouraged to take some night courses at the local university in engineering, which he did (and performed well in) for three years.

Recently, with a respectable (although not expert) engineering background, he was promoted to assistant supervisor in the company's drafting department. Here he had the technical skills necessary to supervise his employees, and the work he supervised was also highly programmed, as in the assembly department. The draftsmen whom he supervised were of diverse ethnic backgrounds, and many of them had been in the department for 8–10 years. There was a feeling on the part of some of the new subordinates that one of them, Fred Keen, should have been promoted to the position Joe was given. This feeling was not too strong, however, as Fred Keen was disliked by certain members of the group.

Joe continued his basic leadership style (as described above) in his new job; but somehow productivity in the drafting department fell. Numerous antagonisms developed under Joe's leadership and a couple of his better subordinates resigned within a period of three months.

Questions for Discussion

1. Can you explain why Joe encountered these problems in his new job in terms of bases of social power?

2. How could Fiedler's contingency leadership model be used to describe Joe's problem?

3. What should be done to correct the situation?

Source: Reprinted by permission from Richards and Greenlaw, *Management: Decisions and Behavior* (Homewood, Ill.: Richard D. Irwin, 1972), pp. 198–199. Copyright 1972 by Richard D. Irwin, Inc.

READING 49
HOW TO CHOOSE A LEADERSHIP PATTERN
Robert Tannenbaum and Warren H. Schmidt

"I put most problems into my group's hands and leave it to them to carry the ball from there. I serve merely as a catalyst, mirroring back the people's thoughts and feelings so that they can better understand them."

"It's foolish to make decisions oneself on matters that affect people. I always talk things over with my subordinates, but I make it clear to them that I'm the one who has to have the final say."

"Once I have decided on a course of action, I do my best to sell my ideas to my employees."

"I'm being paid to lead. If I let a lot of other people make the decisions I should be making, then I'm not worth my salt."

"I believe in getting things done. I can't waste time calling meetings. Someone has to call the shots around here, and I think it should be me."

Each of these statements represent a point of view about "good leadership." Considerable experience, factual data, and theoretical principles could be cited to support each statement, even though they seem to be inconsistent when placed together. Such contradictions point up the dilemma in which the modern manager frequently finds himself.

NEW PROBLEM

The problem of how the modern manager can be "democratic" in his relations with subordinates and at the same time maintain the necessary authority and control in the organization for which he is responsible has come into focus increasingly in recent years.

Earlier in the century this problem was not so acutely felt. The successful executive was generally pictured as possessing intelligence, imagination, initiative, the capacity to make rapid (and generally wise) decisions, and the ability to inspire subordinates. People tended to think of the world as being divided into "leaders" and "followers."

New Focus

Gradually, however, from the social sciences emerged the concept of "group dynamics" with its focus on *members* of the group rather than solely on the leader. Research efforts of social scientists underscored the importance of employee involvement and participation in decision making. Evidence began to challenge the efficiency of highly directive leadership, and increasing attention was paid to problems of motivation and human relations.

Through training laboratories in group development that sprang up across the country, many of the newer notions of leadership began to exert an impact. These training laboratories were carefully designed to give people a first-hand experience in full participation and decision making. The designated "leaders" deliberately attempted to reduce their own power and to make group members as responsible as possible for setting their own goals and methods within the laboratory experience.

It was perhaps inevitable that some of the people who attended the training laboratories regarded this kind of leadership as being truly "democratic" and went home with the determination to build fully participative decision making into their own organizations. Whenever their bosses made a decision without convening a staff meeting, they tended to perceive this as authoritarian behavior. The true symbol of democratic leadership to some was the meeting—and the less directed from the top, the more democratic it was.

Some of the more enthusiastic alumni of these training laboratories began to get the habit of categorizing leader behavior as "democratic" or "authoritarian." The boss who made too many decisions himself was thought of as an authoritarian, and his directive behavior was often attributed solely to his personality.

New Need

The net result of the research findings and of the human relations training based upon them has been to call into question the stereotype of an effective leader. Consequently, the modern manager often finds himself in an uncomfortable state of mind.

Often he is not quite sure how to behave; there are times when he is torn between exerting "strong" leadership and "permissive" leadership. Sometimes new knowledge pushes him in one direction ("I should really get the group to help make this decision"), but at the same time his experience pushes him in another direction ("I really understand the problem better than the group and therefore I should make the decision"). He is not sure when a group decision is really appropriate or when holding a staff meeting serves merely as a device for avoiding his own decision-making responsibility.

The purpose of our article is to suggest a framework which managers may find useful in grappling with this dilemma. First, we shall look at the different patterns of leadership behavior that the manager can choose from in relating himself to his subordinates. Then, we shall turn to some of the questions suggested by this range of patterns. For instance, how important is it for a manager's subordinates to know what type of leadership he is using in a situation? What difference do his long-run objectives make as compared to his immediate objectives?

RANGE OF BEHAVIOR

Figure 1 presents the continuum or range of possible leadership behaviors available to a manager. Each type of action is related to the degree of authority used by the boss and to the amount of freedom available to his subordinates in reaching decisions. The actions seen on the extreme left characterize the manager who maintains a high degree of control while those seen on the extreme right characterize the manager who releases a high degree of control. Neither extreme is absolute; authority and freedom are never without their limitations.

Now let us look more closely at each of the behavior points occurring along this continuum.

The Manager Makes the Decision and Announces It

In this case the boss identifies a problem, considers alternative solutions, chooses one of them, and then reports this decision to his subordinates for implementation. He may or may not give consideration to what he believes his subordinates will think or feel about his decision; in any case, he provides no opportunity for them to participate directly in the decision-making process. Coercion may not be used or implied.

FIGURE 1

CONTINUUM OF LEADERSHIP BEHAVIOR

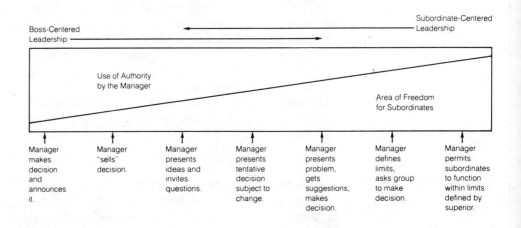

Manager makes decision and announces it.	Manager "sells" decision.	Manager presents ideas and invites questions.	Manager presents tentative decision subject to change.	Manager presents problem, gets suggestions, makes decision.	Manager defines limits, asks group to make decision.	Manager permits subordinates to function within limits defined by superior.

The Manager "Sells" His Decision

Here the manager, as before, takes responsibility for identifying the problem and arriving at a decision. However, rather than simply announcing it, he takes the additional step of persuading his subordinates to accept it. In doing so, he recognizes the possibility of some resistance among those who will be faced with the decision, and seeks to reduce this resistance by indicating, for example, what the employees have to gain from his decision.

The Manager Presents His Ideas, Invites Questions

Here the boss who has arrived at a decision and who seeks acceptance of his ideas provides an opportunity for his subordinates to get a fuller explanation of his thinking and his intentions. After presenting the ideas, he invites questions so that his associates can better understand what he is trying to accomplish. This "give and take" also enables the manager and the subordinates to explore more fully the implications of the decision.

The Manager Presents a Tentative Decision Subject to Change

This kind of behavior permits the subordinates to exert some influence on the decision. The initiative for identifying and diagnosing the problem remains with the boss. Before meeting with his staff, he has thought the problem through and arrived at a decision—but only a tentative one. Before finalizing it, he presents his proposed solution for the reaction of those who will be affected by it. He says in effect, "I'd like to hear what you have to say about this plan that I have developed. I'll appreciate your frank reactions, but will reserve for myself the final decision."

The Manager Presents the Problem, Gets Suggestions, and Then Makes His Decision

Up to this point the boss has come before the group with a solution of his own. Not so in this case. The subordinates now get the first chance to suggest solutions. The manager's initial role involves identifying the problem. He might, for example, say something of this sort: "We are faced with a number of complaints from newspapers and the general public in our service policy. What is wrong here? What ideas do you have for coming to grips with this problem?"

The function of the group becomes one of increasing the manager's repertory of possible solutions to the problem. The purpose is to capitalize on the knowledge and experience of those who are on the "firing line." From the expanded list of alternatives developed by the manager and his subordinates, the manager then selects the solution that he regards as most promising.[1]

The Manager Defines the Limits and Requests the Group to Make a Decision

At this point the manager passes to the group (possibly including himself as a member) the right to make decisions. Before doing so, however, he defines the problem to be solved and the boundaries within which the decision must be made.

An example might be the handling of a parking problem at a plant. The boss decides that this is something that should be worked on by the people involved, so he calls them together and points up the existence of the problem. Then he tells them:

"There is the open field just north of the main plant which has been designated for additional employee parking. We can build underground or surface multilevel facilities as long as the cost does not exceed $100,000. Within these limits we are free to work out whatever solution makes sense to us. After we decide on a specific plan, the company will spend the available money in whatever way we indicate."

The Manager Permits the Group to Make Decisions within Prescribed Limits

This represents an extreme degree of group freedom only occasionally encountered in formal organizations, as, for instance, in many research groups. Here the team of managers or engineers undertakes the identification and diagnosis of the problem, develops alternative procedures for solving it, and decides on one or more of these alternative solutions. The only limits directly imposed on the group by the organization are those specified by the superior of the team's boss. If the boss participates in the decision-making process, he attempts to do so with no more authority than any other member of the group. He commits himself in advance to assist in implementing whatever decision the group makes.

KEY QUESTIONS

As the continuum in Figure 1 demonstrates, there are a number of alternative ways in which a manager can relate himself to the group or individuals he is supervising. At the extreme left of the range, the emphasis is on the manager—on what *he* is interested in, how *he* sees things, how *he* feels about them. As we move toward the subordinate-centered end of the continuum, however, the focus is increasingly on the subordinates—on what *they* are interested in, how *they* look at things, and how *they* feel about them.

When business leadership is regarded in this way, a number of questions arise. Let us take four of special importance.

Can a Boss Ever Relinquish His Responsibility by Delegating It to Someone Else?

Our view is that the manager must expect to be held responsible by his superior for the quality of the decisions made, even though operationally these decisions may have been made on a group basis. He should, therefore, be ready to accept whatever risk is involved whenever he delegates decision-making power to his subordinates. Delegation is not a way of "passing the buck." Also, it should be emphasized that the amount of freedom the boss gives to his subordinates cannot be greater than the freedom which he himself has been given by his own superior.

Should the Manager Participate with His Subordinates Once He Has Delegated Responsibility to Them?

The manager should carefully think over this question and decide on his role prior to involving the subordinate group. He should ask if his presence will inhibit or facilitate the problem-solving process. There may be some instances when he should leave the group to let it solve the problem for itself. Typically, however, the boss has useful ideas to contribute, and should function as an additional member of the group. In the latter instance, it is important that he indicate clearly to the group that he sees himself in a *member* role rather than in an authority role.

How Important Is It for the Group to Recognize What Kind of Leadership Behavior the Boss Is Using?

It makes a great deal of difference. Many relationship problems between boss and subordinate occur because the boss fails to make clear how he plans to use his authority. If, for example, he actually intends to make a certain decision himself, but the subordinate group gets the impression that he has delegated this authority, considerable confusion and resentment are likely to follow. Problems may also occur when the boss uses a "democratic" facade to conceal the fact that he has already made a decision which he hopes the group will accept as its own. The attempt to "make them think it was their idea in the first place" is a risky one. We believe that it is highly important for the manager to be honest and clear in describing what authority he is keeping and what role he is asking his subordinates to assume in solving a particular problem.

Can you Tell How "Democratic" a Manager is by the Number of Decisions His Subordinates Make?

The sheer *number* of decisions is not an accurate index of the amount of freedom that a subordinate group enjoys. More important is the *significance* of the decisions which the boss entrusts to his subordinates. Obviously a decision on how to arrange desks is of an entirely different order from a decision involving the introduction of new electronic data-processing equipment. Even though the widest possible limits are given in dealing with the first issue, the group will sense no particular degree of responsibility. For a boss to permit the group to decide equipment policy, even within rather narrow limits, would reflect a greater degree of confidence in them on his part.

DECIDING HOW TO LEAD

Now let us turn from the types of leadership which are possible in a company situation to the question of what types are *practical* and *desirable*. What factors or forces should a manager consider in deciding how to manage? Three are of particular importance:

- Forces in the manager.
- Forces in the subordinates.
- Forces in the situation.

We should like briefly to describe these elements and indicate how they might influence a manager's action in a decision-making situation.[2] The strength of each of them will, of course, vary from instance to instance, but the manager who is sensitive to them can better assess the problems which face him and determine which mode of leadership behavior is most appropriate for him.

Forces in the Manager

The manager's behavior in any given instance will be influenced greatly by the many forces operating within his own personality. He will, of course, perceive his leadership problems in a unique way on the basis of his background, knowledge, and experience. Among the important internal forces affecting him will be the following:

1. *His value system.* How strongly does he feel that individuals should have a share in making the decisions which affect them? Or, how convinced is he that the official who is paid to assume responsibility should personally carry the burden of decision making? The strength of his convictions on questions like these will tend to move the manager to one end or the other of the continuum shown in Figure 1. His behavior will also be influenced by the relative importance that he attaches to organizational efficiency, personal growth of subordinates, and company profits.[3]

2. *His confidence in his subordinates.* Managers differ greatly in the amount of trust they have in other people generally, and this carries over to the particular employees they supervise at a given time. In viewing his particular group of subordinates, the manager is likely to consider their knowledge and competence with respect to the problem. A central question he might ask himself is: "Who is best qualified to deal with this problem?" Often he may, justifiably or not, have more confidence in his own capabilities than in those of his subordinates.

3. *His own leadership inclinations.* There are some managers who seem to function more comfortably and naturally as highly directive leaders. Resolving problems and issuing orders come easily to them. Other managers seem to operate more comfortably in a team role, where they are continually sharing many of their functions with their subordinates.

4. *His feelings of security in an uncertain situation.* The manager who releases control over the decision-making process thereby reduces the predictability of the outcome. Some managers have a greater need than others for predictability and stability in their environment. This "tolerance for ambiguity" is being viewed increasingly by psychologists as a key variable in a person's manner of dealing with problems.

The manager brings these and other highly personal variables to each situation he faces. If he can see them as forces which, consciously or unconsciously, influence his behavior, he can better understand what makes him prefer to act in a given way. And understanding this, he can often make himself more effective.

Forces in the Subordinate

Before deciding how to lead a certain group, the manager will also want to consider a number of forces affecting his subordinates' behavior. He will want to remember that each employee, like himself, is influenced by many personality variables. In addition, each subordinate has a set of expectations about how the boss should act in relation to him (the phrase "expected behavior" is one we hear more and more often these days at discussions of leadership and teaching). The better the manager understands these factors, the more accurately he can determine what kind of behavior on his part will enable his subordinates to act most effectively.

Generally speaking, the manager can permit his subordinates greater freedom if the following essential conditions exist:

- If the subordinates have relatively high needs for independence. (As we all know, people differ greatly in the amount of direction that they desire.)
- If the subordinates have a readiness to assume responsibility for decision making. (Some see additional responsibility as a tribute to their ability; others see it as "passing the buck.")
- If they have a relatively high tolerance for ambiguity. (Some employees prefer to have clear-cut directives given to them; others prefer a wider area of freedom.)
- If they are interested in the problem and feel that it is important.
- If they understand and identify with the goals of the organization.

- If they have the necessary knowledge and experience to deal with the problem.
- If they have learned to expect to share in decision making. (Persons who have come to expect strong leadership and are then suddenly confronted with the request to share more fully in decision making are often upset by this new experience. On the other hand, persons who have enjoyed a considerable amount of freedom resent the boss who begins to make all the decisions himself.)

The manager will probably tend to make fuller use of his own authority if the above conditions do *not* exist; at times there may be no realistic alternative to running a "one-man show."

The retroactive effect of many of the forces will, of course, be greatly modified by the general feeling of confidence which subordinates have in the boss. Where they have learned to respect and trust him, he is free to vary his behavior. He will feel certain that he will not be perceived as an authoritarian boss on those occasions when he makes decisions by himself. Similarly, he will not be seen as using staff meetings to avoid his decision-making responsibility. In a climate of mutual confidence and respect, people tend to feel less threatened by deviations from normal practice, which in turn makes possible a higher degree of flexibility in the whole relationship.

Forces in the Situation

In addition to the forces which exist in the manager himself and in his subordinates, certain characteristics of the general situation will also affect the manager's behavior. Among the more critical environmental pressures that surround him are those which stem from the organization, the work group, the nature of the problem, and the pressures of time. Let us look briefly at each of these:

Type of Organization

Like individuals, organizations have values and traditions which inevitably influence the behavior of the people who work in them. The manager who is a newcomer to a company quickly discovers that certain kinds of behavior are approved while others are not. He also discovers that to deviate radically from what is generally accepted is likely to create problems for him.

These values and traditions are communicated in numerous ways—through job descriptions, policy pronouncements, and public statements by top executives. Some organizations, for example, hold to the notion that the desirable executive is one who is dynamic, imaginative, decisive, and persuasive. Other organizations put more emphasis upon the importance of the executive's ability to work effectively with people—his human relations skills. The fact that his superiors have a defined concept of what the good executive should be will very likely push the manager toward one end or the other of the behavioral range.

In addition to the above, the amount of employee participation is influenced by such variables as the size of the working units, their geographical distribution, and the degree of inter- and intra-organizational security required to attain company goals. For example, the wide geographical dispersion of an organization may preclude a practical system of participative decision making, even though this would otherwise be desirable. Similarly, the size of the working units or the need for keeping plans confidential may make it necessary for the boss to exercise more control than would otherwise be the case. Factors like these may limit considerably the manager's ability to function flexibly on the continuum.

Group Effectiveness

Before turning decision-making responsibility over to a subordinate group, the boss should consider how effectively its members work together as a unit.

One of the relevant factors here is the experience the group has had in working together. It can generally be expected that a group which has functioned for some time will have developed habits of cooperation and thus be able to tackle a problem more effectively than a new group. It can also be expected that a group of people with similar backgrounds and interests will work more quickly and easily than people with dissimilar backgrounds, because the communication problems are likely to be less complex.

The degree of confidence that the members have in their ability to solve problems as a group is also a key consideration. Finally, such group variables as cohesiveness, permissiveness, mutual acceptance, and commonality of purpose will exert subtle but powerful influences on the group's functioning.

The Problem Itself

The nature of the problem may determine what degree of authority should be delegated by the manager to his subordinates. Obviously he will ask himself whether they have the kind of knowledge that is needed. It is possible to do them a real disservice by assigning a problem that their experience does not equip them to handle.

Since the problems faced in large or growing industries increasingly require knowledge of specialists from many different fields, it might be inferred that the more complex a problem, the more anxious a manager will be to get some assistance in solving it. However, this is not always the case. There will be times when the very complexity of the problem calls for one person to work it out. For example, if the manager has most of the background and factual data relevant to a given issue, it may be easier for him to think it through himself than to take the time to fill in his staff on all the pertinent background information.

The key question to ask, of course, is: "Have I heard the ideas of everyone who has the necessary knowledge to make a significant contribution to the solution of this problem?"

The Pressure of Time

This is perhaps the most clearly felt pressure on the manager (in spite of the fact that it may sometimes be imagined). The more that he feels the need for an immediate decision, the more difficult it is to involve other people. In organizations which are in a constant state of "crisis" and "crash programming" one is likely to find managers personally using a high degree of authority with relatively little delegation to subordinates. When the time pressure is less intense, however, it becomes much more possible to bring subordinates in on the decision-making process.

These, then, are the principal forces that impinge on the manager in any given instance and that tend to determine his tactical behavior in relation to his subordinates. In each case his behavior ideally will be that which makes possible the most effective attainment of his immediate goal within the limits facing him.

LONG-RUN STRATEGY

As the manager works with his organization on the problems that come up day by day, his choice of a leadership pattern is usually limited. He must take account of the forces just described and, within the restrictions they impose on him, do the best that he can. But as he looks ahead months or even years, he can shift his thinking from tactics to large-scale strategy. No longer need he be fettered by all of the forces mentioned, for he can view many of them as variables over which he has some control. He can, for example, gain new insights or skills for himself, supply training for individual subordinates, and provide participative experiences for his employee group.

In trying to bring about a change in these variables, however, he is faced with a challenging question: At which point along the continuum *should* he act?

ATTAINING OBJECTIVES

The answer depends largely on what he wants to accomplish. Let us suppose that he is interested in the same objectives that most modern managers seek to attain when they can shift their attention from the pressure of immediate assignments:

1. To raise the level of employee motivation.
2. To increase the readiness of subordinates to accept change.
3. To improve the quality of all managerial decisions.
4. To develop teamwork and morale.
5. To further the individual development of employees.

In recent years the manager has been deluged with a flow of advice on how best to achieve these longer-run objectives. It is little wonder that he is often both bewildered and annoyed. However, there are some guidelines which he can usefully follow in making a decision.

Most research and much of the experience of recent years gives a strong factual basis to the theory that a fairly high degree of subordinate-centered behavior is associated with the accomplishment of the five purposes mentioned.[4] This does not mean that a manager should always leave all decisions to his assistants. To provide the individual or the group with greater freedom than they are ready for at any given time may very well tend to generate anxieties and therefore inhibit rather than facilitate the attainment of desired objectives. But this should not keep the manager from making a continuing effort to confront his subordinates with the challenge of freedom.

CONCLUSION

In summary, there are two implications in the basic thesis that we have been developing. The first is that the successful leader is one who is keenly aware of those forces which are most relevant to his behavior at any given time. He accurately understands himself, the individuals and group he is dealing with, and the company and broader social environment in which he operates. And certainly he is able to assess the present readiness for growth of his subordinates.

But this sensitivity or understanding is not enough, which brings us to the second implication. The successful leader is one who is able to behave appropriately in the light of these perceptions. If direction is in order, he is able to direct; if considerable participative freedom is called for, he is able to provide such freedom.

Thus, the successful manager of men can be primarily characterized neither as a strong leader nor as a permissive one. Rather, he is one who maintains a high batting average in accurately assessing the forces that determine what his most appropriate behavior at any given time should be and in actually being able to behave accordingly. Being both insightful and flexible, he is less likely to see the problems of leadership as a dilemma.

RETROSPECTIVE COMMENTARY

Since this *HBR* Classic was first published in 1958, there have been many changes in organizations and in the world that have affected leadership patterns. While the article's continued popularity attests to its essential validity, we believe it can be reconsidered and updated to reflect subsequent societal changes and new management concepts.

The reasons for the article's continued relevance can be summarized briefly:

The article contains insights and perspectives which mesh well with, and help clarify, the experiences of managers, other leaders, and students of leadership. Thus it is useful to individuals in a wide variety of organizations—industrial, governmental, educational, religious, and community.

The concept of leadership the article defines is reflected in a continuum of leadership behavior (see Figure 1). Rather than offering a choice between two styles of leadership, democratic or authoritarian, it sanctions a range of behavior.

The concept does not dictate to managers but helps them to analyze their own behavior. The continuum permits them to review their behavior within a context of other alternatives, without any style being labeled right or wrong.

(We have sometimes wondered if we have, perhaps, made it too easy for anyone to justify his or her style of leadership. It may be a small step between being nonjudgmental and giving the impression that all behavior is equally valid and useful. The latter was not our intention. Indeed, the thrust of our endorsement was for the manager who is insightful in assessing relevant forces within himself, others, and the situation, and who can be flexible in responding to these forces.)

In recognizing that our article can be updated, we are acknowledging that organizations do not exist in a vacuum but are affected by changes that occur in society. Consider, for example, the implications for organizations of these recent social developments:

- The youth revolution that expresses distrust and even contempt for organizations identified with the establishment.
- The civil rights movement that demands all minority groups be given a greater opportunity for participation and influence in the organizational processes.
- The ecology and consumer movements that challenge the right of managers to make decisions without considering the interests of people outside the organization.
- The increasing national concern with the quality of working life and its relationship to worker productivity, participation, and satisfaction.

These and other societal changes make effective leadership in this decade a more challenging task, requiring even greater sensitivity and flexibility than was needed in the 1950s. Today's manager is more likely to deal with employees who resent being treated as subordinates, who may be highly critical of any organizational system, who expect to be consulted and to exert influence, and who often stand on the edge of alienation from the institution that needs their loyalty and commitment. In addition, he is frequently confronted by a highly turbulent, unpredictable environment.

In response to these social pressures, new concepts of management have emerged in organizations. Open-system theory, with its emphasis on subsystems' interdependency *and* on the interaction of an organization with its environment, has made a powerful impact on managers' approach to problems. Organization development has emerged as a new behavioral science approach to the improvement of individual, group, organizational, and interorganizational performance. New research has added to our understanding of motivation in the work situation. More and more executives have become concerned with social responsibility and have explored the feasibility of social audits. And a growing number of organizations, in Europe and in the United States, have conducted experiments in industrial democracy.

In light of these developments, we submit the following thoughts on how we would rewrite certain points in our original article.

The article described forces in the manager, subordinates, and the situation as given, with the leadership pattern a resultant of these forces. We would now give more attention to the *interdependency* of these forces. For example, such interdependency occurs in: (a) the interplay between the manager's confidence in his subordinates, their readiness to assume responsibility, and the level of group effectiveness; and (b) the impact of the behavior of the manager on that of his subordinates, and vice versa.

In discussing the forces in the situation, we primarily identified organizational phenomena. We would now include forces lying outside the organization, and would explore the relevant interdependencies between the organization and its environment.

In the original article, we presented the size of the rectangle in Figure 1 as a given, with its boundaries already determined by external forces—in effect, a closed system. We would now recognize the possibility of the manager and/or his subordinates taking the initiative to change those boundaries through interaction with relevant external forces—both within their own organization and in the larger society.

The article portrayed the manager as the principal and almost unilateral actor. He initiated and determined group functions, assumed responsibility, and exercised control. Subordinates made inputs and assumed power only at the will of the manager. Although the manager might have taken into account forces outside himself, it was *he* who decided where to operate on the continuum—that is, whether to announce a decision instead of trying to sell his idea to his subordinates, whether to invite questions, to let subordinates decide an issue, and so on. While the manager has retained this clear prerogative in many organizations, it has been challenged in others. Even in situations where he has retained it, however, the balance in the relationship between manager and subordinates at any given time is arrived at by interaction—direct or indirect—between the two parties.

Although power and its use by the manager played a role in our article, we now realize that our concern with cooperation and collaboration, common goals, commitment, trust, and mutual caring limited our vision with respect to the realities of power. We did not attempt to deal with unions, other forms of joint worker action, or with individual workers' expressions of resistance. Today, we would recognize much more clearly the power available to *all* parties, and the factors that underlie the interrelated decisions on whether to use it.

In the original article, we used the terms "manager" and "subordinate." We are now uncomfortable with "subordinate" because of its demeaning, dependency-laden connotations and prefer "nonmanager." The titles "manager" and "nonmanager" make the terminological difference functional rather than hierarchical.

We assumed fairly traditional organizational structures in our original article. Now we would alter our formulation to reflect newer organizational modes which are slowly emerging, such as industrial, democracy, intentional communities, and "phenomenarchy."[5] These new modes are based on observations such as the following:

Both managers and nonmanagers may be governing forces in their group's environment, contributing to the definition of the total area of freedom.

A group can function without a manager, with managerial functions being shared by group members.

A group, as a unit, can be delegated authority and can assume responsibility within a larger organizational context.

Our thoughts on the question of leadership have prompted us to design a new behavior continuum (see Figure 2) in which the total area of freedom shared by

FIGURE 2

CONTINUUM OF MANAGER—NONMANAGER BEHAVIOR

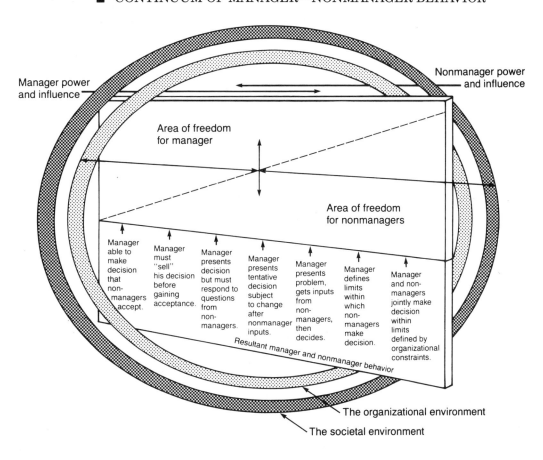

manager and nonmanagers is constantly redefined by interactions between them and the forces in the environment.

The arrows in the exhibit indicate the continual flow of interdependence influence among systems and people. The points on the continuum designate the types of manager and nonmanager behavior that become possible with any given amount of freedom available to each. The new continuum is both more complex and more dynamic than the 1958 version, reflecting the organizational and societal realities of 1973.

Questions for Discussion

1. How important is it that a manager's subordinate know what type of leadership the manager is using?

2. What factors should a manager consider in deciding on a leadership pattern?

3. Do long-run versus short-run objectives influence leadership style selection?

Notes

1. For a fuller explanation of this approach, see Leo Moore, "Too Much Management, Too Little Change," *HBR*, January–February 1956, p. 41.

2. See also Robert Tannenbaum and Fred Massarik, "Participation by Subordinates in the Managerial Decision-Making Process," *Canadian Journal of Economics and Political Science,* August 1950, p. 413.

3. See Chris Argyris, "Top Management Dilemma: Company Needs vs. Individual Development," *Personnel,* September 1955, pp. 123–134.

4. For example, see Warren H. Schmidt and Paul C. Buchanan, *Techniques That Produce Teamwork* (New London: Arthur C. Croft Publications, 1954): and Morris S. Viteles, *Motivation and Morale in Industry* (New York: W.W. Norton & Company, Inc., 1953).

5. For a description of phenomenarchy, see Will McWhinney, "Phenomenarchy: A Suggestion for Social Redesign," *Journal of Applied Behavioral Science,* May 1973.

EXERCISE 50

LEADERSHIP STYLE AND PHILOSOPHY

All of us have an image in our heads of how a leader should act which makes up our leadership philosophy. For the purpose of helping you think more clearly about certain elements of your own philosophy, twenty topic areas of management are presented below. Each has three alternatives. You are first to read all three alternatives so you will have a general understanding of their content. You are then to select the alternative that most nearly corresponds with your own views and assign it a 1; select the one that least corresponds with your views and give it a 3; and finally, assign a 2 to the remaining alternative. Your answer should appear like the following. No two alternatives should receive the same number, and each must be rated.

Example. Personal relationships with employees:

16. __3__

17. __1__

18. __2__

For the purpose of completing this exercise, assume you are in a manager's job, just above the first line of supervision, and that you have five to seven units reporting to you. The supervisors of these units would make up your immediate team. The ratings you assign below indicate how you feel management functions, processes, and what policies should be conducted with your team and throughout the organization generally.

Write your responses in the "Your Answer" column.

Your Answer

I. Leading operating activities:

For the most part I lead by using staff and committee meetings for reviewing progress reports which are thoroughly developed according to our division's regulations.   1. _____

I see myself primarily as a facilitator providing guidance and support for team members in achieving programs we have agreed upon.   2. _____

I determine how my team wants to direct activities, and I usually go along with them.   3. _____

II. Control over operating activities:

I work out with my subordinates the framework for operations and reporting and then provide for maximum self-direction within the confines set up.   4. _____

There is no real substitute for a manager running a "tight ship." It is a manager's responsibility to stay on top of the major operations and the people running them.   5. _____

Source: Reprinted by permission from James B. Lau, *Behavior in Organizations* (Homewood, Ill.: Richard D. Irwin, 1975). Copyright 1975 by Richard D. Irwin, Inc.

Your Answer

Control can be best achieved by following a system of policies, procedures, and requirements so that everyone has the basic framework of guidance as to what is expected.

6. _____

III. Meetings:

I hold a short staff meeting two mornings each week for open discussion and coffee. The real value comes from the feelings of being on the same cooperative team.

7. _____

Meetings and committees are valuable for many organizational purposes, but they must be conducted with agendas and procedures to save time.

8. _____

I find I can keep track of what each person is doing by having frequent individual meetings with each person reporting to me. This almost eliminates the need for group meetings.

9. _____

IV. Concerning status symbols, privileges, and perquisites for managers, my position is:

We all want status. These are part of the reward for demonstrated competence and aggressiveness. To openly and candidly make this known within the organization is an aid in motivating managers.

10. _____

Creating a supportive atmosphere with informality and a minimal use of status-type indicators can contribute to the morale of the employees.

11. _____

Too much emphasis upon status indicators can unfavorably influence communication and the way people interact. More can be gained by stressing what we are trying to achieve together.

12. _____

V. In regard to women wanting equal opportunities for management positions, I believe:

All individuals should be given the opportunity for developing their full potential for management positions regardless of sex.

13. _____

I would give them full consideration, but the fact that women historically have not achieved leadership positions shows the probability of their becoming equal to men in assuming managerial responsibility is questionable.

14. _____

This is best handled by organizational policies which assure systematic review of all women candidates for promotion on a continuing basis.

15. _____

Your Answer

VI. Personal relationships with employees:

We have arrived at a time when warm friendships on the job are just as appropriate as any other type of friendship.　　　16. _____

Maintain good personal relationships on the job but avoid socializing off the job.　　　17. _____

You have to maintain your position with a certain amount of distance both on and off the job.　　　18. _____

VII. A frequent complaint from organizations concerns people who have been employed for many years and seem no longer to be fully productive. Organizational effectiveness can be served by:

Facing up to the situation and realistically finding some way to get rid of the "deadwood."　　　19. _____

Recognizing that humane treatment is foremost, both from the ethical point of view and the effect any company action might have on the other employees.　　　20. _____

Finding different jobs for these people which might spur their interest and use their capabilities.　　　21. _____

VIII. Employees are continuously concerned about fair treatment. I believe:

I follow the company policies as much as possible, because they have been written specifically for the purpose of assuring that employees receive fair treatment in many activity areas.　　　22. _____

The manager is in the position of a judge in determining what is fair, but he always has to be responsive to the problem of how his actions will be perceived by the employees.　　　23. _____

When deciding what is fair, the main thing is to make sure the people working for you know you really care about them.　　　24. _____

IX. There are many views on keeping up productivity in a business office situation. I believe that:

If a relaxed atmosphere is created in an office, the employees will generate their own pressure.　　　25. _____

Wherever possible, methods should be found of setting up work schedules so that pressure comes from the assignment system and work load rather than from the supervisor.　　　26. _____

Keeping people under a certain amount of pressure from the supervisor results in work being turned out at a good rate.　　　27. _____

Your Answer

X. Formal organizational life breeds informal organizations and cliques. I believe:

A well-managed, well-controlled organization minimizes the opportunity for these to become a problem. When informal organizations or cliques do become active, measures can be found to neutralize them.

28. _____

The boss who is known to fight for his people is not likely to have trouble in this regard, since he will probably have the informal organization on his side.

29. _____

The team approach with open communications and a problem-solving orientation can integrate information groups into work activities.

30. _____

XI. How to motivate people to work:

A manager can motivate people by showing drive, enthusiasm, and high commitment for what he is doing. Being an appropriate example is all-important.

31. _____

A manager has to stress results and high standards but should arrange the work in such a way that everyone has the maximum opportunity for self-management.

32. _____

There are two factors that are foremost: first, there is still no substitute for simply being considerate of people, and secondly, they will work hard if they feel they are accepted as a member of the group.

33. _____

XII. When I am looking for leadership talent among my employees, I operate on the assumption that:

The majority of the people have some potential for developing leadership capabilities.

34. _____

It is something you either have or don't have, and the task is to find those who have it.

35. _____

It is most important to make sure that the individuals you select for future leaders will be able to fit into the style and character of the organization.

36. _____

XIII. Delegation is a matter of:

Assigning whatever responsibility you assume the individual will have to shoulder if he is going to make an effective manager.

37. _____

Letting the individual decide when he believes he is ready to assume more responsibility.

38. _____

Gradually releasing responsibility as you observe the individual is ready for it.

39. _____

Your Answer

XIV. In my company, I support a promotion policy that selects:

Tactful, reasonable leaders who keep the people satisfied while attaining reasonably good production.

40. _____

Leaders whose results records show they have high standards and are getting high commitment from people.

41. _____

Leaders who go all out for the people, since they are what makes the company go.

42. _____

XV. Concerning communication problems with subordinates:

If the employees know the boss is open to feedback, they will usually take the initiative to clear up communication problems when they arise.

43. _____

You probably won't have communication problems, if you concentrate on getting all the information out to people so they know what you want them to do to complete their work.

44. _____

The manager has to develop communication skills to persuade, sell, and even negotiate to get the job accomplished.

45. _____

XVI. When conflict arises between employees, I believe:

If a manager creates the climate where everyone feels he is part of the family, disagreements can often be overcome by emphasizing the positive and what we have going for us.

46. _____

Often a manager facing conflict is in a similar role to that developed by labor: he has to examine the issues involved, look for answers acceptable to both sides, and find middle-ground solutions when necessary.

47. _____

Conflict can destroy effectiveness. It must be dealt with firmly so people will know it will not be permitted.

48. _____

XVII. Participative management (letting employees participate in the decision-making processes):

The Main advantage comes from having employees serve on committees and special task forces where their ideas can be used.

49. _____

When people have taken part in a decision, they are more apt to be committed to carry it out.

50. _____

It is needed to give people a sense of personal worth and importance.

51. _____

Your Answer

XVIII. Managing competition between different working elements of an organization:

Stressing common goals among the units or competing against your own record is the most meaningful approach.

52._____

It's natural to want to be on a winning team, which means you want your part of the organization to do better than the others.

53._____

It always exists so the main thing is to make sure your people don't become too obvious about it or let it get out of hand.

54._____

XIX. When employees start expressing their concerns and feelings, I would:

Encourage people to say what they are feeling so management can be responsive to their needs.

55._____

Stress what is logical and rational and tell people to keep feelings and emotions out of our work relationships.

56._____

Keep a low profile, that is, play things in low key so feelings do not get ruffled; make compromises necessary to maintain this atmosphere.

57._____

XX. Completing the annual performance evaluation on employees:

Performance evaluation can be an effective means of developing influence over people; if they know what behavior you are rewarding and correcting, they can better measure up to your expectations.

58._____

The major value of the annual report is that it provides the opportunity to recognize the employee for what he is doing well.

59._____

Performance evaluation can be made meaningful by the superior and the subordinate agreeing upon what goals are to be accomplished and how the expected results are to be evaluated.

60._____

Complete the answer sheet to examine your style and philosophy of leadership.

ANSWER SHEET FOR LEADERSHIP STYLES QUESTIONNAIRE

Copy your answers from the questionnaire on Leadership Style and Philosophy. Total your scores where indicated.

No. of Item	Your Answer	No. of Item	Your Answer	No. of Item	Your Answer	No. of Item	Your Answer
		1.	_____	3.	_____	2.	_____
5.	_____	6.	_____			4.	_____
9.	_____	8.	_____	7.	_____		
10.	_____			11.	_____	12.	_____
14.	_____	15.	_____			13.	_____
18.	_____	17.	_____	16.	_____		
19.	_____			20.	_____	21.	_____
		22.	_____	24.	_____	23.	_____
27.	_____	26.	_____	25.	_____		
28.	_____			29.	_____	30.	_____
		31.	_____	33.	_____	32.	_____
35.	_____	36.	_____			34.	_____
37.	_____			38.	_____	39.	_____
		40.	_____	42.	_____	41.	_____
44.	_____	45.	_____			43.	_____
48.	_____	47.	_____	46.	_____		
		49.	_____	51.	_____	50.	_____
53.	_____	54.	_____			52.	_____
56.	_____	57.	_____	55.	_____		
58.	_____			59.	_____	60.	_____
Total Box A	[ ]	Total Box B	[ ]	Total Box C	[ ]	Total Box D	[ ]

= 120

After you have totaled boxes A through D, mark an X on the corresponding scales on the lower half of the form at a point corresponding to theg number appearing in the box; if box A is 20, for example, the scale on A should be marked at 20. When all four scales have been completed, draw a connecting line between the Xs. This represents your profile for four different leadership styles. Bring your results to class for discussion.

Put an X on the scales below to represent your numerical scores for the boxes above.

_____	A	15	20	25	30	35	40	45
_____	B	15	20	25	30	35	40	45
_____	C	15	20	25	30	35	40	45
_____	D	15	20	25	30	35	40	45

EXERCISE 51
BUILDING THE HOTEL SAN FRANCISCO

In this exercise you will be exposed to different leadership styles. Your instructor will divide the class into groups of approximately five members. Each group will be provided with a building kit containing a supply of computer cards, one ruler, one scissors, one stapler, and a limited supply of tape. The objective is to construct the "Hotel San Francisco." The construction must have high aesthetic appeal and also be able to withstand the "big quake." (The earthquake will be simulated by dropping a book on the structure from a height of approximately five feet.)

A leader for each group will be designated. As soon as the leaders have received instructions and returned to their respective groups, the groups may begin work on their task. You will be allowed twenty (20) minutes for construction.

When the construction period has ended, your instructor will select one person from each group to serve on a real estate appraisal board. The real estate appraisal board will convene to judge each hotel on its aesthetic appeal and then conduct the simulation (book drop) earthquake. Aesthetic appeal plus quake damage should be used to select the "winning" hotel. The decision of the appraisal board is final.

Your instructor will provide you with additional information for completing this exercise.

Source: Adapted from "Using Participative Management" by Samuel C. Certo, Proceedings of the Eleventh Annual Conference of Eastern Academy of Management, 1974. Republished in Certo and Graf, *Experiencing Modern Management,* William C. Brown Company, 1980.

CASE 52
THE SECRET OF BRADFORD'S WAREHOUSE

Robert Bradford was obviously enjoying the press conference being held in his honor:

Reporter 1: Mr. Bradford, were you surprised when the congressional committee investigating defense contracting procedures today singled out your operation and praised it as a model of efficiency?

Bradford: Yes, I certainly was. We in the aerospace business are used to criticism from the Congress and various defense agencies. It was a pleasant change to have one's company lauded for its achievements.

Reporter 2: But Mr. Bradford, the congressional committee specifically alluded to Bradford's Warehouse in its published remarks and not to the Ingersoll-Standard Corporation as a whole. Indeed, other segments of your corporation have come under fire recently for extensive schedule slippages and cost overruns.

Bradford: I haven't seen the entire text of the committee report. If they specifically referred to the Warehouse, then I am certainly honored and share this honor with my entire design and production team.

Reporter 3: Mr. Bradford, could you tell us exactly what is meant by the term, Bradford's Warehouse?

Bradford: Well, about seven years ago Ingersoll-Standard quietly received an Air Force contract for a classified tactical missile system. Even today I am unable to reveal the scope or nature of the equipment involved because of security reasons.

At the time the effort was so security sensitive that the Air Force wished to have the entire project handled in a separate physical area so that all persons without a need-to-know could be easily excluded. The Air Force was also extremely concerned about compressing the time schedule as much as possible.

Ingersoll-Standard responded by acquiring a nearby vacant production facility which subsequently became known as the Warehouse. It was staffed by a small, highly select team of professionals which achieved the results desired by the Air Force. Since that time the same basic team has been involved in several other aerospace programs operating from the same location.

Reporter 2: Mr Bradford, you've mentioned the Warehouse several times but isn't the more usual term, *Bradford's Warehouse?*

Bradford: Yes, I suppose you're right. I've been the General Manager of the Warehouse operation since its inception and my name has become associated with it by many persons both inside and outside the corporation.

Reporter 3: The congressional committee noted the efficiency with which your people have developed complex systems. They said your operation had a remarkably good cost and schedule record which is inconsistent with the prevailing industry record. Would you comment on this?

Bradford: At the Warehouse we strive to meet or exceed all contractual requirements.

Reporter 1: Could you be more explicit? Exactly what is the secret of Bradford's Warehouse?

Source: Reprinted from Robert D. Joyce, *Encounters in Organizational Behavior,* 1972, with permission of Pergamon Press, Ltd., Oxford, England.

Bradford: There is no secret. . .just common sense. First, we're very selective in our use of talent. When a new project comes in we evaluate its manpower needs relative to our available talent. If necessary we "borrow" persons from other Ingersoll divisions. These persons are particularly selected for their past accomplishments, inventive ideas, ability to work rapidly, and their probable compatibility with existing Warehouse personnel.

Secondly, we use only a quarter to a third the number of people usually assigned to a project of equivalent magnitude. In this way we virtually eliminate job overlaps and work duplication. We stretch every bit of creative talent out of each person on the team. Decisions are made at the lowest possible level and formal meetings are kept to an absolute minimum.

We also demand and get maximum design latitude so we don't have to submit time consuming and costly engineering change proposals to the government every time we run into a design snag. We trust our designers and we expect the contracting agency to trust us to meet the design parameters as originally developed.

Lastly, we keep all paperwork to an absolute minimum. We have successfully refused to submit the normal twenty tons of progress reports on projects of this type. Instead we provide periodic reports of our own simplified design.

Reporter 3: Your critics say that your management methods are ruthless. . .that you run Bradford's Warehouse with an iron hand. It is also widely known that you refuse entry to anyone who is not part of the project team. It is even rumored that you refused a visit by a certain general because you felt the facility tour would waste too much time. Is this true?

Bradford: Our work is best accomplished with as few "advisers" as possible. . .whether part of our corporation or not. However, I recall no instance in which a high ranking government official with a need-to-know clearance was barred from the Warehouse. Now, regarding my ruthlessness, I suggest you talk to my people. . .

The news of the congressional committee report had been received about noon and, at the request of local newspapers and the television stations, the press conference had been hastily called that afternoon at the Ingersoll Executive Briefing Room. Many company officials were on hand with Corporate public relations personnel being most visible.

Not all Ingersoll-Standard officials were elated by the publicity. One executive later confided the following information to a reporter with the explicit understanding that it was off-the-record and, if printed, a denial would be issued. Bradford's Warehouse has to be put in its proper organizational perspective. Their output represents less than 15 percent of the total of our aerospace operations. Fortunately, Bob Bradford has a direct telephone line to our president, Mr. Ingersoll. When Bradford wants something he simply phones Ingersoll and he gets it! This fouls up all other priorities and schedules and the rest of us make a poorer showing as a result. It's a classic case of the tail wagging the dog!

Bradford indiscriminately "raids" other projects for people whenever he wants them. I've had several top designers stolen by Bradford. This leaves me with unfilled positions and further schedule delays.

Bradford also consistently circumvents established procedures and someone else has to pick up the broken pieces he leaves along his path. For example, his engineers ignore the Purchasing Department and deal directly with vendors. you can imagine the problems that creates for others.

Next, I suppose Harry Ingersoll will suggest that all managers employ the *miraculous* Bradford methods. That would be analogous to King Arthur asking the knights of the round table to establish priorities in a free-for-all with broadswords! If it comes to that, Ingersoll can expect my resignation. Extending the use of Bradford's management techniques to other parts of the company would signal the end for Ingersoll-Standard in the aerospace industry!

Questions for Discussion

1. What is Bob Bradford's leadership style?
2. Does Bradford deviate from his predominant style? If so, how? Is it appropriate?
3. Should Bradford try to be more consistent in his leadership style?

CASE 53
METRO CITY HEALTH DEPARTMENT

The growth of Metro City during the past two decade has generated the need for continuously expanding public services. As in other cities, tax revenues are generally insufficient to provide all the services demanded by the community. The City Health Department, one of the public agencies most affected by the scarcity of public money, recently felt it might improve the quantity and quality of its required operations at existing funding levels by improving managerial and operating efficiency.

This suggestion for improving efficiency was presented at the monthly executive board meeting by the Department Director. All members of the board agreed that further efficiencies were possible. Indeed, outside critics of governmental operations, notably the largest Metro City newspaper, had frequently cited the City Health Department for specific instances of mismanagement and bureaucratic red tape. Before the meeting adjourned, a committee was appointed to select an independent management consulting firm to review and make recommendations as to how the Metro City Health Department could make the necessary operational changes to provide those public services required of it within the current budgetary limitations.

At the next meeting of the executive board, the committee submitted its findings as to the availability and projected costs for the services of four prominent management consulting firms. The committee's recommendation was, in view of their findings, that the firm of Barton, Bastine, and Bowditch should be contracted to perform this task. This firm had successfully performed on assignments with public service organizations in other major United States cities and the committee was confident that they would be able to provide the desired guidance in this instance as well. The executive board approved the recommendations of the selection committee and the contract was awarded to Barton, Bastine, and Bowditch.

On the first of May, a management evaluation team headed by Daryl Bowditch began its study of the City Health Department. The first task was to analyze the operations of the department and to compare its growth rate, expansion of services offered, and budgetary increases to the changes in city population over the last two decades. Second, a comparison of the services being offered

Source: Reprinted from Robert D. Joyce, *Encounters in Organizational Behavior,* 1972, with permission of Pergamon Press, Ltd., Oxford, England.

by the Metro City Health Department would be made to those offered by health departments in other cities of similar size throughout the United States. Third, an audit of "management attitude" would be used to determine the validity and nature of apparent management inefficiencies.

After several months study, Daryl Bowditch reviewed a rough draft report on all three phases of their work. The first two phases were a confirmation of the feelings of the executive board. The third phase was somewhat of a surprise.

PHASE 1
SERVICES AND
COSTS RELATIVE
TO POPULATION
TRENDS

The consultant analysis of departmental operations revealed that the primary function of the City Health Department is the rendering of services directed toward the prevention of disease. In this capacity, the department coordinated the activities of several official and unofficial agencies which are also directly concerned with disease prevention.

The study also indicated that many of the department's programs are educational in nature—informing the public of potential health problems, the possible dangers, symptoms, and general methods of prevention. Activities include food, meat, and milk inspections, vector control,[1] air and water pollution, and others. An extensive program of services for the economically depressed includes direct medical services for prenatal care, pediatrics, dental health, tuberculosis control, and control and care of venereal disease. The drug abuse problem has also become a major program from the standpoint of education as well as treatment.

PHASE 2
COMPARISON
WITH OTHER
CITIES

Analysis of the programs offered by the City Health Department revealed that the services offered in Metro City do not differ appreciably in scope or quality from those offered in comparable cities in other parts of the country.

The findings of the evaluation team relative to the growth rate of the department in proportion to the city's growth and the expansion of services with time indicated that there was no major disparity between Metro City and others. The team recognized that it certainly would be easier for the department to function more effectively with greater human and financial resources. The findings were, however, that the present level of approximately three hundred employees, mostly professional and technical, and an annual budget of $18.5 million was minimally adequate to deliver the required services.

PHASE 3
MANAGEMENT
AUDIT

The third phase of the Barton, Bastine, and Bowditch study involved an audit of management attitudes. The technique used to gather data for this portion of the study was to personally interview all members of each of the three levels of management starting from the Assistant Directors down. Seventy personal (and confidential) interviews were conducted. The major purpose of these interviews was to determine how each level of management viewed itself and the other two levels. Upon completion of the interviews, the team members compared notes and selected one statement characteristic of the views of the entire class of management toward the other classes. These summary statements were:

Top Management's View of:

1. *Top Management:* "We are doing a beautiful job considering the handicap of a tight budget and incompetent personnel with whom we must operate."

2. *Middle Management:* "Our big problem is uncooperative and incompetent middle management. Why can't these managers do what we want?"

3. *First-Level Supervision:* "These people are lackadaisical but do an acceptable job under the circumstances."

Middle Management's View of:

1. *Top Management:* "These people are unorganized and confused. They have no long-range plans nor firm objectives or goals. They float with the tide."

2. *Middle Management:* "We are ambitious and try to function effectively without knowing what top management wants or expects. We are conscientious but need guidance. We wish we could really measure the results of our operation."

3. *First-Level Supervision:* "These people are lackadaisical but can get the job done if we stay after them."

First-Level Supervision's View of:

1. *Top Management:* "They do a fair job but they don't appreciate our efforts or understand our problems."

2. *Middle Management:* "They don't appreciate our efforts and should use some of our solutions rather than think up their own. We wish they would make up their minds as to which direction we are going. If they want good solutions, they should at least consult with us."

3. *First-Level Supervision:* "We do a good job when you consider the handicaps of the system. It is difficult to see the results of our efforts, much less measure them. No wonder we're glad when five o'clock rolls around each day."

Daryl Bowditch approved the report and had it typed in final form for presentation to the executive board.

Questions for Discussion

1. Do you think the views expressed by the various levels of management are typical in business firms?

2. How can the contradictory views of each management level be altered?

3. What kind of long-range solution will ease the management problems faced by the health department?

Note

1. Vector in biology is an insect or other organism that transmits a pathogenic fungus, virus, bacterium, etc.

CASE 54
THE TROUBLESOME BOSS AT WORLDVIEW TRAVEL

Frank Cashen worked in the computer department at the headquarters of a large chain of travel agencies. As a programmer supervisor, he was responsible for overseeing the department which operated the systems used by the agency for billings and bookings, payroll, payments to travel providers, and so on. Frank reported to Mark Noble, Operations Vice President of the Worldview Travel Agencies, Ltd.

Frank had just come out of his regular Monday morning session with Mark. These sessions were set up to discuss procedural changes being contemplated for the future, evaluation of the ongoing systems operation, and discussions of any operating problems or variances about which top management might be notified. Frank's secretary noticed he was visibly upset as he returned to his office, and telephoned his friend, John Barnes, a data processing manager for another company in town. Frank said to John: "Noble is giving me ulcers. Mark pretends to be friendly, but when I try to explain things to him, he refuses to listen. He says, "My job is to get results, Frank." John responded to Frank: "You shouldn't worry too much about him. Mark is probably going to retire in a couple of years. Worldview's President isn't going to do anything about him. Just tell Mark what he wants to hear. That's what I do with my boss."

As Frank hung up the phone, he began to think about John's advice. Frank was particularly worried because his department was behind schedule on making an important payroll change to implement new tax laws on employee payroll deductions. Frank felt it was not his fault. He had made several suggestions to Mark about how to implement the change, but Mark did not respond. He didn't know if Mark was waiting for more information about the new tax law, or if it was just the typical pattern of Mark's lack of responsiveness to him. In either case, Frank knew that Mark would be really upset if he found out that the department was late in getting the payroll changes prepared.

Frank thought about quitting his job. Other companies would probably hire him with his skills and experience. He had a headache most of the time. Mark never gave Frank any credit for the department's success.

Frank decided to call John again to ask him how he would handle the upcoming deadline that he was sure he was going to miss. John said: "Frank, call the local IRS office and ask them if you can have a few extra days. Work it out with them. Then when Mark asks about it, just tell him things are taken care of."

Although this approach tempted Frank, he worried that it wouldn't work. The payroll had to go out; even if the IRS approved a delay a later change would mean even more reprogramming for the next payroll to account for the tax deductions which should have occurred earlier. Frank also thought about visiting with Mark to discuss his frustration and to ask for temporary additional help to meet the deadline. He thought that Mark might not want to go to that extra expense. And he also believed that John was right when he said, "The old goat isn't going to change at this stage of his career."

Frank also thought about just trying to "tough it out," since Noble was nearing retirement. But another friend suggested that Frank talk to Mark's supervisor, the President of Worldview Travel. Frank could tell the President about the frustrations that Mark was causing for the programming department. His friend suggested that since Frank had a good record with Worldview, and mobility potential to other jobs, that the President would at least listen to what his concerns were.

Frank was perplexed. He was not at all happy with his relationship with his boss. Yet he liked working at Worldview, and otherwise enjoyed his job. He needed a job, of course. But he didn't know how much longer his stomach could tolerate the current situation. Just as importantly, he wasn't sure how to tackle the problem of being late with the payroll change.

Questions for Discussion

1. Should Frank ask the IRS for a delay?
2. Should Frank talk to Mark Noble about the immediate problem (delay)?
3. Should Frank talk to Mark about their working relationship?
4. Should Frank discuss the problem with the President of Worldview Travel?
5. Should Frank quit his job and find another one?
6. Should Frank try several of these approaches over a period of time?

CASE 55
URIS HALL DORMITORY KITCHEN

PART I

The history of the dormitory began in 1957. The building was built to house thirty men, provide food service to these men, and give the needed room for office space. At that time the cafeteria staff included eleven women and one male student worker. The organization of work was as follows. One woman worked during the morning and early afternoons as cashier. Five of the remaining ten worked from 5:00 a.m. until 1:00 p.m., and the other five worked from 1:00 p.m. until 8:00 p.m.

The male student worked in the evenings as a cashier and dishwasher. Two of the women, Mrs. A and Mrs. B, served as the head cooks. One worked in the morning, and the other worked in the evening. Their duties were limited to making up menus and assigning work. Each of the women under the head cook had a specialty such as baking, salad making, or dishwashing, and each ordered her own supplies in light of the scheduled menus.

Because of the relatively small number of people served, the women were not pressured to prepare large quantities of food. The student cashier was occasionally looked upon as an outsider, but generally he was accepted, especially if some strenuous task was necessary. The cooks prepared twenty meals a week (Sunday night being the exception).

The menu was known because it repeated itself weekly with only occasional variations. With only two exceptions the workers had ten or more years of duty in the dormitory when the case writer came upon the scene in 1975. He was impressed with the quality of the food which, although repetitious, everyone agreed was very good.

The organization was as follows. The head cooks supervised the other cooks, the dishwasher, and the cashier. The setup was identical with the two crews. The student worker was treated well by the women because he was helpful when they needed him; he also happened to be the dormitory director's son. The women were all in their middle or late sixties except the cashier who was about fifty years old. They were all either married or widowed and all had one or more children who were no longer living at home.

The women were all skilled in their work, as was evident from the good food. All but one of them, the eldest who did the baking, had completed grade school, although only five had finished high school, and none had attended college. They were all of Protestant background, and all lived in the city or just outside it. The ladies got along together extremely well and were always willing to help each other. They took turns serving at meal time so everyone had a chance to eat, and they frequently rode to and from work together. When any of them became sick, the others would always give everyone a day-by-day account of the stricken individual's condition.

Several of the women attended the same church in town. They all conversed freely and at length at meal time or any other time, and in the case-writer's two years at the dorm, he never knew of any hard feelings among them.

The head cook pretty much let the other cooks carry out their assignments as they wished. Troubles encountered in the job were typically blamed on the dorm

Source: Adapted from a course assignment prepared by Charles I. Case for Professor J. G. Hunt, Southern Illinois University-Carbondale. Reprinted from Dittrich and Zawacki, *People and Organizations* (Homewood, Ill.: Business Publications, Inc., 1981), pp. 301–306. Copyright 1981 by Business Publications, Inc.

director. Working conditions were adequate although not modern. Much of the equipment installed in 1957 was still being used in 1976. Many time-saving devices such as electric can openers and electric dishwashers were not available. The cafeteria was not air conditioned although two large fans were utilized in the summer, and the cafeteria was always warm in winter.

In spite of these less than ideal conditions, the women rarely complained. They seemed to be accustomed to the old equipment and comfortable using it. As for the activities of the people, all of the cooks did part of the buying, and all took turns serving.

The other activities will be described for each group. At 5:00 a.m. when the morning crew arrived, they all turned their attention to having breakfast ready by 7:00 a.m. The women were assigned typical breakfast preparation duties. After breakfast and after they ate and helped the dishwasher get started, each woman began preparing her own part of the noon meal. One woman had sole responsibility for making the various salads, two others prepared the vegetables, one cooked the meat, and the fifth made all of the desserts. This routine was strictly followed unless someone was ill. In this case, one of the women from the evening group worked all day, or all of the women from the morning crew shared their stricken comrade's duties.

The activities of the evening crew were similar. They have specialized jobs, much like the morning crew, in preparing the evening meal. However, after the meal was over at 7:00 p.m., they all helped clean the kitchen up for the next day. In the cleaning up process they assumed the job of cleaning up the area in which they worked to prepare their specialty. They all freely socialized with one another and took pride in their jobs. There were some strong sentiments among the women about their work and their relationship to each other. These women had worked together for a long time, and had built strong and lasting friendships. Although each jealously protected her individual independence in her specialty, there were strong feelings that each owed it to the others to make sure her part was done well and on time. During the few times when someone did not have her part of the meal ready when it was time to begin serving, the sanctions of the other women were overt, verbal, and sharp.

Production was satisfactory in every way. There were very few people who did not like the food. The ladies appeared to be satisfied. They did not seek other employment, which was plentiful.

PART II

In 1975, the dorm was purchased by State University and was rebuilt and considerably enlarged. In the fall of 1977, it emerged with facilities for 278 men and women, a recreation hall, a large dining hall, a library and a chapel.

All of the old crew were invited to work in the new kitchen, and they all accepted the invitation. To accommodate the increased volume, additional people were required, as were clearer lines of organization. Initially, all of the old crew were put together in one group along with one new person. This group worked in the morning. Ten additional women were hired to work the evening shift. Six male students were hired to operate the new automatic dishwasher and take out garbage during the rush periods. A new organizational structure was developed for the growing organization.

A cafeteria supervisor was hired to head the entire cafeteria operation. This woman had a number of years experience in running large food service facilities. She was given responsibility for planning all menus, buying the food, assigning jobs, and scheduling workers. The only authority she was not given was the right to hire and fire workers and to make her own budget. These two functions were assumed by the dormitory director. The work was divided into the following categories: meats, vegetables, salads, desserts, and dishwashing. The morning crew moved its working schedule back an hour. They started at 4:00 a.m. and worked until 10:00 p.m. A head cook was chosen in each group. She was responsible for seeing that things were done when the supervisor was not present.

The activities performed by the groups remained much the same as they were described in Part I. The only difference was that more people were required. The duties called for the combined efforts of more than one woman. The interactions were very limited. This was because the women rarely saw each other, and the two groups prepared their own meals. Thus, the evening crew started making the evening meal from scratch rather than serving what was prepared in the morning. The only exception was that the desserts were all made in the morning.

Brand new equipment was placed in the cafeteria. An emphasis was placed on obtaining equipment capable of preparing large quantities of food in the most efficient manner. The building was air conditioned, well lit, and had been carpeted.

The workers were no longer allowed to order their own supplies. The new supervisor assumed this function entirely. It was necessary to order different kinds and different quantities of food now that 300 were being fed instead of thirty. For instance, the old crew who had been accustomed to cooking rather small roasts were now asked to cook very large roasts. Soon a lot of trouble was evident about the quality of food being ordered. The old crew felt that the supervisor was not doing a creditable job. They made their sentiments well known, both in verbal discussions with the supervisor and in written statements to the director. They claimed the food was impossible to cook, of inferior quality, and a waste of money.

Their second gripe concerned the hiring of a woman to work in the morning who was not of the old group. The women objected to her presence for two reasons. First, she was loud. She was not belligerent or profane, but she had a husky, bellowing voice. She was also given to lengthy seizures of singing at the top of her booming voice. None of the other women possessed these characteristics and they objected rather strongly to the noise.

This was not their most serious objection to her however. This woman, whom we shall call Mrs. Loud, also frequently extolled her own great skill in large kitchens, though she only had one year of experience. Not only did Mrs. Loud boast of her own abilities, she also tried to instruct the other women in the proper method of cooking. Mrs. Loud felt that her supposed expertise qualified her to boss the other women. A long succession of incidents followed in which Mrs. Loud became an increasingly bad influence on the morning crew. Finally, two of the women came to the supervisor and explained that they could no longer tolerate Mrs. Loud and would quit if she was not replaced.

There was also a problem concerning the dishwasher. One woman was assigned the entire job of washing dishes at the old dormitory, and the old crew accepted this as proper procedure. However, the volume of business and mechanics of the automatic dishwasher at the new cafeteria necessitated that the women sometimes help the woman assigned to the dishwasher. This was especially true when the student helpers were not available. Many of the women did not like or accept this situation and were rather upset about it.

They first objected because they felt that the woman assigned to the job was not doing her job properly. It soon became evident that this was not the case. Rather, at times, the volume of dishes simply was too much for one woman to handle. The student workers alleviated the problem to a great extent, but there were still times when the cooks were required to help. Scraping and washing dishes is not the most desirable or satisfying job in a kitchen, or anywhere else for that matter. Each woman was assigned a specialty and took pride in her work, and broadening these duties to include these kinds of activities did not go over well. Long and sad grumbling was often voiced by the cooks who had to help with the dishwasher.

The evening crew was also plagued by some problems. First, there was the problem of adjustment for the new employees. As previously stated, all the old employees were put on the morning shift, so all the people on the evening crew were new. Three of the women had no previous experience working in a large cafeteria, so they had to learn as well to adapt. The part of the job involving cleaning the cafeteria each night also became a problem. The women felt that they were being imposed upon because the morning crew had no such duties. Several of the women had expressed displeasure at the cleaning chore and had said that they would quit "if the opportunity arose for another job."

The third group of people working in the new dormitory was the student workers. Only one student worked at the old dormitory, but the new dormitory required the part-time help of six students. These workers were all young men who lived in the dorm. They worked mainly during the noon and evening meals, where as many as 325 people were served. They worked almost solely on the automatic dishwasher, which was used to capacity during these peak hours. They also did some cleaning chores and stocking, but were mainly limited to washing dishes.

Although these students were generally aware of the problems in the cafeteria, they did not take sides or engage in the squabbling. They came in, did the work, and got out as fast as possible. The cooks and other staff considered these students as welcome help. As one put it, "I don't know what we'd do without them."

The output of the cafeteria during this period was not too desirable. The production of food was adequate, although it was frequently not on schedule or in proper quantities. Morale was not high, and many of the women, both old and new employees, expressed dissatisfaction with their jobs. This dissatisfaction was mainly centered on the assignment of duties, the personalities of fellow workers, and the lack of consideration that the workers felt they were receiving from the management. The director felt that changes were necessary, and he made plans for reorganization to take place on January 1, 1978.

Questions for Discussion

1. In Part I it was noted that the ladies rarely complained about their working conditions. Why?

2. Do you think the dormitory director should have authority to hire and fire workers?

3. Why did the old crew start complaining about the food being ordered?

4. What recommendations would you make to the dormitory director?

CHAPTER 8

COMMUNICATION

● **LEARNING OBJECTIVES**

After completing this chapter you should have:

1. A better understanding of why messages have different meanings for senders and receivers.

2. An understanding of methods and channels of communication.

3. An improvement in your communication skills.

W hen managers apply leadership skills, work with groups, or develop interpersonal relationships, some action is usually required. This action comes in the form of communication—both verbal and nonverbal. Through the presence or absence of body movements, speaking, listening, and writing, we communicate messages to those around us and receive messages in the form of feedback. Some of what you learned earlier about understanding yourself and others also applies here in terms of how we perceive and send messages, for the sender and the receiver are operating under a certain set of assumptions and expectations. This chapter includes material designed to give you experience in understanding and developing your communication skills. Since verbal communication is the most frequent activity managers engage in, this skill can be crucial to your success and effectiveness.

Communications can be considered a six-part process:

1. The sender conceives of a message to convey to a receiver.
2. The sender puts the message in a form he or she thinks the receiver will understand.
3. The sender chooses a method to transmit the message (verbal, nonverbal).
4. The sender chooses a channel of communication (formal, informal).
5. The receiver perceives the message.
6. The receiver decodes and understands the message.

Of course, in the last two phases the receiver may perceive something different than the sender intended. (Have you ever played that party game where a rumor is sent along a line of people and ends up much different from the original version?) The message may be coded incorrectly, the wrong method or channel used for transmission, or the receiver may have a different set of assumptions about what the message meant. Thus, true communication is difficult to achieve. That is why feedback is often important. The receiver becomes a sender and transmits to the original sender what he or she thinks the message meant in the form of appropriate or inappropriate behavior or a response to the message. The

"Martha Burleigh" case helps you explore various aspects of communication in the workplace.

As we briefly mentioned, the channel used to send messages is a major feature affecting communication effectiveness. The reading "The Care and Cultivation of the Corporate Grapevine" introduces you to the informal channel that managers use. But managers are sometimes ambivalent about the grapevine. They are positive toward the grapevine when that grapevine works to communicate their message quickly and the message is well received. You can sometimes obtain greater acceptance of a message by working through informal leaders of a group than by "passing down revelations from on high." But managers become negative toward the grapevine when they feel it is nothing but a rumor mill. In the reading, Davis points out that this problem can be dealt with by the prompt communication of facts.

While the informal channels are often used and useful, managers also use the formal organizational structure and other methods to communicate—both orally and in writing. The "Lazarsfeld's Department Store" case illustrates many ways in which managers and employees communicate, and provides examples of managerial reactions and uses of various communication systems.

The content of communication is also important. But content is affected by the communication process as outlined earlier. In order to understand the communication process better, you might try the exercise "The Meanings in Communication," which deals with the encoding process by which the sender puts a message in a form he or she thinks will be understood. You may find that, as a result of the use of slang, a literal interpretation of messages bears little relationship to the actual content in the mind of either the sender or the receiver.

The exercise "How Would You Reply?" focuses on the encoding and decoding aspects of communication and on feedback. Underlying each message are the thoughts, interpretations, and emotions of all parties to a communication. How supervisors or managers respond to a communication may depend on what they thought the sender meant in the first place. Thus, their response may be one of action or perhaps of feedback to the sender to suggest understanding. Or it may be a request for more information or an interpretation to determine whether they are decoding the message properly.

Responses may be perceived positively or negatively. Managers receiving messages from others need to consider *their* response in this light. "The Taciturn Manager" case also addresses this issue and shows how unintended communication can take place. Here, failures in communicating the true meaning occurred. Through the managers' actions, employees received an incorrect message. Part of this problem, of course, involves the third aspect of the six-part process—the method used to transmit.

In the "Nonverbal Communication" exercise, you have a chance to study another method of transmitting messages. Have you ever heard of body language? It's for real! The spoken word is important, but how you shake hands, your body posture, facial expressions, appearance, movements, and the like, convey an equally important message. "Nonverbal Communication" asks you to analyze what these unspoken messages are and how they affect receivers. ●

READING 56

THE CARE AND CULTIVATION OF THE CORPORATE GRAPEVINE

Keith Davis

The vice-president of a large processing company, one of only a few top officers privy to plans for relocating the company to a nearby suburb, was startled one day to hear his wife upbraid him for not telling her about the move. She had heard the news from her maid.

The wife of a plant supervisor delivered her baby at 11 p.m. A company survey revealed that by 2 p.m. the next day, 46% of the management personnel already knew about the blessed event.

The middle manager of a medium-sized manufacturing company was understandably surprised when a colleague congratulated him on his promotion. The announcement had not even gone through the paperwork yet.

In all these cases, the informal communication apparatus known as the corporate grapevine was at work. With the rapidity of a burning powder train and as elusive as a summer zephyr, it filters through steel walls and glass partitions, from subbasement to the rafters, past the water fountain, the copying room, the manager's door and the porter's mop closet. It cares nothing for civil rights; it has no respect for persons or for the prerogatives of management; it will carve up and serve the big boss, the shop foreman, or the pool typist with fine impartiality.

Wherever people congregate in groups, the grapevine is sure to grow. It may manifest itself in smoke rings, jungle tom-toms, taps on prison walls or just idle chitchat, but it will always be there. Indeed, the word *grapevine* has been part of our jargon ever since the Civil War, when telegraph lines were strung loosely from tree to tree in vine-like fashion and resulted in messages that were frequently garbled.

Because it is able to penetrate the most rigid corporate security with ease and cannot be held accountable for its errors, managers sometimes succumb to the wish that the company grapevine would wither and die. But the weedkiller that can stunt its growth has not yet been formulated. It is as hard to kill as the mythical glass snake that, when struck, broke itself into fragments and grew a new snake out of each piece.

NATURAL AND SIGNIFICANT

For those managers who are so often "the last to know" about the grapevine's latest intelligence, it may be of some comfort to consider that it is a natural, normal part of a company's total communications system and is no more evil in itself than pain or the weather. It is also a significant force within the work group, helping to build teamwork, motivate people and create corporate identity.

The point is that every organization functions under two systems, one formal and one informal. The formal organization is the one usually shown on organization charts in which authority is delegated from one level to another according to a strict chain of command. The informal organization, on the other hand, arises from the social relationships of people, and is neither required nor controlled by management. To serve this informal organization, an informal communication system arises that is variable, dynamic and fickle, running back and forth across organizational lines and rapidly changing its course. Hence, the grapevine.

In a sense, moreover, the degree of grapevine activity is a measure of a company's spirit and vitality. If employees are so disinterested in their work that they do not engage in shop talk, they are maladjusted. If they are so indifferent about their associates that they even eschew chattering about who will get the promotion, who brought in the big contract or which young executive is dating whose secretary, they are patently abnormal. A lively grapevine reflects the deep psychological need of people to talk about their jobs and their company as a central life interest. Without it, the company would literally be sick.

More than merely a device to convey corporate gossip, the grapevine is an influence to be considered in all management actions. Indeed, since the grapevine's influence may be favorable or unfavorable, managers are coming to realize that to get this vine to bear desirable fruit, they must feed, water and cultivate it. To integrate the grapevine's interests with those of the formal organization, they must listen to it, study it, learn who its leaders are, how it operates and what information it carries.

MAKING IT WORK

For every story on the vine, however wild and fanciful, has its root cause. If the grapevine has it that Joe is about to quit, it may mean that Joe's associates wish he would quit, that Joe wishes he could quit, or that Joe's wife wants him to quit. Or something else. A confidential chat with Joe himself can uncover the reasons he is on the grapevine, and maybe even solve whatever the problem may be.

At the same time, the manager who finds himself constantly bypassed by the grapevine should take it as a signal that his own channels of communication can stand some dredging. For example, does he help his people get information when they need it? If so, they will be more likely to return the favor by keeping him informed. Does he talk with his staffers only when official business requires it, or does he keep in touch by chance chats in corridors, the cafeteria or even the men's room? If so, they are more likely to level with him beyond the demands of office protocol.

In this way, the grapevine gives a manager considerable feedback about what his employees are up to. It also helps interpret management to the workers so that they may be more understanding. It is especially helpful in translating management's formal orders into employee language by conveying information that the formal system does not wish to carry and purposely leaves unsaid. The supervisor who comes to work in an ugly mood because he has had a spat with his wife, for instance, can hardly announce that fact to his people. But he can forewarn them informally by putting on the grapevine the admonition, "Don't talk to the boss about a raise today."

Another fascinating feature of the grapevine is its fast pace and canny skill at cracking even the tightest company security screen. Being flexible and personal, it spreads information faster than most management communications systems operate. One company, for example, signed its labor contract at 11 p.m., and had to keep its publications staff busy all night in order to have a suitable bulletin ready for employees arriving at work the following morning. It was the only way that the company could match the grapevine's speed and forestall undesirable rumors about the agreement.

When both the formal and informal communications channels are working effectively, they complement each other. Each carries information particularly suited to its needs and capabilities so that together the two systems build effective communications in the company.

But the two systems can also work at cross purposes, and the manager's job is to try to bring the grapevine into closer harmony with the total needs of the organization and work group. In order to do this, though, he must understand the grapevine's way of life.

Many a "last to know" executive grumbles about the grapevine because he is under the impression that it operates like a long chain in which A tells B, who tells C, who then tells D, and so on until, twenty persons later, Y gets the information—very late and very incorrect. Not so. Some grapevines may operate this way, but research shows that they generally follow a different pattern, which works something like this: A tells three or four others (such as B, R and F). Yet only one or two of these receivers will then pass on the information, and they will usually tell more than one person. Then, as the information becomes older and the proportion of these knowing it gets larger, it gradually dies out because those who receive it do not repeat it.

THE "CLUSTER CHAIN"

This network is a "cluster chain," because each link in the chain tends to inform a cluster of other people instead of only one person. And in every cluster chain, as noted, only a few persons are active communicators on the grapevine for any particular bit of information. In one company whose grapevine activity I recently studied, 68% of the executives knew about a quality control problem, but only 20% of them passed the information along. In another company, when a manager planned to resign, 81% of the executives knew about it, but only 11% spread the news.

The reason everyone in the chain does not become a liaison for every bit of information is that the grapevine is more a product of the situation than it is of the person. People tend to be active on the grapevine when events cause them to be, especially during periods of excitement and insecurity. Given an impending layoff of personnel or the installation of a new computer, the grapevine hums with activity.

This element of cause and predictability is important because it offers management a chance to influence the grapevine. At times when the grapevine is crackling with vibrations, executives need to watch it with extra care and feed it true information to keep it from getting out of hand.

While it is true that some gossipy types are more often to be found working in the grape vineyard than others, there is no evidence that any one person or group consistently acts as liaison to the exclusion of all others. Given the proper situation and motivation, anyone in an organization can become a grapevine activist. In three successive surveys I made of one group of sixty executives, the liaison individuals were different in each instance.

Nevertheless, based on empirical observation, certain conclusions can be drawn about the corporate grapevine. The first, of course, is that the greatest spread of information occurs immediately after it is known. The second is that people are most apt to feed the grapevine when their friends and work associates are involved. This means that if Executive A is to be promoted or Executive B fired, employees need to know the true story as soon as possible. If they are not informed, they will fill in the gaps with their own conclusions.

Since the grapevine exists largely by word of mouth and by observation, it is most active in office situations that regularly bring people into contact with each other. For example, in one company the chief link between two offices was one manager's secretary, who stopped by the other office right after lunch every day to pick up reports. In another office, the link was an accounting clerk who phoned 300 yards across the company property each morning to get certain cost data.

It may be a cliché, but it is nevertheless true that the secretary plays a key role as liaison agent in the grapevine. Since she processes her boss' correspondence, greets visitors, makes appointments and often acts as her employer's confidante, she is strategically located as a communication center in the work system, and is the one most likely to feed the grapevine. On the other hand, I hasten to add that the corporate grapevine is very much a coeducational institution, in which the men are no less active in spreading news than the women.

THE GRAPEVINE VS. RUMOR

If the corporate grapevine enjoys something less than the high regard of management, it is because of its undeserved reputation as a rumor factory. But rumor and the grapevine are not the same; rumor is a part of the grapevine—the injudicious and untrue part that is communicated without factual evidence to back it up. Rumor should, of course, be stopped as soon as possible. For research shows that once a rumor is known and accepted, employees tend to distort future happenings to conform to the rumor.

Take the case of John Worker, who cut two fingers of his left hand at his machine one morning, and was sent to the dispensary for first aid. The farther from John's department the story traveled, the more gruesome were his injuries, until finally the story had him losing his left hand. Alert supervisors at the company, observing the effect of the rumor on morale, promptly investigated the facts and announced over the public-address system that the most serious injury treated that morning were two cut fingers of a machine operator, who received treatment and returned to his job. No mention was made of the rumor itself, but the announcement brought it under control.

Since rumors are generally incorrect, an outcropping of them can be as crippling to an organization as a tornado—and usually cause as much damage. Rumor should be dealt with firmly and consistently, but the manager must also be careful about what he attacks and how he attacks it. It is folly to strike at the entire grapevine merely because it happens to be the agent that carries the rumor. That approach would be as judicious as throwing away a typewriter because of a few misspelled words.

Because its errors are more dramatic and consequently more impressed on the memory, people think that the grapevine is less accurate than it really is. Actually, the reverse is true. My own research indicates that in normal business situations, between 75 percent and 95 percent of grapevine information is correct, even though most of the stories are incomplete in detail.

Of course, that 5 percent to 25 percent error can be vital to the truth of the story. I recall, for instance, one grapevine story about a welder marrying the general manager's daughter that was true with regard to his getting married, the date, the church and other details. The one wrong fact in the report was that the girl was not the general manager's daughter, but merely had the same last name. Yet this one fact made the whole story erroneous—even though the rest of it was correct.

Such inadequacies of the grapevine mean that, in total, it probably produces more misunderstanding than its small percentage of wrong information suggests. And for that reason alone, many a manager is given to fantasizing about the day he can post a notice on the bulletin board saying: "Effective 12:00 noon tomorrow, the grapevine in this office is abolished."

That is mere wishful thinking. For the evidence is rather conclusive that homicide will not work with the grapevine. If we suppress it in one place, it pops up in another.

Moreover, the sinuousness of the grapevine—its ability to move in all directions within and outside the organization—is a fact of corporate life. Those managers who do not accept it, respect it, and cultivate open channels of communication to offset it may continue to find themselves out of touch with what is really going on in the company. They may also be the subject of the next story on the corporate grapevine.

Questions for Discussion

1. Why do managers dislike the corporate grapevine? Is it really the grapevine they don't like, or is it something else?
2. If managers do not get information from the grapevine, can they be effective?
3. How can a manager use the grapevine effectively?

CASE 57
MARTHA BURLEIGH

Ten years after the event John Sedgwick could remember vividly in its every detail what he called the "affaire Martha" and particularly his sense of personal outrage when he first learned of Andrew Joplin's decision. The passage of a decade, during which he had accumulated a substantial amount of administrative experience himself, studied a number of administrators-at-work, and read and thought a lot about administration, had left him still unsure as to whether his boss had shown a deep understanding of human nature in his handling of Martha Burleigh, clerk-stenographer, or whether he had been just plain lucky that the action he took turned out as well as it did.

John Sedgwick at the time had been working for the United States Air Force as a civilian employee in the aircraft structural design division, evaluation section. He was one of four engineers reporting to Andrew Joplin, the section chief. Assignments were divided as follows:

- Sedgwick: heating and ventilating, fire protection
- Anderson: production materials and processes
- Berry: production materials and processes
- Zernia: design strength minima for structural components
- Joplin: supervision, integration of above assignments

Martha Burleigh was the clerk-stenographer for the section. Although she was under Andrew Joplin's direct supervision, she handled the clerical work of the entire group. She was about 40 years old, had been in the section for 15 years, and had the reputation of being the best quality (not quantity) producer among the clerk-stenographers in the aircraft structural design division. She was single and lived at home with her father, mother, and a brother about her own age, also unmarried.

John remembered Martha as sallow in complexion, thin and stringy in build, neat but drab in dress; and as impersonal and withdrawn in her daily contacts with divisional personnel. She wasn't exactly unfriendly, she just wasn't friendly. She addressed herself diligently to her work, did a minimum of talking, and never took part in the give and take of office badinage.

Source: From Austin Grimshaw and John Hennessey, *Organizational Behavior* (New York: McGraw-Hill 1960). Used by permission.

Floor space in the division was allocated to sections on the basis of a fixed number of square feet per employee. Footage assigned to each section was subject to immediate adjustment whenever its personnel increased or decreased. Layout of desks in the evaluation section was as follows (see Stage 1).

Stage 1

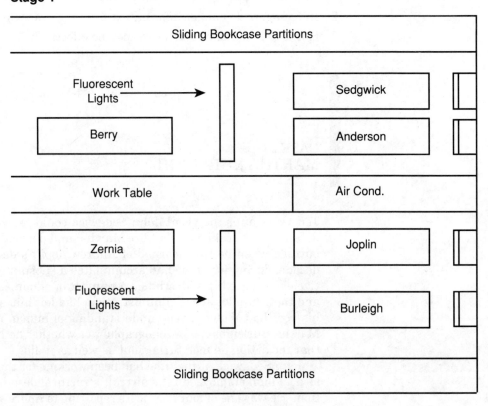

Sedgwick, Anderson, Joplin, and Burleigh had window desks. Berry and Zernia had inside desks. The entire space was brilliantly lighted by fluorescent tubes and there were no shadow areas.

Andrew Joplin, before joining the section as chief a year earlier, had been an aircraft structures engineer. In this position his duties had been entirely technical in nature, with no supervisory responsibility. He was a graduate engineer, 36 years old, with 12 years of continuous service as an Air Force civilian employee. His appointment as chief of the evaluation section, aircraft structural design division, had involved a transfer within the aircraft design organization from one branch to another, an increase in grade and a higher salary. The four engineers under him had all been in the section for varying periods of time when Joplin took over—Sedgwick and Anderson for nearly four years and Berry and Zernia for one and two years respectively. All four had enjoyed working for Joplin and with each other. There was no conflict of interest among them because each had his own specialty.

The trouble with Martha began when Berry quit to take a job in industry. Her space by the window and the desk where she sat were assigned to another section in the square footage readjustment which followed Berry's resignation. He was not replaced. Joplin assigned Zernia to Berry's old location and Martha to the desk vacated by Zernia (See Stage 2). Martha was obviously disturbed. She became more tight-lipped and silent than ever.

Stage 2

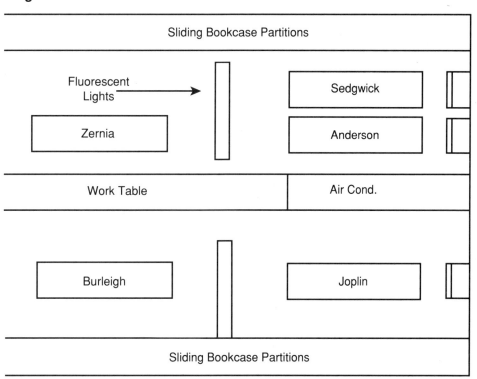

Almost immediately after the move, Martha began to complain that the fluorescent lights bothered her. Joplin had the lights turned 90 degrees in an attempt to stop her frequent references to her newly developed headaches. When she continued to complain, he arranged to have light meter tests made. These indicated that the illumination level at her location was slightly below the recommended standard, so he had blue tubes put in. These brought the lighting level at her desk slightly above standard.

During the following two weeks Martha still fussed about her headaches. She kept aspirin, cotton pads and eyewash, prominently displayed, on her desk and frequently used them. She bought a pair of dark glasses and a green celluloid eyeshade, which she wore constantly. Her production dropped to almost zero. Work she had previously handled in stride had to be sent outside the section to the typing pool, in order to get done within a reasonable time.

Sedgwick, Anderson, and Zernia were upset because Martha was not getting out the work they gave her. Also, they resented her attitude, Zernia, they pointed out to each other and to Joplin, had gotten along all right in the same location and his job involved much more eyestrain than Martha's. They severally said to Joplin: "Let's lay down the law, let her know who's boss around here. Send her to the doctor. If he says she's OK, get her reassigned out of the section and get someone in here who'll get some work done."

Instead of acting on this advice, Joplin horrified the three engineers by trading his window location for Martha's inside space (See Stage 3).

Stage 3

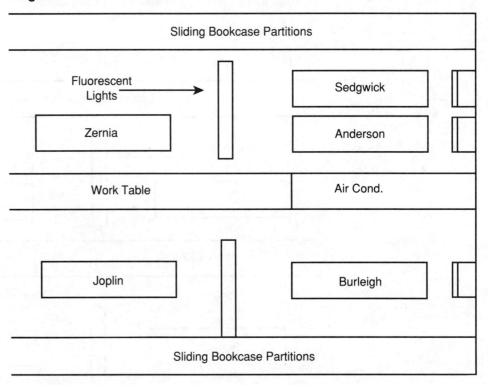

Martha immediately abandoned her aspirin, eyewash, dark glasses, and eyeshade. Her productivity at once returned to its previous norm. She apparently took her return to a window desk as her just due. She made no slightest gesture of demurring when Joplin suggested the shift, nor did she ever thank him for it.

After a few days the section settled back into its former routine. Sedgwick, Anderson, and Zernia, although still upset by Joplin's solution, decided to go along with it. Sedgwick and Anderson, however, did try individually to persuade Joplin to trade locations with them. Joplin refused to do so.

Questions for Discussion

1. Was Martha Burleigh's message received and correctly understood by Andrew Joplin?
2. Did Martha Burleigh's message convey the correct feeling to the receiver?
3. Discuss the methods of message transmission. Were these the best ones that Burleigh may have chosen?
4. Did Andrew Joplin understand the message? Explain.
5. Was the problem handled correctly as far as Andrew Joplin was concerned?

CASE 58
LAZARSFELD'S DEPARTMENT STORE

Mr. Francis Powell, executive vice-president of Lazarsfeld's Department Store, returned from a conference held by the National Retail Dry Good Association, where he had been impressed by a talk he heard on the subject of communications. Soon after his return to the store, he discussed the conference with Ms. Sandra Stone, the personnel manager, and gave her the notes he had taken on that talk. Ms. Stone agreed that relationships between members of the Lazarsfeld organization might be improved if more attention were given to management-employee communications.

A young man, George Peters, had recently joined the Personnel Department and was being trained for the position of employment supervisor. A graduate of the state university, he had worked in a small department store while in college and for two years thereafter. Mr. Peters came to Lazarsfeld directly from that position. It occurred to Ms. Stone that it would be good training and experience for her new assistant if he made a thorough survey of the methods of communication used by the store personnel.

Mr. Peters was given this assignment, which he discussed with both Ms. Stone and Mr. Powell. He was also given Mr. Powell's conference notes, told that he could interview any executive in the store, and asked to complete the survey within a week.

Four days later Mr. Peters presented the following report to Ms. Stone and asked if he could discuss it with her after it was read.

STORE COMMUNICATIONS: REPORT BY GEORGE PETERS

Like many other department stores, Lazarsfeld's has various, established channels for two-way communications between management and workers. A need exists for making these communication channels more effective. This report suggests that improvements in store communications might result in greater employee understanding of store problems and could increase worker productivity, reduce operating costs, and create greater store profits.

Means of Communication

Various types of communication are presently used at Lazarsfeld's. They include the following:

    A. Written Communications. Several media make up this part of the formal system, which is used by management to supply workers with information.

        1. House Organ. Lazar-Life is a monthly publication written and edited by store employees. It is an attractive magazine featuring many employee pictures and brief copy. It concentrates on the "human element," attempting to build group solidarity among store personnel. The store management makes little or no effort to use this medium to tell employees of its philosophy or its problems.

        2. Door Handouts. Employees receive these bulletins when they sign in for work. The handouts announce special events, such as an evening softball game, and emphasize important sales promotions or other events. They are issued once or twice a week. Frequently, they give employees information or instruction from management.

3. *Paycheck inserts. Another reminder that emphasizes important promotions, charity solicitations, or policies is a brief message placed in each employee's paycheck envelope. This method is particularly effective when the store is in the process of a charity drive. In general, the messages in pay envelopes are carefully written; when asking for a contribution, they do not offend the readers. Several supervisors feel that these inserts are less effective when used every week.*

4. *Bulletin Boards. Eleven bulletin boards, placed in strategic locations throughout the store, contain important and current information. Some workers pay very little attention to these postings. Perhaps the material could be presented in a more interesting and readable form. Some employees complain that items on the bulletin board are seldom changed and that current notices are carelessly posted.*

5. *Intrastore Correspondence. One of the most useful channels of communication consists of intracompany correspondence and reports. Written material travels between superiors and subordinates, as well as among people of equal rank. These reports are usually concerned with operating problems and policies, but they frequently clear up misunderstandings and solve problems that reach deep into the human relations aspect of communications. Many individuals in the store do not write letters, memos, and instructions as well as they should.*

B. *Meetings. Department and store meetings constitute another segment of Lazarsfeld's formal communication system.*

1. *Departmental Meetings. In departmental meetings, employees receive merchandise information and hear about changes in operating procedures. New selling techniques are also presented. Their primary function is to stress store operations, policies, procedures, and merchandise.*

2. *Store Meetings. Occasionally a meeting is held on the main floor for all 800 Lazarsfeld employees. Everyone is expected to come to work ten minutes early on store meeting days, but half or more of the store personnel either miss the meetings or come in late. New policies or special promotions are briefly discussed, and detailed explanations are given at the department level. The purpose of the mass meeting is to develop a feeling of group solidarity and to give employees the opportunity to hear a message from "top management." Supposedly, the workers will think that they are in "one, big, happy family," and thereby accept the submitted information more readily. These meetings are not as successful as the speakers think they are. Many employees complain about the early starting time, especially since they receive no compensation for the extra time spent in the store.*

C. *Counseling. In connection with employee attitudes and performance, there are two types of counseling: a six-month interview and the attitude survey. The objectives of both counseling methods are to determine and improve both job satisfaction and job performance.*

1. *Six-Month Interview. Each employee is rated and interviewed by a member of the Personnel Department every six months. An attempt is made to see if an adjustment between job and worker is needed. Compensation problems, promotions, benefits, and transfers are the main topics considered. It is the responsibility of the Personnel Department to cooperate with an employee's supervisor if any action is needed after the interview. These interviews have more form than substance. In many cases, the worker and the personnel counselor have different opinions about needed adjustments. The interviews seem overly guided by what the counselor, who has obtained impressions from other employees, feels is important.*

2. *Attitude Survey. Occasionally, management attempts to determine general employee attitudes toward store policies and operations through questionnaires. These are given to each worker in those departments where morale or productivity seems to be low. Some employees think the attitude surveys are a waste of time. A number of the younger stock boys take the interviews as a "joke," which probably makes their information highly unreliable.*

D. *Informal Communications. Some supervisors and department heads at Lazarsfeld's seem to be unaware of the fact that good management-employee relations depend upon continuous, satisfactory relationships. These managers are frequently skilled in merchandising or sales, but they fail to realize that the cooperation and goodwill of subordinates is necessary in order to have an effective department. Employees holding lower-level management positions do not appear to believe that this is true.*

1. *Manager-Employee Relationship. There is a wide variance in supervisory effectiveness from department to department. In a few departments the employees seem to be reasonably contented and productive. Their bosses treat them as individuals and are willing to listen to their problems and questions. Too many Lazarsfeld supervisors, however, do not know how to develop this open atmosphere. Their employees seem to be afraid and seldom choose to speak with their superiors. Some even refused to talk freely with the author of this report.*

2. *Grapevine. Lazarsfeld's grapevine is, perhaps, the quickest means of communication in the store. It travels up and down the management-employee ladder at a rapid rate.*

Conclusions

Some potential channels of communication in the store have not been included in this study. The most significant of these are the relationships between training supervisors and employees. No doubt the activities of the store's training division could be a more effective channel for management communications. When training new employees and when training current employees for transfer, the training supervisor and the department instructors could pass along more information regarding management policies and practice. Moreover, training supervisors could collect ideas, suggestions, and other information from workers which, in turn, could be helpful to management. Apparently, higher-level executives have seldom participated in training meetings. One supervisor stated that he was sorry his boss couldn't have heard what was said at the last supervisory conference.

At this time, two suggestions might be appropriate. First, it is recommended that the suggestion system, which was discontinued several months ago, be reconsidered. Secondly, it is suggested that this report be carefully reviewed in management and supervisory meetings. Improvements in store communications can be made if the key people in the organization give their attention to the problem.

Respectfully submitted,

George Peters

Less than an hour after Ms. Stone received the report on communications, she called Mr. Peters into her office. "It's a good report, George. You've covered a lot of ground. But don't you think you've been a little too critical in some spots? You've been pretty hard on our counseling program."

"Well, I hope not, Ms. Stone," said George. "I just didn't know how to write the report. I could have made it sound better, but I decided to tell it like it is."

"Oh, it's not so bad—but, take something like the early morning meetings. A few employees gripe about the ten minutes' early start, but do our better people mind? Don't the meetings do more good than harm?"

"Possibly so, Ms. Stone, but I just feel that there have been too many lately. Mr. Bauer had two last week."

"Well, Mr. Bauer is superintendent over the whole store—but he probably does call too many meetings. Did you talk to him about the survey? How did he like it?"

"I think he was too busy to really understand what I was doing," replied Peters. "I had a hard time seeing him and when I did have a chance to get into his office, I waited behind a line of three other people. I don't think he liked the survey."

"But what did he say about the communications in his department?" asked Ms. Stone.

"He said they were good; he thinks there is no problem. He says that when he wants to communicate, he just goes out and talks to whomever he wants to communicate with. Of course, I couldn't ask him many questions."

"I know what you mean George. I need to reach him this morning. I've called three times and I can't get him on the phone."

"Well, I want you to know, Ms. Stone, that I appreciated the opportunity to make this survey. If I seem critical it's just because I want to be of help."

"I'm glad you feel that way," replied Ms. Stone. "We want you to get into these store problems. I'd better mark this report 'Confidential'—and we'll see what Mr. Powell says about it."

"Thanks, Ms. Stone," said George as he left the office.

Questions for Discussion

1. What are the various mechanisms to communicate at the department store? Are they equally effective?

2. Does Mr. Bauer seem concerned about effective communications? Are meetings a good way to communicate?

3. What would you recommend to Ms. Stone regarding issues she should bring up with Mr. Powell?

4. If Mr. Powell agrees with the report's conclusions, what action should he take?

EXERCISE 59
THE MEANINGS IN COMMUNICATION

Below is a list of expressions that are in use today. Try to discern the literal meaning of each expression and then write what you think its slang meaning is. Look for examples of its use by people you talk with on a given day and try to assess whether their meaning is the same as your interpretation. Write other expressions you encounter and what they mean. Does the meaning vary with voice inflection or with how the expression is used in the sentence?

Expression	Literal Meaning	Meaning in Usage
Laid back		
That's where it's at		
Getting his act together		
Too much		
That's cool		
It's history		
Out of hand		
The whole nine yards		
Stressed out		
Out of it		
Later on		
Get real		
She gets off on		
Home boy		
That's heavy		
Chill out		
That gets me down		
Give me a break		
Grass		

EXERCISE 60
HOW WOULD YOU REPLY?

On the following pages, you are presented with number of expressions typical of employees in many different settings. In each instance, you are to presume that you are the employee's supervisor and that the expression is directed to you.

Following each expression are five different replies. Read each carefully. You will probably feel that some of the replies are inappropriate; others may strike you as particularly apt. Try to select from among the five the one reply that you feel would be most effective under the circumstances.

You aren't given much information about the employee—in fact, very little. This may have a lot of influence on the reply you see as best. As you consider each alternative, try to capture your reasons for accepting or rejecting it.

As you complete each item, it will be discussed in class. As the discussions continue, you may find that not everyone agrees on the answers and that some individuals rather consistently respond in a certain way.

1. *Assistant foreman, age 31, light manufacturing:* "Well, yes, there is something on my mind. It's just that I'm wondering what happened on the last promotion deal—you know, when Pete was made foreman there in the other department. I was wondering how come Pete was chosen, and it seemed sorta strange to me. I didn't think he was in line for the job at all. But my real question is what you fellows think of me. I've been assistant foreman now for two and a half years, and I've been in the department here for six, and I, I just wonder; well, to hear people talk, that this is just my job, that here is where I belong, and that's it. I'm assistant foreman till the day I die. I kinda thought my work has always been pretty good. At least, no one has done any griping about it. Seem to have as good a record as anybody else, and I just want to know what the heck it takes to get a promotion around here."

   a. Has something happened, George, that makes you bring this up at this time?

   b. Heck, George, you've been around long enough to know the promotion policies. It isn't going to do any good to just hope you'll get a promotion; you've got to get in and show you've got it on the ball.

   c. Don't be discouraged, George, we like your work. Just be patient and I'm sure a promotion will come along. We'll do all we can to help get you ready for it.

   d. Seems to me, George, that you're being a little impatient and maybe a little jealous of Pete.

   e. In other words, George, you feel kind of puzzled about just where you stand with the company, is that it?

2. *Crew member, age 42, steel plant:* "Look, Sven, you got to pull me off the back-room crew. Me and Pawlitz can't work together. A real blowhard, that Pawlitz. Whatever I do he don't like it; all the time bitchin'. I try. How come you don't get him off the crew, off by himself, like loading out in the yard or something; he's always complaining about the heat anyway. You gotta be blind not to see that he screws up a crew."

Source: From E. H. Porter, Jr., and Eugene R. Streich, *Learn to Listen Effectively* (Published for private circulation only by Systems Development Corporation, Santa Monica, Calif., 1959), pp. 4–10. Reproduced here by permission of Eugene R. Streich.

a. You know there are always two sides to these things. Did you ever stop to think that there might be things you do that start Pawlitz going?

b. Let me look into this. Maybe there is something I can do. Until I can why don't you just keep a stiff upper lip and get along with him as best you can?

c. It's O.K. for you to ask for a transfer but you shouldn't go complaining about other members of the crew. It gets around and makes for bad feelings.

d. Pawlitz is really getting under your skin. Is that what you mean?

e. What's Pawlitz been doing? Tell me about it.

3. *Research scientist, age 37, R & D Division:* "I don't believe we will be able to hold to the project target date for the prototype version, Frank. A lot of reasons, bugs here and there, but mainly because we need another staff person. Wilson is a good man, but young. Michaels leaves something to be desired. He is essentially a sound man, but my God, these new-degree people do need seasoning. You know I wasn't too happy the day you assigned him to the project. Well, that's neither here nor there now. However, I do want you to see the picture here. We're way understaffed in terms of real people."

a. Maybe what you ought to do is to go back and review just how you have things scheduled. See if you've got the best assignment of tasks and men. I don't like to ask for more help until I'm real sure we are at peak efficiency.

b. I gather you feel pretty strongly that that's where the trouble is; not enough experienced help.

c. Do you suppose that your feelings toward new-degree people could be getting in your way of utilizing them effectively?

d. Just how many people do you have who are experienced?

e. I don't know whether we can get any more help with the budget we have, but let me look into it and see what I can do. At least we can try!

4. *Man, age 36, public utility* (has just been reassigned to work under an old friend): "Well, Jack, here we are together again. (Pause.) Guess it will be like old times, hey? Remember how we used to ram the old power report through in three days? Well, I guess you have been keeping the old nose clean since those days. (Pause.) Well, suppose you tell me where I fit in now."

a. Well, suppose we start off with operations. How much do you know about how we do things here?

b. I gather you'd like it to be like old times but you're afraid that it won't turn out that way. Is that what you're saying?

c. We cut plenty of corners back then all right but I've learned since then that's not the way to do it. We'll get along just fine. Our policies and procedures are real clear here.

d. Well, it's not quite the same as then but I sure hope we can be as friendly as we were then. There's no reason I can see why we shouldn't be.

e. I get the feeling that being assigned to an old buddy is kind of "sticking in your craw."

5. *Woman employee, age 29, electronics company:* "Mr. Nelson, somebody will just have to do something about the men swearing and their bad language in the washroom. It carries right through that ventilator opening into the women's lounge, and really, it's just terrible, all that dirty talk. Some of us can hardly stand to go in there. I'm surprised that with your background you haven't said something about it."

   a. Why, I didn't realize at all what was happening. Don't be upset. I'll get maintenance to look into it right away. Everything will be O.K.

   b. What do you mean? What kind of talking is going on?

   c. You feel it's just gone too far; that it's unfair to ask anyone to put up with it?

   d. Maybe you're not feeling too well, Mary. Maybe you're on edge. You've never mentioned this to me before.

   e. Mary, you don't have to listen to it if you don't want to. Just ignore it and see how that works.

6. *Man, age 34, printing and publishing house:* "Look, Walt, I feel funny asking this question, but who in hell do I work for around here? You are the department head, but Hank gives me most of my assignments and kind of checks them over, at least I think he does. Except he doesn't work under you. I keep catching it from Eddie, who really lets me know when something's wrong; but he is only here on loan from the shipping department and won't be around for long. And, now I hear we are going to have some kind of performance review system and I don't want to get caught short on this."

   a. Sounds like you're getting "edgy," Ralph. You talk like a man who is getting anxious about this job, or maybe something at home.

   b. What the hell, Ralph. You know that every so often any supervisor has to cut across authority lines to get the job done right. We're a team here, Ralph. Don't get so excited about the red tape of clear lines of direction.

   c. Seems like things ought to be clear but they aren't, and you don't want to be the victim. Is that it?

   d. What's the matter, Ralph? Are you afraid that no one will speak up for you? How do you think things should be?

   e. Don't worry, Ralph. Even if it's confusing at times as to just who you do get your work from, you're working for me and I'll be the one to speak at performance review time.

7. *Salesman, age 38, building and supply company* (long-distance call to his sales manager concerning an expense-account matter): "That you, Fred? Ah, fine, fine, I'm fine; and you? Good. Say, Fred, what's the idea of bouncing my last two 63's? I just got the note from your gal in the office. Yeah, caught up with me in Denver. What gives? Here I've been going along figuring I'm O.K. on my entertainment, and then, whammo! I thought I was following your thinking on this. Remember, I asked about this when I called from K.C. a couple of weeks ago? Now, you pull this flip on me. Hell, I can't rework it now. I didn't save any of the chits. You know that. Besides, I'm behind on my schedule now."

   a. What do you mean, you can't rework them now, Al?

   b. This comes as a real surprise to you, is that what you're saying, Al?

c. You may have thought you were following my thinking, Al, but you'd better rethink our conversation. Some of those items are just out of bounds. Look'em over again.

d. O.K., Al, tell you what let's do. When you come back in we'll sit down and go over things. I'm sure we can get it ironed out.

e. It seems to me, Al, that maybe you're kind of remembering things the way you want to.

8. *Woman office worker, age 44, insurance company:* "Mr. Whitman, I wish you would do something about moving the water cooler away from where it is along the wall near the mimeo machine. Ah,. . .maybe we could put it way in the back and there wouldn't be so much confusion then. What I mean is that, well, there is a lot of fooling around and disturbance where it is now. You know, all the men hang around because that Gonzales girl is there. And, she is one of those. . .well, she likes it. You can see that just by looking at her with her tight clothes and all, and her bending over the machine all the time. Really!"

a. Gosh, Rose, you shouldn't be upset by that. You know how it is with these young girls. I'm sure nothing is really going on.

b. Has she done anything out of line that you could see, Rose?

c. I gather you feel it's kind of indecent, is that it, Rose?

d. You know how it is as you get older, Rose, the same things we used to do as youngsters look kind of risque now.

e. No, Rose, I'm not going to bother them as long as they continue to get their work done. Maybe you could change your desk so you don't have to look at them.

9. *Carpenter's foreman, age 33, construction company:* "Hey, Bud! Gotta minute? Good. This business with Fred and his materials-handling people has started again. A real hassle this time. They know damn well they are supposed to leave the trusses up against the studs at the garage end of the house. Well, do they? Hell, no! Every time we find'em at the other end, or, even worse, out in front. Man, they weigh 210 apiece. One of my guys has to crawl down off the plate and help tip it up and then climb back up. They have been belly-achin' and I don't blame them. I just talked to Fred about it, but all he did was mumble about how his boys can't always get their trucks in with the mud and blocks all around the place."

a. You jump to conclusions awfully fast, Jack. Sure you're not doing it again?

b. Now, cool down, Jack. Put yourself in his place. You know that you couldn't have gotten back there through this yard yourself. Explain it like that to your men. They'll understand.

c. You feel he's letting them get by with it and then alibiing for them, is that it?

d. What do you think ought to be done, Jack?

e. O.K., Jack, I'll have a talk with him and see if we can't straighten this out.

10. *Student nurse, age 20, lying-in hospital:* "Honestly, Miss Carson, I'm ready to throw in the sponge. I've been ordered, pushed, shoved around today until I just can't take it any more. It's 'Nurse, haven't you told Dr. Stertz

I have to see him?' 'Nurse, my toilet is stopped up.' 'Nurse, when will they bring my baby in?' 'Nurse, they want you down on 2 in the labor room.' My God, I can't be everywhere. And then that old bat in records is on my neck about the file for 324. Good grief, I don't know what happened to that folder, and I told her so this morning."

a. We do not speak of our supervisors in that way. I suggest that you realize that the job is going to be like this—you're a nurse. Learn how to handle it!

b. It's not always easy, that's for sure. You'll get used to the routine before long and these won't be problems at all.

c. Let's see, how long have you been on ward duty now?

d. Maybe you find it difficult when the pace of the work is set by what others want rather than by the way you want it.

e. Seems like everyone and everything is just pounding at you until you can't stand it.

CASE 61
THE TACITURN MANAGER

No sooner had Fred Whitney entered the plant on Tuesday morning than he received a call from the plant manager telling him to come upstairs. Fred did so and went immediately into the plant manager's office. The following conversation took place.

"Fred, you've been on my back for three years to get you some new machinery in your department. Well, now you've got it. Last month I asked the finance department to purchase nine new machines for your people. They agreed and we got a call from the manufacturer late yesterday afternoon. The new machines will be here first thing Monday afternoon.

"That's great, but why didn't you tell me sooner?"

"I wasn't sure the order would be approved, and I didn't want to get your hopes up. However, it's all settled. In the meantime, I want you to have the people working on your nine oldest machines to disassemble them and get them ready for packing. We've managed to sell them to a firm in Illinois, and I want them ready to be shipped first thing Monday morning. It'll probably take your people the rest of this week to tear down the old machines for shipping. Then, on Monday morning they can help install the new ones and get back to work on Tuesday."

On the way to the production floor, Fred felt very good. He could not wait to tell his men the good news. However, then he decided it might be better if he told them nothing. The plant manager had surprised him; why not surprise the men in turn? This seemed like a good idea to Fred. As a result, when he got to the production floor, he told the men working on the old machines that they were to forget about their work assignments and start disassembling the machines immediately. Although the workers seemed confused, Fred did not give them an explanation and they decided not to press the matter any further. By late Friday afternoon the machines were all disassembled and packed for shipment. Fred could hardly wait to see the worker's faces on Monday morning when the new ones arrived.

On Monday morning Fred received another call from the plant manager. He hurried upstairs expecting to learn that the machines had arrived. However, the manager had something else to tell him.

"Fred, what the hell is going on in your department?"

"Nothing, we're waiting for the new machines to arrive so we can start assembling them and get to work. Boy, are the men going to be surprised."

"Oh yeah. Well, here's a surprise for you. Personnel just called in to say that they were quitting, while the other three say they are sick."

"There's got to be some mistake. Why would these guys want to quit? They have been asking for new machines."

"I don't know but I'll tell you this: you'd better find out what's going on and get it straightened out quick."

Fred immediately called one of the workers who had phoned in to say he was quitting.

"George, this is Fred. I was just up to see the plant manager and he tells me you're quitting. What's the problem?"

Source: From *Cases and Study Guide*, by Luthans and Hodgett. Copyright 1973 by McGraw-Hill, Inc. Used with permission of McGraw-Hill Book Company.

"Listen, Fred, I'm not going to sit around waiting to be fired. I spent all day yesterday looking through the want ads and there are plenty of jobs available for machinists. I have an interview in about an hour with another firm."

"But why do you want to quit? What makes you think you'll be fired?"

"Are you kidding? Why would we be disassembling those machines and packaging them if the firm weren't getting ready to lay us off? There's nothing left for us to do. I know someone's getting ready to lower the ax on me."

"But that's not it at all, George. We have new machines coming in to replace those old ones. That's why we were packaging the old ones and shipping them out. We were making room for new ones."

"Well, why didn't you tell us that? The scuttlebutt around the plant was that we were being laid off. You had the nine of us scared out of our wits."

"I didn't tell you about the new machines because I wanted to surprise you."

"Well, you sure surprised me."

Fred spent the next hour calling the rest of the men and explaining the situation. By noon all of them were back in the plant helping to assemble the new machinery.

Questions for Discussion

1. Why did the men get the idea they were going to be laid off?
2. What lesson should Fred have learned?
3. What can Fred do now?

EXERCISE 62
NONVERBAL COMMUNICATION

Below is a list of nonverbal communication methods. Pick a day on which you will attempt to keep track of these messages. Think back at the end of the day to three people you communicated with in some way. Record how you responded to these people in terms of their nonverbal communication media. Identify those that had the greatest and least effect on your behavior.

Medium	What was the message?	How did you respond?	Which affected your behavior most and least?
How they shook hands			
Their posture			
Their facial expressions			
Their appearance			
Their voice tones			
Their smiles			
The expressions in their eyes			
Their confidence			
The way they moved			
The way they stood			
How they smelled			
Symbols or gestures they used			
How loudly they spoke			

CONTROLLING

n Chapter 3, we discussed the planning process and stated that the final stage of planning requires analysis of progress toward objectives. Control is the process that aids the manager in conducting that analysis. The manager first evaluates results in light of specified objectives, and then takes steps to see that those objectives are achieved. Several tools facilitate this process: PERT and some of the decision-making tools and techniques can help, and the budget is one of the more commonly used approaches. Many of these tools are oriented toward controlling things. People, however, are also "controlled." The reading, "Who's in Control Here?" introduces you to some of the people-oriented aspects of control. It will show you that some of the concepts you explored earlier, such as motivation and leadership, are related to control. And, of course, effective control requires good communication. In using these skills for control, firms often set up systems and procedures for managers to use. Several experiences and cases in this chapter help you to see how these might be established and how they operate.

"The LBS Control Problem" is an exercise dealing with a small consulting firm that has not yet established any control procedure for evaluating the quality of its consultations. You will be asked to play the role of one of the consultants in setting up the control system.

The "Donald Jurgensmeyer" case presents a dilemma for several managers who need to control the behavior of a colleague who has developed an alcohol problem.

As a manager, you will be responsible for controlling your own behavior. A crucial issue here will be how you plan your time. Therefore, we have included two exercises—"It's About Time" and "Controlling Your Time"—concerning personal time management.

Of course, humans in the work system respond to various control systems in different ways. The "Anderson Motors" case provides you with an opportunity to examine possible responses to control systems.

The final exercise in this chapter, "Controlling Ethical Behavior" lists various types of behavior in which you may engage as a manager. It is included to help you evaluate and control your own behavior and it relates back to the reading suggesting that personal control is important in organizations. The final case,

"Student Janitors at the Big U," may help you understand what can happen in an organization when control procedures are ineffective (or nonexistent). ●

READING 63
WHO'S IN CONTROL HERE?
Howard R. Smith

Some months ago officials from a sizable organization asked for help in meeting the challenge of inflation and strong competition. In general, they wanted assistance in improving productivity, particularly at the lower levels of their workforce. More specifically, they had in mind some kind of far-reaching, job-enrichment program.

It was obvious that the corporation was already taking some effective actions to relieve its economic crunch. It had made major strides toward controlling a large inventory more economically and had so effectively squeezed down over-head personnel costs that middle-level managers were feeling an acute workload pinch. More had to be done, to be sure; but why this call for outside help from an organization that appeared to be responding effectively on its own?

The answer wasn't immediately obvious, but eventually the real problem emerged: Management had made some important, though uncomfortable, ac-commodations where the organization was "in control"—but felt compelled to ask a group of university consultants for help where management was not in control. More specifically, this organization was "in command" of its destiny at the middle and upper level of its structure, but not at the lowest levels.

THE PROBLEM THAT WON'T GO AWAY

This experience prompted some hard thinking. What if this organization's predicament was an isolated case? Could it be that many large, complex or-ganizations are facing the same difficulty—an inability to "control" workers toward greater productivity?

It was a short step from this thought to Michel Crozier's study of two bureaucracies—one private, one public. The following paragraph from *The Bureaucratic Phenomenon* (University of Chicago–Phoenix, 1967) captures the flavor of that work:

> *Members of higher management are not unaware of. . .[low worker morale], although officially they deny it. They try, however, to explain it away by blam-ing the immediate supervisors. The believe that the cause of the poor morale of the employees—besides the monotony of the task itself—can be found in the supervisors' poor handling of human relations at the primary level. Further-more, they believe it would be almost as difficult to change this situation as to change the work process, since the Agency cannot recruit people of high enough caliber as supervisors. There remains, therefore, only the "solution" of deliver-ing speeches and written instructions advising supervisors to pay more atten-tion to the duties of leadership. This possibility is one of which management avails itself sporadically and with some self-consciousness.*

A longer step in this thinking by Harry Levinson ("Asinine Attitudes Toward Motivation,"*Harvard Business Review,* January–February 1973) noted that we are living these days with what is often called a "motivation crisis." Wouldn't workers "out of control" become a symptom of the crisis?

Then it occurred to me that this country has been seriously concerned about out-of-control workers for three quarters of a century. Was that not exactly the problem Scientific Management so dedicatedly endeavored to solve? And is not the Theory Y family of emphases essentially another way of getting this same discomfort?

It may seem overly dramatic to suggest that we have been trying to work through the same problem for so long—not only without significant success but, in the process, sinking even deeper into difficulty. But that is what has happened. The reason, moreover, is not hard to find. We have persistently attempted to make a motivation "scissors" having only one blade, omitting first one blade and then the other in our efforts to cut through motivational problems.

THE ORGANIZATION-CONTROL BLADE

The two blades required for an effective motivation scissors are well understood in principle. First, there is self-control; what people are and want—deep down inside—must figure substantially in what and how they do. But self-control has to respond to an environment. The organization, therefore, must arrange surroundings and relationships that will help self-control do more nearly what bosses want. Organization control, in other words, needs to do its best to guide self-control or organization control.

Indeed, the importance of these two blades working together is so obvious one wonders how we have continually failed to work at the motivation problem from both directions. But a review of a few high points of employer-employee history during this century permits no doubt that this really did happen.

It is clear that workers out of control was the problem with which Frederick W. Taylor and, after him, the entire Scientific Management movement primarily wrestled. Taylor's epoch-making career was single-mindedly dedicated to lessening what his generation called "soldiering"—workers doing significantly less than they could.

Nor is it surprising that men of that era would very much want to emphasize the organization-control blade of the motivation scissors. They had been born and bred to unilateralness in the relationship between bosses and subordinates. Besides, if workers out of control must be confronted, what would be more logical than to tighten up the control operation?

But emphasis is one thing; a one-bladed scissors is something else. Yet it is easily demonstrated how determinedly one-sided the Scientific Management push was.

SELF-CONTROL AS THE ENEMY

For example, closely controlled workers already had brought motivation matters to the status of a significant problem near the beginning of this century. Thus, there is substance to the accusation that Scientific Management aimed to solve a difficult problem primarily by doing more intensely essentially what had caused it. Furthermore, Taylor himself had a basis for understanding the vicious backlash that can set in when the dimension of self-control is not only ignored but defied. Early in his career Taylor was foreman of a group of workers who were, in the "soldiering" sense, out of control. He told them in no uncertain terms that he knew they were goofing off—and that he, the boss, would correct the situation. A bitter battle ensued as, thus challenged, worker self-control fought back. The outcome could perhaps not quite be called a draw inasmuch as Taylor did get more from his workers. But he was also candid about what he felt he had learned from that warfare. He decided that management-labor interactions could not effectively be built upon an explicitly adversary foundation.

Against that experience, it is puzzling why Taylor seemed so sure that more organization control was the way to go. For as we now so thoroughly understand, the other blade of the motivation scissors, if not invited in the front door, will force its way in the back door, thereby creating an enemy that must be dealt with. In these days when there is so much talk about a motivation crisis in our midst, it is apparent how formidable that enemy can be.

Despite this perversity of organization control dynamics, Taylor and his followers felt that their elaborately revised way of thinking about work and workers would make its way around it. A management program was put together that was to depend as little as was "scientifically" possible on self-control. Thus, a key dimension of "The Gospel of Efficiency" was the so-called "One Best Way." Pursuing the goal of doing many kinds of work "just right," industrial engineers calculated to minute detail what sequence of movements promised to be most productive—so that workers would be thus helped to do the most they were capable of.

BETTER LUCK NEXT TIME

To be fair, Scientific Management probably would have been much less of a one-bladed scissors if the spirit of Taylor's thinking had more thoroughly pervaded practice. A persuasive case can be made for the proposition that a generation of organization leaders effectively sabotaged careful plans to (at least) neutralize self-control as this organization control operation was so meticulously developed. (A classic book of that era—*Scientific Management and Labor*, by Robert A. Hoxie, Appleton, 1915—extensively examined how far practice often departed from the "spirit" of what Taylorites had asked for.)

Especially illustrative is what happened in the incentive compensation realm—Scientific Management's program to give workers their special stake in greater productivity. All too often, when workers on incentive compensation schedules boosted their earnings substantially, managers were easily tempted to substitute organization control for compensation. Bosses would reengineer either method or equipment to bring pay down closer to "what it ought to be." Of course, not many experiences of that kind were needed to convince workers that this game probably could not be won. When this fist in a glove made its presence unmistakably felt, it seemed sensible to stay out of control. That is, here were circumstances almost certain to make self-control an enemy.

Whether broken promises were inherent in Scientific Management is not an issue here. It is enough to note that by the end of the 1920s, it was already understood that little progress had been made toward getting workers more fully under control. Indeed, whatever we may agree the Hawthorne Studies contributed to our thinking, they certainly taught us one thing. Soon after the "Gospel of Efficiency" had been launched with such high hopes, that practice of soldiering reached a high level of sophistication.

What had happened must be counted a remarkable failure—remarkable both in terms of the size of the stakes and in the magnitude of the failed effort. But perhaps the stage was now set for a revised approach that would work more decisively because it could be constructed in large part out of the lessons learned from the failure of "The One Best Way."

THE START OF SOMETHING BIG

Surely the most fundamental of these lessons was a confirmation of the vigorous perversity of an organization control that openly confronts self-control. However, the theory of Scientific Management might have alleviated this difficulty, pressing workers directly and hard for more output boomeranged. The lesson to be learned was that control, as a one-bladed scissors, was not enough.

Note how exactly the basically different approach pioneered by Elton Mayo and Douglas McGregor (Theory X and Theory Y) took up the struggle at this point. On the one hand they were trying to solve precisely the same problem Scientific Management had dedicated itself to. Workers, they also firmly believed, were doing much less than they easily could do. Specifically, they wanted to make a much larger use of the self-control blade of the motivation scissors. If workers could not be induced to do what is wanted or needed by controlling them, perhaps that could be accomplished by doing a lot of "noncontrolling."

This emphasis can be seen clearly in McGregor's use of assumptions as his point of departure (*The Human Side of Enterprise*, McGraw-Hill, 1960). He accused his predecessors of assuming that workers do not want to work (the reason it was thought they must be closely "controlled" into productivity). McGregor's conviction was that a very human yearning/need for work could be unleashed by managers alert to these kinds of possibilities.

In other words, the self-control blade of the motivation scissors was a sort of impatient genie, eagerly awaiting the appearance of organization leaders who would pull the cork out of the bottle. All that was really needed was to get out of the way of self-control. In the first and central Theory Y proposition, McGregor put it this way:

> *The expenditure of physical and mental effort in work is as natural as play or rest. The average human being does not inherently dislike work. Depending upon controllable conditions, work may be a source of satisfaction (and will be voluntarily performed) or a source of punishment (and will be avoided if possible).*

By any standard, Mayo and McGregor were the start of something big. From that point of departure came a human relations movement that thoroughly dominated much thinking about managing work and workers for about two decades. Then, when the extremes of that emphasis began to wear away, there appeared a participative management thrust that is still with us. At the same time a job enrichment effort was developing that is now almost as dominant in thinking about workers out of control as human relations was earlier. That is to say, virtually all widely supported suggestions for bettering organization performance owe a basic conceptual dept to the Mayo/McGregor way of thinking.

Nevertheless, it is no exaggeration to suggest that Theory Y thinking is on the way toward contributing to another remarkable failure. Surely, as judged by such things as systematically deliberate work-pacing, absenteeism, turnover, and sick-leave abuse, workers are as out of control today as the worker group that prompted Taylor's prodigious effort. After all, we commonly refer to our present "worker-out-of-control" problem as a motivation crisis. This is all the more remarkable because a revised approach had an opportunity to build on lessons taught by a predecessor failure, and because men of affairs were all the more under pressure to make a new solution work against the backdrop of earlier high hopes that had been painfully dashed.

ANOTHER ONE-BLADED SCISSORS

Mayo and McGregor should not be held responsible for everything that has happened on the employee-relations front, any more than Frederick Taylor was responsible for the sabotage of a significant dimension of his program by managers. Indeed, it can be persuasively argued that the rest of society after McGregor, just as after Taylor, made a one-bladed scissors out of ideas that would otherwise have been much more useful. This had been so marked during the last two decades that it can be argued that lessons from the Scientific Management era were too well learned as, in a very real sense, we threw out the baby with the bathwater.

McGregor, for example, assuredly did not have in mind abandoning organizational control. Note the phrase, "depending upon controllable conditions," in his central proposition. Moreover, the most seminal chapter in *The Human Side of Enterprise* is entitled "The Traditional View of Direction and Control"—as if he is simply proposing another way of thinking about organization direction and control. Then, after his experience as a university president, he penned several fascinating paragraphs about the boss sometimes having to be the boss, which is often not as much a part of our thinking about what Douglas McGregor was telling us as it should be.

At the same time, however, we have been systematically putting in place programs and institutions that seem to proclaim that getting out of the way of self-control really is enough—that the organization-control blade of these scissors is not very important. (As this is said by Crozier, workers are maintaining their autonomy much more easily than heretofore.)

Thus businessmen who would argue vociferously that money is our most important motivator complain about how high the wage bill is and, at the same time, make little use of that huge outlay for organization-control purposes. Most fringe benefits are thus across-the-board, not relating to performance at all. Many bonus packages are structured as a percentage of regular pay, in no way individualized according to contribution.

Over the years, in all kinds of ways, the organization control exercised over workers by first-level supervisors, the group on whom the principal responsibility for output primarily falls, has been more and more diluted. At the same time, there has been a proportionate diminution of the value of promotion to first-line supervision as an organization-control reward. A high organization tolerance for absenteeism and sick-leave abuse further shields workers from control by the organization. And when all of this is added to the backlash likely to be triggered by command as an organization control, it's small wonder that lower-level managers are often dismayed to discover how puny their influence is over what they are responsible for.

It could be argued that in this stance businessmen have only been following a neglect of organization control as a managerial strategy that had already become much of the warp and woof of this society. And, in truth, both the maturing of the labor union movement and basic trends in public policy have steadily been eroding organization control over workers.

It is not profound to observe that labor union power was developed to curtail the authority of managers. But it is profoundly important that the success of that endeavor contributes powerfully to our new one-bladed scissors approach to motivation. The other side of the leeway to be arbitrary is the flexibility to maneuver organization control toward greater productivity. Union leverage in such things as seniority, layoffs, overtime, worker assignments, and terminations must limit flexibility as it guards against arbitrariness.

The roots of public policy in this field also lie in worker protection. Civil service regulations so elaborately protect workers against arbitrariness that managers are severely restricted in their use of organization control to secure a higher level of output. Indeed, it is a significant commentary on the world we live in that rewarding (punishing) good (poor) employees has become so much trouble for bosses, especially in public bureaucracies, that it is often not done. Public policy, too, has developed programs for protecting workers against unemployment, sometimes even including protection against having to accept work considered undesirable. Such buffers against discomfort make it that much more difficult for organization control to discriminate in favor of better performance.

THAT HELPLESS FEELING

None of this is intended as a diatribe against appropriately protecting workers. The point is that, given whatever objectives are thereby served, such protection will generate consequences that must be lived with. One of the most crucial of these is the erosion of organization control as part of a larger evolution holding us to a one-bladed-scissors motivation strategy. One blade doth not a scissors make—and workers "out of control" is closely analogous with endeavoring to cut with a scissors that is not all there.

Small wonder, then, that our client organization was not well in command in the lower reaches of its hierarchy—and thus was seeking outside help. Small wonder, indeed, if perhaps many organizations, à la Professor Crozier (in *The Bureaucratic Phenomenon*), feel so helpless in this out-of-control situation that they often merely go through the motions of improving matters rather than really shaping things differently.

Questions for Discussion

1. What are the two blades required for an effective motivation scissors?

2. How did the Scientific Management movement evolve? What was the major problem it set out to solve? Has it worked? Why or why not?

3. What is preventing upper-level management from utilizing the "double-bladed scissors" approach concerning motivation of lower level workers? Do you think this will change in the future? Why or why not?

4. How have Elton Mayo and Douglas McGregor (Theory X and Theory Y) contributed in overcoming the problem of motivation? Is Theory Y thinking on the way toward contributing to another failure?

EXERCISE 64

THE LBS CONTROL PROBLEM

You are a member of Lawrence, Blanchard, and Stokes, Consultants (LBS), a new organization involved in managerial and marketing consulting, which has no control procedures to evaluate the quality of services it offers its clients. These clients consist primarily of large- and medium-sized organizations—mainly insurance companies and export marketers—in a large, western port city.

Lawrence, Blanchard, and Stokes has a staff of five consultants, including Messrs. Lawrence and Blanchard and Mrs. Stokes. Messrs. Lawrence and Blanchard, both in their fifties, are MBAs who retired early and sought new careers. Mr. Lawrence, a retired commander, was an operations research consultant in the navy, where he was responsible for equipment supply operations in Vietnam. Mr. Blanchard, retired from Quickie Mart Foods, was vice-president and director of marketing. Mrs. Stokes, age forty-seven, operated her own insurance consulting business in Toronto for twenty years. When her husband was transferred, Mrs. Stokes found a consulting position with the organization. Lawrence, Blanchard, and Stokes hired two additional employees—Dallas Coleman and Russ Spencer. Dallas holds a bachelor's degree in accounting and would like to get an MBA, but he is twenty-one and wants to get some work experience before going back to school. Russ, age twenty-nine, received his MBA after undergraduate school, and did a stint in the Coast Guard. He has a bachelor's degree in finance, an MBA, and worked for two years as a financial analyst.

Lawrence, Blanchard, and Stokes, functioning for two years, has managed to obtain eight major accounts on a continuing basis and approximately thirty accounts on a noncontinuous basis. Annual gross billings for last year were $807,000, with an approximate return on investment of 8 percent. Gross billings for the first quarter of this year were $283,971.

LBS limits its accounts to specific areas of managerial and marketing consulting. For example, LBS consultants work closely with insurance and export company personnel departments to study hiring and training procedures. LBS also studies employee movement patterns within a company and why employees resign. From its analyses, LBS makes personnel policy suggestions. Additionally, it studies the size of an organization in relation to that organization's product, service, and environment, and makes recommendations for changes in the organizational structure. It will advise on one-time, noncontinuous problems of the type discussed above.

LBS's marketing consulting consists mainly of helping export companies with their foreign distribution problems. For example, moving products to coastal areas in the Middle East is easy; however, distributing these products to the interior is hindered by lack of transportation facilities, perishability of products, and inability of U.S. exporters to communicate with members of Middle Eastern cultures. LBS also assists insurance companies' newly formed marketing departments with advertising. Insurance companies, in a highly competitive industry, have found the need for more and continued advertising research, but do not feel qualified to handle the function themselves. LBS has contracted with several insurance companies to carry out advertising research on a continuing basis. It also has several one-time commitments to evaluate the effectiveness of advertising programs in smaller cities near its home office.

Mr. Lawrence, the company's president, plans to call a meeting of all his consultants to address the issue of quality controls for the consulting being done by Lawrence, Blanchard, and Stokes. Although he has some ideas of his own, he does not plan to set forth controls at this time. Instead, he will request that each of you come to the meeting prepared to discuss the types of controls that can be implemented.

Your instructor will divide the class into groups of five persons. Each person will be assigned to play the role of one of the consultants described in the exercise. Before the class in which this exercise will be discussed, think, from the perspective of the role you are playing, about what control processes could and should be implemented in the organization. During the first part of the class period your group will discuss ideas and will develop a control plan. Each group will then present its plan to the class for further discussion.

Your instructor may give you additional guidelines.

CASE 65
DONALD JURGENSMEYER

Donald Jurgensmeyer, age fifty-two, is sales manager for a division of Johnson Manufacturing Company, a large, heavy machinery firm with headquarters in Milwaukee, Wisconsin. He has been employed by the company for twenty-seven years.

His is a typical Johnson Manufacturing success story. He started in a management program for a few dollars a week, and he now supervises salesmen all over the country. With his bonuses, Jurgensmeyer made $75,000 last year.

But Raymond Johnson, the company president, has noticed that Jurgensmeyer isn't his old self; he doesn't seem as alert or as jovial as he used to be. When Jurgensmeyer asks the salesmen how they like working for him, their responses are politely positive, but without the enthusiasm he used to get.

Recently, Elaine Wahl, vice-president of personnel, asked to see Johnson: she wanted to discuss Jurgensmeyer.

Wahl: Ray, I feel we have a real problem on our hands and since he's been here twice as long as I have, I wanted your okay before I tried to do anything. Over the last year or two, I've heard rumors that Don Jurgensmeyer has been hitting the bottle, especially when he's on the road working the territory with our salespeople. I've checked it out, and it's true. This is making a bad impression on the salesforce: What kind of example does he set for these people? I think we ought to try to do something because I'm sure it's affecting his performance.

Johnson: Elaine, That's a very serious charge. You know how we feel about that. I know salespeople traditionally drink more than others. They say they have to entertain buyers and so on. How do you know this isn't gossip started by some fellow who wants his job?

Wahl: I thought of that. I called in several salespeople I hired and respect. I explained I wasn't just digging dirt, that I was concerned about Don—whom I really like. In fact, who doesn't? I asked them if they'd had any experiences along this line. I assured them what they told me would be kept confidential and that the details would not be revealed—that we were just trying to see if Don needed help and if so, what could we do to help him.

Johnson: Well what did you find out?

Wahl: Plenty. I'll read from a report I drafted after one recent territory visit.

Salesman's Commentary

I really hate to talk about Don—first because he's my boss and second because I like him. But I do think he needs help. Last time he came to my territory I picked him up at the airport. He arrived at 7:45 a.m., having flown through several time zones. He suggested we check him into his motel first, so I took him there. It was about 8:30 a.m. when we walked into his room. All the way from the airport he complained. He had just been to a convention of buyers. Over and over he bemoaned that all these guys wanted to do was drink and stay up late. He told me he was very tired and at one point he said, "If I never have to take a drink again in my life, I'll be happy."

As we walked into his room I asked him if he'd had breakfast. He said no, but didn't want any. Then he opened his suitcase and took out a fresh fifth of Scotch. He said to me, "Well, before we get going, what do you say we have a phlegm cutter." With this, he poured himself a water tumbler full of Scotch and downed it. Frankly, I'm not much of a drinker, so I passed it up.

We had an important appointment with my biggest buyer. He's known Don for years and he has always been more likely to give us an order if Don was there. I reminded Don of the appointment several times, but he kept talking about how tough it was in the old days, how lucky we young guys were, and so forth. Finally, even though he was my boss, I insisted we go. We were going to be fifteen minutes late as it was, and I had two days of appointments lined up. Don is a big help in sales and I wanted to make the most of his time. The big buyer kept us waiting thirty minutes. He's always prompt. I made some lame excuse to the buyer's secretary about Don's plane being late causing our delay, but he sent us a message. We were late the rest of the day. Once you get off schedule, you're dead.

At lunch Don had three martinis. In most of the afternoon calls, he said little or nothing. He insisted we knock off at 4:00 p.m., and I had to cancel our last appointment. He said, "Salesmen need to have a good time too. All work and no play, you know."

Frankly, I am amazed at his capacity. He finished that fifth of Scotch by 5:30. We went to a package liquor store where he bought a fifth of gin and a fifth of bourbon. He drank the gin before we went to dinner at 7:30. I can't handle much liquor. I guess I had two or four ounces of it. He had the rest. Then we went bar hopping until 1:00 a.m. I lost count of the drinks. Then we went back to the room and he finished the bourbon by 2:30 a.m.

I called to pick him up the next day at 7:30 a.m. for our appointments. He asked who we were to see in the morning. I told him. He said, "I don't want to waste my time calling on those people. Pick me up at noon." We got through some of the afternoon calls, then I had to miss another call because he insisted he had to leave town early. We didn't make many sales. One customer we called on the first afternoon phoned and said, "Look, next time he comes to town, skip me. The guy was bombed. He just wasted my time."

Don used to be a big help to me. Now much of the time he hurts me with my trade. It's tragic. He really is a talented salesman. I really learned a lot from him.

Wahl: Well, that was typical of the stories I heard. Do I have your okay to do something?

Johnson: Elaine, I had no idea the problem was that serious. Of course you have my okay. But Don has done a lot for this company and for me. You know he has a job here as long as he wants it.

Questions for Discussion

1. Is the situation with Jurgensmeyer out of control?
2. Can managers exercise control to prevent this kind of situation?
3. What can Elaine do? For example, will Johnson allow her to fire Don?

EXERCISE 66
IT'S ABOUT TIME

Below is a list of statements about managers, their work, and their time commitments. First, decide whether you think each statement is true or false. Then consider the implications your answers have for effective time management. Ask yourself: "Are there any techniques to help me manage my time here?"

Circle **T** (True) or **F** (False)

T   F   1. Most managers are overworked because of the nature of the job.

T   F   2. The manager's job is subject to repetitive time patterns.

T   F   3. No manager ever has enough time.

T   F   4. Managers need to make decisions promptly rather than wait for more information.

T   F   5. Most managers probably can find many ways to save time.

T   F   6. Managing time better is essentially a matter of reducing the time spent in various activities.

T   F   7. Managers deal with people and, because all people are important, cannot establish priorities.

T   F   8. Finding a "quiet hour" probably cannot be done in most cases, especially in small offices.

T   F   9. Most managers probably can solve their time problems by working harder.

T   F   10. If you do things yourself, you can get more done in less time. "If you want it done right, you'd better do it yourself" is still the best advice.

T   F   11. Most managers know how they spend their time and can easily identify their biggest time wasters.

T   F   12. If you really managed your time well, you would be working and living like a robot.

T   F   13. If you really try to control or manage your time, you will miss out on many unexpected opportunities that may arise.

T   F   14. It is not necessary to write out your objectives.

T   F   15. The great majority of the results you achieve are produced by a few critical activities.

Source: Adapted from Merrill E. Douglass, "Managing Time Effectively," *Atlanta Economic Review*, 28, May 1978, pp. 48–54.

EXERCISE 67
CONTROLLING YOUR TIME

In this exercise we want to help you analyze how you spend your time and help you develop an effective time use plan.

Pick a typical day next week when you will be engaged in your normal activities (classes, work, meetings, and so on). Carry the time log on the following page with you during the day from the hour you wake up until you retire. When you have a chance, complete the time log by recording the time spent, the activity (code), with whom you spent time, who initiated the activity (code), and any notes you care to make about it. Record any activity that lasts three minutes or longer.

Bring your log to class to discuss how to analyze the results and put together an effective time use plan. You might think about ways to reorganize your schedule by recording total time spent in each activity classification and looking at how your times compare with those of others.

Note: an alternative and perhaps even more useful project is keep a time log for a whole week.

Time Start	End	Total Minutes	Activity	With Whom	Initiation	Action/Notes

Key

Initiation:
O Others initiated
S Self-initiated

Activity
P   Personal time
TT   Travel time
L   Library work
G   Group meetings
C   Class
E   Entertainment
WK   Work (job)
R   Reading and studying
W   Writing
T   Thinking
WT   Waiting time
TP   Telephone
ET   Eating

CASE 68
ANDERSON MOTORS

Jim Anderson, president of Anderson Motors, a large and quite successful automobile agency in Arizona, had just returned from a company-sponsored dealers' meeting in Los Angeles. While there, he had talked at length with Bob Thomas, a dealer from a nearby community, who said he was achieving great success with a new form of electronic market research. When asked for more detail, Bob replied:

"Jim, anyone who had been in this business for a while knows that we really practice a form of variable pricing, that each deal is finally negotiated between the customer and the dealer. All of us want to be as competitive as we can be— no one likes to lose a deal to a competitor down the street—but on the other hand we have got to realize a reasonable margin on both our new and used cars to stay in business."

"In these negotiations it helps tremendously if we can get a feel for what the customer really expects in a car, we put a hidden microphone in each of the little sales offices where we close our deals. Most of our sales involve multiple customers, usually a man and his wife. After getting them to point where they seem really interested in a car, we leave them to themselves in the office for a few moments. Alone, they usually start to discuss the deal. They often express quite openly their feelings about the car they have been looking at and the kind of price they feel they could probably live with. With the use of the mike, we can listen in and decide whether or not we can afford to make a deal that will satisfy them."

"It works like a charm. You ought to come down and see it for yourself."

Jim was intrigued enough by the idea to ride down to Bob's agency with him that evening to inspect his new device. When they arrived at the dealership, the assistant manager told Jim that one of the salesmen, Harold Foster, was in one of the offices at the moment, talking to a young couple about a used car, and that they could try out the system if they wished. Jim indicated an interest and the assistant manager pressed a button.

The salesman's voice was warm and friendly.

"Well, John, now that you have had a chance to test drive the car, what do you think?"

"It's a great car. It's the model and year we have been looking for, but I think that the price is a little high."

"Well, let's see what we can do—I'm sure we can work out something. The high bluebook on your car works out to be about $500, which doesn't take into account that dent in the rear fender that will need to be repaired before we can put it on the lot. The allowance on your car would reduce the total price on the new one, including the radio you said you wanted, to $2,490. How does that sound?"

"It's still too high. Lee Ann and I still owe some money on a loan I had for schooling, and we are expecting a baby next October. We need a good car, but I don't think we can quite swing the $2,500."

"Well, John, you know we want to make you as good a deal as we can, but we have to eat, too. You are getting a lot of extras on this car, like the air conditioning and power steering. It has real low mileage and it's clean, inside and out."

Source: Published by permission of the author, Clinton L. Oaks, Brigham Young University.

"Look, we really like the car, but $2,500 is still too much money."

"All right, John, how much would you be willing to pay?"

"Lee Ann and I have figured out almost to the penny. We think we could manage about $1,900."

"If I could get the manager to knock off $200, would you be interested?"

"No, that would still leave the price more than we can afford to pay. I guess we will just have to look somewhere else."

"Wait a minute, John. I'll tell you what. Let me try to work something out. I'll go talk to the manager and go to bat for you—maybe I can get him to O.K. a lower price."

Jim and Bob heard the door slam as Harold left the sales office. A moment or so later he joined them in the assistant manager's office. As they continued to listen, John and Lee Ann began to talk about the deal.

"Lee Ann, I really like the car; it's just what we have been looking for."

"So do I. Are you sure that we can't spend any more than $1,900?"

"I have it figured out pretty carefully. The maximum we can afford is $2,100. Any more than that would really run us short next fall."

"Well, John, I guess you're right. But it's too bad. We have looked at a lot of places already without finding any cars we liked as well as this one."

John and Lee Ann continued to talk about the features of the car. Harold Foster in the meantime had discussed the deal with the assistant manager and left them to return to the sales office. Jim and Bob again heard the sales office door open and close as Harold returned to his customers. The following conversation ensued:

"John, I told Mr. Blair, our sales manager, that you wouldn't pay any more than $1,900 on this deal. He said we can't let the car go for that. We would lose money on it if we did. He said our rock bottom price was $2,200."

"Lee Ann and I have just been talking it over and we decided that we could possibly go to $2,100. We can't do any more than that."

"John, you sure drive a hard bargain. Look, I'll tell you what I'll do. I'll give it to you for $2,150, and throw in six free lubes and three oil changes. Now that more than makes up for the other $50, doesn't it? What do you say?"

"You've got yourself a deal."

Bob Thomas reached over and turned off the sound system. "Well, what do you think?" he asked. "We have only had the system installed for about six months, but during that time it has substantially increased the percentage of deals we have been able to close. I also have some evidence that our customers are going away a lot more satisfied than they used to be. For example, about a month ago I had a student market research group from one of the local colleges do a study evaluating our dealership image among recent customers. The results were much more favorable than on previous studies. A number of respondents made such comments as, "They had just the car I wanted, and at the right price," "My deal seemed tailor-made for me," and "I have already recommended them to several of my friends."

"Use of the microphone has helped us to cut through our customers' inhibitions and let us know what the customer really wants in a car and can actually afford to pay. As a result, we can usually arrange a deal that satisfies everyone."

"The system has another big plus I haven't mentioned. For the first time our assistant sales manager can listen to each of his salesmen talking to their customers and can even put them on tape if he wishes. This has proved to be a great help in training new salesmen and in retraining those who aren't meeting their quotas."

Jim Anderson wondered whether or not he ought to try what Bob Thomas had called his "electronic market research" in his own agency. "Closing is always a problem," he reflected. "Though after all the fuss in the newspapers these last few years about bugging, I'm not sure I want any part of it. Still, Bob has quite a bit of evidence that the use of the device has actually increased his customer satisfaction and enhanced the reputation of the firm. Isn't that, in the final analysis, sufficient justification to give it a try?"

Questions for Discussion

1. What are the positive and negative aspects of installing the electronic market research?

2. Should Anderson Motors install it?

3. Suppose it is installed. How would Jim respond to:

   a. A customer discovering the device?

   b. Salespersons refusing to work under those conditions?

EXERCISE 69
CONTROLLING ETHICAL BEHAVIOR

Exhibit 1 provides a list of behaviors that you or your peers might engage in when working for a company. Go through each item and circle the number that best indicates the frequency with which you personally would (or do, if you work now) engage in that behavior. Then put an X over the number you think best represents how often your work colleagues would (or do) engage in that behavior. Finally, put a check mark beside the item (in the "Needs Control" column) if you believe that management *should control* that behavior.

EXHIBIT 1
BEHAVIOR IN ORGANIZATIONS

	At Every Opportunity	Often	About Half the Time	Seldom	Never	Needs Control
1. Passing blame for errors to an innocent coworker.	5	4	3	2	1	_____
2. Divulging confidential information.	5	4	3	2	1	_____
3. Falsifying time/quality/quantity reports.	5	4	3	2	1	_____
4. Claiming credit for someone else's work.	5	4	3	2	1	_____
5. Padding an expense account by over 10 percent.	5	4	3	2	1	_____
6. Pilfering company materials and supplies.	5	4	3	2	1	_____
7. Accepting gifts/favors in exchange for preferential treatment.	5	4	3	2	1	_____
8. Giving gifts/favors in exchange for preferential treatment.	5	4	3	2	1	_____
9. Padding an expense account by up to 10 percent.	5	4	3	2	1	_____
10. Authorizing a subordinate to violate company rules.	5	4	3	2	1	_____
11. Calling in sick to take a day off.	5	4	3	2	1	_____
12. Concealing one's errors.	5	4	3	2	1	_____
13. Taking longer than necessary to do a job.	5	4	3	2	1	_____
14. Using company services for personal use.	5	4	3	2	1	_____
15. Doing personal business on company time.	5	4	3	2	1	_____
16. Taking extra personal time (lunch hour, breaks, early departure, and so forth).	5	4	3	2	1	_____
17. Not reporting others' violations of company policies and rules.	5	4	3	2	1	_____
18. Overlooking a superior's violation of policy to prove loyalty to the boss.	5	4	3	2	1	_____

1. Do your colleagues seem to engage in these behaviors more often than you do?
2. Which behaviors tend to be more frequent?
3. How are they different from the behaviors engaged in less frequently?
4. What are the most important items that should be controlled?
5. How should management go about controlling them?

Bring your results to class for discussion.

CASE 70
STUDENT JANITORS IN THE DORMS AT BIG U

In the aftermath of severe budget cuts and enrollment drops, the president of a large midwestern state university (commonly called Big U by people in the area) was concerned with student work jobs. He knew that these jobs were important to maintain enrollment which was now on the upswing. At the same time, because of budgetary constraints, he wanted some assurance that the jobs were being performed efficiently.

To provide him with some insights from an outside observer, the president contacted the consulting firm of Fastrack Associates, Inc. Janet Rainey, one of the firm's brightest consultants, was given this assignment. The president asked her to begin by investigating the janitorial maintenance workers in the housing area since this was an important function and provided employment for a very large number of workers.

STUDENT HOUSING MAINTENANCE

Big U had three separate housing areas, each representing a complex of several dormitories. Maintenance in Big U housing was the responsibility of area heads, each with an area business manager. The area business manager had authority over maintenance foremen and all maintenance personnel in a designated area. Area business managers were not civil service employees but were administrative appointments made by the central Campus Housing Office. They were generally put in this position to prove themselves worthy of higher positions in the Big U. Thus, their actions tended to be aimed at immediate short-run results, especially with respect to building cleanliness.

Under the area business manager was the area maintenance foreman, and reporting to the area maintenance foreman were the janitor sub-foremen. Both the foreman and sub-foremen in each area were full-time civil service employees. Under the sub-foremen were the full-time civil service janitors, student supervisors, and student workers. The number of janitors and students varied from area to area, depending on the number and size of dorm buildings in each complex.

The full-time janitors were all unionized and had passed a civil service exam. All had at least high school educations. There was a forty-hour work week, vacation, and sick leave; hospitalization and retirement plans were adequate or generous compared to some local private industry. Raises in pay were based on negotiations between the union and the Big U Business Office. Seniority largely but not exclusively governed promotions. Time and one-half was paid for overtime.

Although the civil service janitors had no formal authority over student supervisors, sub-foremen generally assumed students would follow directions of those janitors. The student supervisors usually abided by this unwritten rule to the extent that they felt it justified.

Student supervisors and workers were almost entirely undergraduates at Big U. Most worked 20 hours a week and started at the minimum wage. Promotion for students was from worker to supervisor, and was made on the basis of how long the student had been working rather than merit. Though merit was supposed to be used, it was very difficult to apply. Other rewards were ten cents an

Source: Adapted from a course assignment by Joseph W. Chu for Professor J.G. Hunt, Southern Illinois University-Carbondale.

hour raises after 1,500/2,500/3,500 hours and possible merit raises for outstanding work. The latter were sporadic and perceived as being restricted to a small select group of people. Raises and promotions required approval by the area business manager.

With this background knowledge, Janet turned her attention to one of the housing areas thought to be typical at Big U.

THE TURNER POINT DORMITORY COMPLEX

Turner Point consisted of eleven separate dormitories, each housing 120 students. Five dorms were for men, five for women, and one was co-ed. Also included was Boyd Hall, which served as a cafeteria, snack bar, and recreation area. Boyd Hall also housed the offices of the area business manager, maintenance and inventory control, and several offices related to food service.

Each dormitory included three floors, a combination basement-incinerator, and a multi-purpose lounge area just inside the main entrance to the building. This lounge area was used as a classroom in the men's dorms and as a general lounge for couples to sit and talk in the women's and co-ed units.

Each floor of a dormitory at Turner Point has approximately eighteen rooms and a lounge area about 10 feet wide and approximately 225 feet long. This lounge ran the entire length of the building. There was usually a varying number of pieces of furniture in these lounges, and a tiled floor. The furniture consisted of chairs, couches, tables, lamps, and a hair dryer. On each floor there was a mop room containing a sink and facilities for hanging mops, buckets, and cleaning supplies.

Each basement area had a laundry room, housing two coin-operated washers and two dryers. There was lounge furniture similar to that on the three floors above as well as a television set used on a first come–first serve basis.

The incinerator room adjoined the basement and consisted of a large incinerator and steam and water pipes. The incinerator was used to burn trash from each floor. It was fed from the other three floors via a chute. All non-burnable items were carried by the maintenance crew from the building in large trash cans located on each floor. The floors and the basement were connected by three stairways.

MAINTENANCE AT TURNER POINT

Assignments to dormitories were made by the sub-foreman. Typically there was a supervisor (either student or civil service) and from two to six employees assigned per dorm, with the same number assigned to each. Though six workers was considered an appropriate number, because of a worker shortage, two workers plus a supervisor was the typical assignment. All of the janitorial maintenance employees punched in and out at Boyd Hall. From there they would go to their assigned building.

Janet found the task as defined by the maintenance foreman to be simply keeping an assigned building clean. New workers were not told what the job consisted of by the janitor sub-foreman, who usually handled most communication between the students and the foreman. Instead new workers were assigned to a student supervisor who told them what to do as well as how to do it. In turn, these student supervisors were not given any special instructions as to what they should do in their assigned building. They were assumed to know the job because they generally had at least one semester's work experience. The task as related by one student supervisor was to dust mop and buff all floors and lounge areas in a building, sweep the stairs, carry out all trash cans, keep the rooms clean and in general, do anything that makes the building look clean. This included keeping equipment in good condition and informing the sub-foreman of needed supplies.

The equipment provided usually included wet mops, dry mops, sponges and cleaning agents, a buffing machine, and incidental items. The equipment and supplies were adequate for the job.

At the end of every semester student maintenance workers were required to work a minimum of three days. The dormitory floors were stripped and waxed. In general, the dormitory was given a thorough cleaning. The work day was extended to twelve hours at these times, with no overtime pay for student workers. At the beginning of each semester, students were required to sign an agreement that they would work during this break period. Failure to comply usually resulted in termination with a bad recommendation. It was not unusual for dormitory residents to return from a semester break and find personal items missing from their rooms.

The maintenance foreman's job at Turner Point was filled by a civil servant named A. T. Foyt. Foyt had been with Big U for 20 years and was nearing retirement. Generally his behavior was highly commendable and he was reputed to strongly go to bat for his employees. Occasionally his behavior was inconsistent, and at least once he was noticeably under the influence of alcohol.

Janet found that the sub-foreman was a civil service employee who had been with Big U fourteen years. He tended to put off decisions or refer them to Foyt. He was supposed to visit the dorms regularly to check on the janitorial work. During one recent three-month period he had visited each dorm once. He was once seen carrying an armload of supplies out the side door of Boyd Hall.

The Turner Point area had received a reputation as an easy place to work. Janet found that although student turnover was low, many students failed to show up for work at one time or another. This was especially true during exam weeks or after a special event on campus, such as a game or a concert. Extended and continued absences resulted only in reprimands. It was felt that no one would be fired because of the worker shortage.

Inventory control workers shared the same office with maintenance in this complex. These individuals spent much time sitting in the office conversing or playing cards. These activities were in full view of the maintenance employees.

Janet also found it was not uncommon for a student supervisor and subordinates to be in a dorm basement watching television during work hours. There was also a tendency to exceed the specified fifteen minute break allowed each four hours. In many cases these breaks exceeded thirty minutes.

A RECENT DEVELOPMENT

After a recent inspection the current area business manager felt the buildings were not maintained adequately. He set up bi-weekly meetings with the maintenance foreman, the sub-foreman, and the three civil service janitors assigned to Turner Point plus personnel from the Campus Housing Office. No student supervisors were allowed to attend. At one of these meetings the business manager gave his ratings of the buildings and indicated that he felt the student workers were neglecting their jobs. He concluded that the three buildings where civil service janitors were assigned were better maintained. He suggested that eight more civil service janitors should be hired as supervisors, and that student supervisors be eliminated. Such a recommendation had been rejected in the past because of the much higher payroll costs.

Janet wondered what to recommend to the president. She recognized that there were a number of things that could not be changed and that recommendations that added to the current cost were likely to have rough sledding. She knew the president was concerned about student employment; at the same time, if the buildings were not maintained properly, residents and their parents were likely to complain.

Questions for Discussion

1. Are the positions of authority (manager, foreman, etc.) clearly defined in this case?

2. Are the methods of wage payment consistent?

3. Are the job duties clearly stated? Explain.

4. What should be done about A. T. Foyt?

5. What should Janet recommend to the university president?

CHAPTER 10

COMPARATIVE MANAGEMENT AND THE FUTURE

W

hen you finish your formal study of management, we hope you will have a desire to advance in the field. We think, in order to be more successful in this endeavor, you should examine what management might be like in the future. Another aspect of your future career as a manager is likely to be involvement with management practices in other countries. This chapter is designed to start you thinking about these two topics.

A popular subject today is the exploration of reasons why Japanese business firms have been so successful in world markets. Many writers attribute their success to superior management practices. In many cases Japanese managers appear to apply ideas developed in the United States before American managers even consider using them. The reading in this chapter, "Learning from the Japanese," discusses these ideas and encourages you to consider whether Japanese practices can be applied wholesale.

One important aspect of conducting business in world markets deals with relating effectively to the cultural and legal differences of the host country. Business is not done the same way everywhere. This raises ethical and legal issues and requires that managers carefully consider the policies they wish to establish for doing business in various parts of the world. "Breaking in a U.S. Salesman in Latin America" shows you some of these dilemmas and raises the issue of how a manager ought to operate in a foreign assignment.

The exercise "Demography and the Future" gives you firsthand experience in trying to predict the implications of one very important underlying factor affecting the future environment of business and your own managerial career—demography. For instance, what industry should you look to as you begin your career—one that seems to have a good future or one that may be on the decline? How will demographics affect the outlook for that industry? How will birthrates and other factors affect competition for the managerial jobs you will be seeking? Doing some environmental assessment of factors that may affect you in the future will be helpful as you consider embarking upon an exciting, stimulating, and challenging career in management. When you finish this exercise, we recommend that

● LEARNING OBJECTIVES

When you have finished this chapter, we hope you will:

1. Appreciate some of the problems faced when applying management concepts in other countries.

2. Integrate your knowledge about the job of a manager.

3. Be aware of some of the future directions a managerial career might take.

you consider Reading 41 again. Similarly, case 74, "How to Deal with a Revolution," challenges you to consider the managerial complications of technological changes which may impact organizations in the future.

Our last reading, "Breaking Away," provides an interesting look at what some folks like you are thinking about as they graduate from college and begin their careers as managers for the future. You may want to see how your thinking, goals, and expectations compares with the "class of '87."

We hope you have learned from our book. Learning might be defined as attitude and behavior change; the last exercise is designed to help you explore what behavior or attitude changes you might have experienced. "Effective Managers Revisited" allows you to reflect on the job of the manager and asks you to compare your results to those in a previous exercise. We hope this exercise will encourage you to think about and integrate what you have learned in *The Managerial Experience.* ●

READING 71
LEARNING FROM THE JAPANESE: PROSPECTS AND PITFALLS
Robert E. Cole

It has become extraordinarily fashionable in recent years for leading management experts to trumpet the potential for learning from the Japanese. Particular attention has been called to the advantages of Japanese management style and techniques, especially as they relate to the organization and training of the labor force.

What accounts for this surge of interest? The enormity of Japan's economic success as it moved to the second largest economy outside of the communist bloc and its successful penetration of Western markets are clearly the major factors. When you are getting hurt at the marketplace, you are inclined to sit up and listen.

Yet, there are still many American managers who would dismiss the Japanese experience as one that grew out of Japan's unique cultural heritage and therefore could not have much applicability for U.S. firms. The ranks of this core group, while still strong, have been thinned by the recent invasion of Japanese-operated subsidiaries in the United States. The bulk of the reports on this "invasion" have reported the activities of Japanese companies quite favorably. They emphasize their ability to import Japanese management techniques and philosophy and apply them successfully to their management of American workers.

This turn of events has made it more difficult for the doubters to claim these approaches will work only in the rarified atmosphere of Japanese cultural conditions. Above all, the Japanese are now seen as having a winning package that has catapulted them to success. That American managers are beginning to study carefully and apply Japanese practices in this environment is not surprising. Yet, they often make such decisions in the absence of very hard data showing the applicability of these practices. For example, the literature on the practices of Japanese subsidiaries in the United States is very impressionistic and lacks systematic comparisons, not to speak of control groups. Yet, as Herbert Simon (Carnegie Mellon University's Nobel Laureate in economics) has shown us in his observations on the adoption of computers in the 1960s, management decisions are often based on the fads of the moment rather than some carefully calculated economic rationality.

In one sense, then, these developments must be reckoned as quite positive. In the area of worker-manager relationships, American managers have historically kept themselves unusually insulated from the experiences of other industrial nations; one need only contrast U.S. practices with those in Western Europe where large amounts of information and learning experiences are exchanged. No doubt this is a function of the unique relationship worked out in the course of our history between human and national resources in a relatively isolated geographical setting.

What, then, are the prospects of learning from the Japanese in the area of worker–manager relationships? To answer this question, two approaches are useful:

1. Consider the obverse case—that is, what has been the experience with the Japanese in borrowing from the Americans in this area.

2. Consider the concrete example of Japanese quality control circles (QC Circles).

THE PATTERN OF JAPANESE BORROWING

When the United States was unquestionably the most advanced industrial nation in the early postwar period, in addition to being the conqueror and occupying power of Japan, it was not surprising that the Japanese were willing and eager to learn from American management techniques. Generally, the Japanese were willing to make the assumption that American management techniques must be the most advanced, independent of any objective confirmation. These developments were part of a "management boom," as it was called in Japan, during which American management formulas and techniques were introduced into all spheres of business administration from the 1950s, particularly personnel administration.

The attention the Japanese pay to Western developments in management theory and practice is still astonishing. A significant component of the large literature on management and work in the Japanese language consists of translations and analyses of the work of Western scholars. One estimate puts translations alone at 9 percent of the some 1,000 books published a year. The research and proposals of American organizational specialists such as Rensis Likert, Peter Drucker, Chris Argyris, Douglas McGregor, and Frederick Herzberg are widely known, and the use of their ideas is commonplace in large Japanese firms. Indeed, Japanese managers are often surprised when they visit the United States to find such hostility to their ideas on the part of many American managers.

We can get a sense of the Japanese capacity to borrow and adapt Western organizational technology to their own needs through a brief tracing of the introduction of QC circles. QC circles may represent the most innovative process of borrowing and adaptation in the personnel policies of large Japanese companies in the postwar power.

How QC Circles Work

A QC circle is a relatively autonomous unit composed of a small group of workers (ideally about ten), usually led by a foreman or senior worker and organized in each work unit. Participants are taught elementary techniques of problem solving including statistical methods. It is in principle a voluntary study group that concentrates on solving job-related quality problems. These problems are broadly conceived as improving methods of production as part of company-wide efforts. Some typical efforts include reducing defects, scrap, rework, and down-time. These activities in turn are expected to lead to cost reduction and increased productivity. At the same time, the circles focus on improving working conditions and the self-development of workers. The latter includes: development of leadership abilities of foreman and workers, skill development among workers, improvement of worker morale and motivation, the stimulation of teamwork within work groups, and recognition of worker achievements. Above all, the circles involve recognition that hourly workers have an important contribution to make to the organization.

Before 1945, Japan had only moderate experience with modern methods of statistical quality control. An early postwar effort was organized by U.S. occupation officials to have American statisticians go to Japan and teach American wartime industrial standards to Japanese engineers and statisticians. Prominent in this early effort was a series of postwar lectures beginning in 1950 undertaken by Dr. William Deming to teach statistical quality control practices. Indeed, the Deming Prize was established to commemorate Dr. Deming's contribution to the diffusion of quality control ideas in Japan; an annual competition by major firms for the award serves further to promote the spread of these ideas. These various efforts were a major factor contributing to the formal adoption of Japanese Engineering Standards (JES) provided for by legislation in 1949. The Korean War had a further impact on the acceptance of these standards. In order to win military procurement orders from the American military between 1954 and 1961, the quality standards defined by the U.S. Defense Department had to be met.

In 1954 Dr. J. Juran, the noted quality control expert, arrived in Japan for a series of lectures. He emphasized a newer orientation to quality control, stating that it must be an integral part of the management function and practiced throughout the firm. In practice, this meant teaching quality control to middle management.

From 1955 through 1960 these ideas spread rapidly in major firms. But there was a critical innovation on the part of the Japanese. In the Japanese reinterpretation, each and every person in the organizational hierarchy from top management to rank-and-file employees received exposure to statistical quality control knowledge and techniques. Workers began to participate in study groups to upgrade quality control practices. This practice gave both a simple and most profound twist to the original ideas propagated by the western experts. Quality control shifted from being the prerogative of a minority of engineers with limited shop experience ("outsiders") to being the responsibility of each employee. Instead of adding additional layers of inspectors, reliability assurance and rework personnel when quality problems arise, as is customary in many U.S. firms, each worker, in concert with his or her workmates, is expected to take responsibility for solving quality problems.

This pattern of taking ideas developed in America for management employees and applying them to hourly personnel is not unique to QC circles. Rather, it is a distinctive approach adopted by the Japanese manager. For example, the American ideas on career development that have so much currency today in the personnel administration field were developed and are being applied to management personnel in the United States. The Japanese, however, have taken these same ideas and applied them to their hourly-rated personnel.

To fully understand the process of borrowing and adaptation, it is important to understand why these transformations of American ideas take place. What is it about the Japanese environment of the firm in Japan that makes their response so different from American firms in this regard? We can offer three levels of explanation: cultural, sociological, and economic.

In the cultural arena, the Confucianist doctrine of perfectability of man harmonizes nicely with a belief in the educability and the potential of even blue collar workers to contribute to the firm. The Japanese manager tends to view his employees as having sociopsychological needs, which, if nurtured, will yield economic returns to the firm. They see all regular male employees as resources with substantial potentialities for human growth. This contrasts sharply with the doctrine of original sin that characterized our Judeo-Christian heritage. Here the emphasis is on the fundamental weaknesses and limitation of man.

While it is appealing to lay the differences in willingness to invest in training and responsibility at the feet of Confucianism versus Christianity, this explanation is much too simplistic. In constructing a value-added explanation, we can add first a set of sociological factors. A matter of particular relevance here is the impact of racial, ethnic, and religious differences between the managerial and worker classes. Japan is a remarkably homogenous country in race, ethnicity, religion, and culture. To be sure, there is significant Korean and Eta minority, but they are by-and-large excluded from the large-scale manufacturing sector and relegated to various retail and wholesale trades. For all practical purposes this means that the Japanese manager can accept the proposition that the average worker is really not so very different from them and that "there for the grace of God go I." I maintain that this is a profound point critical to understanding the willingness of Japanese employers to invest in the training of and provide responsibility for blue collar employees.

There is a fundamental egalitarianism in Japanese industry that is quite impressive and is apparent to most careful observers: Japanese managers *believe in their labor force.* They believe that given the opportunity, their labor force can and wants to contribute to organizational goals.

Compare this approach to the situation in American industry. We have a management that is largely white Anglo-Saxon Protestant and a labor force that often comprises diverse racial, religious, and ethnic groups. Cultural gaps reflecting the failures of our public school education system are also wider in the United States. These differences make it much more difficult for management to put itself in the role of the ordinary production worker. Rather, this bifurcation of functions by race, religion, and ethnicity makes it much easier for American managers to see themselves as an elite whose superior education entitles them to make all the important decisions. It makes it easier to dismiss the idea that investment in education and training of ordinary blue collar workers or the sharing of decision making with them would make a significant contribution to the firm.

The final factor in this value-added explanation is an economic one. You can believe all you want in confucianism and egalitarianism, but if your firm is not growing, you are not likely to make major investments in employee training and education, particularly if you have high rates of employee turnover.

The difference between the U.S. and Japanese is obvious in this respect. For the better part of the postwar period, Japanese managers have operated in the context of a high growth-rate economy and, until the early 1970s, a labor surplus economy. Investments in education and training that would enable workers to better participate in organizational decisions could be recouped. Promotion opportunities for talented and even not-so-talented workers were quite large. Moreover, the system of lifetime employment, especially in large Japanese firms, meant that the probability of employees staying on at the same firm was much higher in Japanese than in U.S. firms. Under these conditions, it was not unreasonable for Japanese employers to make large investments in employee training and education. It was easier for them to treat all employees as important resources. In the United States, high turnover and sluggish growth rates in many industries made such investment less likely. Employers were more likely to see hourly rate employees as interchangeable parts, particularly in the context of a large army of reserved unemployed.

EFFECT OF QC CIRCLE PRACTICES

The QC circle movement in Japan has grown explosively. The number of QC circles registered with the Union of Japanese Scientists and Engineers (JUSE) increased from 1,000 in 1964 to some 87,000 by 1978. With an average of almost ten members a circle, the membership totalled 840,000. Unregistered QC circles are estimated conservatively to total an additional five times the number of registered circles, with a membership of some four million. With a total Japanese labor force of some 37 million in 1978, this means that approximately one out of every eight Japanese employees was involved in QC circle activity. The movement has drawn most of its members from hourly employees in the manufacturing sector. These summary figures are inflated because the data do not strictly discriminate between QC circles and some other forms of small group activity such as zero-defect programs, industrial engineering teams, improvement groups, and so on. Nonetheless, we are dealing with a movement that has had a significant impact on managerial practices and the degree of employee participation in the workplace.

Three characteristics of the QC circles as they have evolved in Japan are particularly significant.

- The QC circle is not a response to specific problems. Rather, it is a continuous study process operative in the workshop. That is, it functions as monitoring behavior that scans the environment for opportunities, does not wait to be activated by a problem, and does not stop its activities when a problem has been found and solved. This is a rare quality and constitutes an enormous asset where operative.
- Most U.S. motivational schemes assume that workers know how to raise productivity and improve quality but that they are holding back for no justifiable reason. Operator indifference or even sabotage are assumed to be the normal problems which management must combat. Under these assumptions, close supervision and/or financial incentives is the common response. The QC circle, to the contrary, starts with the assumption that the causes of poor quality performance are not known by either management or workers and that analysis is needed to discover and remedy these causes. A corollary of this assumption is that you must provide participants with the tools and the training necessary to discover causes and remedy them.
- Even if the solutions arrived at by workers are no better than those arrived at by technical personnel, we can anticipate that workers will more enthusiastically carry out solutions to problems that they have solved. You tend to carry out with enthusiasm policies where you have been part of the problem-solving process. This is one of the most fundamental of motivational principles.

It should be noted that the QC circles do not always perform in Japanese companies as they do on paper. Because of Japan's remarkable economic success, we have a tendency to see the Japanese as miracle men who never make mistakes. Some of their common problems are:

- For all the emphasis on voluntarism in QC circle activity, there is a great deal of top-down control in many companies. A significant minority of workers see the circles as a burden imposed on them by management rather than their own program. Thus, the circles often take on somewhat of a coercive aspect that is not the best incentive for motivating workers to produce innovative behavior.

- While in theory there is equal emphasis on the development of worker potential and productivity, in practice the emphasis on productivity has played a more prominent role. This leads workers to often question the benefits that the circles have for them.
- As the QC circle movement has developed, there is a tendency toward the routinization of the original spontaneity. This leads to workers going through the motions and turns their participation into ritualistic behavior.

THE PATTERN OF U.S. BORROWING

We are now in the remarkable situation in which the transmission of information on quality control practices is coming, full circle, back to the United States. Over 100 American firms have now adopted or are in the process of adopting some version of the QC circles. They include firms of different sizes, industries, and technologies. Some of the early innovators are: American Airlines, Babcock & Wilcox, Champion Spark Plugs, Honeywell Corporation, Cordis-Dow, Federal Products, Ford Motor Company, General Motors Corporation, Hughes Aircraft, J. B. Lansing, Lockheed Missile and Space Company, Mercury Marine, Pentel of America, Rockwell International, Solar Turbines, Verbatim Corporation, Waters Associates, and Westinghouse Defense and Electronics Center. In truly American fashion, a variety of consultants have sprung up to implement the QC circles, and the circles are now a regular feature in seminars offered by leading management organizations. The American Society for Quality Control is also providing more publicity and information on the subject. Two former employees of Lockheed Missile and Space Company who were involved with the QC circle program have not only set up their own consultant firm but have also established the International Association of Quality Circles (IAQC). In short, a broadly based publicity campaign designed to diffuse the QC circle practice is beginning to develop and accumulate momentum.

Conversations with officials in various companies suggest a variety of incentives, often multiple, responsible for their decision to introduce QC circles. Some of these more commonly mentioned include: need to maintain or improve quality, search for new ways to raise productivity, fear of a plant closing or shutting down of a product line unless more productive methods are found, worry about a direct Japanese threat to one's market position, desire to reduce the likelihood of unionization, desire to improve relations with existing unions, and a concern with reducing the adversary relation between management and workers. In a very real sense, we have a case of solutions chasing problems. The packaged solution, wrapped in the winning colors of Japan, is being exhibited and marketed for all potential buyers. Management, the consumer, is carefully examining the wares and asking if this solution might not speak to some of its problems. Despite the variety of explanations company officials give for their interest, the desire to raise productivity and improve quality seem paramount, often in the face of increasing competition from the Japanese. With these concerns goes the recognition that perhaps they have underutilized the worker as an organizational resource.

If one examines the industry composition of the early innovators, one finds further confirmation of this position. They tend to be characterized by firms in which quality has long been an unusually important consideration such as aerospace, pharmaceuticals, and high technology companies, as well as those firms in which a stronger concern for quality has recently come to the fore (often through the vehicle of increasing numbers of product liability suits) as in the case of the automobile. The auto industry receptivity involves a case in which producers are being increasingly criticized for the quality of their product at the same time that the Japanese are making sharp inroads on their markets backed by substantial evidence for the claim that the Japanese are both more responsive to the consumer as well as producing a high-quality product.

The reaction of Japanese firms operating in the United States is interesting. Pentel of America is one Japanese subsidiary that has a QC circle program here. Its parent firm in Japan is a leading maker of pens and won the 1978 Deming Prize for the most successful QC circle program. Pentel has nonetheless had some difficult start-up problems with its circle program in the United States, as has another major Japanese firm in California, whose efforts to establish a circle program have been resisted by its American managers.

What is perhaps most curious is that a number of Japanese firms with established and successful QC circle programs in Japan have not pushed for their adoption in their U.S. subsidiaries. Matsushita Electric, a pioneer in the Japanese QC circle effort, does not have QC circles in its Chicago Quasar plant. One of the American managers explained to me that they were proceeding very cautiously. (See Cole, "Will QC Circles Work in the U.S.?" *Quality Progress,* July 1980.) By this he seemed to mean that he doubted whether American employees had sufficient organizational commitment to make the QC concept work in America. Many Japanese subsidiaries in the United States seem to be adopting a wait-and-see attitude. For all the ballyhoo about their success in the United States, Japanese managers in this country feel quite unsure of their ability to understand and master the intricacies of American labor-management relations.

Most of the experiences with QC circles have been quite shallow; few companies have had the circles in operation more than two years. Thus, it would be premature to make assessments as to their suitability to the American environment.

There are those who would argue that workers are the same everywhere and that few adaptations will have to be made to fit the circle concept to the needs of American managers and workers. Experience thus far suggests this is a fallacious view and that unless the circles are adapted to U.S. conditions, they will fail here. Just as the Japanese adapted Western ideas on quality control to develop the QC circle, so will the Americans have to adapt QC circles to fit the needs of American management and labor. This has been most vividly demonstrated in the very use of the term *quality control circles.* Many companies have found that this name itself does not sit well with workers and unions; in particular the word "control" has coercive tones that many firms would prefer to avoid. Consequently, they have chosen other names such as *Employee Participation Circles* and *Quality Circles.* Some companies, however, have stuck with the name Quality Control Circles.

A second area in which adaptation is taking place concerns the role of the union. In Japan, the unions have usually been consulted by management at the time of the introduction of circles but have had relatively little to do with circle operations once they were established other than to monitor excessive demands on workers. In heavily unionized industries in America, this does not seem to be a suitable strategy. It was a strategy that was tried in Lockheed Missile and Space Company, which seemingly had the most successful program in the United States. But when a strike occurred and the workers and union did not receive what they felt was their due at the end of the strike, they responded by reducing their participation in the circles. To be sure, there were other important factors involved. But loss of key personnel and failure to institutionalize QC circles were extremely significant in contributing to the decline of circle activity at Lockheed.

In a number of other firms, management has simply installed the circles with only minimum consultation with the unions. The consequences were predictable; the unions saw the circles as just one more attempt to extract increased productivity from the workers without sharing the rewards and/or as an attempt to win the loyalty of workers away from the union. Union leaders put pressure on workers not to cooperate, and the circles either never got off the ground or collapsed soon after they were started.

In one company, a poor choice of circle leader in the trial program nearly wrecked the initiative with circles. A worker hostile to the local union committeeman was appointed as QC circle leader. The union committeeman did everything in his power to sabotage the program and reduce worker participation in the circles. Failure was narrowly avoided by bringing in a national headquarters union official, who was sympathetic to the program. He smoothed the ruffled feathers of the local committeeman and explained the rationale for the program from a union perspective.

If the circles are to be introduced in a union situation, they need to be part of the program. The union needs to have a "piece of the action" so that success rubs off on them as well. Otherwise they will see QC activity as an attempt to weaken the union, as indeed it is in some companies. If management tries to go it alone, the union will find a thousand ways to sabotage the program. In a number of firms, I asked managers responsible for initiating the QC circle program how they would do it if they could start all over. Again and again, the answer came back that "I would begin it together with the union so to create a steering committee for the circles with local union leaders as members."

A third area in which adaptation is occurring concerns the voluntary character of participation. We have seen how the Japanese approach often takes on coercive tones through pressures from either management or peer groups. In the United States the voluntaristic principle will have to be maintained more firmly to fit with the expectations of American workers and unions. Should this not be the case, workers will in all likelihood reject the QC circles; the experiences with the zero defect movement are suggestive in this regard. Adherence to the voluntaristic principle may make getting the circles started more difficult in the beginning. On the other hand, there are far greater rewards associated with the operation of the circles if you stick to a voluntary approach for workers. Genuine enthusiasm for developing innovative suggestions is more likely to emerge.

A related problem of adapting the circles to the United States environment concerns the nature of peer pressure. In large-scale Japanese organizations, for a variety of reasons management has been able to mobilize a good deal of peer pressure on behalf of organizational goals. This was not always the case, but it has been true to a large extent since the early 1960s. Thus, they have been able to use peer pressure on the shop floor to encourage workers to join and participate in circle activities. In the United States, given the adversary relationships that predominate between management and labor, it is difficult to mobilize such pressures. The circles are often seen as just one more in a series of management gimmicks designed to hustle the workers. When I asked one worker why he was suspicious of the circles, he replied, "I'm a union man." He reported that although 40 percent of the hourly rate personnel in the plant were participating in the circles, there was still a lot of resistance, especially from the older workers who didn't see any virtue in circle activity and didn't think they were likely to change the way things had always been done. In expressing their hostility, the noncircle participants referred to those in the circles as "circle jerks," and those in the circles were clearly quite defensive on the subject.

Given this often hostile atmosphere reported in both union and nonunion firms, two strategies seem relevant.

- The volunteers must struggle to develop ways to make their circle activity provide benefits for all workers as a way of proving its worth and making their participation legitimate in the eyes of their co-workers.
- The introduction of the circles must be done carefully and gradually with attention to reaching opinion leaders among the hourly-rate personnel and local

union officials. Ultimately, the opponents of the circles among the shop personnel will change their minds only when they see changes on the shop floor which they believe are serving worker interests.

Still another area in which adaptation of Japanese practices is taking place is that of wage payments for circle activity. In those situations in which circle activity is conducted on overtime, which is often the case in high volume production operations, American managers will have to pay normal overtime rates. This is not always the case in Japan where sometimes nominal payments are made. Given the practice of permanent employment in Japan, circle activity can be seen as just one of a long stream of contributions that the worker makes to the organization and that will be recognized over the long haul in promotion or wage increases.

In the United States the absence of this long-term commitment means that workers expect their rewards to be more immediate. Instead of monetary incentives for circle suggestions, Japanese employers rely heavily on providing recognition to circle participation through a variety of activities. Again, this makes sense in the context of long-term employee commitment. In the absence of such commitment, U.S. managers will have to provide greater financial rewards for circle suggestions. Not all U.S. companies using circles have accepted this position, but one strategy that does seem to be emerging is that the circle suggestions are channeled into existing suggestion systems with any payments being split among circle members.

One additional point deserves mention here. The provision of recognition to circle members can be complementary to the use of financial incentives. Firms with QC circles have generally found that there is an enormous craving for recognition on the part of participating workers that can be met in a relatively cost-free fashion. Management presentations, meeting in management reserved rooms, T-shirts imprinted with the name of the company circle program have all been found to be useful approaches. The point is not that you can buy off the workers cheap through figuring out some gimmick for recognition. Rather, there is a demand on the part of workers for recognizing their dignity as individuals and their ability to make meaningful contributions to their organization. They want to be recognized both financially and otherwise.

POTENTIAL FOR EXPANSION

Potentially one of the most exciting areas for adaptation of Japanese practices lies in the scope of QC circle activity. The Japanese have concentrated almost exclusively on applying the circles to hourly-rated personnel. U.S. companies have recently made a few breakthroughs to salaried personnel, but even here success is far from assured.

This is a case in which U.S. ignorance of Japanese practices may have been an asset. Most U.S. companies adopting circles have not known that the Japanese have not applied the circles very extensively to white collar workers. Consequently, the American companies have not been subject to any restraint in this area that might otherwise have been the case. As a result, a number of U.S. firms are experimenting with QC circles for technical and staff personnel, office personnel, and even union-management circles. It is too early to evaluate such efforts, but there may be something in the U.S. environment that makes circle activity among salaried personnel more feasible than is the case in Japan. It will be an interesting area to watch.

A final area in which adaptation will have to take place and is taking place is in the treatment and behavior of middle management. While strong top-level management support is critical to the success of the QC circle program, it is the lack of middle management support in many adopting American companies that has proved to be the major obstacle to their success. This has not been a major problem in Japanese companies where traditionally a strong consensus has usually been forged between top management and middle management before innovations are introduced. Top management usually works through middle management in implementing the circles; it may be characterized as a top-to-middle-down model. In U.S. companies that have adopted the circles, more often than not, middle management has been bypassed in introducing the circles with predictable results. They came to see the circles as a threat to their own positions and not necessarily incorrectly so. Thus, insuring the cooperation of middle management in the United States requires the initiation of formal guidelines.

Middle management resistance can take many forms. At one point, the staff person in charge of QC circles (facilitator) was astonished to find suddenly that his best circle leader was transferred into a section where there was no opportunity to lead QC circles because of a hostile supervisor in his new department. The facilitator had lost his best leader and gained nothing. When he asked the supervisor who ordered the change his reason for making the transfer, the supervisor replied that it was a normal operating decision. He said he didn't take the circles into consideration in making his decision. It was not that the supervisor was hostile to the circles as much as that he did not see any connections between his responsibilities and circle activity. Consequently, the circles had a low priority vis-á-vis other demands being made upon him. While this was not a conscious attempt at sabotage, it had the same effect.

In another company the circles and the facilitator were instructed to make reports to the manufacturing manager. Middle management felt that the information contained in these reports was a way of checking up on them. They responded by refusing to cooperate with the facilitator. The facilitator, recognizing her problem, asked top management to call off the reports so that she could win the confidence of middle management.

In general, two strategies for involving middle management in QC circles seem advisable. First, a concerted training program involving all middle management supervisors should be established so that even those who do not volunteer to participate will at least understand the program's needs and operation. The emphasis should not be to pressure middle managers into involvement but to win them over gradually through an educational process. It must be made absolutely clear, however, that they will not be allowed to block the program's installation. One way of involving middle managers more fully in circle activity is to create a steering committee in which both union leaders and middle management are well represented.

A second strategy for harnessing middle management cooperation involves performance appraisal. In some companies the degree of success in circle activities is a factor in their performance ratings. When middle managers understand that top management gives the circles high priority, they will have a stronger incentive to pursue circle activity. This kind of restructuring of middle management priorities can take place only when top management is committed to circle activity. The ideal, however, is to get middle managers to see circle activity as a tool for better accomplishing their everyday objectives.

SUMMING UP THE BASICS

Six basic principles of QC circle activity seem operative. They are:

1. *Trust your employees.* Accept that they will work to implement organizational goals if given a chance.

2. *Build employee loyalty to the company.* It will pay off in the long run.

3. *Invest in training and treat employees as resources which, if cultivated, will yield economic returns to the firm.* This involves the development of

worker skills. Implicit in this perspective is that you aim for long-term employee commitment to the firm.

4. Recognize employee accomplishments. Symbolic rewards are more important than you think. Show workers that you care about them as individuals.

5. Decentralize decision making. Put the decisions where the information is.

6. Work should be seen as a cooperative effort with workers and managers doing the job together. This implies some degree of consensual decision making.

A simple examination of these principles should lead most readers to respond, "What's the big deal?—there is nothing new here." We can make two responses to that. First, as noted earlier, while the ideas may not be new with regard to managerial personnel, they are new with regard to blue collar applications. Secondly, all these six principles can be found in any good survey of behavioral science literature in the United States. What is particularly fascinating is that the Japanese have taken many of the basic ideas developed in the American behavioral sciences and acted to institutionalize them in daily practice in their firms.

In thinking about this matter further, consider the following analogy to technological hardware. The transistor was invented in the United States but was initially commercialized most successfully in Japan. Now many Americans like to emphasize that the invention is the really important thing and that took place in America. So they conclude with a sigh of relief that we still maintain our position of leadership. This interpretation totally misses the point! Much of the history of America's successful industrialization can be attributed to our ability to take inventions developed in Europe and commercialize them successfully in the United States. The jet engine, for example, was invented in England but commercialized in the United States. It is just this that the Japanese are increasingly doing to us now, and it is a terrible mistake to downplay the creativity needed to take an invention and adapt it to commercial possibilities. This applies just as much to organizational software (including techniques for organizing the labor force) as it does to technological hardware. Although the management principles operative in the QC circle may not strike an American manager as terribly original, it is the ability of the Japanese to synthesize these principles in a system and institutionalize them in daily practice that is extraordinarily original.

Simon Kuznets, in his pathbreaking study of industrialization (*Modern Economic Growth*, Yale University Press, 1966), maintains that the increase in the stock of useful knowledge and the application of this knowledge are the essence of modern economic growth. This increase, in turn, rests on some combination of the growing application of science to problems of economic production and changes in individual attitudes and institutional arrangements which allow for the release of these technological innovations. As industrialization spread through the world, technological and social innovations cropped up in various centers of development. These innovations were the outcome of a cumulative testing process by which some forms emerged superior to others; each historical period gave rise to new methods and solutions. The economic growth of a given nation came to depend upon adoption of these innovations, Kuznets concludes, by stressing the importance of the "worldwide validity and transmissibility of modern additions to knowledge, the transnational character of this stock of knowledge, and the dependence on it of any single nation in the course of its modern economic growth."

We are dealing here with the borrowing and adaptation of social innovations. Although Kuznets speaks of both technological and social knowledge, his reasoning applies most forcefully to the realm of technological choice. It is here that the selection of the most progressive technique will be made most unambiguously in terms of cost-benefit analysis. For example, the last furnace using a hot blast and a mineral fuel adopted in nineteenth-century America was clearly superior, in terms of reducing costs and increasing productivity, to its predecessor based on charcoal technology. One can make a similar point with regard to adaptation of technology to specific environmental conditions. Thus, to pursue the steel-making example, the basic oxygen furnace developed in Austria depended, in part, for its success on the availability of special heat-resistant brick used to line the converters that were not available outside of Austria. It was not until comparable heat resistant bricks were developed outside of Europe that the basic oxygen furnace became economically feasible in North America and Japan.

With social knowledge and institutional arrangements, the situation is more complex. To be sure, certain institutional arrangements are fairly rapidly grasped under the right conditions as being essential to economic progress. Consider the spread of the joint stock company, double-entry bookkeeping and the diffusion of multidivisional decentralized management structure. Many other institutional innovations, however, are not easily compared and evaluated vis-á-vis existing arrangements. This is because social innovations often interact with a variety of other processes in a way that obscures their respective contributions to economic growth. Furthermore, the output of social innovations is often not as easily quantified as is usually the case with hard technology.

It is the lack of clarity in these relationships and the abundance of unwarranted inferences that lead to an element of fad in the adoption of social innovations and give free rein to arguments grounded more in ideology and power relationships than in tested generalizations. A rapid rate of diffusion of a particular social innovation may reflect these considerations more than the proven superiority of the innovation in question. Ironically, the claims to superiority of one social arrangement over another often are cloaked in the language of objective social science.

Thus, the task of evaluating the applicability of Japanese management practices in the United States and judging what are to be the needed adaptations is a herculean task. Many claims are being made and often by those with vested interests in the outcome. How is one to separate the wheat from the chaff? How are we to insure diffusion of the best practices? There are no simple answers to these questions. The problem is made more difficult by our dependency on consultants for diffusing information on such innovations. Naturally, they treat such information as proprietary. Yet, consultants possess and diffuse both good and bad information in varying proportions. It is extremely difficult for the manager to separate the good consultants from the bad consultants. By the nature of their business, consultants don't like to talk about failure. Moreover, each consultant is devoted to creating a differentiated product that they can market over a broad client base. For all these as well as other reasons, the manager seeking to identify a program in work restructuring that fits his or her needs has great difficulty.

Yet, even here the Japanese case may be instructive. In the case of QC circles, a nonprofit professional association (Union of Japanese Scientist and Engineers) set up a structure that provides for a standardized collection of information (including a central repository) and a "public testing" of strategies and programs. This information is then fed back to individual firms in a variety of packages carefully tailored for different levels of personnel. The Union of Japanese Scientists and Engineers helps develop a consensus on what constitutes best practice and encourages the dissemination of these ideas. It may be time for organizations such as the American Society for Quality Control and the American Society for Training and Development to assume such functions. There is already some movement in this direction, and it is my hope that it will crystallize in a concrete form.

To be sure, even if successfully applied to American firms, QC circles will continue to evolve into new forms of worker participation in decision making. If one could say that their major contribution was to convince American management that hourly-rated workers do have an important contribution to make to the organization and are prepared to do so when given the opportunity, then the innovation will have had a lasting impact in America.

Questions for Discussion

1. What had led Japanese managers to apply American management theory throughout their organizations?

2. What is a quality control circle? How does it operate? What does it do?

3. Why might U.S. managers want to apply Japanese management practices?

4. What "principles" of management are being applied in the use of QC circles? Can these work for everyone?

5. Are there certain types of firms in the United States that are more likely to use Japanese management practices? Which firms would have more difficulty?

6. If U.S. managers want to use these approaches, how should they go about introducing or adapting them into their firms?

CASE 72

BREAKING IN A U.S. SALESMAN IN LATIN AMERICA: TO BRIBE OR NOT TO BRIBE

The Starnes-Brenner Machine Tool Company of Iowa City, Iowa, has a small, one-man sales office headed by Frank Rothe in Latino, a major Latin American country. Frank has been in Latino for about ten years and is retiring this year; his replacement is Bill Hunsaker, one of Starnes-Brenner's top salesmen. Both will be in Latino for about eight months during which time Frank will show Bill the ropes, introduce him to their principal customers and, in general, prepare him to take over.

Frank has been very successful as a foreign representative in spite of his unique style and, at times, complete refusal to follow company policy that doesn't suit him. The company hasn't really done much about his method of operation although from time to time he has angered some of the top company men. As President McCaughey, who retired a couple of years ago, once remarked to a vice president who was complaining about Frank, "If he's making money—and he is (more than any other foreign offices), then leave the guy alone." When McCaughey retired, the new chief who took over immediately instituted organizational changes that gave more emphasis to the overseas operations, moving the company toward a truly worldwide operation in which a "loner" like Frank would

Source: Philip R. Cateora and John M. Hess, *International Marketing* (Homewood, Ill.: Richard D. Irwin, 1979). Copyright 1979 by Richard D. Irwin, Inc.

probably not fit. In fact, one of the key reasons for selecting Bill as Frank's replacement, besides Bill's being a topflight salesman, is Bill's capacity as an "organization" man. He understands the need for coordination among operations and will cooperate with the home office so that the Latino office can be expanded and brought into the "mainstream."

The company knows that there is much to be learned from Frank, and Bill's job is to learn everything possible. The company doesn't want to continue some of Frank's practices, but much of his knowledge is vital for continued, smooth operation. Today, Starnes-Brenner's foreign sales account for about 15 percent of the company's total profits, compared with about 3 percent only ten years ago.

The company is actually changing character from being principally an exporter without any real concern for continuous foreign market representation to worldwide operation where the foreign divisions are part of the total effort rather than "stepchild" operations. In fact, Latino is one of the last operational divisions to be assimilated into the "new" organization. Rather than try to change Frank, the company has been waiting for him to retire before making any significant adjustments in their Latino operations.

Bill Hunsaker is 36 years old with a wife and three children; he is a very good salesman and administrator although he has had no foreign experience. He has the reputation of being fair, honest, and a "straight shooter." Some, back at the home office, see his assignment as part of a grooming job for a top position, perhaps eventually the presidency. The Hunsakers are now settled in their new home after having been in Latino for about two weeks. Today is Bill's first day on the job.

When Bill arrived at the office, Frank was on his way to a local factory to inspect some Starnes-Brenner machines that had to have some adjustments made before being acceptable to the Latino government agency which was buying them. Bill joined Frank for the plant visit. Later, after the visit, we join the two at lunch.

Bill, tasting some chili, remarks, "Boy! this certainly isn't like the chili we have in America." "No, it isn't, and there's another difference too. . .the Latinos are Americans and nothing angers a Latino more than to have a *'Gringo'* refer to the United States as America as if to say that Latino isn't part of America too. The Latinos rightly consider their country as part of America (take a look at a map) and people from the United States are North Americans at best. So, for future reference, refer to home either as the United States, States, or North America, but for gosh sakes not just America. Not to change the subject, Bill, but could you see that any change had been made in those S-27s from the standard model?" "No, they looked like the standard. Was there something out of whack when they arrived?" "No, I couldn't see any problem—I suspect this is the best piece of sophisticated bribe taking I've come across yet. Most of the time the Latinos are more 'honest' about their *'mordidas'* than this." "What's a *mordida?*" Bill asks. "You know, *'Kumshaw,' 'Dash,' 'Bustarella,' 'Mordida';* they are all the same: a little grease to expedite the action. *'Mordida'* is the local word for a slight offering or, if you prefer, bribe," says Frank.

Bill quizzically responds, "How much bribery does it take to make successful sales anyway?" "Oh, it depends on the situation but it's certainly something you have to be prepared to deal with." Boy, what a greenhorn, Frank thinks to himself, as he continues, "Here's the story. When the S-27s arrived last January, we began uncrating them and right away the *'Jefe'* engineer, *'Jefe,'* that's the head man in charge, began extra careful examination and declared there was a vital defect in the machines; he claimed the machinery would be dangerous and thus unacceptable if it wasn't corrected. I looked it over but couldn't see anything wrong so I agreed to have our staff engineer check all the machines and correct any flaws that might exist. Well, the *'Jefe'* said there wasn't enough time to wait for an engineer to come from the States, that the machines could be adjusted locally, and we could pay him and he would make all the necessary arrangements. So, what the hell do you do? No adjustment his way and there would be an order cancelled; and, maybe there was something out of line, those things have been known to happen. But for the life of me I can't see that anything had been done since the machines were supposedly fixed. So, let's face it, we just paid a bribe and a pretty darn big bribe at that—about $50 per machine—what makes it so aggravating is that that's the second one I've had to pay on this shipment."

"The second?" asks Bill. "Yeah, at the border when we were transferring the machines to Latino trucks, it was hot and they were moving slow as blazes. It took them over an hour to transfer one machine to a Latino truck and we had ten others to go. It seemed that every time I spoke to the dock boss about speeding things up they just got slower. Finally, out of desperation, I slipped him a fistful of pesos and, sure enough, in the next three hours they had the whole thing loaded. Just one of the 'local customs' of doing business. Generally though, it comes at the lower level where wages don't cover living expenses too well."

There is a pause and Bill asks, "What does that do to our profits?" "Runs them down, of course, but I look at it as just one of the many costs of doing business— I do my best not to pay but when I have to, I do." Hesitantly Bill replies, "I don't like it, Frank, we've got good products, they're priced right, we give good service, and keep plenty of spare parts in the country, so why should we have to pay bribes to the buyer? It's just no way to do business. Hell, you've already had to pay two bribes on one shipment; if you keep it up, the word's going to get around and you'll be paying at every level. Then all the profit goes out the window— you know, once you start, where do you stop? Besides that, where do we stand legally? Perhaps you have missed all the news back in the States about the United Fruit bribery payment, Japan and Lockheed, the oil companies, laundered money, and so on. Congress is mad, countries are mad, the Prime Minister of Japan, Tanaka, had been ousted because of bribery. I'd say that the best policy is to never start; you might lose a few sales but let it be known that there are no bribes; we sell the best, service the best at fair prices, and that's it."

"Oh boy!!" Frank thinks to himself as he replies, "First of all, I've heard about all the difficulty with bribing governments, but what I did was just peanuts compared to Japan and Lockheed. The people we 'pay off' are small and granted we give good service, but we've only been doing it for the last year or so. Before that I never knew when I was going to have equipment to sell. In fact, we only had products when there were surpluses stateside. I had to pay the 'right' people to get sales and, besides that, you're not back in the States any longer. Things are just done differently here. You follow that policy and I guarantee that you'll have fewer sales and a heck of a lot more headaches. Look, Bill, everybody does it here; it's a way of life and the costs are generally reflected in the mark-up and overhead. There is even a code of behavior involved. We're not actually encouraging it to spread, just perpetuating an accepted way of doing business."

Patiently and slightly condescendingly, Bill replies, "I know, Frank, but wrong is wrong and we want to operate differently now. We hope to set up an operation here on a continuous basis; we plan to operate in Latino just like we do in the United States. Really expand our operation and make a long-range marketing commitment, grow with the country!! And, one of the first things we must avoid are unethical. . ."

Frank interrupts, "But really, is it unethical? Everybody does it, the Latinos even pay mordidas to other Latinos; it's a fact of life—is it really unethical? I think that the circumstances that exist in a country justify and dictate the behavior. Remember man, 'When in Rome, do as the Romans do.'" Almost shouting, Bill blurts out, "I can't buy that. We know that our management practices and techniques are our strongest point. Really all we have to differentiate us from the rest of our competition, Latino and others, is that we are better managers and, as far as I'm concerned, graft and other unethical behavior has got to be cut out to create a healthy industry. In the long run, it should strengthen our position. We can't build our future on unethical practices."

Frank angrily replies, "Hell, it's done in the States all the time. What about the big dinners, drinks, and all the other hanky-panky that goes on? Not to mention Gulf Oil, United Fruit, or our own Congress and 'Koreagate'? What is that, if it isn't *mordida,* the North American way? The only difference is that instead of cash only, in the United States we pay in merchandise and cash." "That's really not the same and you know it. Besides, we certainly get a lot of business transacted during those dinners even if we are paying the bill." "Bill, the only difference is that here bribes go on in the open; they don't hide it or dress it in foolish ritual that fools no one. It goes on in the United States and everyone denies the existence of it. That's all the difference—in the United States we're just more hypocritical about it all."

"Look dammit," Frank continues almost shouting, "we are getting off on the wrong foot and we've got eight months to work together. Just keep your eyes and mind open and let's talk about it again in a couple of months when you've seen how the whole country operates; perhaps then you won't be so quick to judge it absolutely wrong."

Frank, lowering his voice, says thoughtfully, "I know it's hard to take; probably the most disturbing aspect of dealing with business problems in underdeveloped countries is the matter of graft. And, frankly, we don't do much advance preparation so we can deal firmly with it. It bothered the hell out of me at first; but, then, I figured it makes its economic contribution, too, since the payoff is as much a part of the economic process as a payroll. What's our real economic role anyway, besides making a profit, of course? Are we developers of wealth, helping to push the country on to greater economic growth, or are we missionaries? Or should we be both? I don't really know, but I don't think we can be both simultaneously, and my feeling is that as the country prospers, as higher salaries are paid and better standards of living are reached, we'll see better ethics. Until then, we've got to operate or leave and, if you are going to win the opposition over, you'd better join them and change them from within, not fight them."

Before Bill could reply, a Latino friend of Frank's joined them and they changed the topic of conversation.

Questions for Discussion

1. Is what Frank did ethical? According to whose ethics—Latino's or the United States'?

2. Frank seemed to imply that there was a difference between what he was doing and what happened in Japan or with United Fruit. Is there any difference? Explain.

3. Frank's attitude seems to imply that a foreigner must comply with all local customs, but some would say that one of the contributions made by U.S. firms is to change local ways of doing business. Who is right?

4. Should Frank's behavior have been any different had this not been a government contract?

5. If Frank shouldn't have paid the bribe, what should he have done, and what might have been the consequences?

6. What are the company interests in the problem?

7. Do you think Bill will make the grade in Latino? Why? What will it take?

8. How can an overseas manager be prepared to face this problem?

EXERCISE 73
DEMOGRAPHY AND THE FUTURE

The makeup of the population of a given society, changes taking place in the size and shape of that population, and the effects those changes are likely to have is the subject of demography. Managers need to pay attention to these changes and forecast their potential implications because they are likely to significantly impact both their businesses and their careers.

This exercise provided you with an opportunity to gather some data and assess its impact on your future.

First, read the background information. Then, gather the data suggested and answer the questions at the end of the exercise. Bring your findings to class for discussion.

BACKGROUND INFORMATION

What happened to Gerber Products? Why did it add new products beyond its baby food line? American Hospital Supply Company has grown at a phenomenal rate lately. Why? Part of the answer to these questions is that the baby boom became a baby bust. After a steady decline in the U.S. birthrate from the 1800s to 1940, a twenty-year period of increased birthrate occurred in which the population grew from about two children to four children per woman. This was followed by a decline in the 1960s and 1970s. The birthrate (among other variables) has an impact on total population size and affects age range proportions, which, in turn, affect basic demand patterns for certain goods and services.

Another significant feature of birthrate data is the number of families without children. Due to overall lifestyle, a two paycheck family with no children results in different housing patterns, disposable income, and unique consumption patterns. A nation where the average family has two children will have a higher per capita income than a nation where the average family has three children. Disposable income would increase and be used for travel, entertainment, or a house at the beach. Although people would not eat more, they might eat more convenience foods or gourmet foods or go to restaurants more often.

The work force, meanwhile, also begins to take on a different composition. The post-World War II baby boom means more people competing for middle management positions in the 1980s. With fewer full-time students, thousands of teachers are also competing for jobs. A smaller group of young people, those growing up after the baby boom generation, may see a perpetual barrier to success and prosperity. However, the scarcity of young people may place them in demand for jobs requiring youthful energy and fresh training. Demand for specialists may also change. For example, while there may be an oversupply of physicians, there may be less need for obstetricians and more need for specialists in geriatric care.

What some have come to call the "graying of America" could have significant impact on demand patterns for products and services, as well as both threats and opportunities for various segments of the economy in the future. Birthrate data and the population's age composition can give significant clues to the patterns that could emerge in the future, patterns that would affect business and their managers in predictable ways. This exercise seeks to stimulate your thinking about these patterns and their implications for you.

**YOUR
ASSIGNMENT**

1. Gather basic data on the population. Your library should have census data collected by the government. *The Statistical Abstract of the United States* provides convenient reference data.

2. Draw a series of bar charts showing trends for each decade from 1900 through 1980 (every ten years) for the following:

   a. Total population

   b. Number of men and women

   c. Children born per women (births, rates, fertility)

   d. Percent of population by the following age categories: 1–13; 14–21; 22–35; 35–65; over 65.

For each of the following categories of economic activity, indicate what your data suggest. (Check whether the segment will be hurt or helped, and provide a brief explanation indicating which of your charts leads you to your conclusions.)

Economic Segment	Helped	Hurt	Why?	What Chart Supports It?
Advertising				
Autos				
Broadcasting				
Clothing				
Health care				
Housing				
Jewelry and watches				
Life insurance				
Liquor				
Movie theaters				
Restaurants				
Sports and recreation				
Tobacco				
Travel				

1. Comment on how these data are likely to affect you as a manager.

2. Bring your findings to class to discuss and compare.

CASE 74
HOW TO DEAL WITH A REVOLUTION

The Jaycees had gathered for their regular monthly meeting at the local Catfish Cabin restaurant. After dinner, the President introduced the speaker for the evening. Dr. Paul Powell was a noted futurologist at the local university. Dr. Powell's subject was titled "The Home Information Revolution." Excerpts from his speech are summarized below.

"Tomorrow's home telephone system, probably built around a minicomputer, should make those staid instruments of today as obsolete as a jungle drum. We have technology and much of the basic hardware right now to set up a true home communications center. There is a revolution just over the horizon that will vastly simplify consumers' lives to no less an extent than the advent of natural gas and electricity revolutionized kitchens dominated by wood-burning stoves."

Innovations foreseen include: "A small, inexpensive computer that will help strip away paperwork troubles and shopping trips for the home and apartment dweller just as larger models simplified and speeded up today's business."

"With a minicomputer that may cost less than a black-and-white TV, the consumer can use code symbols to do a number of jobs. One set of coded instructions can automatically withdraw $50 from your bank account and transfer it to the ABC Co. to pay off a bill, with a computerized receipt."

"Grocery or department store shopping in the future may well be handled from the living room using catalogues. Pick your items, punch the store and item codes and wait for delivery of the orders that probably will be made up and bagged or boxed automatically."

"We foresee the home being wired with special sensors that will bleep, squeak, or wail out their warnings in case of fire, leaking gas, or the like. Antiburglary devices could report directly and instantly to the nearest police station."

Hospital bills for some patients soar today because of the need to keep them in the hospital so as to keep a close watch on their vital signs. This monitoring could be done at home with equipment that transmits information to the hospital and / or physician automatically and around the clock."

"Electronic mail could be delivered at different rates depending on the time of day or night it is sent. And we may see machines that give the receiver a letter-like copy through facsimile process. Tomorrow's newspapers may be delivered the same way."

"And of course, that same basic minicomputer can order up special TV and movie programs for the home set and enroll you in special courses that are taught via television."

"I think it is important to note that much of what is foreseen for home telephone operations will entail significant energy savings. The energy costs of sending and receiving conventional mail are quite high compared to the electronic version. Centralized and high speed delivery systems for everything from groceries to a new sofa will lessen the need for trips in the family auto."

Several of the Jaycee's in attendance were particularly intrigued by Dr. Powell's remarks. Jack Jacobs operated the local Entre' computer store. On his way out of the meeting, Jack joined into a conversation in the parking lot between Frank Fredericks, the manager of the Safeway grocery store, and George

Garwin, the manager of one of the large local hospitals. As he listened, he realized that Frank and George disagreed with each other about Dr. Powell's remarks.

Frank was of the opinion that even though technology was available, the cost was far beyond the wherewithal of typical consumers. George disagreed. He believed that costs would drop dramatically, and that dual-income families could afford to purchase the technology. Then Frank suggested that even if costs could be reduced as the technology became more widely available and used, shoppers would resist such an approach. Frank believed that consumers would prefer to get out of their homes, thinking that shopping was a social experience. George reminded him of the enormous success of some of the television "home shopping networks," and recalled the growing popularity of catalog shopping.

Meanwhile, Ronald Rea joined the group in the parking lot. He owned a local realty firm. Mr. Rea commented that he was quite taken with Dr. Powell's foresight. He envisioned a time when various properties could be displayed directly to a client's home, instead of wasting time with an agent traveling to disparate locations to view properties. Video displays of homes and commercial properties could be made available instead of a brief listing on a piece of paper. At this point Frank stated that he believed resistance from existing realtors, for fear of losing their jobs, would make it difficult for Ron to try such a thing.

Jack couldn't help but notice that a few other small groups were engaged in similar exchanges elsewhere in the parking lot. In one group the owner of a local travel agency and a bank vice-president were closely questioning Dr. Powell about his thoughts as to the impact of such a revolution on their businesses. And the editor of the local newspaper was asking Dr. Powell if he thought videotex or some such system would affect the classified ads.

In another group, Alice Allen, a local department store manager, indicated she thought that her management activities might force significant changes in the face of such a revolution. Instead of spending time managing a floor-based sales force, she believed that she might have to spend more time with inventory control and delivery systems. In a sense, she thought she would spend less time managing people, and more time managing technology. The local police chief disagreed. He thought that even if burglar devices, fire sensors, and so on were linked to police headquarters, his job would still entail managing people.

Questions for Discussion

1. Do the different reactions of Frank and George to Dr. Powell's speech surprise you? Explain.

2. Could the work environment that a manager controls affect his understanding of the future changes that Dr. Powell is speaking of in his presentation?

3. Do you think that Alice Allen is correct in her assumption that she will have to alter her management style? Explain.

4. Do you think these forecasts will ever happen? If not, why not? If so, how long will it take, and what changes will have to occur?

5. If such a scenario evolves; what would the impact be for various types of business firms and their managers?

READING 75
BREAKING AWAY

Meet Julie Spear Merritt. She is a bright, energetic young woman, a former tri-
athlon competitor, from Houston. For six years, she worked as a geological engineer with Shell Oil Co., helping to select sites for drilling in the Gulf Coast
region. Then, a couple of years ago, she quit. "There was more routine office
work in the job than I wanted," Merritt says. "I was bored." This fall, she plans
to start a new career, possibly working for a small furniture or real estate
development company in North Carolina. She expects to make substantially
less than she was earning at Shell, but that doesn't bother her. "I want to get
up every morning and like what I do."

Julie Merritt is an M.B.A. So, for that matter, is 23-year-old Shawn Hornsby,
an equally bright and energetic young man from north central Illinois. As a
child, he had always assumed that he would someday wind up running the chain
of discount variety stores his grandfather had founded in 1922. But two and a
half years ago, as Hornsby was completing his undergraduate work at Illinois
Wesleyan University, his father decided to sell the company. Shawn went off to
Indiana University's Graduate School of Business not knowing exactly what he
would do when he got out.

Somewhere along the way, he developed the notion of starting his own business, perhaps a chain of fast-food restaurants. His idea was to locate them in
small towns with populations of 10,000 or so, much like the towns where his
grandfather had set up discount stores more than 60 years before. If all goes
well, Hornsby will launch the venture this summer. And he has a partner—his
father. "My father never went to college," he says. "He's learned by doing. But
I think he's impressed with the stuff I've learned at business school. He thinks
I'm different from the M.B.A.s he's read about."

Julie Merritt and Shawn Hornsby are, indeed, different from the M.B.A.s
we've all read about. They are not the smug, pinstriped, fast-track go-getters
who have been blamed for everything from the fatal myopia of large corporations to the rampant corruption on Wall Street. They do not think that two years
in a classroom has taught them all they need to know about running a company.
Nor do they expect to conquer the world at any point in the near future, while
being paid a six-figure starting salary for doing it. Rather, they are the type of
bright, resourceful, roll-up-your-sleeves young people that most growing companies would be happy to have as employees, or customers, or suppliers. The
question is: are they typical of their classmates or the exceptions that prove the
rule?

That's an important question, if only because of the sheer number of M.B.A.s
being unleashed on America these days. This June, the nation's business schools
will graduate the largest class in history, more than 70,000 new masters of business administration. To put this figure in perspective, consider that the class of
'87 is almost as large as the total number of M.B.A.s produced during the entire
decade of the 1960s. We're talking about a thirteenfold increase in business-
school enrollment over the past 25 years, a 50 percent increase over the past 10.
More people are now graduating from business school each year than from medical school and law school combined.

Source: Reprinted with permission, *INC.* magazine, (June, 1987), copyright © 1987 by INC.
Publishing Company, 38 Commercial Wharf, Boston, MA 02110.

The trend, moreover, shows no signs of abating. On the contrary, it has become institutionalized. The number of master's degree business programs has increased 67 percent, from 389 to 650, since 1974, when somebody first began to keep track of such things. Back in 1962, Harvard University alone accounted for some 12 percent of the country's annual crop of M.B.A.s. Today, the figure is 1.1 percent and falling. Meanwhile, more young people decide each year to turn their attention to business, and to get there by way of an M.B.A. degree.

Who are they? Why did they go to business school? Where are they headed, and where do they hope to end up? What do they want from the companies they work for, and what do they expect to find? And how have they been shaped by the events of their times? This is, after all, a generation that grew up after Vietnam and after Watergate. Most of them entered college at about the same time Ronald Reagan became President; now they are graduating from business school as he prepares to step down. By and large, they have no memory of an era when large U.S. corporations seemed invincible to foreign or domestic challenge. Rather, they have seen the decline of one major American industry after another; the rise of the entrepreneur; and, more recently, the scandals on Wall Street. How have these graduates been affected by all this, and what impact are they themselves likely to have on the American economy in years to come?

With such questions in mind, we set out to survey a cross section of the M.B.A. class of '87, as represented by the graduating students at 10 respected business schools around the country. (See "How the Survey Was Conducted.")

We asked them questions on subjects ranging from their family backgrounds to their career plans to their attitudes toward business in general and small companies in particular. In all, we distributed 1,500 questionnaires (150 per school) and received 907 replies

The results provide a portrait of an M.B.A. class that is not only larger than those of 10 or 20 years ago, but different. For one thing, it is much more heterogenous, in part because it includes people who probably would not have gone to business school in the past—people such as Glenda Johnson, a 27-year-old black woman from Miami.

Nine years ago, Johnson was finishing up high school and planning to enroll at Cornell University as a premed student. Then she heard a recruitment speech by Sybil C. Mobley, the dynamic dean of Florida A & M University's business school, who inspired her to switch colleges and careers. This month, she is receiving her M.B.A. form the University of Pennsylvania's Wharton School of Business and heading off for a job as a financial analyst with Burger King Corp., in preparation for owning her own company. "Business is where the best opportunities are," she says. "I think I'll be able to benefit other people as much by being in business as I could have in medicine."

Not that Johnson is typical of the class of '87. Like previous classes, it is predominantly white (81 percent), male (64 percent), and young: two-thirds of its members are 24 to 28 years of age. As for the future, the majority (61 percent) plan to go to work for large corporations (defined as companies with sales greater than $150 million) with another 24 percent headed for midsize companies (with sales between $25 million and $150 million). Their occupations of choice are still financial services (41 percent) and consulting (37 percent), and their salary expectations are still high. On average, the M.B.A.s we polled figure they'll make close to $43,000 in the first year out of business school; five years down the line, they plan to be earning more than $97,000 a year.

But if all this suggests that many of this year's M.B.A.s do fit the popular stereotype, it also tends to hide the large number who don't.

Consider, for example, Steve Prelosky, a 30-year-old engineer at Carnegie-Mellon University's Graduate School of Industrial Administration. Unlike most of his classmates, Prelosky already has a lot of big-company experience. After graduating from Pennsylvania State University in 1979 with a degree in mechanical engineering, he spent six years working for General Electric Co. There he did a variety of jobs, at one point even traveling to the Middle East to sell parts for gas turbine engines. The longer he worked, however, the more convinced he became that his future lay outside a large company. As markets matured, he saw his opportunities for advancement dry up, and—with them—the promise of job security. Finally, he decided to quit and go to business school. "With my wife working and no kids, I felt it was a good time to take a risk," he says.

Last winter, in the midst of his second year, Prelosky got wind of a part-time job with a young Pittsburgh-based company, a $5-million business that produces carbon dioxide for industrial uses. The founder, a friend of his family, was thinking about adding capacity and asked Prelosky to crunch some numbers. "I analyzed the profit-and-loss margins under several different scenarios, things I didn't even know how to do before going to business school." His findings convinced the company to proceed with the expansion—and to offer Prelosky a full-time position on its finance staff.

In the new job, Prelosky expects to have many new opportunities and challenges. "Besides working on the financial end of the business, I plan to have some input into marketing and to bring in some business," he says. His salary is $4,000 or $5,000 less than the $40,000 he was making at GE, but now he has 10 percent of the equity of a growing company. "My goal is to help this company grow and to make sure that we stay lean, because that's our advantage."

Prelosky is not alone in deciding to cast his lot with a smaller company. Of the graduating M.B.A.s we polled, 9 percent said that they plan to seek employment in companies with sales of $25 million or less. That may not sound like many—until you consider that, extrapolated, it represents more people than the entire M.B.A. class of 1962.

Unfortunately, those who do want to work for smaller companies face a vexing problem: finding jobs. While the major corporations, investment banks, and consulting firms make annual pilgrimages to business schools, smaller companies tend to stay away. "Not many of them are big on recruitment," says Lee A. Junkans, director of career services and placement at Duke University's Fuqua School of Business. "So it's up to the student to locate these companies."

That is often a major undertaking. Kay Branz, for example, has been spending hour upon hour reading the classified ads and searching for information about small businesses in the Chicago area, while she finishes up her degree from Northwestern University's J. L. Kellogg Graduate School of Management. "The opportunities aren't staring you in the face," she says. "You have to get out and shake the bushes." In early April, most of her classmates were responding to job offers from large companies. Branz, however, had yet to latch on to anything.

Nor, for that matter, had Steven Szafara, a Philadelphia native who is getting his M.B.A. from Wharton. Szafara, 27, was looking for a marketing or staff job with a small manufacturing business, preferably in the Philadelphia area. "I enjoy creating things," he says. "It's part of my personality." He passed the word to everyone he knew, even some headhunters. "You name it," says Szafara, "and I was doing it." Finally, late in April, he landed a consulting position with an accounting firm—long after most of his classmates had lined up their postgraduation jobs.

There are, of course, some lucky ones who don't have to look far for a small company in need of their services. Carol Sabransky, for one, is thinking about heading back to the chain of pharmacies her father owns. That's not what she had in mind when she enrolled in Indiana University's M.B.A. program in January 1986. After managing one of the pharmacies, on the north side of Chicago, she had decided, at the age of 32, that it was time to move on to bigger things. She thought of becoming a lending officer at a bank, or a brand manager with a large consumer products company. But the more she learned about those options, the more attractive the family business became. The grass, she concluded, is greener on her own side of the fence.

Sabransky is well aware that competition in the retail drug market is getting more and more cutthroat. "These days, it's an accomplishment just to stay alive." But her business-school training has opened her eyes to possibilities she didn't see before. "I'd want to do a lot more market research, but I think there's a way we could expand our business by emphasizing service. And besides," she adds, "I really think I'd get lost in a big company. I need to see the difference I make."

The same goes for Patricia Sheehy, whose father owns several car dealerships in the Northeast. Although she finally accepted a position as a commercial lender in a bank, the 26-year-old M.B.A. from Duke was greatly tempted to return to the family business. "Where else would I have an opportunity to learn about the whole business?" she asks seriously, then laughs. "That's something my father likes to kid me about. He thinks it's funny that M.B.A.s are always talking about finding 'challenging opportunities.' In his day, people looked for jobs."

Sheehy's father is right. The search for "challenging opportunities" is an almost monotonous refrain among this year's graduating M.B.A.s. Overall, they ranked "challenging work" and "company atmosphere" above everything else, even "high salary," as leading considerations in choosing their next job. The large majority, moreover, believe that entrepreneurial companies are best suited to provide those things. According to 65 percent of the respondents, such companies offer the best opportunities for advancement; 76 percent said they have a more challenging work environment; 84 percent said they are more receptive to new ideas; and 62 percent said they provide greater opportunity to build personal wealth. The one thing entrepreneurial companies do not offer, according to 85 percent of those polled, is "more time for family and nonbusiness activities." But, then, this year's M.B.A.s tend toward workaholism; on average, they plan to spend 56 hours a week on their new jobs.

So, given these plans and beliefs, why aren't more of them looking for positions in small, entrepreneurial companies? Perhaps because many of them intend to start their own. Fully one-third of the respondents say that they will start or acquire their own business within 10 years. Another 41 percent say that they might. Only 25 percent dismiss the possibility.

That represents a significant change in the attitude of business-school graduates. Granted, previous generations of M.B.A.s have founded a lot of companies over the years, but it was seldom something they planned on doing when they left business school. Rather, they generally headed off for jobs in large companies with every intention of staying there. Only when career options narrowed at the top did they decide to set out on their own.

Not so the current generation of M.B.A.s. Some of them already have their business plans written and are out looking for capital. Heather Wictum, for one, is in the midst of launching a new toy company, even as she prepares for her graduation from the University of Southern California's School of Business Administration. The company will specialize in what she calls "children's play environments." Its first product, a kit of plastic construction materials, will be aimed at families with little space in a backyard. She hopes to have prototypes ready by July. In the meantime, she is approaching investors for $50,000 in start-up financing.

Wictum, 30, is no novice when it comes to starting businesses. A textile-design major in college, she financed her undergraduate education by designing and selling shirts to a highly specialized market segment: bagpipers. Subsequently, she spent two years managing subcontractors for a San Francisco apparel company. That experience should come in handy in her new venture: in order to keep a lid on overhead, she plans to farm out the manufacturing. "We'll do our own light assembly work and packaging," she says, "and we'll focus on future products."

Peter Francis, a 34-year-old M.B.A. from Stanford University, is taking a different approach. He plans to spend the next few months looking for a small machine shop in the Seattle area, with the notion of purchasing it through some form of leveraged buyout. But that's just for openers. A trained machinist, he eventually hopes to branch out into computer-integrated manufacturing, which he considers a potentially enormous market. "I'll be applying automation to my own company," says Francis, whose father manufactures oceanographic equipment in Massachusetts. "And I hope to become good enough to sell this expertise to others."

Then there are those, such as Linda Steckley, who intended to start service businesses. Steckley, 45, is getting her M.B.A. from the University of Miami, where she has worked for several years as a fund-raiser. Along the way, she acquired great contacts. "But I didn't have the quantitative skills," she says, "and I didn't have the confidence." Now she plans to go into the executive search business, either on her own or as a partner in an existing firm. "Before I did my M.B.A., there was no way I would have started a business."

People such as Wictum, Francis, and Steckley are a distinct minority, however, accounting for only about 5 percent of the graduating M.B.A.s we polled. More typical are those who intend to get some additional experience and seasoning before setting off on their own. Of the M.B.A.s headed for large companies, 25 percent say that they will have their own businesses within a decade. Many, of course, are reluctant to discuss those plans, for fear of antagonizing their next employers. But there are some who talk quite freely about their goals.

Jock Donaldson, for example, is a 30-year-old M.B.A. from the University of Minnesota's Curtis L. Carlson School of Management who has spent the past five years working for a heavy-duty automotive-parts manufacturer started by his grandfather. The company, with annual revenues of $260 million, is now publicly owned and run by professional managers. Donaldson feels that his business-school training has improved his chances for advancement in the company, but he doesn't intend to stay there long. Within the next three to five years, he hopes to buy or become a partner in a small manufacturing or distribution business. "I'd like to see an actual product," he says. "And I'd want it to be an industrial product, as opposed to a consumer one. The consumer is just too fickle for me."

David Lowenstein, a Duke M.B.A., also plans to acquire some big-company experience before going into his own company. The company he expects to go into, however, is his family's electrical supply business. "Business school taught me how to ask tough questions," says Lowenstein, 24. "But I need some really good experience in sales and marketing at General Foods Corp. "My father thinks it's a great company," he says. "And I think it will be a terrific place to learn."

To be sure, most of the would-be entrepreneurs in the class of '87 do not have family businesses to come back to after they've acquired the requisite experience elsewhere. Instead, they plan to start their own. After graduation from Duke's Fuqua School, for example, 25-year-old Steve Layne will "pay his dues" at D'Arcy Masius Benton & Bowles, one of Madison Avenue's premier advertising agencies, where he is taking a job as an assistant account executive. "I hope to absorb as much as I can about how the industry works," he says. "But I can't see myself working for someone else for the rest of my life." He eventually hopes to set up a marketing consulting firm geared toward smaller companies.

Lisa Nelson, an M.B.A. candidate at the University of Texas at Austin, has similar plans. She wants to work for a few years as a commercial loan officer in a bank before starting her own consulting business for minority entrepreneurs. Nelson, who is black, says she got the idea while studying the economics at

Michigan State University. "I was talking to a couple of friends, one in accounting, the other in finance. We all felt that minorities were missing out because so many of them didn't know how to put the pieces of a business together or refine their ideas." At Texas, she pitched the consulting concept to her roommates, both marketing majors, who were interested. "We plan to stay in touch over the next few years," Nelson says.

This is not to suggest that the M.B.A. class of '87 is teeming with future entrepreneurs. Let's face it: those who say they'll start or acquire their own companies may never get around to it. Those who think they just might do it may decide not to. And those who plan to stay in large companies probably will.

But even among the latter there are signs that attitudes are changing in ways that could affect the small-business sector in years to come. Consider Chris Hastings, a Wharton M.B.A. who intends to pursue a career at a major bank. He has no intention of leaving to start his own business—but the idea of lending to large corporations leaves him cold. "A big company like Exxon has plenty of options," he says. "They might get 30 different proposals and, 9 times out of 10, they'll make their decision based on price." Hastings thinks he would get more "psychic satisfaction" lending to smaller businesses, which tend to have fewer options. "It's a lot more exciting," he says, "because they really need you."

So what are we to make of all this? What clues does it give us about the future? After all, the current crop of business-school graduates is bound to influence our world in one way or another, if only by dint of numbers, and there are more M.B.A.s graduating every year. Among them are thousands of prospective employees, managers, partners, suppliers, customers, competitors, bankers, even bosses. And in 20 or 30 years, they will fill the top ranks of U.S. business. How will they lead? What impact will they have?

Thirty-eight years ago, *Fortune* asked similar questions about another group of college students, those who were receiving their undergraduate degrees in June 1949. It was a huge class by the standards of the day, including 150,000 men, 70 percent of whom were veterans. They had grown up during the Depression, gone to war, and come home to build families and careers. Most of them were going directly into business after graduation. (That was before the era of the M.B.A.) Searching for clues about the impact these seniors would have, *Fortune* conducted a survey. Its conclusions are chilling in the accuracy with which they foreshadow the history of corporate America over the next 30 years.

"Looking to big business for security, a cautious generation turns its back on venture," the article's subtitle began. The author, Holly Whyte, went on the explain: "Security, of course, can mean many things. In [the class of] '49s case it is bound up in people. Spiritually, it means working for people, in the sense of service, of justifying one's place in the community. Materially, it is, simply, working under them. The class of '49 wants to work for somebody else—preferably somebody big. No longer is small business the promised land. As for the idea of going into business for oneself, the idea is so seldom expressed as to seem an anachronism. 'I never saw a bunch that so wanted to make this free-enterprise system work,' says a professor of business administration, 'but they are interested in the system rather than the individual enterprise. They will be technicians—not owners.'"

Such attitudes were certainly understandable, given the experiences of that generation, and—at the time—they offered the hope of an economy that would function more smoothly than ever before, Whyte wrote. "If ever there was one, this will be a generation of managers. . . Competence, certainly, '49 will supply in abundant measure, and never has there been a class so absorbed with the techniques—and the desirability—of making business more efficient."

And yet Whyte also expressed a gnawing concern about the class of '49. "Will this community-conscious group furnish any quota of free-swinging s.o.b.'s we seem to need for leavening the economy? Or will it be so intent on achieving a super-lubricated, integrated private enterprise—a sort of socialization by big business instead of government—that it will prefer a static, and thus more manageable, economy to a dynamic one? Will '49s, in short, be so tractable and harmonious as to be incapable, twenty or thirty years hence, of making provocative decisions?"

The answer can be found in the record of the Fortune 500 during the 1970s and early '80s. From that perspective, the class of '87 seems to offer us hope that, after nearly four decades, the pendulum has at least begun to swing back.

HOW THE SURVEY WAS CONDUCTED

Early this year, we set out to survey members of the M.B.A. class of '87 with the goal of gaining some insight into who they are, what they believe, and where they are going. Toward that end, we compiled a five-page questionnaire, which we delivered in late February to 1,500 second-year M.B.A. students at 10 business schools around the country. The schools were: Carnegie-Mellon University's Fuqua School of Business; Indiana University's Graduate School of Business; Northwestern University's J. L. Kellogg Graduate School of Management; Stanford University's Graduate School of Business; the University of Miami's School of Business Administration; the University of Minnesota's Curtis L. Carlson School of Management; the University of Pennsylvania's Wharton School of Business; the University of Southern California's Graduate School of Business Administration; and the University of Texas at Austin's Graduate School of Business.

The schools were chosen with an eye toward obtaining as broad a cross section of the class as possible in terms of geography, type of program, and student background. At each school, we provided questionnaires to 150 randomly selected students. Of the 1,500 questionnaires distributed, 907 were completed and returned, for a response rate of 60 percent. Survey results were compiled by Data Tabulation Services Inc., in Stoneham, Mass. *INC.* special projects editor Sara Baer-Sinnott coordinated the entire process. Research assistance was provided by Teri Lammers.

SURVEY RESULTS

TABLE 1
CLASS PROFILE

Sex			Age			
Male	Female		Under 25	25–27	28–30	Over 30
64%	36%		19%	44%	23%	13%

TABLE 2

WHAT DRIVES THEM?

(On a scale of 1 to 5, with 5 being the highest.)

Ability to provide for self and/or family	4.3
Creative outlet	3.6
Wealth	3.5
Recognition	3.4
Opportunity to contribute to society	3.3
Power	2.8

TABLE 3

AREAS OF INTEREST

	Men	Women
Managing people	27%	39%
Money management/stock market	32%	21%
Sales and marketing	31%	42%
Percent who plan to start/acquire company in 10 years	38%	25%

TABLE 4

THE DIFFERING ATTITUDES OF RECENT COLLEGE GRADUATES AND THOSE WHO'VE BEEN OUT IN THE WORLD

	1985 grads	1963-77 grads
Why attend business school		
To gain new skills	38%	62%
To get a job	42%	25%
Evaluation of fellow M.B.A.s		
Materialistic	53%	38%
Hardworking	65%	79%

TABLE 5
THE JOB CHOICE

By type of company		By size of company	
Financial services	41%	Large, established	61%
Consulting	37%	Midsize (revenues	
Consumer products	26%	$25m.–150m.)	24%
High technology		Small (revenues less	
& electronics	25%	than $25m.)	9%
Investment banking	25%	Self-employed	5%
Food & beverage	15%	Unsure	1%
Other services	15%		
Other manufacturing	14%		
Real estate & construction	13%		
Government	7%		
Energy & mining	6%		
Retail trade	5%		
Education	4%		

TABLE 6
IMPORTANT FACTORS IN CHOOSING A JOB

	Employees of Midsize to Large Companies	Employees of Small Companies	Self-Employed
Challenging work	77%	69%	55%
Feeling of autonomy	15%	28%	45%
Chance for ownership	5%	22%	43%
High salary	25%	12%	32%

TABLE 7

WHAT M.B.A.s THINK ABOUT YOU (SMALL BUSINESS OWNERS)

They are best suited to provide	True	False
More opportunities for advancement	65%	18%
A more challenging work environment	76%	12%
Greater receptivity to new ideas	84%	7%
Greater opportunity to build personal wealth	62%	19%
More time for family & nonbusiness activities	5%	85%

TABLE 8

BELIEFS ABOUT FACTORS IN THE SUCCESS OF A BUSINESS

Solid operating plan	16%
Strong financial backing	5%
A good product or service	34%
Capable managers	27%
Luck	3%
Effective marketing & advertising	5%
Contacts	1%
Research & analysis	1%
Ethical behavior	1%
Other	6%

Questions for Discussion

1. What are the backgrounds and future ambitions of 1987 graduates? Are your ambitions similar?

2. What directions are new graduates moving toward as they seek a job?

3. Compare and contrast the difference between 1949 M.B.A. students and those of today. How do they differ in their desired goals?

4. Has the decline in major U.S. industry affected the attitude of today's M.B.A. graduates?

EXERCISE 76
EFFECTIVE MANAGERS REVISITED

Below is a partial list of behaviors in which managers may engage. Rank these items in terms of their importance for effective performance as a manager. Put a 1 in the space provided next to the item you think is most important, 2 for the next most important item, and so on to 10 for the least important item.

_____ Communicates and interprets policy so that it is understood by the members of the organization.

_____ Makes prompt and clear decisions.

_____ Assigns subordinates to the jobs for which they are best suited.

_____ Encourages associates to submit ideas and plans.

_____ Stimulates subordinates by means of competition among employees.

_____ Seeks means of improving management capabilities and competence.

_____ Fully supports and carries out company policies.

_____ Participates in community activities as opportunities arise.

_____ Is neat in appearance.

_____ Is honest in all matters pertaining to company property or funds.

You may recall that you completed this exercise before. If you saved that exercise from Chapter 1, why not compare results? What, if any, additional behaviors would you include in this list?